CONSPICUOUS CONSUMPTION IN AFRICA

CONSPICUOUS CONSUMPTION IN AFRICA

EDITED BY DEBORAH POSEL AND ILANA VAN WYK

WITS UNIVERSITY PRESS

Published in South Africa by:
Wits University Press
1 Jan Smuts Avenue
Johannesburg 2001

www.witspress.co.za

Compilation © Editors 2019
Chapters © Individual contributors 2019
Published edition © Wits University Press 2019
Images and figures © Copyright holders

First published 2019

http://dx.doi.org.10.18772/22019053641

978-1-77614-364-1 (Paperback)
978-1-77614-365-8 (Web PDF)
978-1-77614-366-5 (EPUB)
978-1-77614-367-2 (Mobi)

All rights reserved. No part of this publication may be reproduced, stored in a retrieval system, or transmitted in any form or by any means, electronic, mechanical, photocopying, recording or otherwise, without the written permission of the publisher, except in accordance with the provisions of the Copyright Act, Act 98 of 1978.

All images remain the property of the copyright holders. The publishers gratefully acknowledge the publishers, institutions and individuals referenced in captions for the use of images. Every effort has been made to locate the original copyright holders of the images reproduced here; please contact Wits University Press in case of any omissions or errors.

Project manager: Alison Paulin
Copyeditor: Alex Dodd
Proofreader: Alison Paulin
Indexer: Margaret Ramsay
Cover design: Hybrid Creative
Typesetter: MPS
Typeset in 10 point Garamond Pro

CONTENTS

ACKNOWLEDGEMENTS
vii

LIST OF ILLUSTRATIONS
viii

1 **THINKING WITH VEBLEN: CASE STUDIES FROM AFRICA'S PAST AND PRESENT**
Deborah Posel and Ilana van Wyk
1

2 **CHANGES IN THE ORDER OF THINGS: DEPARTMENT STORES AND THE MAKING OF MODERN CAPE TOWN**
Deborah Posel
25

3 **CONSPICUOUSLY PUBLIC: GENDERED HISTORIES OF SARTORIAL AND SOCIAL SUCCESS IN URBAN TOGO**
Nina Sylvanus
45

4 **ETIENNE ROUSSEAU, *BROEDERTWIS* AND THE POLITICS OF CONSUMPTION WITHIN AFRIKANERDOM**
Stephen Sparks
63

5 **RECYCLING CONSUMPTION: POLITICAL POWER AND ELITE WEALTH IN ANGOLA**
Claudia Gastrow
79

6 **CHILUBA'S TRUNKS: CONSUMPTION, EXCESS AND THE BODY POLITIC IN ZAMBIA**
Karen Tranberg Hansen
96

7 **JACOB ZUMA'S SHAMELESSNESS: CONSPICUOUS CONSUMPTION, POLITICS AND RELIGION**
Ilana van Wyk
112

8   **PRECARIOUS 'BIGNESS': A 'BIG MAN', HIS WOMEN AND HIS FUNERAL IN CAMEROON**
Rogers Orock
133

9   **YOUNG MEN OF LEISURE? YOUTH, CONSPICUOUS CONSUMPTION AND THE PERFORMATIVITY OF DRESS IN NIGER**
Adeline Masquelier
150

10 **BOOTY ON FIRE: LOOKING AT *IZIKHOTHANE* WITH THORSTEIN VEBLEN**
Jabulani G Mnisi
168

11 **CONSPICUOUS QUEER CONSUMPTION: EMULATION AND HONOUR IN THE PINK MAP**
Bradley Rink
183

12 **THE POLITICS AND MORAL ECONOMY OF MIDDLE-CLASS CONSUMPTION IN SOUTH AFRICA**
Sophie Chevalier
200

13 **MARIGOLD BEADS: WHO NEEDS DIAMONDS?!**
Joni Brenner and Pamila Gupta
214

CONTRIBUTORS
231

INDEX
235

ACKNOWLEDGEMENTS

We gratefully acknowledge the A W Mellon Foundation's financial contribution to the two workshops at the Institute for Humanities in Africa, University of Cape Town, that have resulted in this edited collection. The contributors to this volume have participated enthusiastically and generously; we thank them for their intellectual investment in the project. We would also like to thank the reviewers of the volume and the Wits University Press team.

LIST OF ILLUSTRATIONS

Figure 1   Garlicks store, Cape Town. First appeared in *The Cape Register*, 26 August 1893. Courtesy University of Cape Town Libraries.

Figure 2   A wax-cloth trader arranging her stall in the Lomé textile market. Photograph by Nina Sylvanus.

Figure 3   Photographic collage of Sasolburg cars by Jacques Bernard. Used with permission.

Figure 4   Etienne Rousseau with Elsie Human, wife of CJF Human, Managing Director of Federale Volksbeleggings, at the company's year-end function, 28 November 1975. Courtesy the Archive for Contemporary Affairs, University of the Free State.

Figure 5   President Frederick Chiluba, with wife Regina Chiluba in the background. Photo by Thomas Nsama/AFP/Getty Images. Courtesy Gallo Images.

Figure 6   Wiz kid dress. Photograph by Adeline Masquelier.

Figure 7   Faire le show. Photograph by Adeline Masquelier.

Figure 8   The Good Fellas' designer shoes. Photograph by Mpho Sekatane. Courtesy The Good Fellas.

Figure 9   The Good Fellas buying expensive alcohol. Photograph by Mpho Sekatane. Courtesy The Good Fellas.

Figure 10 The Good Fellas posing at the Civic Centre in Kempton Park. Photograph by Siyabonga Mhlanga. Courtesy The Good Fellas.

Figure 11 Cover image of 2001 edition of the *Pink Map*. Courtesy A&C Maps. © www.mapmyway.co.za

Figure 12 Strands of Marigold hand-loomed beads can be worn in endless combinations to glamorous effect. Photograph by Liz Whitter.

Figure 13 Marigold hand-loomed beads in five variations on the pixellated 'Camouflage' design. Photograph by Liz Whitter.

1 THINKING WITH VEBLEN: CASE STUDIES FROM AFRICA'S PAST AND PRESENT

DEBORAH POSEL AND ILANA VAN WYK

Thorstein Veblen (2003 [1899]) coined the phrase 'conspicuous consumption' in his critique of nineteenth-century American society, as an indictment of the extent to which the need for personal recognition – or 'honour,' as he put it – was vested in public displays of material acquisition. The phrase immediately caught on, infiltrating vocabularies of social commentary and popular conversation in the United States of America (USA) and beyond. In the present moment, more than a century later, it has self-evident resonance with experiences of ostentatious accumulation across the world.

There are some striking resemblances between the USA of the late nineteenth century, about which Veblen was writing, and many parts of the world today – including Africa: buoyant if uneven economic growth; rampant and loosely regulated accumulation; rapid upward mobility in the higher reaches of society coupled with abiding or deepening poverty and marginality for most; insufficient government action to manage or ameliorate the inequalities. The 'Africa Rising' narrative informs some of these trends on the continent. From the early 2000s, a number of influential authors, publications and institutions, including *The Financial Times, The Economist,* the *BBC* and *The International Monetary Fund*,[1] have reported that growing access to the Internet and mobile phones (Mutiga & Flood 2016), an increase in consumer spending and growth in entrepreneurship have marked a new epoch of rapid economic growth across the African continent (Mahajan 2009; Taylor 2014). Combined with the rise of a new middle class, there has been much optimism that this unprecedented growth would translate into increasing incomes across the continent. Critics have pointed out, however, that Africa's 'rise' has not translated into economic democracy, and the small 'middle class' appears more interested in its own meteoric rise and conspicuous consumption than in economic justice (Akwagyiram 2013; Fabricius 2015; Johnson 2015; Wadongo 2014).

As inequalities on the continent deepen, conspicuous consumption has become both the sign of such differentiation and the symbolic register within which much political, social and cultural criticism is couched (Dosekun 2015; Iqani 2016; Mbembe 2004; Spronk 2014). In global news on Africa, conspicuous consumption is often central to the ways in which controversial public figures and events are construed. Consider, for example, the ousting of former Zimbabwean president Robert Mugabe in 2017. Countless articles and commentaries have focused on his, and his family's, opulent lifestyle. 'Gucci Grace' – the satirical name given to his wife – has come under particular scrutiny for her infamous international shopping trips, lavishly expensive jewellery, imported Rolls Royces as well as for the substantial sums she spends on 'spoiling' her two party-loving adult sons (Allison 2017). The alarm over excessive conspicuous consumption in Africa also spills over into trends in popular culture. International media articles on *sapeurs* in West Africa (Doig 2014), mobile phones across Africa (Mutiga & Flood 2016) and elaborate coffins in Ghana (Jansen 2016), for example, are centrally about conspicuous consumption in contexts of extreme poverty.

Under these conditions, then, boldly extravagant consumption, across gender and generation, is read as an emphatic – sometimes hyperbolic – assertion of social, economic and/or political status. Framing African conspicuous consumption in this way is not unique, of course, and as in other cases, reactions and judgements vary. Yet, in the case of Africa, the moral outrage and political scorn that attach to conspicuous consumption seem especially intense. There is no comparably intense public anxiety about the conspicuous consumption of elites in the West who are in many cases far wealthier, often spending money as conspicuously, if not more so, than their African counterparts. This was powerfully illustrated in the recent Paradise Papers exposé, in which international journalists revealed the extent to which the world's super-rich invested money offshore in order to avoid paying domestic taxes.[2] The British monarch, often cited as one of the richest people in the United Kingdom (UK) (see Sherman 2016), was among those on the list (Osborne 2017). However, despite considerable coverage, journalists soon bemoaned the fact that the Paradise Papers did not seem to generate the level of public outrage that they had expected. As one article pointed out, the general public in the UK, Europe and America were more concerned about low-income groups legally exploiting the system than with the dubious tax arrangements and suspiciously lavish lifestyles of the elite (De Vries & Reeves 2017).

The disproportionate moral disdain that attaches to material excess in Africa is not new, having been a prominent and revealing feature of African history from the nineteenth century onwards. Early missionaries and European traders on the continent wrote with alarm about the locals' material demands and excesses (Comaroff 1996: 19–38; Etherington 1978; Ross 1990), especially when it came to local chiefs, kings and other local elites (Collins & Burns 2007: 142–158). As a consequence of such anxieties, a large part of missionaries' 'civilising mission' revolved around teaching locals proper, restrained consumption (Comaroff & Comaroff 1990: 195–216; Etherington 2002: 422–439; Meyer 2002: 753–757). Such patterns of negative framing continued into the twentieth century, as the consolidation of African elites in the post-independence era produced spectacles of wealth and consumerism hitherto unseen on the continent. In many instances, such spectacles became intimately connected with the exercise of power (Bayart 1993; Fanon 1961), with controversial and brutal leaders such as Mabuto Sese Seko (Smith 2013), Uhuru Kenyatta and Joseph Kabila as prime examples.

Conspicuous consumption, therefore, is as much an argument, as it is a public conversation, about 'honour' and power – the factors originally, and famously, posited by Veblen as the primary drivers of such material performances and their effects. Yet, these varied geographies and politics of conspicuous consumption suggest the need for a nuanced engagement with issues of context and history. This collection is an effort to make sense of contemporary versions of conspicuous consumption in Africa and their histories, which, in turn, provides an opportunity to revisit Veblen's early and influential analysis. Contributors engage with varieties of consumerism in a range of specific places and times on this continent, and how they intersect with global genealogies of aspiration, acquisition, status, and conspicuous display.

The collection arose out of a symposium on Conspicuous Consumption in Africa, held at the Institute for Humanities in Africa (HUMA) at the University of Cape Town in December 2014. This symposium posed a number of central questions that undergird the volume as a whole. How do we explain the varied repertoires of conspicuous consumption on this continent, now and in the past? What do these repertoires reveal about the modalities and limits of global and transnational linkages? How have economic, technological, political and social factors articulated with the scale and scope of conspicuous consumption? Why do some variants of conspicuous consumption ignite more argument than others? What are the arguments really about? What are their cultural registers and effects, and how do the dynamics of local and global markets shape these collisions and their impact on political life?

These questions, while grounded in specific case studies, lead back to the concept of conspicuous consumption itself. If the meaning and application of the term seems uncomplicated in everyday parlance, its analytic usage is more elusive, if also powerfully suggestive. So we invited our contributors to grapple with conceptual and theoretical questions too. How is 'conspicuous consumption' usefully and coherently defined? What analytical work do we want the concept to do, and how? In what ways do questions about conspicuous consumption engage with, and contribute to, theories of modernity and its counter assertions in Africa? More broadly, what are the productive theoretical horizons of debate concerning conspicuous consumption in Africa – in particular, the articulations between these processes, and the familiar wirings of power and inequality along lines of class, race, gender, status, religion and generation? Since the concept of conspicuous consumption was produced at the heart of Veblen's *The Theory of the Leisure Class*, which has had a powerful imprint in many historical and contemporary studies of material excess,[3] we invited the contributors to engage these questions by way of the Veblenian conceptualisation, and to consider if and how it helped in making sense of their empirical material.[4]

The chapters in this volume engage with these questions in variegated ways, from the standpoint of different disciplines, geographies and histories, and with varying degrees of engagement with the details of Veblen's writings. No doubt there are several gaps and omissions in the collection. The geographic focus is largely on sub-Saharan Africa, with a concentration on South Africa. Historically too, the volume opens up a few windows, rather than shedding a comprehensive light, on its animating questions. To some extent, this is a consequence of the offerings at the symposium itself. But as editors, we have not set out to produce a geographically or historically complete selection of chapters. Our aim is far more modest: to assemble a selection of empirically diverse renditions of material 'excess', with a unifying conceptual thread deriving from an effort to think with Veblen, and the uses and/or limits of the notion of conspicuous consumption associated with his corpus of work.

In the remainder of this chapter, we provide a brief introduction to some of the key tenets of Veblen's thinking about conspicuous consumption. We then discuss the ways in which the individual chapters advance our understanding of the multifaceted dynamics of conspicuous consumption in Africa's heterogeneous past and present, and finally, summarise the collective verdict on the relevance and utility of the Veblenian conceptualisation.

VEBLEN ON CONSPICUOUS CONSUMPTION

Born in 1857, Thorstein Veblen was the son of Norwegian immigrants to the USA. He grew up on a farm in Minnesota in a financially comfortable but not affluent home. His father, who loomed large in his life, extolled and performed the virtues of hard work and self-reliance, underpinned by a commitment to the authenticity and creativity of manual labour. (The house that Thomas Veblen built is still standing.) These were values that would stay with Thorstein throughout his life (carpentry was one of his abiding hobbies) and would permeate the substance of his arguments – particularly in his valorisation of productive work as the antithesis of leisure and the nemesis of 'the leisure class'.

While originally trained in philosophy, Veblen's first academic job was in economics, at the University of Chicago, where he wrote *The Theory of the Leisure Class* (first published in 1899). He was writing in the midst of huge economic ferment and upheaval, triggered by very rapid industrialisation in the USA, notably in heavy industries, such as coal mining and steel production. The last three decades of the nineteenth century saw a huge increase in the number of mines, factories, machines and the construction of miles of railroads in the USA, which produced gargantuan fortunes for the men who owned them (Spindler 2002: 4–5). This was the period in which multimillionaires, such as Andrew Carnegie, John D Rockefeller, Solomon Guggenheim, Cornelius Vanderbilt and others, accumulated extraordinary sums of money (Holbrook 2010). Their lifestyles evinced their success; America's rich founded their own elite schools and private clubs, and lived in vast mansions filled with rare art and decorative objects and serviced by ornately dressed butlers and footmen. (In 1895, George Vanderbilt built a 250-room Renaissance-style palace, which remains the largest house ever built in the USA.) For Veblen, this was the archetypal 'leisure class': people who made extravagantly good, very quickly and brazenly, and who were intent on declaring their material success as ostentatiously as possible.

At the same time, greater proportions of American people were becoming ever poorer. Chicago was one of the cities in which the brutal inequalities of modernising America were painfully apparent. Alongside the excesses of the rich, the familiar features of extreme poverty, such as disease, overcrowding and premature death, were ubiquitous. Things were particularly bad during a bout of economic depression in 1893–4, with unusually high rates of unemployment and popular disaffection. Veblen was deeply troubled by the poverty around him and vented his spleen by writing satirically about what he saw as the vanities of the leisure class, their absurd and hyperbolic displays of wealth, their cultural pretensions to arcane and useless knowledge, their ostentatious architecture and their deliberately expensive works of art.

While the late nineteenth-century American condition triggered Veblen's critique, he intended his analysis to have a far wider historical and geographical reach, and presented it as a general theory of conspicuous consumption. Theoretically, his writings engaged centrally with both Charles Darwin and Karl Marx – two major thinkers of the day. Veblen treated practices of consumption as unfolding across the *longue durée*, as historical processes that evolved incrementally, without any abiding *telos*. Here, the influence of Darwin's evolutionism was keenly apparent, rendering Veblen's philosophy of history very different from that of Marx. For Veblen, history did not move through radical revolutionary ruptures, with an emancipatory momentum driving it forward; rather, history had a cumulative but directionless dynamic, with the residues of 'archaic elements' retained long beyond their first manifestation, and without any normative progression.

Within this long history, since the onset of what Veblen satirically calls 'barbarian society' (marked by the introduction of property), repertoires of consumption had been a decisive force, rather than something secondary and epiphenomenal, *á la* Marx. According to Veblen (2003: 8), the primary human motivation, which had not changed, was the pursuit of 'esteem' or 'honour' in the eyes of others. (Veblen speaks generically about honour, but in fact the discussion is tacitly more specific, concerning the honour of men.) Honour, in turn, had a profoundly material register. During the initial peaceable phase of human evolution, the so-called primitive savagery phase, honour was secured through productive work. During this phase, where individual ownership was not a dominant feature of economic life, social hierarchies were relatively flat, and social distinctions between classes and employment were inconsistent (4). With the violent and predatory transition to 'barbarism' (Veblen's deliberately counterintuitive term for the advent of property), the basis of esteem shifted to ownership, associated with demonstrable wealth (4–5). Veblen (12–13) explained the transition to private ownership as the result of the male quest for honour during war, a quest that resulted in both private ownership and forms of marriage that survived into the modern industrial era.

The practice of seizing women from the enemy as trophies gave rise to a form of ownership-marriage, resulting in a household with a male head. This was followed by an extension of slavery to other captives and inferiors, besides women, and by an extension of a system of ownership-marriage to women other than those seized from the enemy.

Once established, 'the possession of wealth', he said, 'confer[red] honour' (Veblen 2003: 14), in a hierarchy of social and personal value rooted in hierarchies of material acquisition. As he asserted, 'The end sought by accumulation is to rank high in comparison with the rest of the community in point of pecuniary strength' (16).

In Veblen's view, wealth *per se* was insufficient to confer and retain honour; the possession of wealth had to be visible and public, 'for esteem is awarded only on evidence' (Veblen 2003: 131). The point of 'pecuniary strength' was to make it conspicuous, to show it off to selected others. This happened in two ways. The first was through exemption from work (productive work) – that is, in becoming leisurely. 'Conspicuous abstention from labour therefore becomes the conventional mark of pecuniary achievement and the conventional index of reputability' (19). The second was through the conspicuous consumption of material goods – a 'wasteful' practice, in Veblen's eyes, as it had no productive purpose or rationale. For Veblen, as societies became more complex over time, this became the dominant repertoire for the production of honour and esteem.

Veblen used the term 'conspicuous consumption' without defining it, as though its meaning was self-evident. In fact, its usage was abidingly imprecise, sliding between different and inconsistent versions. In some instances, he implied that conspicuous consumption was 'consumption in excess of the subsistence minimum' (Veblen 2003: 35). Used in this way, conspicuous consumption includes all consumption for any purposes other than meeting basic needs – be it status-driven or not (as in displaying family heirlooms for the sake of their sentimental associations, or assembling large collections of stamps, fridge magnets, or porcelain frogs for the fun of it). Used in this way, the term 'conspicuous consumption' would have no necessary association with excess, encompassing relatively modest and discreet ornamentation (such as a bowl of flowers in the hall, an indulgent birthday celebration, a second pair of shoes) for reasons other than meeting basic needs. The 'conspicuousness' of the consumption practices would tacitly refer to the ways in which they clearly exceeded those minima.

On other occasions, however, Veblen sees conspicuous consumption as far narrower and more specific, going well beyond consumption for purposes other than meeting basic material need. For example, he writes of 'the conspicuous consumption of valuable goods', these being 'the right kind of goods', evidently 'expensive', and paraded in 'excess' (Veblen 2003: 36). Here, conspicuous consumption is understood in relation to public codes of extravagance and excess, pertaining to what is socially recognised as the 'right' sorts of goods to confer social standing. Thus, eating gargantuan quantities of cabbage would likely not qualify, whereas lobster feasts would. Unlike the more inclusive references to conspicuous consumption, these narrower renditions suggest the necessity of an audience, as well as a tacit social grammar of conspicuous consumption – a shared set of understandings as to what constitutes the kinds of goods worth consuming in 'extravagant' ways in order to produce 'honour'.

These conflicting renditions of the notion of 'conspicuous consumption' are overlaid by other inconsistencies and ambiguities. For example, Colin Campbell (1995: 37–47) points out that Veblen's account elides versions of conspicuous consumption as a deliberate, motivated practice and as an unintended effect of decisions taken for other reasons. A person may acquire an expensive imported car for the express purpose of impressing others; or because s/he relishes the experience of driving a top-end, well-engineered vehicle. The social status that the car confers would then be an effect of, rather than the primary motivation for, the act of conspicuous consumption. Clearly, Veblen's usage of the term 'conspicuous consumption' is as vague and mercurial as it is suggestive and tempting – a point to which we return later in our discussion.

One of the more striking, and prescient, strands in Veblen's account of conspicuous consumption is the direct link he draws between it and patriarchy (loosely understood as male domination). Historically, for Veblen, the emergence of the leisure class – that grouping whose ownership of property enabled conspicuous leisure and conspicuous consumption – was bound up in the first instance with the capture and enslavement of women. *The Theory of the Leisure Class* built on Veblen's very first publications, which included articles on 'The Barbarian Status of Women' (1899) and 'The Economic Theory of Women's Dress' (1894). The first form of ownership, Veblen argued, was the ownership of women, seized during combat with enemy societies. (His data here is a random assortment of anthropological writings, with a particular interest in what he had read about the Vikings.) Marriage then evolved as a mimicry of such conquest, with men able to demonstrate their superior honour by way of the women they married and displayed. Women's exemption from manual labour became a statement of the social standing of their husbands; likewise, a wife's conspicuous consumption – her dress in particular – testimony to the 'pecuniary strength' of her husband (Veblen 1894: 202). There is thus a full chapter in *The Theory of the Leisure Class* devoted to dress. 'The first principle of dress is conspicuous expensiveness', writes Veblen: to lay claim to social honour, a man has to have a wife clad in extravagant clothes, way beyond the functional necessities of her daily life.

> No apparel can be considered elegant, or even decent, if it shows the effect of manual labour on the part of the wearer, in the way of soil or wear. The pleasing effect of neat and spotless garments is chiefly, if not altogether, due to their carrying the suggestion of leisure – exemption from personal contact with industrial processes of any kind. (78)

For Veblen, if conspicuous consumption emerged as a practice characteristic of the top end of the social hierarchy, its pursuit came to define the material habits of those lower down too. Veblen introduced the concept of 'pecuniary emulation' to refer to a restless ambition on the part of those of relatively meagre means to consume more, to elicit greater 'esteem' in the eyes of those at the top. Veblen would have been unsurprised at the history of capitalism in the twentieth century, with the working classes having been less inclined to lead the revolution than Marx had anticipated. From Veblen's perspective, the working class was more likely to aspire to resemble the bourgeoisie than to want to bring them down.

Marx, of course, also recognised this phenomenon at play; but he deemed it 'false consciousness', which would give way once the working class could see through this mystification and recognise its true objective interests in a more equal economic and social order. This was not so for Veblen. For him, the process of emulation was more complex and intractable than false consciousness. It is not that the have-nots were elaborately duped into something they did not understand. Theirs was a more active, complex complicity with the trappings of wealth, which made for processes with greater psychological complexity and social traction than the idea of false consciousness could muster. 'Barbarian society' produced a material commodification of esteem and social standing with which those at the bottom of the heap became preoccupied, because (as Veblen saw it) it offered them real and enduring, if ultimately wrong-headed and superficial, psychological and social satisfaction.

Some of Veblen's most scornful commentary took such practices of emulation as its target: 'Very much of squalor and discomfort will be endured before the last trinket or the last pretence of pecuniary decency is put away' (Veblen 1899: 40). And, 'People will undergo a very considerable degree of privation in the comforts or the necessaries of life in order to afford what is considered a decent amount of wasteful consumption' (77).

As we suggested at the outset, elements of Veblen's argument gained a great deal of traction in popular debate. His book, *The Theory of the Leisure Class*, was also widely reviewed – often negatively – in scholarly circles (Tilman 1992; Spindler 2002). One of the reasons for the intensity of interest was surely the novelty of Veblen's approach to questions of economic behaviour, including his insistence on the centrality of consumption as a major driver of human history. Veblen's depiction of conspicuous consumption is therefore a tempting invitation to pull together psychological, social, cultural and economic factors in making sense of the urge to consume beyond the functional necessities of material subsistence. Indeed, Veblen's genius as an economist was to see economic, social and psychological processes as fundamentally interlinked, *contra* the premise that economies have inner 'iron laws' that can be fathomed without making reference to how societies change over time, and to the psychological dynamics, along with the social norms and values, that shape them. This put him profoundly at odds with the canon of his discipline, which analysed economic behaviour as the utility-maximising action of *homo economicus*, a creature of rational and individual self-interest. In the universities of Veblen's time, cultural norms in far-flung places were what anthropologists studied, the human psyche the domain of psychologists, and social inequality a sociological preoccupation. But he disavowed the rapidly sedimenting disciplinary boundaries that took psychology, sociology and anthropology out of economics, and that removed affect from considerations of self-interested reason. This made him one of the earliest assertively interdisciplinary scholars. John Patrick Diggins (1999: xiii) calls him 'the pioneer of economic anthropology'; he could equally well be called the pioneer of cultural sociology.

If the provocations of his interdisciplinarity were one reason for Veblen's wide readership, the originality and self-evidence in his account of conspicuous consumption surely also animated interest. This was an obviously striking feature of the society of his day, yet it had not been subjected to any serious study or commentary. Veblen was the first scholar to detect the power of consumption patterns in driving wider social and cultural shifts (Spindler 2002: 124). The tenets of his analysis of conspicuous consumption and pecuniary emulation were remarkably prescient as the era of mass consumerism dawned in the twentieth century. Unsurprisingly, as the global hegemony of consumerism grew increasingly evident from the 1960s, Veblen's work enjoyed a new surge of interest and commentary. Yet there are many facets of Veblen's analysis that have justifiably attracted criticism. His invocation of a long history of conspicuous consumption rooted in the transition to 'barbarian society' is high on generality and low on evidence and contextual detail. Many commentators have simply discarded the historical evolutionism of the account, inspired by Darwin, as unpersuasive (in Tilman 1992: 73) and unnecessary to more selective engagements with the kernel of his thesis about the symbolic powers and drivers of material consumption. Some who regale the merits of Veblen's work are nevertheless unconvinced that it offers a general theory of conspicuous consumption across time and space. In the words of C Wright Mills (2002 [1951]: 115), for example, 'Veblen's theory is not "The Theory of the Leisure Class". It is a theory of a particular element of the upper classes in one period of the history of the nation. It is a criticism of the *nouveau riche*, so much in evidence in Veblen's formative time, the America of the latter half of the nineteenth century' (cf. Davis 1992: 223).

The theoretical challenge, then, is how to think productively with Veblen, rather than engaging or applying his analysis comprehensively; how to use his writings as suggestive beginnings, rather than fixed endpoints, of any study. In the remainder of this introduction, we suggest how we might do so, and how the chapters in this volume take up this challenge.

DIFFERENT READINGS OF VEBLEN

Even if we acknowledge, with C Wright Mills (2002), that we should not read Veblen as offering anything like a general theory of 'the leisure class' but rather a theory of its characteristics in late nineteenth-century America, there remain different ways of reading that account, linked to different ways of thinking with this work in relation to different geographies and histories of conspicuous consumption.

Veblen's writings on conspicuous consumption and emulation are suggestive rather than exhaustive; they are provocative and revealing, but often vague and incomplete. This allows for varying interpretations of his central arguments. In one reading, Veblen makes the strong and comprehensive case that conspicuous consumption is an inevitable – and more or less exhaustive – feature of the material culture of 'the leisure class'. Likewise, the lower classes engage in emulation as a matter of course, as part of the way in which hierarchies of honour work in materially unequal societies.

If this is how Veblen is read, then the account of conspicuous consumption becomes far too blunt and homogenising. It becomes far more productive to retrieve the analysis as one that offers a much weaker set of propositions about conspicuous consumption, as one dimension (among others) of the material culture of 'the leisure class' – and one that takes shape under particular conditions. As several chapters in this volume show, this approach then yields far richer, more layered accounts of conspicuous consumption than Veblen's own writings suggest.

Critics have also drawn attention to the unrelenting spleen in Veblen's writings about conspicuous consumption. In his eyes, there was absolutely nothing redeeming about the practice at all. It was nothing more than 'trash', as Adorno (1941: 389) put it. This normative freighting weighs heavily in his historical analysis, detracting from any claims to scholarly objectivity. As Bernard Rosenberg puts it, 'while chuckling over the aphorism that "cheap clothes make a cheap man", Veblen practically says that cheap clothes make a fine man. The one is as manifestly wrongheaded an aesthetic as the other' (quoted in Tilman 1992: 253; see also Davis in Tilman, 223). For Veblen, it was entirely unthinkable that there was anything legitimately pleasurable or respectable in the act of conspicuous consumption. This is a point of vehement critique from Adorno – remarkably, given Adorno's own scathing critique of the superficiality of capitalist consumerism.

> Veblen's image of society is based not on the ideal of happiness but that of work ... The happiness that man actually finds cannot be separated from conspicuous consumption. There is no happiness which does not promise to fulfil a socially constituted desire, but there is also none which does not promise something qualitatively different in this fulfillment. Even the commodity fetishist who has succumbed to conspicuous consumption to the point of obsession participates in the truth-content of happiness. (Adorno 1983: 82–3)

A more interesting and open analysis of conspicuous consumption, then, would leave aside the unilateral judgement of its ethical or normative value or lack thereof. This also enables a more complex, varied enquiry into the motives and effects of such practices – including a range of affective dimensions that Veblen's scorn simply obliterates.

If we read Veblen in these ways – as having produced a suggestive and provocative lens on aspects of material culture in unequal, modern societies, rather than having provided a fixed and comprehensive theoretical template – then the question of what we mean by conspicuous consumption returns to centre stage. If not all the consumption practised by the leisure class is 'conspicuous', then how do we recognise those instances thereof that are? And if the practice of conspicuous consumption is always historically embedded, in relation to particular social grammars of consumption, can we posit shared characteristics across these different places and times? Are we referring to one recognisable practice with a series of necessary, defining features, or a concept which acquires its meaning through family resemblances (as per Wittgenstein)?

With these questions in mind, we turn to the individual chapters in the collection, each of which contributes particular angles and aspects of a composite analysis.

THE CONTRIBUTORS

Deborah Posel writes about the pursuit of conspicuous consumption as an integral part of Cape Town's transformation from a colonial town to a modernising city. Here is a case of the collective pursuit of honour as an exercise in status-making, but with dimensions largely absent in Veblen's account – in particular, the close articulation between hierarchies of social and political standing, and the making of a colonial racial order. Spectacles of material abundance among Cape Town's largely white elite became part of the making of class and racial distinction, illustrating this grouping's position at the helm of a growing city that could take its place within the sophisticated world of goods, at the same time as creating a racial hierarchy that would extrude almost all but its affluent white inhabitants to the margins of that world. Veblen had little to say about the regulation of conspicuous consumption: its insertion into the field of political and economic governance. In Posel's chapter, these connections are central. Her chapter focuses in particular on the advent of department stores in Cape Town – an institution designed as a veritable cornucopia of stuff on sale: huge in scale, in volume of trade and in the range of things on offer. First established in Cape Town from the late nineteenth century, such stores became both sites and symbols of Cape Town's commercial, aesthetic and scientific prowess, while the act of shopping enabled a declaration of sophisticated modernity, an insertion into a wider world in which the very latest fashions, styles and technologies circulated with mounting rapidity. That most of the shoppers were white and affluent was anything but incidental. The much acclaimed, glorious extravagance of these stores illustrated a version of whiteness at its class apex, thoroughly entangled with the joys and expectations of material abundance, at the cutting edge of what the world of global commerce had to offer. As this took root in segregationist South Africa, it would stand in stark contrast to its formative binary: what white consumers perceived to be the alarming, altogether improper, material excesses on the part of black consumers.

The entanglement of colonialism with conspicuous consumption and its shaping of a racial order was, of course, not unique to South Africa. While Togo had a very small colonial settler society, similar processes were at work here. In her chapter, Nina Sylvanus shows how sophisticated sartorial fashions among colonised Togolese threatened the colonial project's civilising mission, demanding both regulation and intervention. However, as she also shows, this was a highly gendered project precisely because the colonial public sphere centered on the social production of the male world of civil service. Thus, while Togolese dandies were closely scrutinised, their female counterparts could develop an autonomous aesthetic of sartorial excess. Sylvanus demonstrates that this aesthetic, known as *pagne*, allowed a complex project of self-making and status performance for individual women, tempered only by local expectations of respectable femininity. As such, *pagne* became an emancipatory project that allowed women to fashion a public culture in which they were central. In postcolonial Togo, the public display of *pagne,* and its continued role in self-making, points to important historical continuities in women's sartorial fashions. In a context of economic hardship, *pagne* also allows women to fashion themselves in ways that are aspirational and circumvent established class positions. Sylvanus's engagement with Togolese fashion over time upsets the certainties of Veblen's gender and class distinctions. Unlike Veblen, who insisted that women's dress functioned to increase the pecuniary repute of men, she puts dress forward as an autonomous female project, which is of political and social import. Unlike Veblen's study of the American leisure class, Sylvanus looks at conspicuous consumption in the long shadow of colonialism, arguably a system in which honour was writ on a larger scale than in Veblen's version of the household or class.

Stephen Sparks' chapter explores the contested politics of conspicuous consumption in the making of Sasolburg – a town on the Witwatersrand buoyed by the establishment of Sasol, the lucrative oil-from-coal enterprise, in turn intertwined with arguments within the wider politics of Afrikaner nationalism. Sasol not only lubricated the commercial fecundity of the town, it also became the institutional and symbolic milieu of a new cohort of white Afrikaners with mounting prominence and influence within the Afrikaner *volk* (nation): at the cutting edge of global science, champions of modernising progress, youthful and internationally connected. Focusing on a biography of one of the leading figures in this cohort, Etienne Rousseau, Sparks examines how this scientific, cultural and ideological trajectory took root in Sasolburg and shaped the consumption of its white inhabitants, across the class spectrum. As domestic purchasing power grew from the mid-1950s, so too did the enthusiasm for the world of stuff. Predictably for a town symbolising the power of petrol, cars were at the forefront of that, at least for the men about the town. For women, it was the homemaking project that shaped their consuming selves, as Sasolburg's economy boomed in tandem with the rest of the country during the 1960s, and as flows of imported goods, particularly from the USA, entered the homes of the affluent as well as the aspirant upwardly mobile. Yet these changes were neither seamless nor uncontroversial. Anxieties about the moral degradation associated with materialist preening were predictable, given the salience of a Calvinist sensibility in the community at large. And in Rousseau's case, such concerns collided with his personal ambitions to ride the new economic and cultural wave, and his internal conflicts about indulging in a life of extravagant travel and leisure. As Sparks concludes, however, the drive to prosper largely triumphed, and Sasolburg's consumerist trajectory was set. It's a story that confirms many of Veblen's central theses – about the ways in which conspicuous consumption becomes a stage for the enactment of gendered status-seeking. But like Hansen, Posel and Van Wyk, Sparks extends these arguments to underline the politics of the process, and the ways in which displays of material abundance intersect with the making of political identities – in this case, in the intimate spaces of the (white) home, and in the (white) public space of an emerging town. The chapter also tacitly unsettles a reading of Veblen that assumes the hegemony of consumerist status-seeking to be self-evident and stable.

Like Sparks' chapter, Claudia Gastrow's chapter deals with elites who have unfettered access to the proceeds of a petro-economy. Her chapter underlines the global registers of arguments about conspicuous consumption in Africa, how its (contested, contradictory) meanings are inextricable from the continent's colonial history and the racist legacies thereof. Angola's first family is among its most extravagant and profligate consumers, making no efforts to hide their considerable wealth from national and international media. On the contrary, these are heralded as markers of the nation's, as much as their individual, business prowess, which is in turn presented as a sign of 'Africa rising' – the successful entrepreneurship that marks Africa's transcendence of its lineage of economic victimisation. As Gastrow comments, such meanings have become possible exactly because colonial rule manipulated black people's access to consumable goods in line with presumed racial hierarchies of worth. Getting rich, and flashing that wealth around, became a language of anticolonial dissidence, demonstrating an agency and confidence to break the presumed rules of properly modest black African consumption. Here then is a version of the 'honour' conferred by conspicuous consumption that derives from a contradictory mix of both emulating and defying the material repertoires of the colonising power. Angola's elite, however, has a notorious history of equally flagrant corruption; its conspicuous consumption is typically the result of ill-gotten gains. Claims to material honour, then, have little traction among the majority of Angolans, who contest bitterly the brazenly 'bling' lifestyles of their rich and famous in the midst of dire national poverty, and recognise the corrupt affluence for what it is. Abroad however, in the racially prejudicial world of American reality television, in which flashy consumerism becomes the icon of power and glory on the 'dark' continent, the fact of such demonstrable wealth on the part of an individual black African can produce a surprised respect simultaneously coupled with confirmation of the continent's inherent corruptibility.

While Gastrow's chapter deals with the ways in which an African elite has utilised global registers of racism to fend off accusations of corruption, Karen Tranberg Hansen's chapter deals with one who famously could not: Frederick Chiluba. By the time of his trial in Zambia, former president Chiluba had become internationally synonymous with large-scale corruption. Local reactions to his indictment, however, were muted – until investigators discovered Chiluba's cache of clothes and money stored in 21 trunks and 11 suitcases in a warehouse owned by one of his co-accused. The trunks revealed a stupendous stash of designer clothes, shoes and accessories, much of it unused. This discovery galvanised public interest and outrage at Chiluba's manifest 'greed'. But, as Hansen shows, this accusation was contextual and deeply political. While Chiluba was in political favour, locals had widely copied his New Culture suits and colourful ties, but it was only once he fell afoul of local opinion that his sharp outfits were deemed excessive. In her reading of the Chiluba scandal, Hansen shows that his preoccupation with dressing well was integral to the way in which he crafted his public persona; Chiluba loved the dramaturgy of power. In contrast to his dressed body, Chiluba's trunks became symbolic of political greed. Veblen's focus on clothes and fashion does not go beyond individual status-seeking to the body political, which Hansen shows, is sartorial. Nor does Veblen allow for the pleasurable play with fashion that was central to the way in which Chiluba crafted his public persona.

Ilana van Wyk's chapter deals with another African leader (and his family) who has amassed enormous wealth through the state: South Africa's Jacob Zuma. Her chapter takes on the vexed question of why it is virtually impossible to shame him, and why shame (and Veblen's 'honour') should be such a powerful register through which to address conspicuous consumption. Here, Van Wyk unpacks the productionist religious ethic that animates Veblen's criticism of both the leisure class and conspicuous consumption. Unlike many of his contemporaries (and economists today), Veblen included religious office holders and institutions in his discussion of conspicuous consumption, but assumed that his puritanical values were universally shared. Van Wyk shows that these values continue to shape negative popular ideas about consumption and debt today. Like Gastrow, Van Wyk looks at Zuma's contemporary 'audience', but finds that many of them are not only appreciative of the ways in which he flaunts 'his' wealth; they are also receptive to his complaints that criminal accusations against him stem from sinister plots. She ascribes much of this support to a new religious ethic,

Neo-Pentecostalism, which has infused South African public culture. In its emphasis on the prosperity gospel and spiritual warfare, Neo-Pentecostalism embraces conspicuous consumption as a sign of divine favour and encourages believers to consume (usually beyond their means) as an act of faith. Jacob Zuma, like many other African leaders, is well versed in this theology and frequently draws on it to justify his transgressions and to attack his opponents. Van Wyk shows that his followers not only recognise him as a man of faith but actively engage in the same register, leading to an increasingly Pentecostalised public space where conspicuous consumption is not 'simply' aspirational but carries the weight of religious conviction.

In his ethnography of an elite man's funeral in Southwest Region, Cameroon, Rogers Orock holds a close lens to the social construction of 'big men' (and 'big families') in West Africa. Although he agrees with Veblen that conspicuous consumption and conspicuous waste play a central role in class differentiation, he shows that cultural and structural factors could imbue it with considerable anxiety and vulnerability. In a Cameroonian context of high social and economic inequality, where access to new forms of consumption and enrichment is limited, conspicuous consumption is a deeply serious stage on which 'big men' (and families) have constantly to affirm their status through a 'logic of inflation'. Since being 'big' in Cameroon goes beyond the display of expensive material objects to encompass also one's ability to look after people, it necessarily entails the intimate and domestic lives of 'big men'. These lives are often painfully exposed at funerals, where the social costs of bigness are dramatised in frequent family conflicts and social claims that do not hold up to scrutiny. At these 'orchestrated social dramas', the complex domesticities that arise from 'big men's' inflated sexual appetites also come to the fore and threaten both the deceased and his family's reputation or 'bigness'. Orock argues that both the sociopolitical value and the vulnerabilities that conspicuous consumption generate could only be realised in a social context where its lavish display is culturally evaluated. While Orock's chapter pays attention to the gendered repertoires of conspicuous consumption in Cameroon, he also reveals the intimate and domestic lives of 'big men' as an overlooked register of conspicuous consumption among the leisure class in Africa.

Adeline Masquelier's chapter finds subcultures of conspicuous consumption in Niamey, the capital of Niger, among the ranks of poor young Muslim men, whose material indulgences constitute a lexicon of youthful male dissidence. Economically insecure, alienated and bored, many such youths gather socially in *fadas* – groups that provide a space of refuge, solidarity and fun, as a bulwark against their economic insecurities and the social constraints of their Muslim milieu. These *fadas* instantiate a version of 'waithood' – anticipating, often dreading, incipient adulthood. Their conspicuous consumption has become a dominant and eloquent repertoire within that space, as a means of talking back to the many constraints of a disciplined Muslim adult life. Alcohol flows freely and often expensive African-American hip-hop clothing – associated with their 'gritty images of heroic masculinity' – is celebrated in an expression of connectedness to the 'global popular culture' fashioned by global neoliberal markets.

Efforts to impress their male peers and attract female interest are central factors here, with strong echoes of the familiar Veblenian argument. But these practices of status-seeking are more variegated and culturally complex than in Veblen's rather attenuated account – especially with respect to the generational dynamic, and its intersections with the pursuit of a heroic masculinity forged in the interstices of poverty and religious regulation. Here are young men deliberately not emulating the ways of their social superiors in the older generation; their status-seeking is vested in their transgressions, even if these will likely give way in later years as they embrace the dominant norms of Muslim adulthood. Masquelier's account also foregrounds questions of affect – beyond Veblen's censorious disapproval of any hedonistic materialist excesses. The young men of the *fadas* seek and find pleasure and emotional solace in their lifestyle – even if their enjoyment is tinged with the anxieties about their incipient adulthood.

Jabulani Mnisi's chapter on *izikhothane* in Johannesburg echoes Masquelier's in its focus on a much-derided youth subculture, which embraces spectacular forms of conspicuous consumption. *Izikhothane* are young men from South African townships who vie for 'respect' by theatrically destroying expensive consumer items in competitive dance-offs. In the townships, *izikhothane* are anomalous for the abandon with which they spend money and the hyperbolic extent of their 'waste', both conditions that scandalise their thrifty elders and a censorious media. While their competitions resemble the potlatches referenced by Veblen, they differ in the important respect that they are hosted by men who are socially immature and economically marginal. These facts are obvious to their audiences and threaten the supposed 'honour' that the young men are trying to secure for themselves. However, as Mnisi shows, while *izikhothane* would love to inhabit a masculine ideal untouched by poverty, their competitions are geared to impress their peers at school – not with their riches, but with their ability to hustle and to take risks. While women often feature as 'trophies' in these competitions, it is the conviviality of the lifestyle that attracts many *izikhothane*: an easy-going brotherhood in which the difficulties of their home lives recede. Participants also imagine the *izikhothane* lifestyle as a short, enjoyable hiatus between their youth and more conventional and arduous adult plans. And unlike Veblen, who insists that people in the lower classes merely emulate their social superiors, Mnisi shows that *izikhothane* are deeply original in the ways that they assemble and don their finery.

Bradley Rink's chapter considers the commercialisation of homosexuality in an affluent suburb of Cape Town's Atlantic Seaboard popular with foreign tourists – a process very familiar in other parts of the late-modern capitalist world. Sexuality has long been closely associated with an erotics of 'stuff', in historically contextual forms and fashions. Rink offers a case study of how this connection has been shaped in post-apartheid South Africa, and how it has turned queer men into avid consumers, in the name of their sexuality. His discussion focuses on The Pink Map – a tourist guide to queer spaces in De Waterkant, Cape Town, that has been in circulation since 1999. In the early years of its existence, the imagery included in the map showcased the *frisson* of the nearly nude male body as the basis for mapping sexual desire onto the geography of this part of the city. A mere three years since the promulgation of the new Bill of Rights and its provisions of sexual equality, The Pink Map was initially a celebration of the newfound visibility of gay life – a proud geographical 'coming out', welcoming gay men into the open. But as the years have passed, the Map has changed, its representations of gay life increasingly preoccupied with the local geography of an exultant consumerism. Food and fashion now dominate, as the novelty of sexual emancipation in South Africa has receded. The meaning of gay conspicuous consumption in an area such as De Waterkant is thus one strand in a wider sociopolitical transformation, as the contours of the post-apartheid order have changed. But Rink situates these historical realignments more widely too, arguing that the case of De Waterkant is also a localised example of a more global trend, in which the initially transgressive idea of a 'gay village' has given way to a gay consumer 'lifestyle village', promoting the cornucopia of copious shopping as the gateway to a pleasurable existence. Adding a close consideration of sexuality to the analytic mix, Rink also underlines the need to set the idea of conspicuous consumption into motion – geographically and historically, mapping its changing forms and what these reveal about closely aligned shifts in the politics of identity in neo-liberal times.

While Veblen concentrated on the pecuniary habits of the leisure class, he insisted that no social class stood outside the matrix of reputability. However, it was from the middle classes down that a 'curious inversion' (Veblen 2003: 38) happened in the gendered construction of conspicuous consumption. Here, by necessity, men engaged in productive labour, while the duties of securing reputability through conspicuous consumption and leisure devolved to their wives. In the middle and lower classes then, the reputability – or 'decency', 'good name' and 'self-respect' (40) – of the household rested on the wife's (and children's) conspicuous consumption and vicariously reflected on the male head of the household (38–41). In this deeply patriarchal system (35), Veblen described the middle and lower middle classes as conservative and thrifty (18) but despite their parsimony, insisted that conspicuous consumption was an abiding preoccupation in their domestic sphere (32).

Sophie Chevalier's chapter questions the centrality that Veblen accorded to conspicuous domestic consumption among the middle classes by looking at the food provisioning and food consumption patterns of the lower middle class in Durban, South Africa. In a society where debates about conspicuous consumption and class stir up considerable racial anxieties, especially around the definition of so-called 'black diamonds', she shows that the lower middle class consciously subscribes to a different register. Even though food is their single biggest monthly expense, Chevalier argues that instead of conspicuousness, lower middle class food consumption is guided by a moral economy that emphasises careful budgeting, sharing and community belonging. What emerges is a consciously self-controlled consumer who restrains her excesses, even during festive periods, in the interest of others. While this restraint might stem from a different moral order from the one that informed Veblen's thesis, it is also fundamentally tied to the precariousness of this class. The middle class in Durban is also, unlike Veblen's middle classes, marked by the fluidity of household compositions, which sees adults routinely sharing food with poorer family members. Veblen (2003: 154) seems to have been baffled by such affective and non-conspicuous forms of consumption, saying that the 'impulse of charity or of sociability … tends in a direction contrary to the underlying principles of the institution of the leisure class'.

The final chapter by Brenner and Gupta breaks the mould set by the other chapters, each of which complicates and diversifies Veblen's analysis, but with a version of conspicuous consumption essentially in line with Veblen's, as publicly recognisable extravagant excess (whether intended as such or not). Joni Brenner has been the link between the Zimbabwean women who weave Marigold beads and the discreet commercial market for these beads in her home, the occasional pop-up shop, occasions such as the Johannesburg Art Fair – and any academic conference that Brenner attends, where they are voraciously consumed. This includes the conference that seeded this volume. In many ways, the consumption of these beads is the very antithesis of the phenomenon Veblen describes as ostentatious acquisition and display to champion male honour according to the dominant social standards of extravagance and luxury. Brenner and Gupta thus juxtapose the Marigold beads to diamond jewellery, which would fit more comfortably into the Veblenian mould. But the excited frenzy of the bead's consumers also makes a case for a more flexible and nuanced notion of conspicuous consumption – one which is wholly shorn of Veblen's moralistic disdain, open to the pleasures of the thing itself, and yet acknowledges nevertheless the integral connection between material display and the claim to social status. Marigold beads are bought, given and worn mainly by women, but a particular stratum and type of women: intellectual, arty, or professional people, whose social distinction manifests, in part, in their disavowal of 'bling'. As per Veblen, their consumption of the beads is conspicuous in being purely decorative (as opposed to functional). By conventional standards of 'bling', these beads are relatively invisible and inauspicious. Yet for those who wear them and the small numbers who see and record their presence, the beads confer the cachet of exclusivity: they are not cheap, nor are they readily available. Wearing them creates an inner circle of those who recognise each other as having similarly 'sophisticated' tastes and style. Here then, is a very different kind of conspicuous consumption, which defamiliarises the Veblenian norm. The chapter is an outlier in the volume in many ways, and yet integral to the overall story that the collection tells in that it urges those who might be quick to dismiss the Veblenian consumer as other than themselves to recognise a not wholly dissimilar pattern in the connection between the recognition of a social elite and its material ornamentation.

In all, then, the chapters in the volume illustrate a variety of contextual and structural factors driving the pursuit of conspicuous consumption that Veblen's account underplayed, or wholly omitted. Generation, race, sexuality, national identity, religion and political power have all emerged as formative fault lines and processes with which the dynamics of conspicuous consumption are thoroughly intertwined. The volume has also demonstrated a far more variegated, and interesting, affective register of conspicuous consumption than Veblen, in his moralistic contempt, was willing to acknowledge: from exuberance, pleasure, happiness and care through to longing, uncertainty, anxiety and insecurity. Our relationships to the promise of material abundance are emotionally and psychologically moored in ways that bear far fuller analysis than Veblen was open to. Overall, the volume demonstrates that the motivations for, and consequences of, conspicuous consumption are more layered and situated than we find in the sparseness of Veblen's version. And conspicuous consumption emerges here as a site of inner/private and outer/public contestation, rather than an entirely complacent and consensual way of being, in the manner suggested by Veblen's account.

Conspicuous consumption, then, may take different forms in different places and times. *And yet*: there is a unifying strand across all these chapters, running through all the discussions of contextual specificity and variability. In every chapter, a performance of a form of material abundance is rendered as having been understood and received as an expression of social standing, within the particular audiences for which it is performed – even if this does not entirely exhaust or explain that performance. The volume produces many different versions of a formative link between the pursuit of conspicuous consumption and hierarchies of status and recognition – varied though these may be. These links are mediated and dense; they take shape in different ways in different contexts – but they are there, abidingly, nonetheless. The concept of conspicuous consumption underlines the ways in which status-seeking, in its various modalities, is woven into the fabric of inequality and power, on one hand, and the vagaries of identity-making, on the other. This surely makes it a central and revealing aspect of any efforts to fathom the history of Africa's projects of modernity, and their global lineages and legacies. Whatever the excesses, oddities and limits of Veblen's original thesis, his central proposition seems abidingly relevant, and fruitful to think with.

REFERENCES

Adorno, T. W., 1941, 'Veblen's Attack on Culture', *Studies in Philosophy and Social Science* 9: 389.

Adorno, T. W., 1983, *Prisms*, The MIT Press: Cambridge.

Akwagyiram, A., 2013, 'Africa Rising – But Who Benefits?', in *BBC Africa*, viewed 12 August 2017, available from: http://www.bbc.com/news/world-africa-22847118.

Allison, S., 2017, 'Grace Mugabe: The Rags to Riches Rise and Fall of "Gucci Grace"', in *The Guardian*, viewed 15 November 2017, available from: https://www.theguardian.com/world/2017/nov/15/grace-mugabe-the-rags-to-riches-rise-and-fall-of-gucci-grace.

Bayart, J.,1993, *The State in Africa: The Politics of the Belly*, Longman: London & New York.

Campbell, C., 1995, 'Conspicuous Confusion? A Critique of Veblen's Theory of Conspicuous Consumption', *Sociological Theory* 13(1): 37–47.

Collins, R. O. & Burns, J. M., 2007, *A History of Sub-Saharan Africa*, Cambridge University Press: Cambridge.

Comaroff, J., 1996, 'The Empire's Old Clothes: Fashioning the Colonial Subject', in D. Howes (ed.), *Cross-Cultural Consumption: Global Markets, Local Realities*, 19–38, Routledge: London and New York.

Comaroff, J. & Comaroff, J. L., 1990, 'Goodly Beasts and Beastly Goods: Cattle and Commodities in a South African Context', *American Ethnologist* 17(2): 195–216.

Davis, F., 1992, *Fashion, Culture, and Identity*, University of Chicago Press: Chicago.

De Vries, R. & Reeves, A., 2017, 'Why do People Care More about Benefit "Scroungers" than Billions Lost to the Rich?', in *The Guardian*, viewed 18 November 2017, available from: https://www.theguardian.com/commentisfree/2017/nov/15/benefit-scroungers-billions-rich-paradise-papers-tax-avoidance.

Diggins, J. P., 1999, *Thorstein Veblen: Theorist of the Leisure Class*, Princeton University Press: Princeton.

Doig, S., 2014, 'Meet the Dandies of Brazzaville', in *The Telegraph*, viewed 19 November 2017, available from: http://www.telegraph.co.uk/men/fashion-and-style/10564648/Meet-the-dandies-of-Brazzaville.html.

Dosekun, S. O., 2015. Fashioning Spectacular Femininities in Nigeria: Postfeminism, Consumption and the Transnational. PhD thesis, Kings College London.

Etherington, N., 1978, *Preachers Peasants and Politics in Southeast Africa, 1835–1880: African Christian Communities in Natal, Pondoland and Zululand*, Royal Historical Society: London.

Etherington, N., 2002, 'Outward and Visible Signs of Conversion in Nineteenth-Century KwaZulu-Natal', *Journal of Religion in Africa* 32(4): 422–39.

Fabricius, P., 2015, 'Africa Rising or Africa Uprising?', in *Mail & Guardian*, viewed 19 November 2017, available from: https://mg.co.za/article/2015-11-11-africa-rising-or-africa-uprising/.

Fanon, F., 1961, 'Pitfalls of National Consciousness – Decolonization', *New Agenda: South African Journal of Social and Economic Policy*, 2017 (66): 36–40.

Holbrook, S. H., 2010, *The Age of the Moghuls: The Story of the Robber Barons and the Great Tycoons*, Transaction Publishers: New York.

Iqani, M., 2016, *Consumption, Media and the Global South: Aspiration Contested*, Palgrave Macmillan: London.

Jansen, C., 2016, 'How Ghana's Top Fantasy Coffin Artist Has Put the Fun in Funeral', in *The Guardian*, viewed 19 November 2017, available from: https://www.theguardian.com/world/2016/nov/24/paa-joe-ghana-fantasy-coffin-artist-casket-funeral.

Johnson, S., 2015, 'Slowdown Calls "Africa Rising" Narrative into Question', in *The Financial Times*, viewed 19 November 2017, available from: https://www.ft.com/content/93d5c572-7bf6-11e5-a1fe-567b37f80b64.

Kistner, U., 2015, 'Trading in Freedom: Rethinking Conspicuous Consumption in Post-Apartheid Political Economy', *Critical Arts* 29(2): 240–259.

Mahajan, V., 2009, *Africa Rising: How 900 Million African Consumers Offer More Than You Think* (4th edn.), Wharton School Publishers: Upper Saddle River.

Mbembe, J-A., 2004, 'Aesthetics of Superfluity', *Public Culture* 16(3): 373–405.

Meyer, B., 2002, 'Commodities and the Power of Prayer: Pentecostalist Attitudes towards Consumption in Contemporary Ghana', *Development and Change* 29(4): 751–776.

Mills, C. W., 2002 [1951], *The Theory of the Leisure Class*, in I. L. Horowitz (ed.), *Veblen's Century: A Collective Portrait*, Transaction Publishers: New Brunswick and London.

Mutiga, M. & Flood, Z., 2016, 'Africa Calling: Mobile Phone Revolution to Transform Democracies', in *The Guardian*, viewed 22 November 2017, available from: https://www.theguardian.com/world/2016/aug/08/africa-calling-mobile-phone-broadband-revolution-transform-democracies.

Osborne, H., 2017, 'Revealed: Queen's Private Estate Invested Millions of Pounds Offshore', in *The Guardian*, viewed 18 November 2017, available from: https://www.theguardian.com/news/2017/nov/05/revealed-queen-private-estate-invested-offshore-paradise-papers.

Plotkin, S., (ed.), 2017. *The Anthem Companion to Thorstein Veblen*, Anthem Press: London.

Ross, R. J., 1990, 'The Top Hat in South African History: The Changing Significance of an Article of Material Culture', *Social Dynamics* 16(2): 90–100.

Sherman, E., 2016, 'Queen Elizabeth: A Look at 90 Years of Vast Wealth and Perks', in *Fortune Magazine*, viewed 18 November 2017, available from: http://fortune.com/2016/04/21/tqueen-elizabeth-birthday-net-worth/.

Smith, D., 2013, 'Mobutu Sese Seko's Body to be Returned to Democratic Republic of the Congo', in *The Guardian*, viewed 23 November 2017, available from: https://www.theguardian.com/world/2013/oct/25/mobutu-sese-seko-remains-repatriated-congo-zaire.

Spindler, M., 2002, *Veblen and Modern America: Revolutionary Iconoclast*, Pluto Press: London.

Spronk, R., 2014, 'Exploring the Middle Classes in Nairobi: From Modes of Production to Modes of Sophistication', *African Studies Review* 57(1): 93–114.

Taylor, I., 2014, *Africa Rising? BRICS – Diversifying Dependency*, James Currey: Oxford.

Tilman, R., 1992, *Thorstein Veblen and His Critics, 1891–1963: Conservative, Liberal and Radical Perspectives*, Princeton University Press: Princeton.

Veblen, T., 1894, 'The Economic Theory of Women's Dress', in *The Popular Science Monthly* 46: 198–205.

Veblen, T., 1899, 'The Barbarian Status of Women', *The American Journal of Sociology* 4, 503–514.

Veblen, T., 2003 [1899], *The Theory of the Leisure Class*, Edwin Mellen Press: Lewiston.

Wadongo, E., 2014, 'Africa Rising? Let's be Afro-realistic', in *The Guardian*, viewed 20 November 2017, available from: https://www.theguardian.com/global-development-professionals-network/2014/nov/07/africa-rising-lets-be-afro-realistic.

NOTES

1. In 2014, the International Monetary Fund held a conference entitled 'Africa Rising: Building to the Future' (see https://www.imf.org/en/News/Articles/2015/09/28/04/53/sp052914).
2. In November 2017, the German newspaper *Süddeutsche Zeitung* obtained information on the Paradise Papers and shared it with the International Consortium of Investigative Journalists who then published their findings in a range of publications, including *The Guardian*, the *BBC* and *The New York Times*.
3. Perhaps because Veblen himself was an early, and pioneering, interdisciplinary writer, his work has engaged the attention of scholars across a range of disciplines and fields of study – well beyond economics, his 'home' discipline (See for example, Plotkin 2017).
4. See also Ulrike Kistner (2015) on conspicuous consumption in South Africa post-apartheid.

2 CHANGES IN THE ORDER OF THINGS: DEPARTMENT STORES AND THE MAKING OF MODERN CAPE TOWN

DEBORAH POSEL

One of the strands in Thorstein Veblen's *Theory of the Leisure Class* that commentators tend to ignore – for good reason – concerns his remarks about the relationship between consumption patterns and race.[1] Giving an evolutionary account of the 'dominating influence … of the dolicho blond type of European man' (Veblen 2003: 104), Veblen reproduces a racialised hierarchy of 'civilisation', but within an anachronistic account (both conceptually and historically) that carries little interest in current debates or commentaries. His text, then, has little to contribute on what is arguably a critical dimension of conspicuous consumption in racialised societies – namely, the ways in which this consumer practice is fundamentally shaped by the intersections between the racial order and the material order of things. Yet despite these obvious gaps, Veblen's insistence on the importance of the realm of material consumption in producing social hierarchies and their symbolic grammars is absolutely pertinent – not least in the making of race.

In the same period about which Veblen was writing, but far away, in the modernising colony of the Cape, a distinctive regime of conspicuous consumption was emerging within the middle and upper echelons, largely (although not exclusively) white. New notions of material abundance intersected with practices of race, as well as class and status, becoming central to the configuration of Cape Town as a worldly port city.

From the late nineteenth century, unprecedented volumes and varieties of stuff became available within South Africa. This was a consequence of both global and national developments. As Christopher Alan Bayly (2004: 472) puts it, this period was marked by a 'great acceleration' – 'the dramatic speeding up of global social, intellectual and economic change' – including in the movement of things and people around the world. More effective global networks of trade enabled, *inter alia*, by the advent of steam ships moved greater quantities of goods around the world more frequently than before. That these were available for circulation was a consequence, in turn, of recent technologies of mass production and scientific invention, created and driven by burgeoning markets for their consumption. Within South Africa, harbours were upgraded to expedite growing networks of import and export trade, railways were built to enable transportation from coastal to inland destinations, while new consumer markets were buoyed by the growth of the diamond and gold fields.

As the country's foremost port, Cape Town was a critical node in these processes, and as a result, was transformed from a small colonial town into 'a modern planned city' (Bank & Minkley 1998/9: 7). As the mines and their environs expanded, so too did the demand for manufactured goods, most of which were imported and transported via Cape Town. Industrial activities in the city also flourished, although on a far smaller scale than on the Rand, with 'small factories erected, machines imported and more workers employed' (Bickford-Smith 1995b: 130). The economic slump of the 1880s gave way to a period of vigorous economic growth – albeit with the Anglo-Boer War as something of a dampener. A building boom erupted during the 1890s, leading to a refashioning of the architecture and physical infrastructure of the city, as the local council – dominated by ambitious, prosperous merchants – underwrote and championed the aspiration to modernise. Indeed, mercantile interests were at the forefront of the economic and political changes afoot. Their efforts coincided too, with processes of Anglicisation, aligning Cape Town with the British metropole, and away from its earlier Dutch colonial attachments. The main street, previously named in Dutch as 'Heerengracht', was changed to Adderley Street and the architecture of new buildings mirrored the Victorian styles of the British metropole, as grand, sometimes multi-storeyed, constructions replaced the lower-lying Cape Dutch colonial vernacular. With the means and incentive to expand their premises, 'by 1894, Cape Town merchants had largely rebuilt the heart of the city' (Bickford-Smith 1995b: 130). In this, new and/or enlarged wholesale and retail premises were prominent. Investments in upgrading the physical infrastructure of the city (funded by municipal revenues accruing from the building boom) were also spearheaded by leading wholesalers and retailers who dominated local government, and for whom substantial investments in the urban infrastructure (roads, drainage systems, etc.) were also good for business.

The population grew exponentially too, with increased international immigration and national migration between 1891 and 1904 bringing some 40 000 whites and

30 000 Asians and Africans into Cape Town (Bickford-Smith 1995b: 131). By 1904, this was South Africa's largest and most cosmopolitan city – a place of growing inequality that also saw the emergence of a more assertive and formative racial hierarchy than in the past. The advent of department stores at the turn of the twentieth century was one small but important slice of this new material and social order. It is a history about which little academic analysis has been produced.[2]

THE EMERGENCE OF DEPARTMENT STORES

The advent of the department store represented a significant shift in a longer history of the popularisation of shopping[3] and, as Walter Benjamin (2002) recognised, a cultural and social milestone in the theatricalisation and aestheticisation of consumption. Many of the department stores' defining features had a longer historical lineage: as Frank Trentmann (2016: 191) argues, 'virtually all its innovations can be traced back in time … What department stores did was to bring together these various innovations under one enormous … roof' – a major innovation in and of itself.

The first department stores appeared in Britain and France from the mid-nineteenth century, followed by the USA, and some British colonies – notably Australia. They took shape somewhat differently in particular places and contexts, ranging from top-end through to somewhat more modest structures and offerings. Still, the institution of the department store exhibited some shared features, which are worth establishing briefly before considering the case of department stores in Cape Town in more detail.

The economic logic that drove the development of department stores was the pursuit of much-increased profitability based on the rapid turnover of a wide range of goods located under a single roof, to which a comparably voluminous stream of customers would have access. This was predicated on a repertoire of retail sale based on fixed prices, kept down by the lower mark-ups made possible by large volumes of goods sold (Pasdermadjian 1954: 3). The economic challenge, and opportunity, created by the department store was thus to engineer a dramatic escalation in the demand for consumer goods by changing the place and appeal of the experience of shopping in everyday life in those places where these new stores took shape.

For this reason, the architecture, aesthetics and public representation of the department store were crucial. The department store proffered a new 'shopping experience' – as that upon which the enterprise would pivot. With *Le Bon Marché* having captured the Parisian bourgeois imagination from the mid-nineteenth century, the French realist novelists identified the changes: in Honoré de Balzac's words, these spaces would become 'great poem[s] of display' (cited in Benjamin 2002: 3), in what Emile Zola famously called 'cathedrals of commerce' (2008: 234).

In the biggest and best of the department stores, the shopping experience was infused with a heady sense of worldliness – borne of having access to a profuse variety of goods from many and distant parts of the world. As Paul Lerner puts it, department stores produced statements of an 'aspirant internationalism': 'department stores not only promoted the international origins of their stock, but they represented themselves as gateways to the wider world in both metaphorical and literal ways' (2010: 397).

In this respect, the department store was closely aligned with the phenomenon of industrial exhibitions (another important repertoire of nineteenth-century modernity) that 'displayed the products of the world in a way that blurred the lines between culture and commodity' (Trentmann 2016: 193). In the best department stores, goods were on offer not merely from within the familiar routes of exchange within the British Empire: Japan, the USA, Paris and other European centres of fashion became sources and icons of the very latest in style, taste and progress. To shop in such spaces – and go home with goods from exotic and far-flung places – was to partake of a culturally sophisticated world imagined on a grand canvas beyond the parochial confines of everyday life.

Exoticism and excited modernity went hand in hand with what Rosalind Williams calls a 'democratisation of luxury' (1991: 11), but perhaps more appropriately, the extension of aspirations to 'luxury' beyond aristocratic elites and the prosperous top-end of the bourgeoisie. For of course, the constraints of class would be increasingly prominent, as the capitalist order of the nineteenth century exacerbated inequalities of wealth and economic opportunity. The department store – particularly in its most up-market incarnation – would not be a store for any 'riff-raff'. But in extending access to larger numbers of shoppers who could afford to pay for 'quality goods' at 'low prices', the department store enacted a distinctive and seductive compound of 'luxury' and 'bargain', of particular appeal to the growing ranks of middle-class consumers. Indeed, prefigured by the advent of the shopping arcades documented by Walter Benjamin, the department store marked the beginning of the mass enchantment with shopping in spaces of spectacle.

Close attention was paid to the architecture of department stores, as typically bold and innovative spaces, inside and outside. In order to accommodate the requisite range and volume of goods, the building had to be capacious, encompassing several storeys taking up a large footprint on the ground. When budgets permitted, such scale also offered the opportunity for grandiose and spectacular construction, using the very latest in scientific technology and building methods. This was the era in which skyscrapers first appeared, enabled by the pioneering use of steel girders in their construction. Iconic department stores soared skywards on the strength of such steel frames. The use of sheets of glass – made possible by new technologies of glass manufacture – enabled the insertion of large display windows rendering storefront displays visible to passers-by on the street who might then be tempted to indulge further by entering the shop and its promise of profusion. The insertion of electric lighting to illuminate the windows at night added sophistication and glamour to the window-shopping experience. Lifts and elevators – themselves a symbol of the modern cutting-edge of the times – graced the interiors of many department stores, facilitating more efficient mobility through the different storeys of the building, at the same time as enacting the semiotic coupling of stylish 'progress' with the newfound abundance of all manner of stuff. Harrods in London installed its first 'moving staircase' in 1898, boasting that it moved up to 4 000 customers per hour (Trentmann 2016: 195), an astounding number of people to be traversing the premises of one store at the time.

The interiors of department stores were typically more lavish and elaborate than more ordinary shops. At the top end, considerable expense went into creating spectacles of opulence, with well-appointed fittings, using expensive materials to make grand and alluring statements about the stature of the enterprise. Special attention was paid to female shoppers – a critical, and growing, constituency for department stores – with a 'feminine' aesthetic self-consciously deployed in well-appointed changing rooms and 'restroom' facilities. Many department stores also introduced bandstands and/or tea rooms as part of their interiors, to entice shoppers to extend the time spent in the store, and to add to the perception of the shopping experience as leisurely and enjoyable in and of itself. For women with time on their hands, the department store thus became a new kind of public space: one in which they felt safe to gather independently of men, with socialising and shopping merging into a single activity (Bowlby 2000: 8–9). This is not to say that male customers were not also wooed: dedicated sections and styles for male customers were imbued with more 'masculine' appeal.

In short, the central achievement of the department store was to infuse a newly burgeoning velocity and scale of retail trade with a distinctive 'structure of feeling', to use Raymond Williams' (1977: 133–135) phrase: pleasure, awe and endless temptation in the midst of an abundance of things, in turn bound up with performances of modernising worldliness and sophistication. All of this was on offer across the spectrum of the middle classes, widening the seduction of fashionable abundance beyond the narrow confines of rich elites.

GARLICKS AND STUTTAFORDS IN CAPE TOWN

As suggested earlier on in this chapter, several historians of the Cape have rightly stressed the need to take account of the growth of commerce in nineteenth-century Cape Town – and the political muscle of those who promoted it (often themselves leading businessmen in the colony) – as critically formative factors in the history of the emergent city at the turn of the century (Bickford-Smith 1995b; Bank & Minkley 1988/9;

Worden, Van Heynigen & Bickford-Smith 1998). The development of the department store forms part of this story of the commercialisation of everyday life in the colony and its impact on the changing colonial order.

Writing in 1861, an unnamed 'lady', recently arrived in Cape Town, was relieved to discover the degree of material comfort among the colony's propertied elite, notwithstanding the fact that 'the place was in its infancy as to riches, conveniences, taste and luxury' (A Lady 1998: 37). Referring to the homes of the 'ladies of the garrison', the author registered her initial surprise at:

> how very well-ordered are the appointments of many of these houses. They are generally situated in the suburbs – called the 'Gardens' – and besides being provided with stables and coach-houses, have flower-pots and verandahs loaded with bloom. Most of the drawing-rooms are very prettily furnished, with profusion of vases, easy chairs and walnut and rosewood articles 'deluxe'. (A Lady 1998: 11)

The shops of the time did not disappoint her either, particularly in the range of goods available at the venerable Fletchers store – a mainstay of the colonial household and of the hawkers and country storekeepers who sourced their goods from this 'mammoth establishment' offering 'the sale of everything essential to household expenditure, except bread, meat and drink' (A Lady 1998: 11). Notions of 'everything essential' within the town's elite and emergent middle class – as well their conception of 'a mammoth establishment' – would undergo a noticeable shift in subsequent decades, not least with the establishment of Garlicks and Stuttafords, Cape Town's two flagship department stores.

The 'lady' author of *Life at the Cape* also noted disapprovingly the scorn affected by Cape Town's landed elite towards the pursuit of 'business' – a sign, in her eyes, of a snobbish colonial insularity. 'To see women [of white Cape Town society], who have perhaps never moved in Europe in other than third-rate middle class society, turn up their chiselled noses at good-natured, and by no means vulgar, Africanders, *because* their husbands are engaged in business, is one of the saddest proofs of insular pride and power of human conceit' (A Lady 1998: 38).

John Garlick, founder of the Garlicks emporium and influential local politician, was one among several leading English-speaking businessmen who played a key role in transforming that perception, elevating – indeed, glorifying – commerce as a respectable and ennobling pursuit, and one of the vanguards of British colonial 'progress' and 'civilisation'. Garlick, by all accounts, was a consummately skilled entrepreneur-cum-politician, who had assimilated well into the genteel hierarchies of the colonial order. He had first arrived in Cape Town in 1872, at the age of 20. By the mid-1880s, he had acquired a reputation as one of the town's most effective merchants. An article recounting the success of the 1884 Industrial Exhibition in Cape Town (in which Garlick had played a major role), described him as 'one of those quiet, unobtrusive, kindly men, who accomplished more than those who may be described as "hustlers"'(Official Programme 1914: 31). Others also publicly hailed his virtue as a businessman, in 'the application of enterprise and commercial vigour', 'a true spirit of enterprise, a vigorous capacity for making all things turn to account, and judicious employment of means' (*Excalibur* 1886). Veblen would have approved: here was a man who embraced the ethos of hard work, was absorbed in the details of his enterprise, and was an astute and visionary businessman, who prided himself on being abreast of the very latest trends in fashion and technology. Yet, *contra* Veblen, it was exactly this ethos of hard work and productivity that engineered the city's access to a new order of the 'conspicuous waste' that the acerbic economist so scorned. Garlick's hard work went into using the department store and its regime of conspicuous consumption to help shape Cape Town's sense of its worldly progress and colonial modernity – at the same time as making himself rather rich.

Garlick's first large store was opened in 1875, on the corner of Bree and Strand streets in central Cape Town. An advertisement in *The Cape Mercantile Advertiser* promised 'an entirely new stock of General Drapery, Hosiery, Haberdashery, Millinery, Boots, etc. etc. which Garlick will offer at very low prices for Cash' (Rosenthal 1960: 6). The new shop drew rapt admiration from *The Cape Register* in 1886 – not for any grandiosity in its architecture and fittings, but rather for the hive of activity and the mounds of stuff it accommodated. So successful had Garlick been in attracting throngs of customers that the need for a new and better shopping space had become abundantly clear, said the text. Seven years later, in 1893, the more magnificent spectacle of the new Garlicks emporium was opened on the corner of Adderley and Waterkant streets – perhaps *the* prime retail site, with a commanding position in the visual iconography of the emerging city, and one of the first buildings upon which the eyes of immigrants or visitors would alight upon disembarking from ships in the harbour.

It would prove to be a very expensive venture. The required investment was made possible by the considerable profitability of Garlick's first store, along with the success of his other shops set up near the diamond fields in Kimberley. With no shortage of cash, Garlick was set on creating an architectural and commercial landmark. He wrote to his aunt in England, 'I am building a new store and expecting it to be the biggest and best in South Africa when it is finished' (Rosenthal 1960: 257). Garlick was closely involved with every step of the construction process. In lavishing his attention on the project, he dug deep into his pockets to fund it: 'I want it of the best quality', he insisted – and wanted it known, publicly, that no expense was spared (Rosenthal 1960: 260).

And he intended thereby to break the mould of retail trade in Cape Town: 'to bring the whole of the outfitting and tailoring business down' (Rosenthal 1960: 258). If quietly spoken, Garlick's intentions were anything but quiet, aiming to make 'not only commercial but engineering history' (Rosenthal 1960: 259).

Indeed, the most salient, and significant, feature of the store was its hubristic ambition, and the attendant spectacle. By local building standards, it was huge, spanning an entire block and rising up a 'towering five storeys' (Rosenthal 1960: 259). The exterior was architecturally elaborate, replete with 'ornamental ironwork, the statuary along the roof, the mock Renaissance turrets, porticos and other trimmings' (Rosenthal 1960: 259). A monumental sign on the roof named the store, visible from afar (see Figure 1). The 'chief entrance' (one of three) was particularly grand, having 'a handsome tiled floor, on either side [of which] are large ornamental iron gates' (*The Cape Register* 1893). The interior too made a bold and extravagant statement – with many departments, spread across two floors, abundantly stocked, generously proportioned and expensively furnished – including 'costly counters and fittings of mahogany and brass', and 'good quality leather' (Rosenthal 1960: 261). When the *Cape Argus* announced the opening of this store in September 1893, it underlined this commitment to opulence:

> In regard to the furniture of the building, which has been supplied by the well-known firm H.E. Richold, it may be mentioned that it is of the most elaborate description throughout. The waiting and retiring rooms for ladies are provided, with artistic settees, easy chairs, tables and Turkish carpets, which given them an appearance of great cosiness and comfort. (*Cape Argus* 1893)

The desires and tastes of women shoppers were prominent in the aesthetic and contents of the store. With a keen eye to this constituency, Garlick retained the services of buyers in Europe as well as London: with Parisian fashion iconic of worldly style, he insisted that while most imports came from Britain, the key fashion items had to come from Paris, along with other orders placed in Vienna and Milan (Rosenthal 1960: 30). The interior of the store included 'two ladies' fitting-on rooms … and Mr. Garlick has brought out two English dressmakers, who will each attend to the wants of lady customers. There is also a Ladies' waiting room, comfortably furnished, and provided with lavatory etc.' (*The Cape Register* 1893).

The store was also technologically cutting-edge – a point of particular pride and attentiveness on Garlick's part, recognising that this would be a central element of how the enterprise represented itself and captured the public imagination. The display windows comprised 'twelve of the largest sheets of plate glass ever imported into Cape Town, each 42 inches by 51' (Rosenthal 1960: 266). In addition to embellishment by 'special brass fittings of the newest patterns' (*The Cape Register* 1893), the windows also boasted fitted mirrors, to maximise the visual impact of the displays to passers-by. In his commissioned commercial biography of Garlick, Rosenthal notes three other technological innovations that would distinguish the store from anything else in the country at that time, and bring it on par with the more sophisticated department stores elsewhere in the world: the installation of a lift; electric lighting; and a sprinkler system.

Two lifts were installed (one for customers, the other for goods) – the country's first. *The Cape Register*'s article on the opening of the store in 1893 noted 'a very handsome passenger lift, constructed by Messrs R Waygood & Co, made of walnut and satinwood, and fitted with an ornamental brass rail, [which] ascends to all floors, and is in charge of a competent man'. The reassuring lift operator notwithstanding, Garlick was not happy with this first installation, and soon made enquiries about a replacement that was even more modern – in fact, globally cutting edge, with only one then in place in New York. In 1898, he wrote to Messrs Crossman and Brothers in New York:

> I see an account of the inclined elevator in use at Messrs Bloomingdale Bros Store in New York. Can you get full particulars? I may say we find considerable difficulty in getting customers on to the First Floor showrooms. They are not used to Elevators and feel it is too much trouble to go up one floor only and it is too much trouble for them if they can get the same things elsewhere on the ground floor in the immediate neighbourhood. Consequently I think this 'inclined elevator' would answer. Will you personally go into the question, try it and get a lady friend or two – one of them of nervous disposition, if there are any such women in America – to try it also, and let us have the result. (Garlick 1898)

Lighting such a huge store was a formidable technological challenge, requiring the installation of 'a four horse power Otto Gas Engine of the latest pattern, which is used for the whole of the large electric light machinery' (*The Cape Register* 1893). If a dark interior would have been symbolically catastrophic, the new source and scale of lighting made a powerful impact in and of itself.

A fire in the premises would have been equally disastrous, hence Garlick's investment in a new and elaborate sprinkler system, described by *The Cape Register* (1893):

> Each floor is protected by a number of automatic sprinklers the invention of the firm of Witter & Son, Bolton, these are placed at certain distances in the ceilings, throughout the building. It is an automatic arrangement which opens of itself in case of fire.

Provision for the entertainment of customers became part of the sociality of the store. Some time after the initial construction, a 'high class tea room' (Rosenthal 1960: 268) was added, which might have been particularly tempting for the women customers who frequented the store to shop and socialise. Christmas performances, with special provision for children, became a regular occurrence.

Given the scale of his investment and the need to move large volumes of stock quickly so that fashions did not stale, Garlick also understood the importance of aggressive marketing. Frequent and large advertisements were placed in all the newspapers. Their format broke the then dominant mould of modest, informational text shorn of emotional hype, simply listing inventories of goods. The adverts for Garlicks were hyperbolic in comparison, and avowedly emotive, in line with the intended spectacle of the shopping experience. Typically, it was a 'huge' sale that was being advertised in large bold type, enacting the quintessential duo of 'quality' and 'bargain' that characterised the department-store formula. A typical example was an advertisement placed in the *Cape Argus* in 1895 – two columns wide and extending the full length of the page (far larger than any other advertisement in the paper) for 'astounding bargains in all departments':

- 'thousands of pounds worth of fashionable wearing apparel at unheard of prices'
- 'thoroughly genuine and important reductions in every section of our gigantic stock'
- 'Avail yourself of the bargains. **Be in Time.** There is something to astonish you in every department.'
- 'Gentlemen, hurry and see what you can get for your money in our Outfitting Department.'
- 'Boys clothing at less than half usual price'
- **'We mean to make this the Record Sale. The bargains we are offering are simply irresistible.'**
- 'Young and old should come: all will find genuine goods at prices hitherto deemed impossible.'
- GENUINE BARGAINS FOR **CASH ONLY**'
- 'Don't miss it, come yourself and bring your friends with you.' (*Cape Argus* 3 July 1895; bold font as in the original)

The language of advertisements such as this made clear that Garlicks was not marketed merely for the Cape Town elite. Here was a space that offered a 'gigantic stock' of desirably 'fashionable' and 'astonishing' goods to consumers beyond the small upper stratum. Indeed, Garlick was forthright in recognising that the success of the shop would depend on drawing in sizeable numbers from lower down the social ladder too. Thus, when detailing the need for a handrail for the lift, he noted that 'the class of people we get here are not careful and cannot be relied upon in the same way they can be in England' (Rosenthal 1960: 263). This would include English- and Cape

Dutch-speaking 'country cousins', as Garlicks put it, (Rosenthal 1960: 264), similarly inexperienced in the sophisticated ways of the English upper classes.

The Stuttafords department store, which took shape incrementally from 1872, was not dissimilar. Samson Stuttaford had arrived in Cape Town from England in 1854 (18 years before Garlick), and entered the drapery and haberdashery trade. With more experience and time in the colony than Garlick, Stuttaford (in partnership with his brother and W Thorne) had established an international trading network before his department store opened up, producing, *inter alia*, 'South Africa's first direct commerce with Japan' in 1871 (Rosenthal 1949: 14). In 1898, Stuttafords became a public company, having announced profits of a staggering £140 000 over the previous three years (Rosenthal 1949: 144).

The Stuttafords department store began on the corner of Adderley and Hout Street, after Stuttaford purchased the building in 1872 for £10 000 – a 'breathtaking price by the standards of the period' (Rosenthal 1949: 8). Rather than one spectacular construction process (as had been the case with Garlicks), the Stuttafords store was upgraded and extended over time. In 1892, one James Salter-Whiter, who visited South Africa to investigate its commercial prospects (and promote them in Britain), included a description of the Stuttafords store in his account of his travels. He declared himself 'astonished' at the scale and prosperity of 'the shopping establishments' in Adderley Street, then the only street 'running direct to the sea'. His verbally ostentatious text drew attention to the 'magnificent large drapery establishment of Messrs Thorne, Stuttaford and Co'.

> In examining their windows, with articles of every description therein displayed to tempt the curiosity and desire of the public, from a silver knife to the richest brocaded silks, velvets and laces … one can but fancy he is in Regent Street or New Bond Street. (Salter-Whiter 1892: 29)

There was more to come. After the Garlicks store went up in 1893, competition between the two flagship retail stores became intense. Stuttafords underwent serial upgrading, prodded by Garlicks' innovations. By 1900, an extravagant renovation was on the cards:

> Owing to the great expansion of trade in South Africa, the Directors have considered it wise to undertake certain alterations to the front and interior of the Cape Town premises, which will give increased facilities for dealing with the larger number of customers who have to be accommodated. (Rosenthal 1949: 58)

This would include the addition of 'some stupendous balconies, running along the whole length of their Adderley Street frontage and around the sides [and] a huge sign, "Thorne, Stuttaford and Co.", done in metal and overhanging Adderley Street' (Rosenthal 1949: 29).

The size of the premises was also much enlarged through the purchase of adjoining stands (Rosenthal 1949: 57), comparable to the commanding Garlicks site. In 1901, a sprinkler system was added, along with a new 'pneumatic cash carrying system' (Rosenthal 1949: 57). In 1906, 'owing to the up-to-date nature of the showrooms of our competitors' (Rosenthal 1949: 56), the shop interior was again upgraded; six years later, new lifts were installed along with even more modern counters.

Garlicks and Stuttafords both sought the distinction of being the first to import and sell the very latest in fashion and/or technological design, so 'novelties were quickly seized upon' (Rosenthal 1949: 44). While the first cameras had been available at Stuttafords in 1892 ('the earliest to cater for the amateur photographer'), Garlicks was the first to import a typewriter (Rosenthal 1949: 44). Stuttafords had imported 'the Safety Bicycle' in the late 1880s which gave 'women the chance to take to the open road' – suitably attired of course – also thanks to provision by Stuttafords (Rosenthal 1949: 37). In 1908, Stuttafords pioneered the idea of 'having demonstrations on the floor of the shop' (Rosenthal 1949: 72). Each innovation offered the opportunity to use the language of distinction to advertise its virtues. In the 1910 Union Pageant advert, Stuttafords described itself as 'the largest retail store in South Africa', with 'the finest and most up-to-date Hairdressing and Shaving salons in South Africa'.

As the competition between these department stores ratcheted up, so did their efforts to lure as many customers as possible. Like Garlicks, Stuttafords would open its doors beyond the urban colonial elite, to less sophisticated 'country cousins'. As Rosenthal put it, '"Cape Dutch" was never recognised as a handicap in serving the public. Stuttafords saw to it that if anyone from the country came in and wished to be attended to in his own tongue, there was someone on hand who could understand him' (Rosenthal 1949: 34). And the department store's advertisements appeared in both Dutch and English.

CONSPICUOUS CONSUMPTION AND RACE

The hyperbole, spectacle and grandiosity of Cape Town's first department stores was very much in line with this genre of shop worldwide. But as in the case of these other contexts, it is worth reflecting on the wider social and political significance of exactly these characteristics. Why go to such great lengths and expense in styling, equipping and advertising these early Garlicks and Stuttafords department stores? Beyond the profitability of the department store business to its owners, the question invites reflection on the wider significance and impact of these department stores in their particular time and place.

The introduction of department stores was central, rather than incidental, in the development of Cape Town as a commercially vibrant, internationally prominent port city, and in the ways in which it was imagined and marketed by its political and commercial leaders. Indeed the department store offered a metonym of the city's advancing and worldly prosperity. It constituted a particular symbolic universe, as much as a physical and material space of experience. Cape Town's leading newspapers and colonial magazines were run by the same commercial elite that sponsored the city's new shopping genre, as their coverage of the department-store phenomenon showed. Although the amount of written material is relatively scant, it displayed that symbolic world, defined by some key semiotic markers and their interrelationships.

In ways that reproduced the defining economic and cultural logic of department stores globally, the abiding motif within these local representations was that of *abundance*: an abundance in the scale of the shops, the extent of their innovation and in the cornucopia of stuff that they offered for sale to an eager consuming public. The rapt enthusiasm for a glorious material plethora was already evident in an article in 1886 written about the old Garlicks, not long before the even greater splendour of its new building in 1893. The writer registers his sense of the watershed that the abundance of stuff represented, as a change in the material *and* social order of things in the colony. Below 'the apparently stagnant surface of colonial life', he wrote, 'something abnormal, something separate from the great upper strata, is in fiery and vigorous motion below' (*Excalibur* 1886). Rather more 'ordinary' people – the ranks of the worthy and respectable middle strata – were being tempted by the mounds of stuff to which they now had unprecedented access.

> The large block of masonry at the corner of Strand and Bree-streets has many compartments and departments, all 'chock-a-block' with goods, which, like the charms of the classic Egyptian, have an 'infinite variety' that age cannot wither nor custom stale – the fact being that they have no time to moulder in the shelves, and the customers move to and fro in a laden procession. The stock is diversified and curious … you can get all your external wants supplied at Garlick's – no matter if they comprehend a lady's desire in satin and fine linen, a pair of stout inexpressibles, or a relay of colonial leather … The stock scattered, or deftly pressed into niches and shelves, about the several departments, approximates in value to over £25,000; and this stock is continually being replaced, the custom being regular and increasing at a ratio that ought to be – and no doubt is – gratifying to the enterprising merchant. (*Excalibur* 1886)

As the preceding account has shown, by the next decade, the material profusion was accelerating even further, as Garlick and Stuttaford competed to bring 'the latest fashions' and technological innovations onto the commercial menu of colonial Cape Town. It was all about range and scale – and conspicuously so: heaps of stuff, of 'astonishing' variety and novelty, in huge spaces offered to throngs of customers. In 1894, Stuttafords produced a catalogue advertising all its wares that ran over 700 pages, 'handsomely bound in cloth with the firm's coat of arms embossed upon it in red and gold' (Rosenthal 1949: 34). And associated with such overtly voluminous consumption was a new vocabulary of 'needs' and desires: the material accoutrements of colonial life were becoming more variegated and more expansive as the menu of popular desire grew more sophisticated, more worldly.

This newfound and extravagant abundance was rendered as a glorious achievement, a spectacle to behold. Far more than merely a rapidly enlarging heap, this was material abundance of a particular type and significance: formed at the junction of commerce, art and science. A busy commerce in things was aestheticised, the longing to be fashionably up to date was commercialised, and the newest technologies and scientific advances became profitable, while their scientific accomplishment added to the *frisson* of their purchase – a sense of living in exciting and progressive times, despite inhabiting the colonial margin. Descriptions of the exterior and interior of Garlicks and Stuttafords emphasised their aesthetic sophistication, as the hallmark of their size and scale, in turn made possible by the very latest in building technology and design. Garlick had made the symbolic connection between the art and the commerce of the enterprise materially explicit: *The Cape Register* noted that 'twelve statues emblematical of the various arts in connection with the business, [were] on different parts of the building' (1893). And their symbolic fusion with modern science was enacted in the hitherto unimaginable size and height of the structure itself, and in the many 'firsts' (in commodities and technologies) that these stores conspicuously brought to Cape Town. *The Cape Register* deemed Garlicks, in all, 'an ornament to the city', hoping that it would be emulated by other businessmen similarly inspired to such 'handsome' ways of doing business (1893).

The first 'shopping demonstration' introduced at Stuttafords in 1908 enacted this junction of commerce, art and science exactly. 'A number of invitation cards were sent to the ladies of the Peninsula requesting their presence' at a series of demonstrations to promote sales of 'the Perfection Blue Flame Stove' (cited in Rosenthal 1949: 72), the very latest addition to the Stuttafords repertoire. Chairs were set out for 'a large gathering of people' to witness the modern wonder – with suitably cutting edge, artistic accompaniment:

> A few minutes prior to the commencement of the demonstrations, all are enlightened by the selection of high-class music on a fine 'Pathescope' which is the name for the latest improvement in musical reproduction. (cited in Rosenthal 1949: 72)

For those who partook of it, this symbolic trinity repositioned the colony and its inhabitants in a rapidly changing, modernising global world. The *Cape Argus* heralded the new Garlicks department store as an exemplar of South Africa's 'civilised' progress on an international stage:

> These new premises are the headquarters of a gigantic business, built up within the last fourteen years, and now extending over all the civilized parts of South Africa, as well as, indirectly, beyond. (*Cape Argus* 1893)

The language of 'modern civilisation' undergirded *The Cape Register*'s judgment of this commercial and architectural innovation too.

> Our merchants are now actuated by a desire, not only to vie with each other in extending business to the extreme limits of South Africa, but to erect buildings which will be an ornament to the city, and become a suitable, and convenient home for the display of those luxuries which modern civilization not only requires, but demands. (*The Cape Register* 1893)

When the flagship Garlicks store opened in 1893, *The Cape Register* recorded it as 'mark[ing] a new era in the history of Cape Town', partaking more assertively of the global profusion of new and wonderful stuff. And the official catalogue to the 1904 Cape Town Industrial Exhibition proclaimed Cape Town as 'now essentially progressive, determined to maintain its place of proud pre-eminence as the golden gateway to South Africa', not least thanks to:

> the palatial structures of the merchant princes of modern Cape Town ... A thousand things of which he had no felt need would meet his eye in each palace of competing magnificence. Bewildered and bewitched he would contrast the meagre measure of mere necessities with which he had one to be content with the affluence and luxury so profused displayed on every side. (Official Catalogue 1904: 117)

This version of conspicuous consumption went beyond a matter of personal status and honour (as portrayed in Veblen's account); it became a symbol of colonial progress and global positioning – a confident claim to worldly sophistication, replete with the requisite profusion of material 'luxury'.

The department store, and all that it represented, took shape in Cape Town at the same time as its racial order was sedimenting, with political moves towards greater racial segregation, and the growing ideological traction of Social Darwinism (Bickford-Smith 2001: 126–163). How then did these new representations articulate with the changing colonial order?

An answer to the question requires establishing, in the first instance, who the imagined beneficiaries of such civilised and civilising 'progress' were, and how they received the invitation to partake.[4]

There are several indications that these stores kept their premises clear of any 'undesirables' – to maintain the 'civilised' and stylish atmosphere, as well as to ensure the safety the female clientele. Rosenthal speaks of an atmosphere of 'strict decorum', enhanced by the presence of 'shop walkers' who monitored the premises with 'considerable authority' (Rosenthal 1949: 34). As in the profitable conjunction of 'quality' and 'bargain', these stores did not confine themselves to the colonial elite. But their appeal required nevertheless that the 'bargains' were not available to the struggling masses either. Everything about the shop – from the elaborately stylish entrance, tiled floor and embellished shop windows to the well-appointed counters and interior fittings – would have excluded those who were not appropriately dressed. Class constraints then, were tacit, if not also explicit, in the interventions of the 'shop walkers'.

The imprints of race seem no less important. There were no legal barriers preventing 'non-white' customers from entering any Cape Town stores. And it is clear from aspects of Garlick's correspondence that many of the customers at his Cape Town store were not white. For example, in writing to his shipping company and comparing his business in different parts of the Cape Colony, he noted:

> The trade here [in Cape Town] is different altogether to the trade in Port Elizabeth, Kimberley or King Williamstown and neighbourhood. These stores have a large Native population to cater for – whilst our trade is entirely with Europeans and with Coloured people dressed according to European ideas. (cited in Rosenthal 1949: 54)

Given the demographics of the town at the time, such 'Coloured people' would have been mostly Cape Malay; the dearth of African middle-class inhabitants of Cape Town would likely have limited their numbers to only a handful of the clientele in the city's department stores.

In some respects, therefore, these department stores were formally racially open spaces from the outset, and indeed remained so, even as other public places and institutions were being racially segregated. Yet repertoires of racial separatism were evident in Garlicks (and likely in Stuttafords too). *The Cape Register* (1893) made reference to Garlicks' provision of separate work spaces for coloured and white tailors on one of the upper storeys in the store. Toilet facilities were available in both Garlicks and Stuttafords. The dominant (white) mindset of the city included an understanding that toilet facilities should be racially segregated.[5] In the absence of any explicit reference to such facilities in Garlicks or Stuttafords for 'non-whites', it seems safe to assume that these were reserved for white customers – which would thus have signified unambiguously the differential status of 'non-white' customers in the store. While 'non-white' customers were permitted entry into this space of newfound material temptation, this was coupled with clear markers of racial prohibition too.

Symbolically the department store was surely a space of whiteness. Most, if not all, of the attributes of whiteness and its purported superiority – 'civilisation', 'progress', superior rationality manifest in scientific advance, superior aesthetic sensibility, respectability and gentility – overlapped with the semiotic markers of the material abundance associated with the department stores. This was abundance of a glorious, elevating variety – a normative judgement of the achievements of 'civilisation' at its apex – which, in the Social Darwinist terms of the times, was distinguished by its whiteness. It contrasted markedly with a parallel symbolic universe, in which the material abundance associated with 'non-white' people presented a racial affront, an unseemly racial mimicry. The latter association was there, ever so discreetly, in the judgement of the 'lady author' of *Life at the Cape* when she recounted a visit to 'the house of Mrs Samodien, on the occasion of her marriage'. A detailed description of the hostess revealed her to have been elaborately dressed in 'all her finery' to the point that her 'richly draped figure … was really almost elegant' (A Lady 1960: 55). A similar unease with 'non-white' excess was evident in white social critiques of coloured peoples' parades and carnivals of the time, as occasions of undue 'hedonism and ostentation' (Bickford-Smith 1995a: 447), as well as in white distaste at the figure of 'the black swell' on the Kimberley diamond fields – men who paraded their good fortune in extravagant dress (Magubane 2004: 160–66). A writer for the *South African Spectator* in 1902 put it thus:

> … we should aim at the production of good black men and not attempt to make impossible white men out of good black men and thereby waste excellent raw material. To civilise and enlighten from habits of savagery and ignorance is preferable to that form of transformation which is effected by masquerading in borrowed and ill-fitting plumes; affecting mannerisms is grotesque and unbecoming and unnecessary. (cited in Magubane 2004: 179)

In his book, *A Commonwealth of Knowledge*, Saul Dubow considers the 'overlapping, interlinked networks of power and authority that significantly shaped the Cape's distinctive colonial identity' (Dubow 2006: 1). For Dubow, it was the colony's 'considerable repository of scientific and societal knowledge', produced and collated in museums, libraries and literary journals, that was uppermost in the 'means by which the [white] colonial middle class established its public presence' (Dubow 2006: 1). Dubow's account focuses on the mid-to-late nineteenth century, much of it predating the period of transition discussed here. If there is validity in the arguments made here, then we need to take account of the ways in which a 'commonwealth of things' helped constitute the white colonial middle class in the late nineteenth and early twentieth century and was insinuated into their notion of superior 'civilisation'.

The symbolic and material matrix of whiteness in Cape Town, as well as in South Africa at large, would shift in various ways as the twentieth century took shape – affected by the fluidity of other social cleavages. In speaking back to Veblen, this chapter is not intended to assign any fixed meanings to the practice of conspicuous consumption in the racial world of modernising South Africa, but rather to underline the historically variegated, but always fundamentally formative, connections between material performances of abundance (and lack), and the racial hierarchies that assigned differential levels of 'civilisation' on the basis of racial classification.

REFERENCES

A Lady, 1998, *Life at the Cape over a Hundred Years Ago*, Struik: Cape Town. (Originally published as a series of letters in the *Cape Monthly Magazine* during 1871–1872.)

Bank, A. & Minkley, G., 1988/9, 'Editorial: Genealogies of Space and Social Identity in Cape Town', *Kronos* 25: 7.

Bayly, C. A., 2004, *The Birth of the Modern World*, Blackwell: Oxford.

Benjamin, W., 2002, *The Arcades Project* (translated by H. Eiland and K. McLaughlin), Belknap Press: Cambridge and London.

Bickford-Smith, V., 1995a, 'Black Ethnicities, Communities and Political Expression in Late Victorian Cape Town', *Journal of African History* 36(3): 443–475.

Bickford-Smith, V., 1995b, *Ethnic Pride and Racial Prejudice in Victorian Cape Town*, Wits University Press: Johannesburg.

Bowlby, R., 2000, *Carried Away: The Invention of Modern Shopping*, Faber and Faber: London.

Cape Argus, 1893, 'A great business', 1 September, National Library of South Africa.

Cape Argus, 1895, 3 July, National Library of South Africa.

Cape Provincial Archives, KAB 3/CT 4/1/4/1, 'City Engineer to Mayor H. Liberman, re Industrial Exhibition: Sanitary Arrangements', 2 December 1904.

City Engineer to Mayor H. Liberman, re Industrial Exhibition: Sanitary arrangements, 1904, 2 December, Cape Provincial Archives KAB 3/CT 4/1/4/1.

Dubow, S., 2006, *A Commonwealth of Knowledge: Science, Sensibility and White South Africa 1820–2000*, Double Storey: Cape Town.

Excalibur, 1886, 'A look in at Garlicks', 25 June, National Library of South Africa.

Flanders, J., 2011, *Consuming Passions: Leisure and Pleasure in Victorian Britain*, Harper Press: London.

Garlick, J., 1898, 'Garlick to Messrs Crossman and Brothers, NY', 27 July, University of Cape Town, African Studies Library, Garlick Papers BC 292, B2.2.

Kenny B., 2018, *Retail Worker Politics, Race and Consumption in South Africa*, Palgrave: London.

Lerner, P., 2010, 'Circulation and Representation: Jews, Department Stores and Cosmopolitan Consumption in Germany, c. 1880s–1930s', *European Review of History* 17(3): 395–413.

Magubane, Z., 2004, *Bringing the Empire Home: Race, Class and Gender in Britain and Colonial South Africa*, University of Chicago Press: Chicago and London.

Official Catalogue of the Cape Town Industrial Exhibition 1904–5, London: Maclaren, National Library of South Africa.

Official Programme of the South African Industrial Exhibition, 1914, Business Service and Organising Bureau: Cape Town, National Library of South Africa.

Pasdermadjian, H., 1954, *The Department Store: Its Origins, Evolution and Economics*, Newman Books: London.

Rosenthal, E., 1949, 'Across the Counter, Down the Years: A History of Stuttaford and Company Ltd. Department Stores of Cape Town, Johannesburg and Durban', University of Cape Town Library, African Studies Collection.

Rosenthal, E., 1960, 'The Garlicks Story', University of Cape Town Library, African Studies Collection, BZCD 942816.

Salter-Whiter, J., 1892, *A Trip to South Africa,* Sutton: Surrey, viewed 22 October 2018, available from: https://books.google.co.za/books?id=k8IRAAAAYAAJ&printsec=frontcover&dq=a+trip+to+south+africa&hl=en&sa=X&redir_esc=y#v=onepage&q=a%20trip%20to%20south%20africa&f=false

The Cape Register, 1893, 'Garlick's new premises', University of Cape Town, African Studies Library, Garlick Papers BC 292, B2.1

Trentmann, F., 2016, *Empire of Things: How We Became a World of Consumers, from the Fifteenth Century to the Twenty-First*, Harper Collins: New York.

Veblen, T., 2003 [1899], *The Theory of the Leisure Class*, Edwin Mellen Press: Lewiston.

Williams, R. H., 1991, *Dream Worlds: Mass Consumption in Late Nineteenth-Century France*, University of California Press: Berkeley and Oxford.

Williams, R., 1977, *Marxism and Literature*, Oxford University Press: Oxford and New York.

Worden, N., Van Heynigen, E. & Bickford-Smith, V., 1998, *Cape Town: The Making of a City*, David Philip: Cape Town.

Zola, E., 2012 [1883], *The Ladies' Paradise*, Oxford University Press: Oxford.

NOTES

1. See Veblen, 2003, chapter 9, on 'The conservation of archaic traits', 98–112.
2. A noteworthy exception, albeit dealing mainly with a later period, is Bridget Kenny, 2018, *Retail Worker Politics, Race and Consumption in South Africa*, Palgrave: London.
3. Judith Flanders (2011: 42–3), for example, suggests that in several parts of the West, the eighteenth century saw a significant expansion of access to shops and their (still limited) goods on offer – that is, initially preceding the Industrial Revolution, and accelerating beyond it.
4. I have to proceed here with a degree of caution, borne of limited documentation of the immediate and direct effects of these new modes of shopping on everyday life in Cape Town. I have drawn heavily on a relatively small archive of newspapers, magazines and the histories written by the popular historian Eric Rosenthal (who was commissioned to write the stories of several commercial undertakings, including Garlicks and Stuttafords).
5. For example, an account of the 1904 Cape Industrial Exhibition, held on Greenpoint Common, indicated that there were separate toilet facilities for 'European women' and 'Coloured females' (City Engineer 1904).

3 CONSPICUOUSLY PUBLIC: GENDERED HISTORIES OF SARTORIAL AND SOCIAL SUCCESS IN URBAN TOGO

NINA SYLVANUS

In the history of African consumption and concerns with the body, the use of imported goods, especially cloth, is long-standing in the making of 'vernacular cosmopolitanisms' (Bhabha 1994). Such imports serve as ingredients to vernacular dramaturgies of power, often performed through the aesthetics of excess. There are numerous examples of conspicuous displays of wealth and power through adornment: from the 'big men' styles of local chiefs to contemporary politicians (South Africa's Julius Malema's pink suits, most recently); from colonial dandies to contemporary Congolese *sappeurs* (Gondolo 1999), via Ivorian *bluffeurs* (Newell 2012) or South African township youths burning designer clothes in the style of *izikhothane* (Mnisi, see chapter 10, this volume). Although the conspicuous display of wealth through sumptuous attire is primarily written about in relation to men, especially so-called 'big men', there are numerous historical and contemporary examples of the centrality of women's fashions: the decadent styles of Senegalese *diaranka* in Dakar (Mustafa 1998), the flamboyant fashions of Asante Hightimers in Ghana (Gott 2009), or the entrepreneurial styles of 'big women' or 'female Alhajis' in Nigeria (Bastian 1996).

Concerns with material abundance and ostentatious display are not unique to West Africa. Nor are moral evaluations about the appropriateness of the accumulation of wealth and the flashy display of material objects – what Veblen (2009 [1899]) famously called conspicuous consumption. While Veblen wrote in a different time and place, scorning the ostentatious wealth of the late-nineteenth-century American leisure class, his insights (albeit evolutionary and misogynist in scope) about status performance through conspicuous consumption have traveled and continue to bear relevance in other temporal and geographic contexts. How might Veblen's concept of conspicuous consumption help theorise West African, and specifically Togolese, notions of status performance and material abundance from the mid- and late colonial period to the contemporary context of economic crisis and rampant inequality? Specifically, how might thinking with an avowedly female aesthetic of sartorial excess, one which Veblen failed to conceptualise as an autonomous female project (not fashioned in relation to men), further our understanding of conspicuous consumption in colonial and postcolonial Africa? Veblen's interest in women's nineteenth-century fashion was determined by his thesis that the leisure class was driven by a way of life given over to the maintenance and acquisition of the honourable repute of men. Thus, his attention to the quantity, quality, scarcity and comfort of women's dress (corset-based fashions that differentiated the leisure-class madame from the working-class maid) was to show how such forms of dress worked to maintain the pecuniary repute of men.

How does this apply to the case of West African wax-print fashion and to the meanings Togolese women attach to an aesthetics of excess, bearing in mind that the history of colonial regulation that informed these meanings and the practices associated with them was less interventionist vis-à-vis women than men? To what extent are these meanings and practices fashioned in relation to men?

The avowedly female aesthetic of excess in West Africa must be understood as a complex project of public self-making and status performance. This project is not only deeply gendered and shaped by a differentiated politics of colonial regulation and its postcolonial afterlife, but it is also an emancipatory project that enables women to fashion a (visual) public culture, a 'zone of cultural debate' (Appadurai & Breckenridge 1988: 6) in which they take centre stage.

In the historical context of urban development in Togo, *pagne* (a woman's garment that is both tailored and wrapped) became the dominant aesthetic regime through which women claimed a place in public life amidst forms of colonial regulation that made male dress the focus of attention/intervention. The wax-print aesthetic emerged as the sartorial style of choice through which Togolese urbanites chose to express themselves in the gendered public sphere of colonial and postcolonial Togo. In this context, the material dimensions of class and style are entangled with colonially derived notions of modernity, as well as with the temporality of the newly independent nation. Even though Togo was never a settler society – hence, notions of class were not as racially coded as in South Africa, for example – opportunities for upward mobility were racialised and deeply gendered. Women's fashion did not fall under the colonial radar in the same way as men's fashion, the conspicuous styles of which were anxiously monitored by the colonists. The meanings and practices associated with the politics of women's *pagne* style and forms of public self-making differed from the flamboyant dandy fashions that men performed as part of the new colonial division of labour. However, in a reversal of sorts, women's fashion changed in the context of the postcolony with women conspicuously performing fashionability both by conforming to accepted norms of female respectability while also fashioning their own agendas outside the family, signs of which were already apparent during the colonial era.

Togolese women's *pagne* style is one of historical sartorial continuity. Their public visibility and status performances at a time of colonial regulation (and its postcolonial aftermath) were achieved through the display of dress (whereby choosing the right quality of cloth, the right texture, pattern and colour play a key role) as a project of public self-making. It is a project that contrasts with Veblen's historical case study and questions his notion of conspicuous consumption in relation to gender. Women's sartorial expressions were significant in an era of early postcolonial nationhood and culminated in a sartorial event in contemporary Togo. An event that epitomises an avowedly female aesthetics of excess, it demonstrates how the performance of conspicuousness is not determined by class as a position in a complex economic structure (Marx & Engels 2004) or as a system of social classification (Weber 1978), nor is it a form of Veblenesque status emulation (2009) or a template for social mobility. Rather, what the performance of conspicuousness in this context shows is how the ability to establish and maintain a proper kind and degree of consumerism in a context of spiraling inequalities and ongoing economic crisis, challenges older templates of establishing identity as a fixed structural class position predicated on social hierarchy.

CLOTH AND CLOTHING

West Africa's sartorial landscape is dominated by three kinds of garments: *boubou* (a long, loose robe worn by women and men), *pagne* and Western-style clothing. Of course, there is tremendous regional variation within these styles, which are constantly shifting in interaction with various internal and external influences. The visual significance of *pagne* in women's daily life is especially potent. *Pagne* is a French term used throughout Francophone West Africa to denote African print cloth. It can be one piece, or three (*le complet*), affordable or extravagant, and has ritual and utilitarian functions that make it part of every woman's life cycle in many parts of West Africa. In Anglophone West Africa, *pagne* translates as 'wrapper'. I prefer to use the French term throughout this chapter because of its rich etymology on the one hand, and its ontological and signifying characteristics on the other. This type of cloth is generically known as African print, a category that includes Dutch wax cloth (see Figure 2) and Ivorian, Nigerian, Chinese wax cloth, as well as various grades of 'fancy' cloth (Sylvanus 2016).

The ability to read and evaluate *pagne* includes knowing its history and context, and identifying its place in a hierarchy of value denoted by origin and quality. Togolese use the terms *tsigan* ('big one') to indicate a high-value *pagne*, while *tsivi* refers to the 'small' value of the cloth, also called *petit pagne* (small *pagne*). European-imported wax cloth is *tsigan*; it provides maximum 'sparkle' and is preferred by fashion-conscious urbanites. The innovativeness in design and the colourfastness and high-quality cotton of the resin-resist wax print firmly locate that cloth in the high-value register. By contrast, the less durable, roller-printed 'fancy' print is *tsivi*. Historically, these two types of factory-printed cloth have dominated West African markets; together they fall under the umbrella category African print cloth. Although inferior in quality to resin-resist printed cloth (hereafter referred to as wax print or wax cloth), the much more affordable fancy print aesthetic has long generated its own visual culture. Both wax and fancy prints give material and visual form to the changing cultural norms and values that have shaped urban life in colonial and postcolonial West Africa.

In Togo, *pagne* is at once perceived as traditional and modern, classic and cutting edge. *Pagne* can be tailored into stylish garments, or it can be wrapped and knotted around the body. It is a material that is appreciated sensually, but which simultaneously conveys coded messages. It is vibrant matter with material agency, and yet it is manipulated by its wearer and brought to life by the body. It is an ordinary object that patterns women's everyday interactions inside the home, features at the heart of many urban living arrangements, is used at work, in the market, on the streets of Lomé and on the public stages that kin-related life cycle events provide. While men also wear tailored *pagne*, especially shirts, women's investments in *pagne*'s material and visual infrastructure are of an entirely different kind. If *pagne* is part of women's moveable wealth, it is also part of women's social and aesthetic projects.

In urban Togo, the successful tailoring of individual style and a social skin – a process requiring cultural expertise, savvy and knowledge of the cloth's material properties – is contingent upon a larger politics of reputation and recognition that hinges on the value of public appearance. Presenting the self in public is a performative and embodied act that is carefully crafted for the critical gaze of different social groups, including elders. While this bears some resemblance to the social scenarios theorised by Veblen, such evaluations are never made with regard to the symbolic significance of women's dress for men, but rather vis-à-vis a woman's ability to conform to accepted norms of female respectability while performing sartorial distinction, not as an extension of a man's or a kin group's repute, but rather for the making of the self. The act of wearing *pagne* both dresses a woman's subjectivity and extends and locates her in specific social and urban spaces.[1]

Normative ideas about gender and a woman's worth are dominant cultural representations through which Togolese interpret women's fashions. In this way, a *grande personne* (an established person) is said to have arrived in society. Her respectable sartorial display both situates and highlights her social status. Reputation attached to a particular form of respectable femininity hinges on social constructions of success, maturity, and financial well-being. This distinctly feminine project takes place in an urban context where men tend to wear tailored *pagne* shirts, mostly during leisure time or more formally during ceremonial functions, while women create spectacular and singular bodily performances with their *pagne*. And so it is women, not men, who are at the centre of social spaces during the kin-related life-cycle events such as weddings, baptisms and funerals that regularly take place in Lomé's many neighbourhoods (explored further in the third part of this chapter).

CONSUMERISM AND URBAN GRAMMARS OF STYLE IN COLONIAL TOGO

Attention to the historical Togolese use of *pagne* materials requires consideration of the dressed body as more than a self-fashioned semiotic assemblage. The gendered politics of appropriate dress and style in contemporary urban settings, where claims to modernity, tradition and heritage are made, negotiated and transformed, come together in women's fashions dominated by the visuality of wax print materials. However, the development of this print aesthetic occurred at the intersection of colonial institutions and new ideas about progress, wealth, success and independence with older traditions of presenting the body through possession. A long history of sumptuary statuses characterises this region, with people not just wearing animal skins or using bodily modifications to constitute or contest power, but also desiring prestige goods ranging from high-end locally woven cloth to various kinds of manufactured imports. During the colonial period, emergent hierarchies of taste laid the foundation for practices of gendered distinction through the language of fashion. After independence, fashion became a way of expressing the new, modern self formed within the context and heritage of the Togolese nation. As trade in wax cloth played a central role in regional economic development throughout the colonial period, as well as defining the style of independent Togo, the material was already significant before being reinterpreted by urban women aspiring to successfully navigate the changing norms of postcolonial society and its dialectics of tradition and modernity.

In this area of West Africa, cloth and adornment have long played major roles in the political economy as well as in the production and reproduction of political and social life. The long-held power of the dressed body and the aesthetic of public appearance were exemplified in Togo by the sumptuous styles of local chiefs, whose adornment effectively communicated the dazzling wealth and authority they extended through tribute and kinship systems. Togolese consumption of imported and domestic cloth and clothing was therefore already well established by the early twentieth century but had to adapt to new urban settings of work and leisure time when a new corps of fashion setters and fashion talk emerged.[2] Togolese fashion became socially relevant in the new urban context of Lomé's colonial public sphere.[3] The city grew rapidly between 1930 and 1950, doubling its initial population of 15 000 in the span of two decades (Marguerat 1992: 4).[4] The developing city offered a multifaceted stage for showcasing identities and aspirations visually marked in acts of display. Dress and style, and the desired ability to consume well, provided a visual language for expressing and claiming particularly urban statuses.

Viewership and talk about dress informed and shaped consumerist desire and tactics for style and distinction, as well as Togolese aspirations to membership in the colonial city's new 'communities of taste' (Phyllis 1995: 2). Indeed, Lomé was a crucial site for acquiring knowledge about clothing styles as well as 'insights into how to pursue and compete over them' (Hansen 2000: xx). Without going so far as to argue that the colonial city functioned as a dialectical space of freedom and constraint in the Simmelian (1950) sense, or that consumption provided an unrestricted domain for social action divorced from economic structures, I would nevertheless like to suggest that Lomeans experienced the urban predicament as a space where new personal identity spaces formed and where new social hierarchies detached from the values and norms of kinship could be asserted, challenged and reenacted. This was primarily true for the urban individual whose liberation from the constraints of rural society and its social bonds provided freedom while urban society simultaneously generated new constraints in the form of estrangement. As in other parts of colonial Africa, clothing became 'the most readily available practice for popular expressions of African aspirations' (Hansen 2000: 52). Being well-dressed effectively communicated refinement and social success measured against new sensibilities of time and space brought on by urban employment, waged labour and education. This had different implications for men and women, the latter being initially excluded from colonial institutions of education and civil service.

During the colonial era, a race- and gender-tiered hierarchy emerged from these communities of taste, one that would take on novel meanings in the early postcolonial period. This hierarchy fashioned men's and women's work and leisure spaces differently, privileging Europeans and upwardly mobile Togolese men, while relegating lower-class men and women to different subordinate positions. While Togolese men in urban Lomé readily adopted Western clothing and spent a considerable amount of their wages on trousers, shirts and suits, women shaped an innovative urban clothing style based on the print aesthetic of imported *pagne* materials. The social relevance of dress was a topic of conversation that concerned both Togolese and Europeans, but interestingly, women's colourful dress styles did not receive the same colonial scrutiny. This had important implications for the ways in which women fashioned themselves in urban Togo during much of the colonial and postcolonial era. Of course, women were not detached from the order of society and the family, and indeed had to conform to a degree of sartorial regulation in terms of gendered decency and respectability (for example, legs and the upper body had to be covered), yet women also pursued their own agendas. While such individualised forms of dress – using several layers of cloth to wrap the body – could be highly conspicuous in the Veblenian sense, Veblen paid no attention to the kinds of aspirational and agentive projects of sartorial ostentation women concerned themselves with. Then again, Veblen's leisure class individuals were not colonial subjects.

Europeans – at the top of the colonial hierarchy – carefully monitored men's sumptuary regimes, especially the flamboyant fashions of the Togolese dandy whose impeccably dressed body became a battleground for debates about appropriate dress and whether colonial subjects should have clothing needs (dress) or clothing desires (individual style/collective fashion). As elsewhere in colonial Africa, the Togolese dandies essentially threatened European sophistication, yet they were crucial to the functioning of the colonial economy as workers and consumers. They often worked as clerks in European firms or in the colonial administration, where they outshone European dress competence through their highly refined style and elegance.

If the replacement of indigenous dress by Western-style attire was considered a visual signifier of cultural advancement by both colonial subjects and colonisers, the colonisers disavowed Togolese creative engagements with fashion as mimicry. As mimicking subjects, Togolese dandies could never be more than an inferior copy of the superior original (the white coloniser) and thus, by extension, of modernity.[5] Europeans often portrayed the creative ways in which Africans involved themselves with matters of dress in mocking terms. Hansen (2000) describes how the dandy in colonial Zambia was mocked for being 'infantile' and for lacking cultural capital. The dandies' excess became the focus of colonial fears because their cosmopolitan-inflected sartorial arrangements were essentially more 'modern' than those of the colonisers. What emerges from such accounts is a long-held European ambivalence regarding African dress because it exposed 'the tenuous fictions of the "civilizing mission" by enacting the part of civilized African with ease' (Burke in Poiger, Weinbaum, Thomas, Ramamurthy & Dong 2008: 366).

Dress and fashion gave expression to endogenous hierarchies of race and gender among Lomeans that made the colonial elite uneasy. Indeed, the growing importance of dress and style in the context of rapidly expanding urban spaces was not only anxiously monitored by Europeans, but also vividly commented upon by Togolese who used the language of civilisational progress to mark social difference. Educated French-speaking Togolese, so-called *evolués*, benefitted from the colonial contract because they enacted the values of France's civilising mission.[6] Westermann (1938: 351–2) describes how one such *evolué*, Martin Aku, considered illiteracy to be synonymous with poor taste in matters of dress. Aku's literacy analogy is interesting in relation to the cultivated knowledge required to read the language of dress: dressing appropriately required erudition and dress competence, two elements Aku believed to be directly related to the project of education and, by extension, civilising modernity. Upwardly mobile Lomeans used the language of dress and style to mark social distance from less educated, and by extension, less 'civilised' groups and individuals. In this way, the Lomean elite re-appropriated such registers of progress to dismiss uneducated lower-class dandies as 'lacking proper taste' and measured dress competence. Thus what emerges is a racial and gendered hierarchy, dominated by male elite fashion-setters imitated by successively lower classes of aspiring urban subjects. Women, on the other hand, occupied a separate place altogether.

Africanist historians of gender (Allman, Geiger & Musisi 2002) have shown that the colonial public sphere was deeply gendered: it was centered around the social production of the world of civil service, which was male. Women stood on the margins of this world and were not subject to the same kinds of social engineering in the marketplace where they worked and were taxed. Europeans saw Togolese women's work in the market as a 'natural' inclination to help feed the nation and presumed that women adorned themselves out of female vanity. By contrast, flamboyant Togolese men threatened not only European sophistication but also 'native' tendencies toward a vernacular idiom of prestige – to be sumptuous like a chief – that Europeans imagined to be aspirational.

Hierarchies of taste and style, as well as criteria for public evaluations thereof, reflected this gender divide. Because women were merely thought to 'occupy half of the [public/private] "dichotomy"' (Allman, Geiger & Musisi 2002: 3), I suggest that women's aesthetic regimes of the body were not considered as seriously as men's and thus fell off the colonial radar. Within Lomean society however, female sartorial practices were monitored vis-à-vis gendered expectations and new normative forms of respectable and appropriate femininity, in particular pertaining to the length of the wrapper, the accurateness with which the skirt was wrapped around the waist, or the precision of the fold. As large amounts of new imported *pagne* materials found their way into West Africa, and into Togo in particular as its regional trading centre (Sylvanus 2016), so did increased access to sewing machines that enabled new interpretations of European tailoring techniques and style. The *pagne* cloth's material qualities – its solid cotton texture, colourfastness and rich visuality – made it especially suitable for experimenting with form and style, giving custom-made expression to women's sartorial self-making.

But urban Togolese women did not invent their styles in a vacuum; their dazzling print aesthetics were hybrids. The *taille-basse,* a low-cut bodice with a flounce over the waist, was modeled after form-fitted European garments and arose during the colonial era at the intersection of colonial institutions, the technology of the sewing machine, and local interpretations of European tailoring techniques and styles. The so-called *marinière*, a hip-length blouse also developed during the colonial era, is another example of hybrid style. It was influenced by missionary activity and shaped by the new visions of Christianity and its gendered ideals of propriety, decency and respectability. Over time, women developed these styles as the dominant form of dress, adapting conventional ways of draping cloth and ascribing meaning to *pagne*. As an elderly woman explained to me, the art of draping *pagne* was the quintessential style of 'traditional Africa'. Twentieth-century city women, on the other hand, no longer just wore a wrapper around the waist; instead they combined it with tailored blouses to form a new urban aesthetic. The tailoring of new garments ranged from fashionable urban adaptations of the missionary-influenced *marinière* to the fitted, hip-flounced *taille-basse* (camisole) style worn with a tailored skirt and reminiscent of Dior's post-war New Look. Though the colonial elite expressed its disquiet about local men's extravagant dress, the new styles and visual materiality women produced and launched into a competitive public sphere did not contradict colonial domestic virtues of cleanliness and propriety.

After independence in 1960, women became the leading fashion setters. Their hybrid styles were being reinterpreted anew as new wax-print (*pagne*) patterns featuring iconic symbols of modernity (cars and buses, and later cell phones and computers) and abstract designs provided the body with a new idiom by which to make its mark. Since women are often the centre of social space, especially during ceremonial occasions, their carefully styled appearances are visually so dominant that men's sartorial arrangements are a mere backstage and solicit little, if any, attention. This is in sharp contrast to the colonial dandy we encountered earlier. Against the backdrop of a fast-growing cityscape, women made *pagne* and the print aesthetic socially relevant as a measure of distinction, social skin-making, success, fashion and the nation (Sylvanus 2016).

STYLING THE NATION: EMBODYING MODERNITY

As with other African countries recently liberated from colonial rule, Togolese sought out unique means of expression against the backdrop of a nation in the making. During this period of self-assertion and optimism in the 1960s and 1970s, the Togolese nation was 'dressed' economically, politically and culturally. In describing this period, Togolese citizens often use the language of modernity to express particular ideas and views about being-in-the-world that they fashioned in relation to a leap in education, urbanisation and employment, rather than referring to a particular historical condition.[7] As Victoire Bellow's[8] view of her 25-year-old self in the early 1970s attests:

> I was working as a secretary at BCEAO [bank], I had a good salary and I enjoyed reading French novels and magazines and Ghanaian advice columns in my free time. I was independent and living a modern life. I enjoyed going out with my girlfriends. Any social

occasion was an excuse for dressing up, for making a new outfit. I liked wearing French-style dresses, but I also wore *pagne* in modern cuts and miniskirts. (Victoire Bellow, interview with the author, April 2004)

Victoire's experience of modern personhood is linked to work and the new possibilities and forms of leisure and success it enabled. This view also reflects changing gender roles and working relationships between men and women. Making a new outfit provided ample space for crafting her public appearance. In cosmopolitan fashion, this 'modern girl' looked both to and beyond the metropole as she styled her social life, thereby expressing herself as simultaneously contemporary and traditional.

As scholars of consumption and modernity have argued, desires for modernity are often aspirations to simultaneity with cosmopolitan worldliness (Poiger, Weinbaum, Thomas, Ramamurthy & Dong 2008). References to modernity are often references to new or modern lifestyles achieved by the acquisition of technological fetish objects such as television sets, radios, bikes and Vespas, and bring to mind ideas (and nostalgias) of being connected to the world or participating in simultaneous time. It is perhaps not surprising that a series of precisely such objects of modernity (radios, cars, buses, fans) appeared on some of the most popular *pagne* patterns around this time. Embodying Togolese modernity, as it were, women like Victoire made their mark in public venues by creating spectacular and singular performances with their new *pagne*.

Illustrating the 'emancipatory value of both modernity and capitalism' (Burke in Poiger et al. 2008: 363), detached from the dictates of kinship relations yet connected to the world, Victoire and other women like her fashioned lifestyles in both the public and the private sphere. In addition to exercising economic control over her household expenditures, Victoire's urban identity centered on the consumption of things from all over the world (France, Ghana and Togo).

Commodities, apparel, fashion and public appearance were crucial to the making of new identities and the making of the Togolese nation. Being modern in early-1970s Togo drew on a variety of sources. For Victoire, making claims to cosmopolitan simultaneity involved not just wearing Western-style clothing, but also *pagne* in modern cuts that reflected Togolese optimism about their new nation's future. Women's fascination with newly tailored forms of *pagne* also gained nationalist currency through Madame Dinah Grunitsky Olympio,[9] a presidential ambassador whose sartorial choices helped shift the print aesthetic from the realm of dress into the realm of fashion. During one of the presidential couple's first official outings, the First Lady of Togo wore an elegantly tailored outfit made from a wax-print pattern instead of displaying herself in her usual European-style two-piece suit. The positive reception of her outfit in the media positioned Togo as resolutely nationalist-modern in relation to other nations with a similar nationalist outlook, like Ghana, for example. In this way, the materiality of the print aesthetic and its tailored style gained political and resolutely national significance – with an internationalist outlook articulated through its presidential, rather than aristocratic or chiefly, ambassador. Madame Olympio gave currency to a look that cohabited with European clothing styles used as office wear, yet powerfully embedded the *pagne* print aesthetic in the order of the new nation.[10] 'Her style gave the message that you could be a modern, educated woman, wear *pagne* and be proud of being Togolese,' explained an observer of the time whom I spoke with in 2010. By inscribing this reinvented hybrid style with Togolese hierarchy and value, urban Togolese inspired by Madame Olympio reformulated conventions of dress in relation to age, gender and respectability. By the 1980s, the convention of the tailored print aesthetic became the dominant cultural form through which urbanites crafted their public appearances and performed social distinctions.

CONSPICUOUS STYLE: PERFORMING A FEMALE AESTHETICS OF EXCESS

In 1994, the West African CFA franc lost half of its value. In the aftermath of state-owned enterprises collapsing in the late 1980s, structural adjustment programmes and austerity measures profoundly changed what it meant to be a Togolese citizen and a consuming subject. The doubling of prices produced new kinds of inequalities and polarisations as uncertainty and economic hardship came to mark ordinary citizens' everyday lives. Before the devaluation, essential consumer items, like Dutch wax cloth, were available to most consumers; after, they quickly turned into near-luxury goods. What, then, were the implications for peoples' ability to establish and maintain a proper a degree of consumerism? What did conspicuous consumption look like in this new context of inequality, and in whose eyes? How did these categories map onto people's own perceptions of their status?

In the past, Vlisco had been known throughout West Africa as the much-desired, Dutch manufactured Dutch wax cloth, distributed by women traders on West African markets since colonial times. Hit by the 1990s currency devaluation, and the proliferation in the 2000s of Chinese upstart brands copying Dutch designs (see Sylvanus 2016), the company has reinvented its image as a luxury brand. While exclusive Dutch wax prints have, in fact, become investment pieces rather than fashion pieces (with the exception of elite consumption), counterfeits from China have become a viable alternative for many Togolese, allowing fashion to be performed more democratically.

The performative efficacy and the centrality of the conspicuously sartorial became crudely apparent to me when my friend, Belinda Akoussah[11] invited me to accompany her to a baptism in April 2008. In Lomé, baptism and other ceremonial life-cycle rituals are very much part of a popular urban culture. The scene is generally the street itself, blocked off by fences semi-enclosed with tent-like coverings. Family and kin networks typically organise baptisms, and neighbours, friends and extended family attend in large numbers. Women are generally dressed in *pagne* for such gatherings. Although they experience social pressure to maintain a reputation of respectable femininity, women make *pagne* work for them and have their own agendas. While the shape of the body that wears the *pagne* contributes to the success of its reception, the other modality of evaluation is visual: the self-image a woman imprints when she has crafted a complete outfit to wear to a public occasion.

Baptisms often become public ceremonial sites of sorts, and there were at least 300 people at the baptism Belinda and I attended. When we arrived, loud music was blaring out of speakers and the scene was filled with Lomeans of all ages who gathered on plastic chairs surrounding the stage where a master of ceremonies moderated. Upon entering the scene with my friend, the importance of the visual became especially apparent to me. We had rushed to the event, walking fast, but when we approached the public scene, Belinda slowed down. In fact, her entire bodily demeanor changed, as if she had grown taller. Just before entering the space of the event, Belinda took out a tissue from her white purse. She dabbed off the sweat from her forehead, and then wiped the dust from her white high heels. Next, she checked the position of her maxi-skirt's slit, caressed her short-sleeved bodice to smooth it, and finished off with a final adjustment of her hairdo. She verified her impeccable look one last time by adjusting her white earring clips and pulling her purse firmly under her arm. As if she were going on stage, I could sense her anxious excitement about what was about to happen: the imprinting of her image. In slow movements, she presented her crafted appearance to the public gaze. Belinda postured for a moment and placed her hands on her hips as if she hesitated to take a left turn, but then walked straight ahead in slow confident buttock-rotating gait, passing along the first row of plastic chairs lined up in front of the stage. She knew, she told me earlier, that those white shoes, purse and earrings would make an impression with the telescopic effects of her *pagne*'s highly sought-after pattern.

Belinda seemed pleased with the production of her image-imprint. She did indeed catch the attention of the audience, who inspected her outfit from head to toe as she walked down the aisle-like corridor in front of the chairs facing the stage. Some turned their heads. Some seemed amused – others, more inquisitive, seemed to exchange commentary about Belinda's self-presentation. But what kind of recognition was she after? She seemed to know only a few people at the event; some of her girlfriends were there as well as several of her clients. What did recognition in the eyes of friends and strangers produce? Throughout the baptism, Belinda kept commenting on other women's outfits, 'See the girl there, in the official *pagne* [the *pagne* chosen by the family for this event and which supporting kin wore to signify their alliance], the one whose back is almost nude? Eish, what a *faux pas*! She'll forever be known as *petite*, or *la bonne* [domestic worker]; nobody will take her seriously.' She contrasted this woman's failed look with what she considered a proper, yet 'boring' look, pointing at a mother who wore the same fabric as a wrapped skirt with a wide blouse and the third piece in her hand. 'She's really traditional, and people will respect her for that, but her *pagne* has no shape, maybe she didn't have extra money to spend on the tailor, unlike the Madame over there. Oh, she's so elegant and her *pagne* is so beautiful.' Belinda's critical evaluations of other women's styles were competitive in nature. With each assessment, she compared herself to other women's displays of dress and attitude, while also gathering information about current and future trends. Distinguishing herself from *la petite,* whom she looked down upon as lacking the necessary social skills required for having dress competence, Belinda also diminished the mother in her traditional unfitted outfit, whom, she speculated, lacked the means for fashionability. Her confident, and often critical, judgements of other women's outfits seemed to make fashion both an alienating and an aspirational project. Belinda's long-term ambition was to look like the elegant Madame whose cultivated style she hoped to achieve one day.

Several of Belinda's friends and clients came up to her during the baptism to greet her and acknowledge her appearance; she certainly received the desired recognition from her peers. It was only shortly before we left the event that I came to understand the larger context of this competition. Near the exit was a table covered with photographs of the event, and people were looking at their snapshots. The presence of photographers hired for events like these is a common practice; pictures are usually developed within two hours and are available for purchase upon the wrapping up of festivities. Belinda was eager to evaluate her own image. She counted the number of snapshots taken of her, including the ones where she was slightly out of frame, and seemed happy with a count of 15. After counting the pictures, she hesitated for a moment at the table, and then purchased an image where she figured centre stage. 'I will put this one up in my salon, so everyone can see,' she said. Belinda's quest for public recognition exceeded the context of the actual event. Not content to simply gain the admiration of clients and peers, she wished to make her imprint memorable and widely known. I read Belinda's desire to be recognised as unique and inimitable, so that every woman who admired her daring also wanted to be in the same way memorable and inimitable, as part of a larger politics of reputation and recognition.

Ironically, I encountered Belinda's printed image a few weeks later at a family lunch gathering organised by a wealthy cloth trader. As her children and grandchildren gathered in the trader's living room, where Johnny Walker, sparkling wine and soft drinks accompanied our appetisers, one of her daughters pulled out pictures from the baptism I had attended with Belinda. When I explained that I had been at the event, they enquired who this hairdresser friend of mine was. Upon a more careful look at the photographs, I identified Belinda in the background of one of the pictures. 'Oh, her! Yes, I remember this girl, she was definitely trying to make an impression!' the trader's daughter commented.

'Let me see,' exclaimed her mother. She adjusted her glasses and carefully inspected the photo, 'Eish, what a flash!' A long conversation ensued, which hinted at the ideal of how a woman is supposed to look and thus by extension at the possibility of failure. One daughter commented, 'She's dressing above her station,' while her sister found her 'savvy, but trying too hard'. The women reached a consensus that Belinda's fashion statement was overly ambitious. In fact, the cloth trader said that the *pagne* she wore was not a Dutch wax at all, but a Ghanaian print, 'A nice one, but not a Dutch; she surely couldn't afford it.' Her daughters wondered whether the purse was leather or plastic.

Speculations abounded in their discussion. Belinda was not of the same social class, and they mocked her for trying to dress above her station. Excluded from elite consumption and its vectors of social mobility, the women explained that the kind of cultivated dress appearance a woman ideally wants to make at any social event – whether she wants to go for a more 'conservative-classical' or a provocative fashion look – is linked to *elegance cultivée*. This Bourdieusienne cultivated style is acquired over years. It involves seeing and observing, but also learning from the matrilineal line.

Togolese politics of reputation and recognition are tied up in long-held social hierarchies of class and taste. As elsewhere, elites have vested interests in upholding social boundaries through sartorial practices. What constitutes appropriate dress etiquette and style requires social consensus, while the individual cultivation of taste requires knowledge acquired over time and institutional mediation (Bourdieu 1979). To create such a sartorial style is hard work. It is available only to those sufficiently 'cultivated' and involves both the act of conforming to conventions of dress (of knowing how to dress appropriately, when and where), while also demanding a unique interpretation of the garment (involving taste, skill and bodily technique). When I asked whether Belinda could ever achieve this kind of cultivated elegance, they laughed. 'Well, she can, but she has a long way to go; for now she looks like one of those girls in an Ivorian soap opera and not like a *grande personne* (respected adult),' the trader explained.

The evaluative talk surrounding *pagne* contributes to the construction of women's selves as well as society. The daily spectacle of opulent dress on the streets of Lomé is performance-based and carefully assessed, and as Hansen (2013: 1) reminds us, 'what we see, regarding dress, depends on what else we have seen'. In this way, a woman's social skin, made up of personal style, expression, expertise and social skill, is subject to critical judgement. As in other parts of the continent, or with any sumptuary regime for that matter, debates over dressed bodies can be heated because conflicting values can come into play across class, gender and generational divides. Women's dressed bodies assume different meanings depending on the context where they are presented and by whom they are seen. Women's dress practices are continually involved in a politics of reputation that changes with adult femininity.

But was Belinda's look a failed one? In the eyes of the elite, her look was at best dismissed as frivolous, at worst as put on. Yet for Belinda the fashions of the elegant Madames were aspirational, not delimiting. Instead of imitating a look she could not afford, Belinda styled herself independently and showed her determination to one day be as successful and as rich as the cultivated upper class Madame. Meanwhile, being compared to an Ivorian soap actor was not a bad reputation to have for this ambitious hairdresser, even if it did not infer the desired status of *grande personne*. Belinda was on her way, moving forward, and she explained that she 'did not need a sugar daddy' to finance her investments in style. She was determined to make it on her own terms. Belinda wanted to create her own imprint, regardless of whether the Madame was mocking her for now; after all, her image circulated and generated talk, testifying to the desired ability to consume well.

Belinda's avowed aesthetics of excess in times of economic hardship trouble conventional accounts of excess that tend either to focus on men as a regulatory device to control women's power, or, as with Veblen, to focus on the way women's conspicuous dress practices help to maintain a husband's 'honorable repute'. As Belinda's account makes clear, she is neither interested in having her sartorial consumption sponsored by a man, nor is she invested in upholding anyone but her own status or aspirational projects. (This also reminds us of Victoire's story.)

Belinda's case starkly highlights the limitations of an application of the Veblenesque model to contemporary and past modes of conspicuous consumption in Togo. At the very least, it suggests that his theorisation does not travel easily across temporal and geographic divides, because in Togo women have their own agendas when it comes to fashioning themselves in public. And yet, the stakes in participating in any cultural economy of style are high, which was also the case with Veblen's American leisure class. Belinda flaunted the style of the Togolese leisure class, but this was not her audience. Her carefully crafted aesthetic of excess appears to be much more about an urban identity and claiming a social and economic position (impressing those who look up to her as a trendsetter, including hairdressing clients, not unlike the way Victoire spoke about her modernist aspiration) in a context in which opportunities for upward mobility are increasingly constrained by economic precarity. Belinda's desire for conspicuous style was both aspirational and performative.

Perhaps the question is not so much whether Veblen is relevant in the Togolese or the African context – or if theory is always limited to its historical context – as much as it is about considering how categories of class map onto peoples' own perceptions of their statuses.

REFERENCES

Allman, J. M., 2004. 'Fashioning Africa: Power and the Politics of Dress', in J. Allman (ed.), *Fashioning Africa: Power and the Politics of Dress*, 1–12, Indiana University Press: Bloomington.

Allman, J., Geiger, S. & Musisi, N., 2002, *Women in African Colonial Histories*. Indiana University Press: Bloomington.

Appadurai, A. & Breckenridge, C., 1988, 'Debates and Controversies: Why Public Culture?', *Public Culture Bulletin* 1(1): 5–9.

Bastian, M. L., 1996, 'Female "Alhajis" and Entrepreneurial Fashions: Flexible Identities in Southeastern Nigerian Clothing Practice', in H. Hendrickson (ed.), *Clothing and Difference: Embodied Identities in Colonial and Post-Colonial Africa*, 97–132, Duke University Press: Durham.

Bhabha, H., 1994, *The Location of Culture*, Routledge: New York.

Bourdieu, P., 1979, *La Distinction*, Minuit: Paris.

Burke, T., 1996, *Lifebuoy Men, Lux Women: Commodification, Consumption and Cleanliness in Modern Zimbabwe*, Duke University Press: Durham.

Gondolo, D., 1999, 'Dream and Drama: The Search for Elegance among Congolese Youth', *African Studies Review* 42(1): 23–48.

Gott, S., 2009, 'Asante Hightimers and the Fashionable Display of Women's Wealth in Contemporary Ghana', *Fashion Theory: The Journal of Dress, Body and Culture* 13(2): 141–76.

Hansen, K. T., 2000, *Salaula: The World of Secondhand Clothing and Zambia*. University of Chicago Press: Chicago.

Hansen, K. T., 2013, 'Introduction', in K. T. Hansen & D. S. Madison (eds.), *African Dress: Fashion, Agency, Performance*, 1–14, Bloomsbury: London.

Marguerat, Y., 1992, *Lomé: Une Brève Histoire de la Capitale du Togo*. Karthala: Lomé.

Marguerat, Y. & Peleï, T., 1992–96, *Si Lomé m'était contée…* Volumes I, II & III, Presses de l'Université du Bénin: Lomé.

Martin, P. M., 1995, *Leisure and Society in Colonial Brazzaville*, Cambridge University Press: Cambridge.

Marx, K. & Engels, F., 2004 [1848], *Manifesto of the Communist Party*. Penguin: London.

Mustafa, H., 1998, *Practicing Beauty: Crisis, Value and the Challenge of Self-Mastery in Dakar 1970–1994*, PhD dissertation: Harvard University.

Newell, S., 2012, *The Modernity Bluff: Crime, Consumption and Citizenship in Côte d'Ivoire*, University of Chicago Press: Chicago.

Poiger, U., Weinbaum, A. E., Thomas, L., Ramamurthy, P. & Dong, M. Y. (eds.), 2008, *The Modern Girl around the World: Consumption, Modernity and Globalization*. Duke University Press: Durham.

Simmel, G., 1950, 'The Metropolis and Mental Life', in *The Sociology of Georg Simmel*. The Free Press of Glencoe Collier-MacMillian Ltd: London.

Sylvanus, N., 2016, *Patterns in Circulation: Cloth, Gender and Materiality in West Africa*. University of Chicago Press: Chicago.

Veblen, T., 2009 [1899], *The Theory of the Leisure Class*, (M. Benton ed.), Oxford University Press: Oxford.

Weber, M., 1978, *Economy and Society: An Outline of Interpretive Sociology*. University of California Press: Oakland.

Westermann, D., 1938, *Afrikaner erzählen ihr Leben: elf Selbstdarstellungen afrikanischer Eingeborener aller Bildungsgrade und Berufe und aus allen Teilen Afrikas*. Essener Verlagsanstalt: Essen.

NOTES

1. Thus, successfully claiming a place in society requires controlling these gazes through a complex corporeal aesthetic and practice that involves animating cloth so that it enlarges the woman – makes her a *grande personne*, simultaneously big, established and impressive – while also conforming her to gendered expectations of appropriate femininity.
2. Unlike other colonial capitals, which were designed as racially segregated spaces working to instill new colonial boundaries of time and space (see Martin 1995), the majority of Lomé was owned by affluent indigenous plantation owners. In Lomé's mixed neighbourhoods, employment-seeking migrants, public works employees, traders and civil servants would meet at church, the market and other public spaces.
3. The new public sphere emerged in colonial Lomé at the intersection of various French institutions/infrastructures of education and civil service. Economic opportunity and migration brought on a new sphere of anonymity.
4. Lomé's growing population was made up of socially, economically and ethnically diverse groups, among them wealthy plantation and property owners (issue of cosmopolitan Afro-Brazilian commercial elite), traders, civil servants and clerks, market women, skilled and unskilled workers, fishermen, voodoo priests, as well as a small European population made up of French colonial administrators, missionaries and merchants. New forms of social interaction and social mixing were now possible in the context of a rapidly transforming urban society and its new spaces of work, life and leisure.
5. Africanist scholars have worked hard to undo the binary assumption that the West 'has fashion' while the 'rest has dress' (Allman 2004). Until recently, African dress was not considered fashion because fashion is regarded as innovation – the dynamic interplay between *imitation* and *differentiation* to use Simmel's terminology (1904) – with the implicit assumption that innovation can only take place in the metropole of modernity and not in the periphery of 'tradition'.
6. Forming an assimilated modern elite, they had white-collar jobs *and* the possibility of citizenship recognition within French colonialism. This French-made elite not only held political membership in a city council structure but also social membership in various clubs and literary societies such as *La Cosmopolite*, *La Moderne* or the *Club littéraire et artistique de Lomé*.
7. Togolese employ the language of 'tradition' in contradistinction to 'modernity' to talk about urban ceremonial practices, which are often adaptations of rural kin-based conventions. In this way, tradition and modernity refer to different conventions that are differently valued or thought to express different spaces rather than different times.

8   Not her real name. I have adopted pseudonyms to protect the anonymity of my sources. Also, for stylistic purposes, I have chosen to refer to her by first name for subsequent mentions.
9   Madame Dinah Grunitsky Olympio was the widow of Sylvanus Olympio, the assassinated first President of the Republic of Togo.
10 Togolese women working in the public sector often wear European-style clothing for office wear.
11 Not her real name. I have adopted pseudonyms to protect the anonymity of my sources. Also, for stylistic purposes, I have chosen to refer to her by first name for subsequent mentions.

4 ETIENNE ROUSSEAU, *BROEDERTWIS* AND THE POLITICS OF CONSUMPTION WITHIN AFRIKANERDOM

STEPHEN SPARKS

At the beginning of *Rip van Wyk*, South African filmmaker Jamie Uys' 1960 remake of Washington Irving's Rip van Winkle story (Uys 1960), an Afrikaner farmer who has been asleep for 100 years wakes up (the year is 1959) to discover that a hyper-modern, gleaming factory has been built on his former farm. In an amusing scene, a bewildered Rip van Wyk walks through the factory and imagines himself to be under attack by its hissing and belching machinery. He then makes his way to the centre of a bustling and sleek downtown shopping district, where modern cars zip past alarmingly and stylishly dressed shoppers walk in and out of shops stocked with an abundance of consumer items. Uys shot these scenes in the then freshly built company town of Sasolburg, established in the early 1950s by the oil company Sasol – one of the apartheid state's prestige projects – on coalfields and farmlands in what was then the northern Orange Free State province of South Africa, about an hour's drive from Johannesburg.

Through much of the next few decades, Sasolburg became a key site for the elaboration of a new modernised Afrikaner identity and imaginary: what I have dubbed the Apartheid Modern (Sparks 2012). Sasol managers, such as Etienne Rousseau, saw themselves as modernisers responsible for transforming *platteland* Afrikaners into modern subjects. Neglected by historians, Rousseau was a prominent and memorably dyspeptic critic of wasteful consumption under apartheid. Consumption was necessarily a central component of the nationalist modernising push. One of the ways in which Sasolburg was celebrated under apartheid was as a space where white residents – primarily, though not exclusively, Afrikaners – would be incorporated into a racially circumscribed, property-owning utopia, analogous in some ways to the similarly circumscribed 'Consumer Republic' described by Lizabeth Cohen for the post-war United States (Cohen 2004). Thorstein Veblen (2007 [1899]) did not anticipate this: with his narrow focus on status-seeking and 'pecuniary emulation' he was conspicuously uninterested in the ways in which nationalist politics might facilitate the embrace of consumption as a marker of national prowess, as a vehicle for ethnic catch-up, or for the development of particular kinds of 'citizen-consumers' (Cohen 2004; Maclachlan & Trentmann 2004; Posel 2010).

The project of ethnic catch-up (pursuing the status and material accoutrements of Anglo-South African elites and middle classes), which Afrikaner modernisation and embourgeoisement[1] represented, was not without its ambiguities, however. Much of Jamie Uys' *oeuvre* 'highlighted Afrikaner anxiety of entering into modernity' (Tomaselli 2006: 117) and in *Rip Van Wyk* this reticence is hinted at in the bewilderment of the title character as he encounters the factory and its hurried shopping district and traffic. Etienne Rousseau was a modernising technocrat, not a backward-looking figure, but the subjects he and other members of Sasolburg's elite envisioned inhabiting their town were circumscribed in an important respect: they were to be *respectable* moderns.

Rousseau and his ilk retained a marked ambivalence about affluence and its effects, especially in relation to working-class Afrikaners, the primary beneficiaries of white supremacist uplift. This ambivalence had particularly South African and indeed Afrikaner nationalist inflections, but Rousseau shared his residual nervousness with post-war elites elsewhere who worried similarly about the morally corrosive social and cultural consequences of newfound affluence (Trentmann 2016: 300–307; Horowitz 2004: 203–224).

Broedertwis (brotherly feud) within Afrikaner political and intellectual circles, between so-called *verkrampte* (narrow-minded) and *verligte* (enlightened) camps, provides a specifically South African context for understanding Rousseau's ambivalence. Customarily presented in binary terms, this rift dates back to the 1960s in the historiography. Advocating an uncompromising, purist Afrikaner nationalist path, *verkramptes* envisioned a strictly Afrikaner state which would defend 'traditional' Afrikaner culture and set its face against reforming the apartheid system (Serfontein 1979; O'Meara 1983; 1996; Giliomee 1992). The *verligtes,* by contrast, adopted a more pragmatic stance, embracing a broader vision of whiteness incorporating non-Afrikaans-speaking whites, accepted the growing convergence of Anglo and Afrikaner capital and the desirability of carefully managed reforms to the apartheid system. Some important creases have been introduced in the literature. O'Meara's (1983) insistence on directly mapping *verligte* and *verkrampte* onto class geographies of Western Cape Afrikaner bourgeoisie and Transvaal petite bourgeoisie respectively has been qualified in his own later work (1996) and by

Giliomee (1992), while Posel (1991) and Lazar (1988) have both tracked intra-Afrikaner debate and tensions over the meaning and direction of *apartheid* back to the late 1940s.

This chapter introduces an additional crease via a new periodisation drawn from a close reading of Rousseau's biography. *Broedertwis* tensions may have only become visible in a highly politicised form at a later point, but their pre-history can be traced to earlier moments in the biographies of Afrikaner professionals rising through the ranks in the pre-war years. *Verligte* and *verkrampte* tensions were a fight within Afrikanerdom over the legitimacy of contesting dispositions towards the future. A key source of debate was the capacity of the cross-class Afrikaner nationalist alliance to reconcile personal ambition and entrepreneurial subjectivities with the levelling ethnic language which helped bring the National Party to power in 1948. The account in this chapter of Rousseau, a recent Stellenbosch University graduate furtively reading American self-help literature during his lunch break in his office in the late 1930s, suggests that members of the rising Afrikaner professional classes had to negotiate the tensions between these contesting dispositions – *verligte* ambition and *verkrampte* asceticism – at the most personal of levels, some decades before these issues burst into clear view under National Party rule.

Anxieties about consumption – in relation to too much alcohol at a business meeting, for instance – underpinned the sense of ambivalence felt by the likes of Rousseau. This makes intuitive sense: in a pioneering article, Albert Grundlingh (2008: 157) suggested that divisions between v*erligtes* and *verkramptes* owed as much to dissension provoked by shifting consumer practices within Afrikaner communities as it did to more proximate political debates about 'immigration policies, the question of housing for black diplomats, Maoris in the New Zealand rugby team and the role of English speakers in the National Party'.

The *verligte/verkrampte* dyad has been somewhat overstated in conventional accounts of *broedertwis*. In practice, these categories could be brought into unexpected relation with one another. Etienne Rousseau frequently sounded like a *verkrampte* moraliser in his criticisms of consumer practices, but these anxieties about the effects of Afrikaner upward mobility and consumption on worker discipline were the complaints of a *verligte* engineer who saw the white working class as insufficiently productive and overpaid and of an pessimistic moderniser, unconvinced, after overseeing the development of Sasol's company town, of the ability of working-class Afrikaners to remake themselves into respectable moderns. This modernising politics was haunted by the possibility that popular forms of consumption – such as the messily improvised shelter erected around a motor car in lieu of a garage – might express an irredeemable unrespectability.

While he remained fundamentally committed to defending white rule, Rousseau emerged as a *verligte* critic of job reservation and an enthusiastic advocate of liberating Afrikaner entrepreneurs and managers from the 'smallness and envy' of Afrikaner nationalist pieties of old. A defender of the growing convergence of Anglo and Afrikaner capital, he argued that job reservation encouraged laziness and lowered productivity among white Afrikaner workers who demanded higher wages and, he suggested, engaged in unrestrained consumption. Rousseau's attacks on the ill discipline of white Afrikaner workers may have had the ring of *verkrampte* laments, but I argue they should instead be seen as part of the *verligte* project of delegitimising Afrikaner white workers and their *verkrampte* political supporters. In so doing, Rousseau joined a chorus of voices questioning the continued usefulness of the historic Afrikaner nationalist cross-class alliance (O'Meara 1983; 1996). Having resisted *verkrampte* objections to the convergence between Anglo and Afrikaner capital, Rousseau worried that South Africa's conspicuously consuming business elites might jeopardise the legitimacy of the enlarged Anglo-Afrikaner capitalist class into which he and his Afrikaner peers were being incorporated during the 1960s.

MAKING (*ORDENTLIKE*) MODERN AFRIKANERS

Although he was very much a poster-child for the Cape Afrikaner nationalist bourgeoisie, it is important to remember that Rousseau was also the inheritor of a Promethean modernising tradition initiated by (and strongly associated with) Jan Smuts, incorporating fellow Afrikaner parastatal-builders like Hendrik van der Bijl and HJ van Eck (Sparks 2016). These Afrikaner technocrats were from different generations but they had followed similar educational itineraries, including training at Stellenbosch University, as well as in Germany and America, before finally taking up senior technocratic positions managing South Africa's parastatals. It was in this forward-looking modernising spirit that Rousseau envisioned a retooling of Afrikaner religiosity and identity to better align with the realities of industrial modernity. Speaking at the opening of a new Dutch Reformed church in Sasolburg in 1969 – when *broedertwis* conflict was at the first of its peaks – Rousseau observed: 'our churches acquired their character and traditions on the platteland', and that the Dutch Reformed church's religious vocabulary was 'interspersed with references to the land' with figures of speech 'seldom drawn from technical and industrial life' (*Sasol Nuus* 1969). A contemptuous paternalism underpinned these remarks; in the privately uttered words of Rousseau's colleague and successor as Sasol managing director, David de Villiers, the Sasol project 'took a bunch of blanket kaffirs', brought them to Sasolburg and turned them into 'thoroughly sophisticated people' (De Villiers n.d.). Remarkably, in this instance, De Villiers used a derogatory racialised metaphor conventionally applied to rural Africans to refer instead to rural Afrikaners, an increasing number of whom had moved off the land to urban areas like Sasolburg and into the protected industrial occupations offered by the industrial parastatals.[2]

The accoutrements of white English-speaking South African material sophistication and abundance – strongly inflected with Americana – were increasingly refigured in the early apartheid years as the property of a new breed of Afrikaner moderns. Envisioned in part as a vehicle for uplifting and reforming *backvelder*[3] Afrikaners, Sasolburg was celebrated as 'one of the few towns that has boasted modern facilities in every home since its establishment' (Ferreira 1967). The middle-class aspirational ideal entailed houses stocked with modern consumer products and appliances, and dutiful housewives using Sasol by-products to keep both home and garden fastidiously neat and hygienic (*Sasol Nuus* 1963; Day 1974). White working-class residents – especially women – who battled to attain this ideal because their homes, backyards and behaviour did not meet exacting measures of *ordentlikheid* (respectability) were the subject of much opprobrium (Mrs Moore to Town Clerk 1965; Mev. Erasmus to Town Clerk 1966; Mr Jenkinson to Town Clerk, 1971; Sparks 2012).

If gendered homemaking was at the centre of the project of respectable consumerism, so too was a particular vision of car ownership. As William Beinart (2001: 182) has noted, car ownership in South Africa significantly increased during the first three decades of apartheid. Sasolburg owed its very existence as a supplier of petrol to this fact of expanding car ownership and concomitant fuel demand. As the photographs taken by Sasolburg residents included in the collage in Figure 3 illustrate, the local car licence plates in the town during apartheid were distinctively marked with the letters OIL, celebrating the commodity which constituted the lifeblood of their town. Car ownership was therefore necessarily tied up with a strong sense of local identity. Of course, not all white (never mind black) residents were financially well off enough to be car owners, though they surely aspired to be, surrounded as they were with Sasol's muscular iconography of oil, cars and speed.[4] For much of the 1950s, 60s and 70s through to today, the popular Sasolburg Volkswagen dealership, Dutton Motors, has catered to both the upper end of the local market (via Audis) and its lower end (via the Beetle and a range of more affordable second hand vehicles).

These 'OIL' licence plates drew conspicuous attention to the provenance of Sasolburg cars – a significant source of anxiety for Sasol managers such as Rousseau. Editorials in the company magazine *Sasol Nuus* (which doubled as the local newspaper) warned residents: 'We can be proud of the letters [but] they bring responsibilities … every one of us is an ambassador for Sasol and its products. If we are not courteous and careful, Sasol and everything it stands for will be branded and we will lose friends and clients' (*Sasol Nuus* 1955). There were commercial considerations at play, certainly – residents as brand ambassadors – but in the emphasis on manners there was also anxiety about the brash comportment of the local white working-class car culture (*Sasol Nuus* 1959a). The houses aimed at the working-class rental market were initially built without garages or canvas carports. In the late 1950s, one of the 'fathers' of the Afrikaner Nationalist 'Economic Movement', the then Minister of Economic Affairs, Nico Diederichs, echoed local complaints about the unsightliness of working-class consumption. The improvised carports and garages erected by residents of the town's cheaper rental homes to protect their cars had a 'disfiguring' effect on the town, he agreed. (Diederichs to Cilliers 1959).

If white working-class Sasolburgers' improvisations around cars reflected the enthusiasm with which they – and the town – embraced 'automania' (McCarthy 2009) as a form of conspicuous consumption, the town's elite's embrace of consumerism was evidently a qualified one. *Sasol Nuus* editorials repeatedly celebrated the fine balance struck in the local culture: 'Where else can one shop at modern, attractive shops in a village where you know all the friendly shop assistants?' (*Sasol Nuus* 1959b). There were subtle local restraints on conspicuous forms of display. After its formal establishment in the early 1960s, the local town council decided to do without the customary 'mayoral limousines and chains as well as wood-panelled Council chambers' (*Sasol Nuus* 1962). Max Kirchhofer, the Swiss planner commissioned by Rousseau to design Sasolburg, personally vetoed local advertising signs which grew 'ever more conspicuous, with coloured lights assailing the passer-by with spurts of flashes in ever increasing intensity' (Kirchhofer to Town Clerk 1968). Bus-stop advertising was similarly rejected: 'What does it benefit a man waiting for a bus or merely walking in the street or driving a car to be exhorted by methods of shock treatment designed for effect over appreciable distances that he must drink beer of a certain brand, smoke cigarettes with a snob appeal and buy this or that for his health or self-respect?' (Kirchhofer to Town Clerk 1966) Beyond the 'modern things for modern people' (*Sasol Nuus* 1970) promised to clientele by a Sasolburg shop, the local bourgeois vision of virtuous abundance emphasised refinement in the form of *conspicuously* cultured forms of consumption which Veblen would have recognised as status-generating: the top local high school piped classical music through the school during recess and Sasol dedicated its philanthropic efforts to sponsoring the arts, building a world-class theatre in the town which would host international ballet and opera performances. The theatre in question was named after Rousseau, a conspicuous monument to the refinement of Sasol's 'founding father'.

'TO BE SEEN AS PART OF THE TOWN'

Born in 1910, Rousseau grew up in a petit-bourgeois Western Cape Afrikaner home, the grandson of Pieter Daniël Rossouw, a Dutch Reformed church minister and important figure in the late-nineteenth century Afrikaans language movement. Rousseau's father spent much of his working life as a school inspector in Cape rural districts. After completing a stellar MSc in chemical engineering at Stellenbosch – the Alma Mater of many senior Sasol figures – Rousseau worked at Iscor, the South African Torbanite Mining and Refining Company (Satmar), and Sanlam's investment wing, Federale Volksbeleggings, before being appointed to head up the newly established state corporation Sasol at the age of just 40.[5] The virtues of hard work and thrift were strongly emphasised in Rousseau's upbringing; they were also important ideological girders of the Afrikaner nationalist movement which helped catapult him to the pinnacle of professional networks by mid-century (O'Meara 1983).

There was also a notable generational inflection to Rousseau's thinking with respect to spending, shaped in powerful ways by the Great Depression. Completing his MSc at Stellenbosch in 1930, he recalled the heightened sense of obligation he experienced in his effort to pay back the money his parents spent on his university education (Rousseau n.d.). Rousseau and his first wife, Darlene Gerdener, similarly emphasised discipline, saving and cultural refinement in the rearing of their own children (Rousseau 1990: 45). The children acquired conspicuously elite cultural tastes at school and home but their son recalls how his school uniform was repeatedly 'patched up' when he was growing up in Sasolburg; new school uniforms were seldom acquired 'because Mum and Dad wanted us to be seen as part of the town' (Rousseau 1990: 54). In this way, what Veblen (2007) called 'invidiousness' was downplayed, a residue of the levelling impulses of pre-war Afrikaner nationalist cultural politics. Rousseau's commitment to thrift was real enough, however: he refused to accept his annual retainer as a member of the Board of Directors at Federale Volksbeleggings when his travel commitments with Sasol meant he was unable to attend board meetings (Rousseau 1951).

Rousseau (see Figure 4) was, however, driven by personal ambition in ways which he often felt needed concealing. During his lunch breaks at Iscor in the late 1930s he would furtively read American self-help books, closing them and putting them away as soon as anyone entered his office (Rousseau 1990: 20). Similar tensions and temptations had to be navigated while travelling overseas on Sasol business. The customary string of mistresses appears not to have materialised, but in the United States he developed a love for 'fat Havanas' and for the wide variety of Martini drinks on offer, while in Japan he 'learned to appreciate *Sake*'.

On one such trip, getting information out of a senior chemist at a major American company entailed drinking 'seven martinis one Saturday afternoon'. This, in turn, necessitated a hot bath and exercising to 'sweat it out'. That he succeeded in getting the information out of the chemist apparently justified the method (Rousseau 1990: 24). Rousseau's interest in self-help literature endured, with American minister and motivational speaker Norman Vincent Peale, author of *The Power of Positive Thinking*, becoming a firm favourite. He had been an avid reader of *The Economist* since at least the 1950s, and he and his senior colleagues at Sasol and other parastatals became increasingly insistent by the 1960s that despite heading up a state-owned and subsidised company, they too were businessmen subject to the allegedly disciplining effects of the market (De Villiers 1975; Sparks 2016).

THE MANAGERIAL REVOLUTION

The ambitions of Rousseau's new class of Afrikaner parastatal managers – the ambitions he concealed when he read self-help literature in his earlier years – were not to be thwarted. He criticised National Party proposals for enhanced parliamentary control over state corporations by invoking 'centuries of experience' in the business world, which he suggested indicated that efficiency would follow from allowing a board of directors to run state corporations 'like private undertakings'. Despite intermittent treasury resistance to Sasol using state subsidies and tax monies to expand into the private sector, the company began to expand energetically into the wider chemical industry in the 1960s and 70s. It entered into partnerships with myriad private sector companies, including the likes of the Anglo-American owned African Explosives Chemical Industries (AECI). Rousseau defended such expansions as 'the legitimate aspirations of the state corporations' (Sparks 2016: 722).

The '*broedertwis*' within Afrikanerdom provides the critical context for understanding Rousseau's position here, though not in ways typically described in the literature. Rousseau had intimate familiarity with these cleavages within Afrikanerdom. In the late 1950s the Sasol project, together with other parastatals, attracted *verkrampte* criticism for the number of English-speaking South Africans and foreigners among their senior technical staff. Responding to these criticisms, Rousseau privately despaired at the lack of qualified Afrikaners, defended the necessarily cosmopolitan make-up of Sasol's staff and celebrated the new Anglo-Afrikaner white South African identity which he suggested was emerging at Sasolburg (Sparks 2012). The old *Sappe*[6] bogeyman of 'disloyal' Afrikaners who supported Jan Smuts and 'South Africanism' lurked here.

In October 1964, the 25th anniversary of the 1939 *Ekonomiese Volkskongress* (Peoples Economic Congress) – the original event where the project of *Volkskapitalisme* was chartered – was held in Bloemfontein (O'Meara 1983). At the celebration, Rousseau made a speech which was a very deliberate *verligte* intervention into the controversy provoked just a few months before when Harry Oppenheimer of Anglo-American gifted its subsidiary, General Mining, to Afrikaner owned mining house Federale Mynbou. Rousseau's message was clear. It was not 1939 anymore. Afrikaner investment capital had come into its own in the aftermath of Sharpeville[7]; there were now Afrikaner managers and entrepreneurs and, in the spirit of the Managerial Revolution (which he explicitly invoked, in English), managers in the public and private sector should be free to pursue 'necessary' partnerships and deals 'with other groups' (that is to say, Anglo capital), without fearing the loss of Afrikaner identity or the constraints imposed by what he explicitly described as the 'smallness and envy' of the past ('*Die Nywerheidswese en die Jong Afrikaner*', Unknown newspaper 1964). In this way he legitimised the ambitions nurtured by his earlier reading of self-help literature, and his more recent reading of *The Economist*.

'ECONOMICALLY RICH AND SOFT'

This brave new world which Rousseau helped bring into being was not, ultimately, entirely to his liking. Throughout the 1960s and 1970s, in both private correspondence and a series of public speeches widely reported in South African newspapers, Rousseau attacked what he perceived to be the decline of self-discipline, of thrift and of the work ethic – core tenets of the Afrikaner nationalist ambience out of which he emerged – and bemoaned the ascendency of rampant forms of wasteful and conspicuous consumption. These jeremiads ran along two axes: he criticised ordinary consumers – he chiefly had Afrikaners in mind – for indulging in instant gratification, and he condemned the ascendency of the corporate expense account and associated forms of conspicuous consumption among South Africa's business elites.

Like other elite Afrikaner observers at this time, described by Grundlingh (2008), Rousseau believed that the economic boom of the 1960s and the increased occupational mobility enjoyed by Afrikaners had been accompanied by unprecedented cultural shifts. Grundlingh (2008) suggests *broedertwis* tensions may have been as much about differing dispositions towards consumption as a disagreement over National Party racial policies, with *verkrampte* Afrikaners objecting to the ostentatious consumer habits of *verligte* Afrikaner *nouveau riche*. Rousseau presents us with a more complicated case, employing the kind of moralising language more often associated with *verkrampte* critics to mount a *verligte* attack on the Afrikaner working class.

Rousseau warned that Afrikaner worker demands (through their trade unions) were spinning out of control and rising wage bills could not be sustained. His fiscal conservatism echoed similar arguments about union profligacy and inflation being made contemporaneously in the West (Tomlinson 2012: 67). 'The man in the street' needed to realise that 'money does not grow on trees; that it has to be worked for,' he complained. 'The idea of saving for the future has faded,' an 'I want it all, now!' attitude had developed. 'People want bigger houses, better cars, larger domestic appliances and more sophisticated electronic equipment.' 'Austerity, frugal living and wise saving' had fallen by the wayside (Rousseau 1971; *The Star* 1971b). There was a 'growing lack of fear of debt' (*Cape Times* 1966), the white (again, largely Afrikaner) worker was 'demanding more for himself' and 'receiving more in wages than he produced in goods'. During the 'fat years' of the post-Sharpeville boom period workers had become 'economically rich and soft' and 'developed a state of mind whereby they demand a larger slice of the cake, not because of increased productivity but because they feel it is their right' (*Financial Mail* 1970).

These criticisms by Rousseau of white Afrikaner worker demands and consumer habits were a slap in the face for *verkrampte* figures like Albert Hertzog who – in the context of ongoing *broedertwis* contestations – argued that Afrikaner workers interests should lie at the centre of Afrikaner nationalism. They were twinned with increasingly sceptical remarks by Rousseau, beginning in the early 1960s, about apartheid job reservation policies: a critical bulwark of white worker privilege which *verkrampte* politicians defended fiercely. Rousseau came to see the shortage of skilled labour (artificially) created by job reservation as a drain on South Africa's human resources. This was certainly true of the majority of black South Africans but somewhat more originally he focused on the consequences for white children who left school early to take up supervisory or white collar jobs, earning what Rousseau described as 'lopsidedly high wages' in sheltered jobs protected from competition. This encouraged laziness. The lack of competition lowered the standard of work, thereby raising capital costs (*Zionist Recorder* 1962; *The Star* 1971a). By attacking job reservation – a *verkrampte* holy-cow – Rousseau joined those elite Afrikaners who were signalling their willingness to detach themselves from the Afrikaner working class which had proven a key part of the Afrikaner nationalist alliance since the 1930s and 40s.

'BUSINESS HAS BRED A NEW ARISTOCRACY'

In addition to these shifts, the increasing convergence of Anglo and Afrikaner capitalist interests in the 1960s – which Rousseau thought desirable – provides important context for his unsparing criticism of the consumer habits of South Africa's business elite. The ascendency of the corporate expense account drew particular ire. In 1969 he warned that 'business has bred a new aristocracy', and the 'expense account has become a way of life' (Rousseau to Thompson, 4 Nov. 1969). Accusing businessmen of ill-discipline and of abusing alcohol and becoming rowdy on late afternoon airplane flights, Rousseau warned that 'millions of Rands a year' were being lost 'through lack of productivity because officials and directors did not feel like working in the afternoons after business lunches' (*Cape Argus* 1970). Businessmen were buying up 'slices of scenic country' and 'limited beach areas' for their private occupation. They wanted 'bigger and better offices, private dining rooms, more luxurious motor cars, trout and game farms and skiing holidays in Europe' (*The Star* 1971b). 'If they are allowed to go much further,' Rousseau wrote, 'I can see us business leaders with a justified revolution on our hands' (Rousseau to Thompson, 4 Nov. 1969). He did not specify whether he had in mind white or black South African workers in mind – he was painting in broad brushstrokes – but significantly, many of these concerns were expressed in correspondence with an official of the New York-based Conference Board, an organisation established in 1916 to shore up flagging public confidence in business in light of escalating tensions between labour and capital in the United States (Gitelman 1984). Rousseau was similarly anxious about the consequences of a conspicuously consuming business class for the legitimacy of capitalism in South Africa. 'We as business men must realise,' he wrote – again seemingly happy to collapse any distinction between a parastatal manager and a capitalist – that the time when 'the average business man was out to make money regardless of the effect on governments, countries or peoples' is over (Rousseau to Thompson, 7 Sep. 1966; *Cape Argus* 1964).

Why pay attention to this cranky engineer-moralist? Rousseau's stature and influence at the commanding heights of the apartheid economy and state provides an obvious answer. His creation, Sasol, played a central role in the growth of the South African 'commodity plastics *filière*' over the last half century (Crompton 1994). While Sasol's claims to by-product ubiquity were initially somewhat exaggerated, by the end of the 1960s the parastatal could legitimately claim to be contributing by-products to plastic toothbrushes, nail polish remover, makeup, floor polish, wax and much else besides. If South African consumer modernity was the world that Sasol helped make, Rousseau had necessarily been at the forefront of these developments. On his frequent overseas tours on business he was constantly on the lookout for possible new product lines which Sasol could develop for both the domestic and international export markets. Speaking to members of the South African motor industry in 1967, he reported being impressed on his travels in Europe and America by the 'new and original types of service stations':

> Some service stations are combined with restaurants, dance halls, cinemas, amusement parks and all types of diversified commerce where the motorist can stop and can attend to a number of purchases and services apart from those directly applying to his motor car … our marketing methods must be tailored to suit the type of young customer … these young people influence fashions, their buying power is large and, what is even more important, the future is more theirs than ours. (*Automobile in SA* 1967)

In short, for all that it possessed a reputation as a bastion of the apartheid state's isolationism and nativism, Sasol was simultaneously linked into a thoroughly global and techno-scientifically precocious Americanised consumer modernity, which it both impersonated and in turn actively participated in.

If apartheid South Africa was a Consumer Republic, both Rousseau and Sasolburg in their own ways epitomised the ambivalence which characterised aspects of Afrikaner engagement with consumption. Sasolburg was celebrated as a consumer utopia of sorts, a vehicle for the 'democratisation' of consumption for the benefit of *platteland* Afrikaners – though not black South Africans – however, as with elites elsewhere, in South Africa, the likes of Rousseau came to regard the generalisation of growing affluence as an ambiguous creature. Democratising consumption meant heightened visibility of unsightly, conspicuous forms of consumption which reminded Sasolburg's elites of the 'unrespectable' origins of the white Afrikaner working class. It also stimulated fears of the enervating effects of Afrikaner upward mobility and consumerism on the social discipline of Afrikaner workers.

Though in his jeremiads he often sounded like a dyspeptic *verkrampte,* Rousseau's attacks on white Afrikaner worker ill-discipline were, in fact, part of a concerted attempt at delegitimising Afrikaner white workers and their *verkrampte* political supporters. Having resisted *verkrampte* objections to Afrikaner embourgeoisement, Rousseau began to fear that South Africa's conspicuously consuming business elites might jeopardise the legitimacy of the enlarged Anglo-Afrikaner capitalist ruling class into which he and other elite Afrikaners were being incorporated during the 1960s.

There would be a series of ironic twists in the tale. The most obvious one is the fact that Sasolburg, for all of Rousseau's ambivalence, undoubtedly became a showpiece for Afrikaner consumption and aspiration. In his capacity as the apartheid state's oil tsar committed to Apartheid Survivalism in Sharpeville's aftermath, Rousseau recommended the establishment of the Strategic Fuel Fund (SFF) so that the state could acquire stock piles of strategically important fuels in preparation for an anti-apartheid oil-boycott. After the Iranian revolution, much of South Africa's crude oil supplies were secured through intermediaries of dubious standing, such as Mario Chiavelli, who received astronomical premiums for their role in facilitating the shipments and used these monies to fund notorious exercises in conspicuous consumption (Sparks 2017; *Glasgow Herald* 1984). So great was the association of the SFF with corruption, easy money and conspicuous consumption that it became a running joke at the time that its acronym stood for 'sex for free' (Anonymous, Interview 2009).

The corporate restraint which Rousseau believed held the key to the legitimacy of Anglo-Afrikaner capitalism has floundered in South Africa, as it has elsewhere (Piketty 2014: 298–300). One of Rousseau's successors at the head of Sasol recently attracted opprobrium for an annual R54-million annual remuneration package (*Business Report* 2013). In perhaps the greatest irony, Rousseau's protestations about a lack of (white) worker restraint in terms of wage demands and consumption were made just a few years before the explosion of black worker protest in the Durban strikes of 1973. Having been preoccupied with disciplining the desires of white workers, Rousseau would soon be calling for fiscal restraint as organised black labour's wage demands became increasingly strident (*Rand Daily Mail* 1973; 1977). With the forcing open of the protected high-wage enclave previously reserved for white workers, black consumer desire could be given increasingly free rein, at the very least among a new labour aristocracy.

REFERENCES

Anonymous, 2009, Interview by author, Natref operator, Sasolburg 2009.

Automobile in SA, 1967, 'Dr Rousseau's Advice to the Motor Industry', January.

Beinart, W., 2001, *Twentieth-Century South Africa* (2nd edn.), Oxford University Press: Oxford.

Business Report, 2013, 'Sasol Boss Paid R54m', iol.co.za, 11 October.

Cape Argus, 1964, 'Rousseau Criticizes Sumptuous Living', 2 October.

Cape Argus, 1970, 'Businessmen Deny They Misuse Drink', 14 March.

Cape Times, 1966, 'Economic hardship ahead, S.A. told', 17 September.

Cohen, L., 2004, 'A Consumers' Republic: The Politics of Mass Consumption in Postwar America', *Journal of Consumer Research* 31(1): 236–239.

Crompton, R., 1994, *The South African Commodity Plastics Filière: History and Future Strategy Options*, Doctoral dissertation, Howard College: University of Natal.

Day, D., 1974, 'The Use of Sasol Products in Our Everyday Lives,' Johannes Meintjes Collection, Sasolburg Public Library, Sasolburg, 15 May 1974.

De Grazia, V., 2005, *Irresistible Empire: America's Advance through Twentieth-Century Europe*. Harvard University Press: Cambridge.

De Villiers, D., n.d., 'Commentary', Johannes Meintjes Collection, Sasolburg Public Library, Sasolburg.

De Villiers, D., 1975, 'Acceptance Speech' for Rand Daily Mail Business Achievement Award for 1975, Sasol 1 Archive, 4/1/4, Sasolburg, 24 November 1975.

Diederichs, N. to C. F. Cilliers, 1959, 28 July, National Archives, MES 218, H 46/6 v. 1 and 46/7.

Erasmus, Mev. to Town Clerk, 1966, Sasolburg Town Clerk Files, 18/10/25, Complaints.

Ferreira, N., 1967, 'Ons Kyk Terug' Johannes Meintjes Collection, Sasolburg Public Library, Sasolburg.

Financial Mail, 1970, 'AHI: Time for Change', 1 May.

Giliomee, H., 1992, '"Broedertwis": Intra-Afrikaner Conflicts in the Transition from Apartheid', *African Affairs* 91(364): 339–364.

Giliomee, H., 2003, *The Afrikaners: Biography of a People*, University of Virginia Press: Charlottesville.

Gitelman, H., 1984, 'Management's Crisis of Confidence and the Origin of the National Industrial Conference Board, 1914-1916', *The Business History Review* 58(2): 153–177.

Glasgow Herald, 1984, 'South Africa enmeshed it its own web of secret oil deals', 3 May.

Grundlingh, A., 2008, '"Are We Afrikaners Getting too Rich?" Cornucopia and Change in Afrikanerdom in the 1960s', *Journal of Historical Sociology* 21(2/3): 143–165.

Horowitz, D., 2004, *The Anxieties of Affluence: Critiques of American Consumer Culture, 1939–1979*, University of Massachusetts Press: Amherst.

Jenkinson, Mr to Town Clerk, 1971, Sasolburg Town Clerk Files, 18/10/25, Complaints, 4 January.

Kirchhofer, M. to Town Clerk, 1966, Sasolburg, Precinct 15, Part 1, Sasol 1 Archive, Sasolburg, 17 January.

Kirchhofer, M. to Town Clerk, 1968, Sasolburg Town Clerk Files, 30 March.

Lazar, J., 1988, *Conformity and Conflict: Afrikaner Nationalist Politics in South Africa, 1948–1961*, Doctoral dissertation, University of Oxford: Oxford.

Maclachlan, P. and Trentmann, F., 2004, 'Civilizing Markets: Traditions of Consumer Politics in Twentieth-Century Britain, Japan and the United States', in M. Bevir and F. Trentmann (eds.), *Markets in Historical Contexts: Ideas and Politics in the Modern World*, Cambridge University Press: Cambridge.

McCarthy, T., 2009, *Auto Mania: Cars, Consumers, and the Environment*, Yale University Press: New Haven.

Moll, T., 1991, 'Did the Apartheid Economy 'Fail'?' *Journal of Southern African Studies* 17(2): 271–291.

Moore, Mrs to Town Clerk, 1965, Sasolburg Town Clerk Files, 18/10/25; *Klagte*, 12 October.

O'Meara, D., 1983, *Volkskapitalisme: Class, Capital and Ideology in the Development of Afrikaner Nationalism, 1934–1948*, Ravan Press: Johannesburg.

O'Meara, D., 1996, *Forty Lost Years: The Apartheid State and the Politics of the National Party, 1948–1994*, Ravan Press: Johannesburg.

Orwig, S., 2002, 'Business Ethics and the Protestant Spirit: How Norman Vincent Peale Shaped the Religious Values of American Business Leaders', *Journal of Business Ethics* 38(1&2): 81–89.

Piketty, T., 2014, *Capital in the Twenty-First Century* (trans. Arthur Goldhammer), Harvard University Press: Cambridge and London.

Posel, D., 1991, *The Making of Apartheid, 1948–1961: Conflict and Compromise*, Clarendon Press: Oxford.

Posel, D., 2010, 'Races to Consume: Revisiting South Africa's History of Race, Consumption and the Struggle for Freedom', *Ethnic and Racial Studies* 33(2): 157–175.

Rand Daily Mail, 1973, 'Higher Pay Will Mean Loss of Jobs', 2 April.

Rand Daily Mail, 1977, 'Black Wage Realism Urged', 3 June.

Rousseau, E., n.d., 'Commentary', Johannes Meintjes Collection, Sasolburg Public Library: Sasolburg.

Rousseau, E., 1951, 'Memo', Sasol 1 Archive, Sasol General, 31 June 1951.

Rousseau, E., 1959, 'Melbourne Memo' 18/1/11, Australia, 25 June 1959 Sasol 1 Archive, Sasolburg.

Rousseau, E., 1971, 'Economic Prospects for South Africa over the Next Five Years', 12 March.

Rousseau, E., 1975, 'The Coal Renaissance: A South African Point of View', The Robens Coal Science Lecture, London, 6 October.

Rousseau, E., 1976, 'South Africa's Economic Situation', 9 August, Etienne Rousseau Papers, PV 556/10: SASOL; Archive for Contemporary Affairs, University of the Free State, Bloemfontein.

Rousseau, E. to G. Clark Thompson, 7 September 1966, Etienne Rousseau Papers, PV 556/10: SASOL; Archive for Contemporary History, University of the Free State, Bloemfontein.

Rousseau, E. to G. Clark Thompson, 4 November 1969, Etienne Rousseau Papers, PV 556/10 SASOL; Archive for Contemporary Affairs, University of the Free State, Bloemfontein.

Rousseau, E. to Nico Diedrichs, 30 September 1959, MES 218, H4/7 Sasol Algemeen, National Archives of South Africa, Pretoria

Rousseau, E. to Nico Diedrichs, 11 March 1964, SAB MES 219, H4/7/1/SASOL Algemeen, National Archives of South Africa, Pretoria

Rousseau, L., 1990. *PER 80 Gedenkboek P. Etienne Rousseau*, Cape Town: Rubicon Press.

Sasol Nuus, 1955, Editorial, October.

Sasol Nuus, 1959a, 'Besoekers by Sasol', February.

Sasol Nuus, 1959b, 'Shopping in Sasolburg', October.

Sasol Nuus, 1962, Editorial 'Carry on the Good Work', August.

Sasol Nuus, 1963, 'Chemical Expansion at Sasolburg', March.

Sasol Nuus, 1969, 'Our Chairman About the Relationship Between Church and Industry at Sasolburg', July.

Sasol Nuus, 1970, Uniewinkel advertisement, December.

Serfontein, J. H. P., 1979, *Brotherhood of Power: An Exposé of the Secret Afrikaner Broederbond*, Rex Collings: London.

Sparks, S., 2012, 'Apartheid Modern: South Africa's Oil-from-Coal Project and the Making of a Company Town', Unpublished DPhil dissertation, University of Michigan: Ann Arbor.

Sparks, S., 2016, 'Between "Artificial Economics" and the "Discipline of the Market": Sasol from Parastatal to Privatisation', *Journal of Southern African Studies* 42(4): 711–724.

Sparks, S., 2017, 'Crude Politics: The ANC, the Shipping Research Bureau and the Anti-Apartheid Oil Boycott', *South African Historical Journal* 69(2): 1–14.

The Star, 1971a, 'Give bigger jobs to Africans: Rousseau', 20 November.

The Star, 1971b, 'Good Life Must Be Worked for', 17 March.

Tomaselli, K. G., 2006, *Encountering Modernity: Twentieth Century South African Cinemas*, Rozenberg Publishers: Amsterdam.

Tomlinson, J., 2012, 'Thatcher, Monetarism and the Politics of Inflation', in B. Jackson and R. Saunders (eds.), *Making Thatcher's Britain*. Cambridge University Press: Cambridge.

Trentmann, F., 2016, *Empire of Things: How We Became a World of Consumers, from the Fifteenth Century to the Twenty-First*, Allen Lane: London.

Uys, J., 1960, *Rip van Wyk*. Jamie Uys Filmproduksies: South Africa.

Veblen, T., 2007 [1899], *The Theory of the Leisure Class*, Macmillan: New York.

Unknown newspaper, 1964, 'Die Nywerheidswese en die Jong Afrikaner', 5 October.

Zionist Recorder, 1962, 'Sasol Chief Uneasy', 12 October.

NOTES

1. The process whereby previously poor and/or working class Afrikaners became middle class.
2. Seventy-five per cent of Afrikaners had moved to urban areas by 1960. Statistics cited in Giliomee (2003: 405).
3. A derogatory term typically invoking a stereotype of an unsophisticated, rural Afrikaner, unfamiliar with city life and culture.
4. My thanks to Deborah Posel for this point. I greatly appreciate her close reading of multiple versions of this essay.
5. Iscor was the South African Iron and Steel Corporation, a state-owned parastatal, and Satmar was the South African Torbanite Mining and Refining Company.

6 '*Sappe*' survived as a reference to Jan Smuts' old South African Party, which merged with Barry Hertzog's National Party in 1936 to form the United Party. Hertzog was unable to carry many hardline Afrikaner nationalists with him into the new party (and coalition government) and when World War II started he too returned to the Afrikaner nationalist fold because of his insistence on a position of neutrality instead of support for the Allied effort against the Nazis. The use of '*Sappe*' to characterise Afrikaners who continued to support Smuts' United Party after 1939 thus carried perjorative meaning in Afrikaner nationalist circles.

7 On March 21st, 1960 at Sharpeville near Vereeniging, police shot at a crowd of African protesters, killing 69 people and injuring 180 others. Fearful of significant political fall-out, in the immediate aftermath significant capital left South African capital markets. Much of this capital returned as soon as it became clear the South African state had control, but in the interregnum Afrikaner finance moved into the vacuum and took advantage of diminished share prices to increase their shareholdings in a range of industries where previously it had little standing. The extent to which South Africa's post-Sharpeville economic performance was impressive in global terms has been called into question as has the sustainability of that growth given the structural weaknesses of an economy depended on gold price related windfalls and the skills and consumption of a white minority. See Moll (1991) and O'Meara (1996: 171–175).

5 RECYCLING CONSUMPTION: POLITICAL POWER AND ELITE WEALTH IN ANGOLA

CLAUDIA GASTROW

In 2015, Angolans were shocked by the airing of an episode of the American reality television show *Say Yes to the Dress*.[1] The show generally follows a set script where an enthusiastic, but nervous, bride, accompanied by close friends and relatives, frequents an upscale bridal store in order to find her dream dress. The ultimate aim, of course, is to 'say yes to the dress', a moment that is usually accompanied by gasps, tears and smiles from the bride and her party as they see her in 'the dress' for the first time and imagine her perfect wedding and happy future. Everything seemed to be going perfectly to script when *Say Yes to the Dress* followed the wedding party of Naulila Diogo, daughter of the then Angolan Minister of Territorial Administration, Bornito de Sousa,[2] as she arrived at the exclusive New York City-based bridal boutique Kleinfeld, accompanied by her mother and bridal party to purchase nine Pnina Tornai dresses. Two were for her, each decorated with hand-stitched Swarovski crystal details and additional luxuries, such as French lace and a tulle skirt that took 300 hours to make. Her mother had a hand-dyed pink dress, also with hand-stitched crystal details. The episode described Diogo as 'Angolan royalty' and gushingly explained that the over-US$200 000 bill that she had footed for the dresses was the most anyone had ever spent on the show. Diogo explained that she wanted her wedding of 800 people to be 'bigger and better' than any of the other weddings she had attended. Between the crystals, attendants and multiple dresses, it was a veritable orgy of conspicuous consumption, tied up in reality-television packaging as a model to be admired and emulated. The problem, however, was that the audience was not confined to the United States.

Dismayed Angolans eventually viewed the episode when it began to circulate online, and raised objections. The show had aired during the first year of the country's economic bust, following the fall of the international oil price near the end of 2014. Angolans wanted to know exactly how the daughter of a government minister could afford to spend US$200 000 on dresses. Discussion in response to the show was a means of pointing to the excesses of the Angolan political elite – a means of throwing the conspicuous consumption of a minority back in their faces as a critique of the extremely unequal conditions of life that characterise Angola.

The response of De Sousa, however, was not one of humility or shame. Instead, he accused Club-K[3], the website that had 'broken' the story, of being engaged in 'dirty' journalism. He pushed back against the negative framing of the story, stating that Angolans should look at the 'positive side' of his daughter's purchase of the dresses. Tornai had decided to open up her first bridal store in Africa in Luanda. This development 'put Angola on the international fashion circle, putting at the disposal of Angolan brides (and taking away the arguments of their fiancés) high quality options, without them having to spend money on overseas trips' (*RedeAngola* 2015). De Sousa's response appeared out of touch in suggesting that trips overseas were a cost with which the majority of Angolans should concern themselves. More significantly, his words echoed an increasing number of similar claims being made by Angolan elites over the years in defence of conspicuous consumption. While De Sousa focused on a reinterpretation of his daughter's purchases as promoting Angola's international image, others defended their actions by dismissing the often pathologised and racialised representations of African consumption.

Angolans are openly critical of their elite's conspicuous consumption. Thorstein Veblen (1994 [1899]) argued that conspicuous consumption, which was often a form of 'wasteful consumption' in that the goods consumed were not required for basic survival, was a mark of economic power and therefore 'repute'. However, he also noted that consumption was not the only means through which repute was accumulated. The contemporary world he described was also characterised by a counteracting orientation, which he referred to as the 'instinct of workmanship' (57). This instinct favoured activities and forms of accumulation that were identified as 'productive' and 'efficient'. Consumption should therefore not be entirely wasteful, but rather needed to show its use and purpose. What counted as 'waste', as Veblen (60–61) pointed out, however, was ultimately extremely subjective, rather than easily identifiable. So the question of what constitutes wasteful consumption lies at the heart of struggles over legitimate consumption, and it is in this respect that elite consumption in Angola becomes politicised and controversial.

In Angola, significant conspicuous wealth is often associated with corruption. This is perhaps unsurprising given the political connections of many prominent entrepreneurs, who include the children of former President José Eduardo dos Santos, high-ranking generals, and ruling-party stalwarts. Angola is perhaps one of the archetypal examples of the 'privatisation of the state', in which laws and institutions are turned towards private ends for financial accumulation and political power (Messiant 2004; Soares de Oliveira 2015). Importantly, much of the wealth in Angola flows from its offshore oil platforms. The state presents itself officially as the guardian of oil on behalf of the people, through the vehicle of the state oil company Sonangol, and is responsible for ensuring that the promised prosperity of oil is realised. When oil wealth transforms into conspicuous consumption on the part of those with close connections to revenues, commodities become an index of the wasteful usage of public funds. With access to ruling party and state connections being the surest way of accessing the flows of oil revenues, the wealth enjoyed by the elite is then widely viewed as having been siphoned off at the expense of the poor majority. What should have been the benefits of oil accruing to 'the people' instead congeal in designer wedding gowns and first-class flights. Conspicuous consumption, when it lacks the accompanying support of the 'workmanship instinct', leads to ill repute. The accumulation of goods by Angolans associated with the state becomes viewed as wasteful expenditure of the public purse and a product of suspect business practices rather than as an indication of entrepreneurial success.

Accusations of corruption and excess are familiar terrain in disscussions about African wealth. Classic accounts of African politics focus on tropes of eating: the extravagant consumption of women and goods as a means of garnering and performing power (Bayart 1993; Mbembe 2001). In particular, analyses of African elite consumption as being driven by greed and based on illegality rather than legitimate wealth have a long history. Fanon (1963) was one of the earliest critics of an emerging postcolonial elite, which he decried for its parasitism and lack of vision. Describing it as 'mediocre in its winnings, in its achievements and its thinking' he argued that its members engaged in conspicuous consumption in order to 'mask its mediocrity' (120). For him, the consumption practices of the postcolonial elite were a form of crass mimesis which sought to capture the signs of colonial bourgeois power, while lacking the substantive education and drive to build the wealth that underlay it. Subsequent analyses of class on the continent described the wealthy as a '*comprador*' class building their wealth from their ability to act as intermediaries for neocolonial capitalist interests (Sklar 1979). With a recent surge in interest in 'the middle class' in Africa, more complicated accounts have emerged of what constitutes class and wealth in African countries, most focusing on the fraught relationship between consumption and income (Lentz 2015; James 2015; Southall 2016). However, the whiff of illicitness is difficult to dispel for Africa's hyper-rich, especially those who appear to have obvious links to political power. It is exactly the association of wealth with illegality that Angola's elite is increasingly trying to combat publicly. In so doing, they draw on African critiques of antiblack racism to paint critiques of their consumption – even by fellow Angolans – as politically misled and racially prejudicial.

Battles over legitimisation and critiques of elite conspicuous consumption in Angola unfold across specific controversies about elite spending within the context of contemporary Angolan politics. These contestations about conspicuous consumption get to the heart of local contests over legitimate power, but also internationalised discourses in relation to legitimate consumption, thus constituting a site of political struggle mediated by transnational framings of African consumption. Ultimately, critiques and counter-critiques of conspicuous consumption have become a crucible for the negotiation of race, consumption, and legitimacy in contemporary Angola.

CONSUMPTION AND POWER IN ANGOLA

Historically, consumption in independent Angola has been heavily mediated by personal and political connections. In 1977, two years after the country's independence, the ruling Popular Movement for the Liberation of Angola (MPLA) declared Angola a one-party Marxist-Leninist state. However, the implementation of a socialist political and economic agenda was accompanied by the emergence of a system of patronage politics focused on access to goods and favours (Messiant 2004). At independence, a large number of companies were nationalised, the currency, the kwanza, was fixed, and price controls introduced (Aguilar 2001). The purchase of consumer goods was now meant to take place in *lojas do povo* (People's Stores), with people using ration cards assigned to them through their workplaces (Tvedten 1997). Not all *lojas de povo* were equal, however. Higher-ranking civil servants and party members had access to stores with more and better goods. Those working in the diamond and oil business had access to foreign currency and shops in which they could purchase goods with forex at subsidised rates (Bhagavan 1986). These discrepancies in access to goods were justified as a means of maintaining the best talent in the country (Wolfers & Bergerol 1983).

The gradual collapse of Angola's economy, in combination with the already-existing link between a state-created hierarchy and formal access to consumer goods, entrenched a system of favours and personal connections for access to goods. Shortages of goods were frequent in the normal *lojas do povo*, due not only to the inefficiencies of the planned economy, but also the devastating effects of civil war, which had broken out even before the declaration of independence in 1975. As the war continued, local agricultural and industrial production steadily collapsed. The destruction of infrastructure made the transportation of goods increasingly difficult. To survive, Angola, and especially the coastal cities, became ever more reliant on imports funded by the country's oil reserves (Dos Santos 1990). By the 1980s, products such as meat, eggs and fruit became increasingly scarce in official stores, leading to an explosion in the parallel economy, which Angolans referred to as *candonga,* and an increasingly complex system of *esquemas* (schemes) to access basic goods (Dos Santos 1990; Schubert 2000).

Those with access to better and more varied goods in state stores had an advantage in terms of the profits they could reap from *candonga*, and the profits were high. Hodges (1987) states that in 1986, a kilogram of rice cost 25 kwanza in the state stores, but sold for 2 000 kwanza on the parallel market. People who worked in factories, the ports, and other positions where they could access goods, could pilfer and siphon off goods and enjoy the profits (Dos Santos 1990). As public services collapsed, identity documents, medical services, and licences of various kinds all became available through *candonga* (Schubert 2000). Formal employment positions then, while symbolically important (Rodrigues 2006), were economically more significant for the *esquemas* they enabled than for the money earned from them (Schubert 2000). Personal connections became central to consumption, with elites highly dependent on the MPLA for the maintenance of their status, so that, as Messiant (1992: 23) argued, the 'parallel economy, grafted mainly on nomenklaturist[4] privileges and redistribution (or pilfering or theft), is in practice the main mechanism of income distribution'.

The links between political relationships and economic power were exacerbated in the 1990s in the wake of the MPLA's abandonment of socialism. In 1991, the MPLA and Union for the Total Liberation of Angola (Unita) signed the Bicesse Peace Accord, leading to constitutional reforms that introduced a system of multiparty democracy. The MPLA officially abandoned Marxist-Leninism and began a process of privatising state-owned enterprises and property. The privatisation process was extremely opaque, with those with connections to the MPLA generally being favoured for acquisitions (Aguilar 2001). However, while a minority enriched themselves through the introduction of economic reforms, the majority suddenly felt themselves scrambling to survive in an economy in free fall. The return to war in late 1992 led to the ongoing destruction of the formal economy outside of the oil sector and in turn increased reliance on the informal sector. In the cities, the population became ever more dependent on expensive imported goods, even for basic necessities, leading to runaway inflation, which peaked at 12.035 per cent in July 1996 (Hodges 2004). By the early 2000s, surveys revealed the urban population to be significantly more impoverished than it had been a decade before (29). These developments then, showed the limits of a system based on clientelist redistribution. While those with relevant connections might have been satiated, millions of Angolans lived outside of, or with little connection to, the kinds of opportunities that would open up the doors of consumption and comfort.

At the heart of this inequality was the system of patronage and illicit financial spending that had emerged around the oil economy (Hodges 2004; Messiant 2004; Soares de Oliveira 2015). As far back as the 1980s, the Presidency had negotiated oil-backed loans with international creditors to pay for weapons and food through the national oil company, Sonangol (Soares de Oliveira 2015). Millions of dollars therefore bypassed official institutions and were spent in unknown ways (Hodges 2004). Money was siphoned to the top and divested from on-the-ground needs, such as health and education, so that even as state institutions became increasingly incapacitated, those who 'occupied' the state became empowered and wealthy (Messiant 2004). It was exactly this system of oil-loans, personal political connections, enrichment at the top of the state and impoverishment of the majority that set the stage for an explosion of conspicuous consumption on the part of the Angolan elite and the subsequent tensions over it that emerged following the end of Angola's civil war in 2002.

Angola's civil war came to an abrupt end in the first half of 2002, following the killing of Jonas Savimbi[5] by MPLA troops in February of that year. On 4 April 2002, the MPLA and Unita signed the Luena Memorandum of Understanding, which formally brought the war to an end. The end of the conflict coincided with a boom in the international price of oil, Angola's primary export. The country suddenly moved from being heavily indebted to flush with cash, as oil profits rolled in. The rush of petro-dollars fuelled what Schubert (2018: 1) refers to as a 'culture of immediatism: a get-rich-quick ambient and desire for instant material gratification which permeated everyday life in the "turbo-charged economy"'. Elite Angolans' lifestyles were the models of these desires performed through practices of conspicuous consumption. Even as the majority of Angolans continued to struggle with access to basic services and dignified living conditions, the oil platforms pumped millions of barrels which congealed in the Toyota Prados, designer handbags, lavish parties and spacious new apartments of those who enjoyed access to contracts and connections. This was the 'new Angola', an oil party for some, a dream for others, and a country constantly on display. Angolan wealth came to international attention, as Angolans began to purchase significant shares in international businesses – especially in Portuguese banks and media – resulting in the publication of a book with the sensationalist title *Os Donos Angolanos de Portugal* (The Angolan Owners of Portugal) (Costa, Louçã & Teixeira Lopes 2014).

As the world struggled in the midst of the 2008 global financial crisis, Angolan conspicuous consumption, buoyed by the international commodity boom, fed dreams of the 'Africa Rising' narrative, suggesting that the long-dismissed continent was now breaking through into a new era of capitalist success. Angola's wealthy began to become infamous for their purchase of high-end real estate in Portugal and for shopping trips to Dubai, Lisbon and Rio de Janeiro. In 2012, it was estimated that at least 30 per cent of the market for luxury goods in Portugal was made up of Angolan wealth (Negrao 2012). Angolan investors spread their wings, with investments made in banking, food processing, media and luxuries with then President José Eduardo dos Santos's daughter, Isabel dos Santos, purchasing De Grisogono, the Swiss luxury jewellery company. They thus came to be counted among the 'super-rich' Africans with whom Europe and the United States were increasingly enamoured, fulfilling similar tropes of glamour and wealth in the Lusophone world to those being embodied by Nigerians in English-speaking countries.[6] However, even as some commentators fawned over the investments, describing Portugal as lucky to have them, and even as the stream of visits of world leaders to Angola legitimated the balance of wealth in the country, these elite displays of wealth could not escape the whiff of the illicit. Reports on high-level corruption continued to emerge.[7] Transparency International consistently ranked the country as one of the most corrupt in the world, and a growing number of academic works highlighted the suspect international financial relationships through which the Angolan boom was produced (Burgis 2015; Soares de Oliveira 2015). Most recently, a prominent member of the MPLA, Lopo do Nascimento, described the country's post-conflict national reconstruction as akin to 'opening a window and throwing money out' in reference to the wasted show projects and excessive corruption that characterised it (Onishi 2017). Elites have often responded to such criticism by attempting to reframe the meaning of their consumption. Nowhere has this perhaps been more evident than in disputes over the actions and purchases of those who, for many years, stood at the heart of power – former President José Eduardo dos Santos's children.

THE PRESIDENT'S CHILDREN

'Are you suffering from corruption fatigue?' asked the article published on corruption watchdog *MakaAngola*'s website in May 2017 (Dos Santos 2017). The article covered the latest scandal linked to one of President José Eduardo dos Santos's children, the 25-year-old Eduane Danilo dos Santos, more generally known simply as Danilo. At the 2017 amFAR[8] Gala at Cannes, frequented by, among others, actor Will Smith, model Bella Hadid and musician Nicki Minaj, the president's son had outbid others at the accompanying auction to purchase a watch for €500 000. This was in the middle of Angola's most serious economic crisis in a decade. With the crash of the international oil price in 2015, ordinary Angolans' salaries had steadily depreciated and foreign exchange had become virtually unavailable except at exorbitant prices on the parallel market. The sight of the president's son blowing half a million Euros on a watch infuriated people.

The watch quickly became yet another marker of the perceived capture of the state purse by the presidential family, and the callousness with which this money was spent. With formal avenues of protest largely shut down in the country, Angolans took to social media, sending mocking photographs via WhatsApp of, among other things, oversized watches, a car steering wheel covered with watches and drawings of watches on people's wrists, writing messages underneath, such as 'My watch cost 1 million USD', 'Danilo the people don't have medicine'.[9] Danilo dos Santos subsequently took to Facebook to explain his actions, claiming that the watch had merely accompanied the more significant purchase of a collection of prints by photographer George Hurrell for Dos Santos's association *Espirito de Criança*[10] (*RedeAngola* 2017). This donation would, he claimed, contribute to combating HIV and AIDS at an international level. Nevertheless, criticism of the purchase continued, with Angolans perhaps agreeing with the comment made by Will Smith at the auction itself. Smith asked if Dos Santos was not a bit young to have that amount of money.

Former President José Eduardo dos Santos's children have been increasingly embroiled in controversy. Most of these controversies revolve around the sources of their riches in the context of the ongoing impoverishment of the majority of the Angolan population. Their conspicuous consumption and lucrative business deals have earned them ill repute, even as they indicate their strong links to power and wealth. They thus, in many ways, embody Veblen's understanding of conspicuous consumption. The more they consume and enrich themselves, the more the basis of their wealth is questioned. While Danilo dos Santos's actions at Cannes were his first foray into the critical public eye, José Eduardo dos Santos's other children have been subject to public criticism over a much longer period. His two eldest sons, José Eduardo Paulino dos Santos ('Coréon Dú') and José Filomeno de Sousa dos Santos ('Zenú'), have both been subjects of controversy. Coréon Dú is a musician and television producer, who owns Semba Communicação, a 'branding and communication agency'.[11] In addition to developing a number of television programmes for Angola Public Television (TPA), in 2012 this company was controversially given $40 million by the Presidency to promote Angola's public image (Marques de Morais 2012). This, in essence, meant that President dos Santos had handed over $40 million to his son. Zenú was made head of the country's Sovereign Wealth Fund in 2013. Their sister Welwitschia dos Santos 'Tchizé' is a member of parliament and co-owner of Semba Communicação with her brother. However, the most famous of the Dos Santos siblings is José Eduardo dos Santos's eldest daughter, Isabel dos Santos, currently ranked as Africa's wealthiest woman and former head of Sonangol.[12]

Isabel dos Santos's fortunes became more visible following the end of the civil war. In 2013, *Forbes* identified her as the wealthiest woman in Africa, with her personal wealth estimated at approximately $3 billion (Dolan & Marques de Morais 2013). Among other things, she had significant investments in Angola's diamond industry, a 25 per cent stake in Angola's largest mobile telecommunications company Unitel, and investments in the oil, cement and banking sectors (Dolan & Marques de Morais 2013). Despite her denials, her wealth is suspected of being a product of her position as the President's daughter and the benefits that have accrued therefrom. Her rejection of these suspicions has involved a growing public relations engagement to promote her as an example of hard work and business acumen. Perhaps the first very public example of this strategy was an interview with the *Financial Times*, in which she claimed to have sold eggs as a child to fund her 'sweet tooth', as 'proof' of her having had an entrepreneurial spirit from a young age (Burgis 2013). Angolans responded by posting pictures on social media of her carrying golden eggs, and generally mocking the idea that the president's daughter would have engaged in such activities. The political and nepotistic underpinnings of her fortune have become even more apparent since her father relinquished power in 2017, as the new incumbent, João Lourenço, has systematically revoked contracts previously awarded to her, in the process highlighting how much of her previous empire hinged off family relationships (Marques de Morais 2018). Nevertheless, Isabel dos Santos has continued to insist on the legitimacy of her fortune, particularly using social-media platforms, such as Twitter and Instagram, to post photographs of herself at work and attending meetings to attempt to cultivate the image of a hardworking woman. She increasingly accuses those who criticise her as promoting 'fake news'.

The most adept at trying to repackage the image of dubious wealth, however, has been Isabel dos Santos's husband, Sindika Dokolo. Dokolo is the son of deceased Congolese businessman Sanu Dokolo and Hanne Kruse, a Danish employee of the Red Cross who met his father in the 1960s when she worked in the Democratic Republic of Congo. Dokolo's father was a close friend of then Zairean statesman Mobutu Sese Seko, and during the time of his rule, Sanu Dokolo set up the Bank of Kinshasa from which he earned considerable wealth (Collier 2015). Dokolo met Isabel dos Santos in the late 1990s, and they subsequently married in 2003. Dokolo has earned his name internationally through the Dokolo Foundation, which collects and promotes African art, especially making waves for its active attempts to repatriate African art that was stolen during the colonial period.

The Dokolo Foundation first made international headlines in 2006 when it won the call for the African Pavilion for the 2007 Venice Biennale. However, controversy soon followed. In early 2007, an article for *Artnet Magazine* entitled 'Art and Corruption in Venice' highlighted the suspect sources of Dokolo's wealth (Davis 2007). The article claimed that 'the unsavory political and business activities of the people behind the collection are raising questions that could well prove an embarrassment to the venerable art fest,' going on to explain that Dokolo had been the benefactor of suspected corrupt activity on the part of his father, and more recently had been directly linked not only to the Dos Santos family, long accused of significant corruption, but to diamond companies in Angola that had been exposed for partaking in significant human rights abuses in the country's diamond-producing areas, including 'murders, tortures and rapes' (Davis 2007). Dokolo's involvement in the Venice Biennial then, rather than being a moment of African pride, threatened to 'drag to light bitter questions about the relation between African elites and the vast majority of Africans' (Davis 2007). Other notable figures in the international world of art also began to step forward. Chika Okeke-Agulu (2007: 1) wrote a scathing article, which described the Dokolo Collection as representing an 'unprecedented connection between art patronage and state depredation', and went on to argue that 'we cannot afford to accept any suggestion, even of the subtlest kind, that the survival of contemporary African art depends on the patronage of robber barons. And that is why the decision to highlight – to celebrate and authorize – the Dokolo Collection at the 52nd Biennale is most unfortunate.' In reaction to these controversies, Cameroonian artist Barthélémy Toguo withdrew from the Pavilion, refusing to have his name associated with Dokolo. The artistic director of the Venice Biennale claimed to be ignorant of the sources of Dokolo's wealth, but tried to suggest that the significance of the collection should be judged separately from the background of its patron (*Artnet News* 2007).

Dokolo, however, hit back. The first move was to send an attorney's letter to *Artnet Magazine* insisting that the blogpost be removed. This did not happen, but the magazine did publish Dokolo's right of reply, which hit at the heart of discomforts in relation to critiques over African wealth. Dokolo accused the author of the article, Ben Davis, of misconstruing the sources of his wealth, unfairly dragging his family into the spotlight, and essentially of being a shoddy journalist (*Artnet News* 2007). However, his significant move came near the end of the letter, where he asked, 'Would this basic journalistic work have been neglected if I had been a European or American collector?' followed in the next paragraph by a more substantive reference to the problematics of the representation of African wealth:

> I would like to conclude by questioning the 'why' of this article. Why not take any time for research or analysis? Why this taste for immediate caricature when it comes to African elites? Like my father before me, I have decided to fight preconceived ideas so that Africans would have a strong point of view on the world that would be their own. My weapon is this collection and the impact it will have on the African public. (*Artnet News* 2007)

In this statement, Dokolo made explicit what the attempts to refashion images of his wife and her family's elite consumption as hard work and philanthropy do more subtly. That is, Dokolo accused those who criticised his wealth as basing their arguments on historically racialised and prejudicial stereotypes of African consumption. While opportunistic, such attacks on critics are powerful exactly because they resonate with a widely acknowledged problem – namely, racist portrayals of life on the African continent, especially consumption.

Although Angolan wealth has been praised and supported by many in Portugal, the racist underpinnings of understandings of African wealth remain ingrained. In 2014, for instance, a major Portuguese comedy show featured a segment in which an actress in blackface played an Angolan woman, accompanied by her sons dressed in gold chains and listening to hip-hop music, tearing through stores stating, 'I'll buy it all' (Ames 2015). The appeal to what Matlon (2016: 1018) has described as racialised 'icons of hyper-capitalist consumerism' – congealed in the hip-hop stardom, the use of blackface, and the reported crude performance of desperate consumption – indicated the extent to which Angolan luxury was discursively constituted as racial excess by a (white) international gaze.

Caught between images of deprivation and excess, discussing African consumption is inherently a politically loaded issue. The very construction of race in some African countries hinged off the denial of consumption to the black majority, meaning that the making of black deprivation was central to the production of racial differentiation (Posel 2010). Afro-pessimist[13] scholars have equally highlighted how practices of consumption engaged in by black subjects are almost always rendered as pathological (Marriot 2017). In the anti-black historical construction of consumption then, whiteness 'represents … the limit that separates production from conspicuous consumption' (Marriot 2017), meaning that consumption by black people almost always spills into tropes of greed, excess and luxury. International racialised frameworks are exacerbated in the case of Africa by Afro-pessimist tropes that always already define African leaders as 'corrupt and incompetent compradors' (B'béri & Louw 2011: 338), making the possibility of an open discussion of African consumption difficult. Given these racist framings of African consumption, asserting the legitimacy of and demanding the right to conspicuous consumption can be understood, as Posel (2010) has argued, as a radical political act.

It is against these tropes that Dokolo and other Angolan elites act when they claim to be consuming in the interests of the nation, to be promoting philanthropy, or presenting their incomes as a product of hard work rather than nepotism and corruption. They are claiming that, in Veblen's words, their consumption is evidence of an 'instinct of workmanship' (Veblen 1994 [1899]: 57) rather than simple waste. Critiques of their actions, which suggest otherwise, are, they suggest, steeped in racism and the pathologising of Africans. Their words resonate for many exactly because of the awareness of prejudicial views of African consumption from outside the continent, and the ongoing struggle by Africans of various income strata to claim membership of a global community which structurally excludes them (Ferguson 2006). Dokolo has been the most vocal voice of this recycling of conspicuous consumption into an attempted legitimacy. In a 2015 interview, Dokolo struck directly at what are usually presented as Afro-pessimist tropes – representations of African poverty and the stereotyping of the African elite as corrupt. Apparently dismissing accounts of incredible wealth disparities in Angola, he was cited as arguing that, 'there is nothing more racist than this idea that African elites are Africa's problem ... that there are some nice Africans and then a few other Africans who live off the suffering of most Africans' (Minder 2015).

However, there is an ambiguity about the audience at which Dokolo and others' protests are directed – a product I would argue, of the uncanny ways in which African elite consumption is discursively constituted at the intersection of historical international discourses of race and local political contestations. On the one hand, it seems clear that elite responses to critics are aimed at a (white) international audience that is hypocritically torn between desiring African wealth and pathologising it through racist stereotypes. On the surface then, it would appear to be a radical act of rejecting racialised colonial hierarchies that continue to shape international understandings of acceptable consuming subjects. Nevertheless, elite responses are simultaneously regressive when it becomes clear that the most significant critics are not international observers, but Angolans themselves. It is Angolans who post pictures mocking Danilo dos Santos's watch purchase, circulate cartoons of Isabel dos Santos selling golden eggs, and denounce elites for hoarding wealth. It is Angolans who accuse their leaders of 'waste'. To suggest that their criticisms are products of racialised pathology undermines the political legitimacy that underlies these everyday expressions of anger. As such, I would argue that the cleverness of Dokolo's discourse is also its weakness. In presenting criticisms as stemming from external sources, rather than internal ones, he erases and fails to address the growing frustration with the status quo evident in protests, rumour and comedy in Angola. What appears on the surface then to be a radical decolonial critique of the intertwined structures of race and economics is more fundamentally a tool of repression, wielded not merely to criticise external critics but to ignore or discredit local ones.

While José Eduardo dos Santos may no longer be in power, the new political elite have already become the object of Angola's gossip. In March 2018, the same website that broke the *Say Yes to the Dress* story, reported that Jéssica Lorena Dias Lourenço, the daughter of recently elected President João Lourenço, had spent $200 000 on a chartered flight to the United States in order to give birth to her child (Club-K 2018). With stinging insight, it reminded its readers that this was the same amount of money that Ms Diogo had spent on her wedding party's dresses. It commented that some members of the ruling MPLA were concerned that the current presidential family 'might adopt the habits of José Eduardo dos Santos's daughters, of giving birth to their children outside of the country, to the detriment of the hospitals which the the government, during election campaigns, claims to have constructed' (Club-K 2018). While Lourenço remained silent on the matter, the cycle of conspicuous consumption and critique continues.

If patronage, cooption, the manipulation of legislation and threats of violence have historically been the means through which the MPLA state and especially its elites have maintained their privileged position, the management of representation and discourse is clearly another primary arena. Ultimately, what this brief discussion of attempts to recycle scandals regarding elite conspicuous consumption in Angola shows is how the political ambiguity over African consumption can become a tense site for a simultaneous defence and critique of the political power and corruption of that elite. For while Angolans themselves might criticise José Eduardo dos Santos's family, those who are criticised opportunistically represent those very criticisms as being drawn from Afro-pessimist tropes which pathologise African consumption, rather than from genuine grievances about corruption and the abuse of power. In doing this, they not only conflate local anger with historical discourses that pathologise African consumption, but they paint themselves as victims of racism, rather than perpetrators of corruption. They are only able to do this because framings of African consumption lie at the intersection of transnational racialised discourses that uncannily intersect with legitimate political grievances voiced by Angolans themselves – because it is impossible to discuss African consumption outside of the histories of colonialism and racism which constantly try to represent black consumption as pathological.

Chimamanda Adichie (2009) has warned against the 'danger of a single story' in which reliance on stereotypes renders representations of people and places incomplete and simplified. Such advice would be well heeded for discussions of conspicuous consumption in Africa. However, it should also be heeded when analysing attacks by African elites on critics of their conspicuous consumption. Subsequent to Dos Santos stepping down, many of the accusations made against his children appear to have been validated, with both Isabel dos Santos and Filomeno dos Santos facing charges for suspect business practices (Marques de Morais 2018, Deutsche Welle 2018). The accusations of nepotism and corruption cannot simply be dismissed. What emerges is a fraught landscape in which African consumption becomes a site for negotiating political and ethical status, as the argument over what constitutes 'waste' becomes subject to multiple interpretations. In a moment in which African elites are increasingly mobilising luxury consumption as a means to consolidate their power and image locally and abroad, contestations over the question of conspicuous consumption in Angola suggest a curious thing: radical critiques of stereotypes can at times be repressive, while true critique of the political context might align with stereotype. The tussle to control the narrative about consumption lies at the heart of contemporary practices of legitimation, critique and dissent in Africa.

REFERENCES

Adichie, C. N., 2009, 'The Danger of a Single Story', *TED Talk Conference*, viewed 25 November 2017, available from: https://www.ted.com/talks/chimamanda_adichie_the_danger_of_a_single_story

Ames, P., 2015, 'Portugal is Becoming an Angolan Colony', in *Politico*, viewed 25 November 2017, available from: https://www.politico.eu/article/angola-portugal-investment-economy/.

Artnet News, 2007, 'Update on Dokolo in Venice', viewed 12 August 2017, available from: http://www.artnet.com/magazineus/news/artnetnews/artnetnews5-18-07.asp.

Aguilar, R., 2001, 'Angola's Incomplete Transition. Discussion Paper No. 2001/47', World Institute for Development Economics Research. United Nations University.

Bayart, J., 1993, *The State in Africa: The Politics of the Belly*, Longman: London and New York.

Bhagavan, M. R., 1986, *Angola's Political Economy 1975–1985*. Research Report No. 75, Scandinavian Institute for African Studies: Uppsala.

Burgis, T., 2013, 'Lunch with the Financial Time: Isabel dos Santos', in *Financial Times*, viewed 15 August 2017, available from: https://www.ft.com/content/6ffd2edc-955e-11e2-a4fa-00144feabdc0.

Burgis, T., 2015, *The Looting Machine: Warlords, Oligarchs, Corporations, Smugglers, and the Systematic Theft of Africa's Wealth*, Public Affairs: New York.

Club-K, 2018, 'Filha do PR freta avião para ter bebé em Washington' in *Club-K*, viewed 25 July 2018, available from: http://www.club-k.net/index.php?option=com_content&view=article&id=31367:filha-do-pr-freta-aviao-privado-por-200-mil-dolares&catid=8&lang=pt&Itemid=1071

Collier, D., 2015, *Repainting the Walls of Lunda: Information Colonialism and Angolan Art*, University of Minnesota Press: Minneapolis and London.

Costa, J., Louçã, F. & Teixeira Lopes, J., 2014, *Os Donos Angolanos de Portugal*, Bertrand Editora, Lisbon.

Davis, B., 2007, 'Art and Corruption in Venice', in *Artnet Magazine*, viewed 8 August 2017, available from: http://www.artnet.com/magazineus/news/artnetnews/artnetnews2-23-07.asp.

De B'béri, B. E. & Louw, P. E., 2011, 'Afropessimism: A genealogy of discourse', *Critical Arts* 25(3): 335–346.

Deutsche Welle, 2018, 'Angola: Former president's son charged with fraud amid crackdown on corruption', in *Deutsche Welle*, viewed 25 July 2018, available from: https://www.dw.com/en/angola-former-presidents-son-charged-with-fraud-amid-crackdown-on-corruption/a-43156212

Dolan, K. A. & Marques de Morais, R., 2013, 'Daddy's Girl: How an African "Princess" Banked $3 Billion in a Country Living on $2 a Day', in *Forbes*, viewed 15 August 2017, available from: https://www.forbes.com/sites/kerryadolan/2013/08/14/how-isabel-dos-santos-took-the-short-route-to-become-africas-richest-woman/2.

Dos Santos, D., 1990, 'The Second Economy in Angola: *Esquema* and *Candonga*', in M. Los (ed.), *The Second Economy in Marxist States*, 157–174, MacMillan: London.

Dos Santos, D. Q., 2017, 'All the President's Children', in *MakaAngola*, viewed 12 August 2017, available from: https://www.makaangola.org/2017/05/all-the-presidents-children/.

Fanon, F., 1963, *The Wretched of the Earth*, Grove Press, New York.

Ferguson, J., 2006, *Global Shadows: Africa in the Neocolonial World Order*, Duke University Press: Durham and London.

Hodges, T., 1987, *Angola to the 1990s: The Potential for Recovery*, Economist Intelligence Review: London.

Hodges, T., 2004, *Angola: Anatomy of an Oil State*, James Currey: Oxford.

Jarvis, A-A., 2015, 'Rich, urban, and entrepreneurial: Meet Africa's new super-rich with a taste for London lifestyle', *Evening Standard*, 11 June, viewed 17 January 2018, available from: https://www.standard.co.uk/lifestyle/london-life/rich-urbane-and-entrepreneurial-meet-africa-s-new-super-rich-with-a-taste-for-the-london-lifestyle-10308970.html.

Jenkins, D., 2014, 'The Nigerians Have Arrived', *Tatler*, 24 November, viewed 17 January 2018, available from: https://www.tatler.com/article/the-nigerians-have-arrived.

James, D., 2015, *Money from Nothing: Indebtedness and Aspiration in South Africa*, Stanford University Press: Stanford.

Lentz, C., 2015, 'Elites or Middle Classes? Lessons from Transnational Research for the Study of Social Stratification in Africa', Working Paper. *Department of Anthropology and African Studies,* Johannes Guttenberg University: Mainz.

Marques de Morais, R., 2012, 'Dos Santos: Nepotism and Corruption in CNN Broadcast Deal', in *MakaAngola*, viewed 15 August 2017, available from: https://www.makaangola.org/2012/01/dos-santos-nepotism-and-corruption-in-cnn-broadcast-deal/.

Marques de Morais, R., 2018, 'Isabel dos Santos: The fall of Africa's richest woman', *MakaAngola*, viewed 26 July 2018, available from: https://www.makaangola.org/2018/07/isabel-dos-santos-the-fall-of-africas-richest-woman/

Marriot, D., 2017, 'On Decadence: Bling-Bling', in *E-flux*, viewed 18 August 2017, available from: http://www.e-flux.com/journal/79/94430/on-decadence-bling-bling/.

Matlon, J., 2016, 'Racial Capitalism and the Crisis of Black Masculinity', *American Sociological Review* 81(5): 1014–1038.

Mbembe, A., 2001, *On the Postcolony*, University of Chicago Press: Chicago.

Messiant, C., 1992, 'Social and Political Background to the "Democratisation" and Peace Process in Angola', In *Seminar Democratization in Angola*, 13–41, Leiden: September 18.

Messiant, C., 2004, 'The Eduardo dos Santos Foundation: Or, How Angola's Regime is Taking Over Civil Society', *African Affairs* 100: 287–309.

Minder, R., 2015, 'Collector Fights for African Art', in *New York Times*, viewed 12 August 2017, available from: https://www.nytimes.com/2015/07/10/arts/international/collector-fights-for-african-art.html.

Negrao, V., 2012, 'Angola: Turistas Gastam Milhões em Portugal', in *Global Voices*, viewed 25 November 2017, available from: https://pt.globalvoices.org/2012/08/13/angola-turistas-gastam-milhoes-em-portugal/print/.

Newell, S., 2012, *The Modernity Bluff: Crime, Consumption and Citizenship in Côte d'Ivoire*, University of Chicago Press: Chicago and London.

Okeke-Agulu, C., 2007, 'Venice and Contemporary Art', *African Arts* 40(3): 1–5.

Onishi, N., 2017, 'Angola's Corrupt Building Boom: "Like Opening a Window and Throwing Money Out"', in *New York Times*, viewed 12 August 2017, available from: https://www.nytimes.com/2017/06/24/world/africa/angola-luanda-jose-eduardo-dos-santos.html.

Posel, D., 2010, 'Races to Consume: South Africa's History of Race, Consumption and the Struggle for Freedom', *Ethnic and Racial Studies* 33(2): 157–175.

RedeAngola, 2015, 'Foi um manobra journalistica bem "conseguida" (entende-se: "bem suja")', viewed 8 August 2017, available from: http://m.redeangola.info/ministro-do-territorio-responde-polemica-sobre-compra-de-vestidos/.

RedeAngola, 2017, 'Eduane dos Santos pede desculpa mas polémica com relógio continua', May 28.

Rodrigues, C. U., 2006, *O Trabalho Dignifica o Homem: Estratégias de Sobrevivência em Luanda*, Edições Colibri: Lisbon.

Schubert, B., 2000, *A Guerra e as Igrejas: Angola 1961–1991*, P. Schlettwein Publishing: Basel.

Schubert, J., 2018, 'A Culture of Immediatism: Co-optation and Complicity in Post-War Angola', *Ethnos* 83(1): 1–19.

Soares de Oliveira, R., 2015, *Magnificent and Beggar Land: Angola Since the Civil War*, Hurst: London.

Southall, R., 2016, *The New Black Middle Class in South Africa*, James Currey: Oxford.

Sklar, R., 1979, 'The Nature of Class Domination in Africa', *Journal of Modern African Studies* 17(4): 531–552.

Tvedten, I., 1997, *Angola: Struggle for Peace and Reconstruction*, Westview Press: Boulder.

Veblen, T., 1994 [1899], *The Theory of the Leisure Class*. Dover: Mineola.

Wolfers, M. & Bergerol, J., 1983, *Angola on the Frontline*, Zed Press: London.

NOTES

1   To see excerpts from the show featuring Ms Diogo see: https://www.youtube.com/watch?v=TFioQLLuGY0, viewed 8 August 2017. The full episode appears to have been removed from the internet.

2   Following the August 2017 election, Bornito de Sousa became Vice-President of Angola.

3   Club-K, 2015, Filha do ministro angolano compra vestido de USD 200 mil, viewed 8 August 2017, available from http://club-k.net/index.php?option=com_content&view=article&id=21...ra-vestido-de-usd-200-mil&catid=8:bastidores&lang=pt&Itemid=1071.

4   Messiant uses this term in an almost identical way to the manner in which it was used when discussing the institutional structure of the Union of Soviet Socialist Republics. The nomenclatura were members of the ruling party who had been appointed to key positions in the administration of the state. In Angola, this resulted in these individuals not only holding immense power, but

enjoying unusual privileges and access to funds that were not available to those who were on the outside of this protected circle of the party-state.

5   Jonas Savimbi was the longtime leader of Unita, the political grouping that fought against the MPLA from independence in 1975 until 2002.
6   For gushing reporting on the new Nigerian elite and their presence in the UK see Jenkins (2014) and Jarvis (2015).
7   Angolan anti-corruption watchdog organisation *MakaAngola* has consistently produced detailed reporting on corrupt dealings linked to the Angolan elite. See makaangola.org for details.
8   The Foundation for Aids Research.
9   Photographs sent to the author via WhatsApp.
10 Spirit of the Child.
11 http://www.semba-c.com/pages/view/35/semba-comunicacao
12 In November 2017, Ms Dos Santos was removed from her position as head of Sonangol following the stepping down of her father in September 2017 after 38 years in power, and the election of João Lourenço as the new president of Angola.
13 There are two related, yet distinct, uses of the term Afro-pessimism in current literature. The one, represented by scholars such as Jared Sexton and Frank B. Wilderson III, generally seeks to theorise the subject position of blackness, most notably through the history of slavery and the position of abjectness. The second, seen in the work of Ebanda de B'béri and Eric Louw (2011) and Achille Mbembe, critiques what they describe as 'Afro-pessimist' discourses, that, similarly to Orientalism, produce a framing of Africa and Africans defined through Western-constituted prisms of meaning. Within these frameworks, Africa and Africans become reduced to tropes of lack, negativity and absence. In B'béri and Louw's (2011: 337) words, 'Afropessimism produces the meaning that something is wrong with Africans. The heart of this discourse derives from the fact that Africans are failing to live up to a set of criteria generated by Westerners who want to develop Africa.'

6 CHILUBA'S TRUNKS: CONSUMPTION, EXCESS AND THE BODY POLITIC IN ZAMBIA

KAREN TRANBERG HANSEN

By the time of his indictment for corruption, former second republican president Frederick Chiluba of Zambia was already well known for being a great dresser. In one of the first internal criminal trials of an African leader for corrupt activity, the legal prosecution (2003–2009) was followed closely both locally and abroad. While the legal proceedings in Zambia dragged on, a special task force was established to investigate the allegations. When, in 2005, several metal trunks and suitcases were discovered in a warehouse in Lusaka, the capital, revelations about the former president's stunning wardrobe attracted sensationalist attention. Commenting on the revelation of the contents of his stored trunks, Chiluba said, 'Old pictures are there, so you can see how I used to dress ... I was one of the sweetest guys on the street, an entertainer, a politician, a unionist, a man of God. Amen' (*The Post* 2005b). The revelations proved to be a turning point on which Chiluba's fondness for spectacular dress morphed into his stored wardrobe and in turn became emblematic of corruption. Consider the news-in-brief section in *The New York Times* on 15 March 2005, which, drawing on Reuters, reported the following:

ZAMBIA: INVESTIGATORS SEIZE EX-PRESIDENT'S SHOES
Former President Frederick Chiluba reacted angrily to the seizure of his warehoused wardrobe by investigators, including 100 pairs of shoes, 300 shirts and 150 suits. He said it was meant to embarrass him, but investigators said they wanted to show how he abused

his office during his 10-year rule, which ended in 2002. He was charged with corruption in 2003, but has been free on bail. 'What they have done is to bring my underpants out to the general public,' Mr. Chiluba said. 'It is sad that the fight against corruption is being reduced to discussing suits, ties and shoes. Zambians know me and know that I have always dressed very well from the 1960s.' (*The New York Times* 2005: A8)

To be sure, corruption and ostentatious consumption offer juicy news copy and provide dramatic accounts of the lavish lifestyles of former powerful leaders who have fallen from grace. Among the most obvious examples are Mobutu Sese Seko of Zaire (Wrong 2000: 211–231), Jean-Bédel Bokassa of the Central African Republic (Titley 2002), and Omar Bongo of Gabon (Ngolet 2000). Much like in the media, corruption linked with the amassing of vast personal wealth is a standard topic in African Studies (Bayart 1993; Mbembe 2001), as are fraud and widespread misuse of economic resources for personal gain at different levels of society (Olivier de Sardan 1999; Smith 2007). But other than in passing or from a normative perspective, few scholars have engaged seriously with the material culture of consumption and its play in the expression of power.

Former president Chiluba's dressed body invites attention not only because of the flair it added to his corruption trial but also because of its entanglement with the body politic of the nation. Thorstein Veblen's (1953 [1899]) notion of conspicuous consumption may illuminate some aspects of the former president's fondness for bespoke suits and handmade shoes. Coming from a humble background, Chiluba grew into adulthood after Zambia became independent in 1964, advancing through the ranks of the trade union movement. Zambia's copper-based economy boomed during the late 1960s, when the first-class trading areas of towns previously restricted to white customers attracted eager African clients. 'I have always dressed nicely from the 1960s,' Chiluba was quoted as saying. 'I have always worn double-breasted nicely tailored suits' (*The Post* 2005b: 4). Indeed, he was very particular about clothes, honing his style, always performing in public.

But in our twenty-first century world, expensive garments and eye-catching accessories do not signal status and honour as straightforwardly as they might have done in industrialising America when Veblen wrote, or even in Zambia in the 1960s when Chiluba began wearing custom-made suits. The better classes, in Veblen's account, abstained from productive work while they emulated one another, impressing their importance on others through conspicuous leisure and consumption. But the moral edge in Veblen's view of conspicuous consumption as the waste of a leisure class that consumed without producing does not translate well across time and space. And dress does not play the unequivocal role of expressing conspicuousness that it might have done in Veblen's time. In today's world of mass consumption and fast fashion, including in highly unequal countries like Zambia, dress is a contested cultural medium that both transcends and blurs the relationship between stratification and consumption. What is more, writing as an economist about a phenomenon he viewed largely in negative terms, Veblen was primarily concerned with the conspicuous display of status. As fashion scholar Elizabeth Wilson (1987: 50–53; 245) has pointed out, in Veblen's world there is no place for the irrational or the non-utilitarian, for pleasure, and for the usefulness and playfulness of fashion, which was central to Chiluba's crafting of himself as a public persona.

To what extent does a political leader's standing depend on his ability to present himself before the public? Intrigued by excessive ostentation in Nigeria, political scientist Jean-Pascal Daloz (2003) projected a comparative study of Nigeria, France and Scandinavia to explore whether power needs to express itself by means of costly external displays. Departing from Daloz's structures of political competition, Deborah Posel (2010) has suggested that consumption practices in post-apartheid South Africa have been shaped by a peculiar type of capitalism that has depended on the racial regulation of consumption. A similar relationship in Zambia might help explain some of the antecedents of Chiluba's love of clothes.

Attempting to understand Chiluba's preoccupation with dress and why his stored wardrobe so vexed local and foreign observers invites a shift of perspective from Veblen's fairly one-dimensional and moralistic emphasis on the relationship between extravagant dress and claims to honour and status. Clothing and dress practice are salient political matters (Allman 2004); so too are the former president's dressed body and the material artifacts at play in crafting his political persona. Body politics are sartorial and the body surface is a highly charged site that makes dress and apparel powerful matters with bearing on grand questions such as the constitution of society and the roles of its citizens. Chiluba's dress practice had bearing on his self-realisation and the consolidation of his presidential power as well as on the social context of persons with whom he was involved (his co-players and minions). Conspicuous consumption, excess and their shifting evaluations are perhaps best explored as a contextual and political matter. In this instance, Chiluba's clothing consumption came to be viewed in negative terms rather than as a positive display of power.

BACKGROUND

Frederick Jacob Titus Chiluba (See Figure 5), Zambia's first multi-party elected president following former president Kenneth Kaunda's almost 20 years of one-party rule (1972–1991), held office for two terms, from 1991 to 2002. He represented the Movement for Multiparty Democracy (MMD), a party that he had helped organise. Prior to the 1991 election, Chiluba had held a variety of jobs, some of them menial, before being employed as an assistant accountant at Atlas Copco, a Swedish firm, on the Copperbelt. He rose through the ranks of the trade unions to become, in 1974, the Chairman General of the Zambia Congress of Trade Unions. A northerner from Luapula Province, his origins were humble. Born in 1944 of a Zambian mother at a mission hospital across the Congo border, it remains uncertain whether his father was Zambian or Congolese.[1] To 'Plot-Number-One' in Lusaka, as the presidential residence, State House, is colloquially referred to in Zambia, he brought along his wife, Vera. Towards the end of his second term as president and after 33 years of marriage, he divorced her. During his first term in office, Chiluba received an honorary doctoral degree from the University of Malawi and a master's degree in political science from Warwick University in the United Kingdom (UK). It is widely believed that his assistant, Richard Sakala, had written the thesis. The former president was always referred to as Dr Chiluba, or colloquially as FJT (the initials of his first three names: Frederick Jacob Titus).

In the early years of his presidency, Chiluba was the darling of international donor organisations and evangelical Christians. He was a personable man with oratorical gifts, a born-again Christian who brought the passion of the pulpit to his speeches. Soon after taking office, he declared Zambia a Christian nation. After close to 20 years of Kaunda's command economy, the market was opened up, several state-owned firms and companies were privatised, and International Monetary Fund- and World Bank-supported structural adjustment programmes were implemented. But the donors' initial enthusiasm declined soon after his election to a second term. The benefits of liberalising Zambia's resource-rich economy had not filtered down to the country's large and absolutely poor population (at that time, more than 70 per cent of the population lived on less than one United States dollar per day). As Zambia's rating on the United Nations Development Programme Human Development Index plummeted, critics talked about the liberalisation of poverty. Accusations of corruption began to entangle Chiluba and several others with, among other matters, an aborted arms deal, a copper and cobalt marketing scam, and the disappearance of 763 petrol tankers that were destined for the Zambia National Oil Corporation.

THE MONEY MATRIX

In 2002, Levy Mwanawasa, a lawyer and former vice-president, succeeded Chiluba as president. Soon after his accession to office, President Mwanawasa asked parliament to lift the immunity from prosecution that Chiluba enjoyed for cases that arose while he had been the head of state. The members of parliament met his request with massive support: 140 votes to zero. In his address to parliament, Mwanawasa referred to embezzlement and theft, including, according to Jan Kees van Donge (2008), a payment of US

$1.1 million to Chiluba's tailor, Boutique Basile, an exclusive gentlemen's outfitters in Geneva, and one of US $90 000 to his daughter, Helen Chiluba, who was schooling in Europe. Other payments were later revealed, including payments made between 1995 and 2001 to, for example, his second wife, Regina, to the amount of US $352 000, payments to Fine Jewelers in Washington of US $30 000, donations of US $70 000 to American fundamentalist churches, and many others. The payments were funnelled through an account, Zamtrop, set up in London by the office of the president during the Kaunda era. In addition, there were alleged payments of US $20.5 million to a Congolese businessman for arms that were never delivered. In his speech to parliament, president Mwanawasa also mentioned the petrol tankers that had vanished (Van Donge 2008: 75–76). There were additional allegations.

A special task force, established by presidential decree and financed by the international donor community, handled Chiluba's prosecution. The case involved several other accomplices, including the director general of the intelligence service, a former minister of finance, the director of loans and investments at the ministry of finance, the secretary to the treasury, the chief justice, the auditor general, the Zambian protocol officer at the High Commission in London, and the chief executive officer (CEO) and executive director of a company called Access Financial Services (AFS). The chief accused were former president Chiluba, intelligence director Xavier Chungu, and CEO of AFS Faustin Kabwe.

In spite of the extent of publicity in Zambia about the accusations of corruption, few resulted in prosecution. Procrastination in the courts hampered the repossession of properties, especially in Europe (Van Donge 2008: 76). The cases dragged on, because of legal technicalities and due to Chiluba's health problems. For medical reasons, he flew to South Africa for treatment several times. In 2007, the Zambian state launched a civil case at the High Court in London. In the Court's judgement, the owner of Boutique Basile in Geneva was requested to return to the task force more than US $1.2 million (plus costs) that he had received from the Zamtrop account for Chiluba's bespoke suits, handmade shoes and accessories (*Times of Zambia* 2008). The owner, Antonio Basile, wept on several occasions when the extent of his wrongful dealings with Zambian government money was revealed in court.[2] The London Court also found sufficient evidence linking the former president and some of his senior associates to a conspiracy to rob their country's government and the people of US $41 million and ordered them to pay 85 per cent of what they had allegedly misappropriated. The money had been transferred to London bank accounts, ostensibly to repay government debts, but siphoned off for other purposes such as expensive clothes, school fees, motorbikes and a beauty therapy course (*News from Zambia* 2007). Chiluba refused to recognise the British High Court's judgement, which was not registered by the Zambian courts.

That was the London case. The trial in Zambia dragged on for six years until after Mwanawasa's death in 2008. The Zambian judgement of ex-president Chiluba and his co-accused, the two leading businessmen from AFS, CEO Justin Kabwe and director Aaron Chungu, took place in January 2009 in the Magistrates Court of Zambia in Lusaka. The three accused originally faced 169 charges with theft of public funds of more than US $40 million. The state dropped several charges because of a lack of evidence, with the result that the trio was charged with theft of US $500 000. The case alleged that money was diverted from the ministry of finance into an account held by the London branch of the Zambia National Commercial Bank, and that a UK-based investment banking firm, with the help of two UK law firms, moved money into a variety of offshore accounts, trust funds and investment portfolios (Anon 2009: 5). Ever creative with colloquialisms, people in Zambia referred to the financial resources Chiluba and his associates paid out to both local and foreign individuals and institutions as the 'Money Matrix'.

Chiluba and his co-accused denied all charges. When questioned in court about the sources of the money, Chiluba consistently argued that he had received funds from private well-wishers and supporters in Zambia and elsewhere (Anon 2009). The final judgement was delivered in mid-August 2009. Chiluba was acquitted. The prosecution found no record of his alleged thefts but sentenced his co-accused, Faustin Kabwe and Aaron Chungu, to three years each for being in possession of suspected stolen money.[3] When the chairperson of the task force, Maxwell Nkole, decided to appeal the case, Rupiah Banda, who had become president upon the death of Levy Mwanawasa in 2008, relieved Nkole of his duties, arguing that his contract had expired. At the end of October 2009, the task force on corruption was disbanded and merged with the anti-corruption commission. Meanwhile, a number of cases of alleged embezzlement of public funds involving former president Chiluba and several others remain unresolved.

THE DRESSED BODY OF THE PRESIDENT

Consider Chiluba's dressed body. As Terence Turner (1993: 15 [1979]) noted when he coined the notion of the social skin, the body surface is a major stage for the enactment of social reproduction. The body surface plays this role because of its unique ability to mediate between self and society. And because this mediation changes across time and place, there are 'no bodies in a general sense but rather specific bodies, marked by gender, sexuality, class and ethnicity, for instance' (Parkins 2002: 5).

Chiluba was a man of diminutive stature, less than five feet tall, shoe size six, with a light complexion, speculated to reflect his Congolese background. When he assumed the presidency in 1991, his sharp double-breasted suits achieved overnight popularity. Judging from photographs, the suits in the trunks were in fairly neutral colours, not the yellow and creams that the former president favoured while in office. Chiluba accessorised his suits with multi-patterned silk ties and matching pocket handkerchiefs. His shirts were hand-embroidered with his monogram, while his custom-made Italian shoes had platform heels (elevator heels) that added two inches to his diminutive stature. Some shoes were made of 'exotics', a trade term for reptile skin, others of ostrich, and still others of satin. The trunks also contained monogrammed silk pyjamas.

The body is 'never simply a neutral clothes horse' (Parkins 2002: 5). The effects the dressed body provokes for its wearers and its viewers are always and everywhere situated (Entwistle 2000: 80), and therefore bound up with the local body politic in complicated ways. In Zambia, the details of the former president and the first lady's dress were observed with excruciating detail and commented on widely (Hansen 2000: 93).

In his dress style, Chiluba, who presented himself as the embodiment of a new era, provided instant relief from the drabness and austerity of Kaunda's dress regimen. Throughout most of Kaunda's presidency, the safari suit had been *de rigueur* for men in power. Over the years, Kaunda's safari suit had evolved from a colonial-inspired bush suit to a Nehru or Mao-influenced jacket with a small collar. Kaunda usually carried a large white handkerchief (into which he frequently wept), which Chiluba exchanged for silk ties and matching pocket handkerchiefs. Dubbed 'New Culture', Chiluba's distinct dress style was initially copied by civil servants and office workers alike, the latter often sourcing their garments from *salaula* (imported secondhand clothing) markets and calling on tailors to alter large single-breasted suits into double-breasted suits without vents at the back (Hansen 2000: 92). President Chiluba occasionally varied his sartorial presentation, dressing 'like Cuban President Dr Fidel Castro when he was in a militant mood' (*The Post* 2005b: 4). He was also seen sporting Mao-styled high-collared, single-breasted jackets that were rumoured to be gifts from his Congolese friends. The evolution of Chiluba's double-breasted suit hints at inspirations ranging from zoot suits, to preppy, to retro.

Chiluba's first wife, Vera, joined him at Plot Number One when they moved from Ndola on the Copperbelt into State House in Lusaka in 1991. A short, light-skinned woman, Vera liked to dress in *chitenge* (printed fabric) outfits in bold colours and big head-ties or hats. Some observers questioned the qualifications of her fashion advisor. Hailing from an even more humble background than Chiluba, Vera and her flamboyant attire drew the nation's attention as she travelled across the country, promoting the Vera Chiluba charitable initiative, called the Hope Foundation, donating maize grinding mills, *salaula* and blankets to peasant women and the urban poor. Her initiatives and mannerisms received considerable negative scrutiny in the media (Hansen 2000: 95). Long before he divorced Vera in 2001, Chiluba spent large amounts of money on his secretary, Regina, at least according to the court case against him. After leaving office, he married Regina, who was deemed a more stylish and elegant woman than Vera.

At the outset of a new democratic era in Zambia, New Culture was available to anyone. In addition to referring to a dress style, the term New Culture was also used to describe the shift of political and economic orientation after the change from a one-party state to a multi-party regime and the opening up of markets. But New Culture soon lost its political lustre and its fashion appeal became threadbare. The initial enthusiasm about the president, his dress style and the new regime barely lasted into Chiluba's second term. The privatisation of major assets, including the mines, was slow, and did not get under way until the late 1990s. Around that time, accusations began to be made by members of the opposition and from within the ranks of the governing party that Chiluba and his friends had committed a variety of fraudulent acts (Van Donge 2008: 75).

CHILUBA'S TRUNKS

In March 2005, task force investigators found 21 trunks and 11 suitcases containing personal effects that had been placed in storage when Chiluba moved out of State House. They were stored in a warehouse owned by his friend, CEO Faustin Kabwe of AFS, the company at the centre of the plunder of state funds. The Bank of Zambia had liquidated AFS. When efforts were made to repossess the warehouse, task-force investigators discovered some of Chiluba's excesses. An inventory revealed the trunks' contents of more than 150 bespoke suits, 300 shirts in their original cellophane wrappers, more than 100 pairs of custom-made shoes and lots of neckties. There was money, including cash, and brown envelopes containing money as well as cheques. The task-force investigators also found Chiluba's academic degree certificates, some photographs and books.

The exposure of the contents of Chiluba's trunks made front-page newspaper headlines in Zambia and was picked up by the international news wires. The trunks and their contents were the subject of a biting editorial in *The Post*, at that time the chief opposition newspaper in Zambia:

> It is saddening to see [the former] president having a hundred of pairs of shoes stashed away in a warehouse. And we are not talking about cheap shoes but tailor-made ones of all colours – that make the rainbow look inadequate – with high heels made from the most expensive of all sorts of skins in the world (*The Post* 2005a).

What was at issue, *The Post* editorial observed, was not that Chiluba had so many clothes but that they would have cost much more than his official income. As the paper argued:

> Chiluba by his known earnings and declared assets was neither a millionaire nor a billionaire. We say this because we know how many suits, shirts and shoes he went with into

State House in November 1991. He couldn't afford it. Chiluba only started buying and wearing these expensive things, including gold watches and chains, when he had direct control of the Zambian taxpayers' money. (*The Post* 2005a)

Reactions such as these convey deep-seated public scepticism about political leadership. Chiluba and his associates were not common burglars and thieves operating from the townships but rather the powers-that-be who felt entitled to a lifestyle far beyond the imagination of ordinary Zambian citizens.

A THRESHOLD OF THE BODY POLITIC

It was the storing of Chiluba's wardrobe of stupendous proportion, especially his Italian designer suits and high-heeled shoes in the trunks in the AFS warehouse that caught both local and international attention. Because clothing always sends mixed messages, Chiluba's dress practice no longer provoked imitation. In the view of the Zambian citizenry, a threshold had been reached and the ex-president's dressed body had become the flashpoint. It is not surprising that the revelation of the contents of the trunks and suitcases did not sit well with Chiluba (*The Post* 2005b). 'The government has exposed my underpants to embarrass me,' he complained. But he laughed, he said, 'when he read in *The Post* editorial that he did not have many suits when he went to State House in 1991'. Holding forth on a matter he knew well, he asserted that he had always dressed in smart double-breasted suits with matching shoes:

> During the first strike I quenched in 1968 in Ndola, I wore a nice yellow double-breasted suit with matching shoes ... Zambians know that I have numerous clothes and shoes of all colours and from way back. I love colours and I am not allergic to them. I am proud to wear that which I find pleasing in my eyes ... Old pictures are there, so you can see how I used to dress. (*The Post* 2005b: 4)

Chiluba's self-aggrandisement depended on lavish consumption and the transfer of gifts to relatives and friends. The legal charges made against him started and ended with money (*The Post* 2006). One observer, a political scientist, has suggested that the former president's most immediate use of money served to gratify his vanity. 'Chiluba's political style towards the end of his rule,' claims Jan Kees van Donge (2008: 84), 'was fuelled by money, but much more as a display of vanity than as a means of building support'. But there is much more to it than that. There are several issues to consider: firstly, the president, secondly, the citizenry and the nation, and thirdly, the president's allies. Chiluba's comments clearly indicate that he took great delight in the demonstrative effect brought about by being well dressed – in short, he loved the dramaturgy of power. This observation pertains to the individual issue concerned with what a person can do with clothing: in this case, showing off.

But the sumptuous attire – diamond-studded gold watch, signet ring and gold chains – that Chiluba liked to wear did not in and of itself confer power. For this, we turn to the president's dressed body, his entire gestalt (Eicher & Roach-Higgins 1992: 13) that was at the heart of the body politic at a time when New Culture suits had quite clearly lost their sheen. The politics announced by the term had failed to improve the welfare of the citizenry. The evidence in the trunks was just 'too much'. It was over the top. The trunks' revelations crossed the threshold of two otherwise incommensurable value registers between Chiluba's individual dress endeavours on the one hand, and his role as head of state, leading the nation on the other (Guyer 2004: 42; Barber 2007).

DRESS AND POWER

Historically, in this part of Africa and elsewhere, people paid intense attention to their dressed bodies and the effects that dressed body presentations make on the people who surround them. They still do. Leaders everywhere make an impression by the manner and style of their dress, which are commented on widely. Dressing up in all the colours of the rainbow, the diminutive Chiluba might have played the political types of both chief and big man (Sahlins 1963), pooling as a chief, and redistributing as a big man, with the wads of money from the trunks and the cash in brown envelopes and cheques representing payments for special favours.

But how do we reckon with the garments and accessories in Chiluba's stored trunks? Long ago, before the money economy had thoroughly penetrated this region, clothing and apparel served as a store of value (Hansen 2000: 35, 42; 2015: 209) to be used, redistributed and exchanged over time. But in today's global world of mass-produced goods and constantly changing styles, clothing and apparel no longer serve as important resources for accumulation and redistribution.

Chiluba's stored wardrobe displays desire and vanity as well as need. In addition, there is an aspect of greed, which according to AF Robertson (2001: 5) is a matter with which scholars have a hard time coming to terms because we fail to view people as embodied meaning makers. 'Greed', he says, 'is doubly interesting because it is both an aspect of our own growth (I can feel greedy) and one of the ways we come to terms with growth socially – measuring, criticizing, commenting on one another' (2001: 8). He goes on to note that 'when greed is evoked in political contexts it has the leveling effect of reducing comparison to the human body' (2001: 28). 'Kleptocrats from around the world', Robertson (2001: 28) continues, 'have profited hugely from this deception, scaling-up their needs to fit their own estimation of their political status'. In Robertson's analysis, asking whether Chiluba deserved numerous bespoke suits and handmade shoes, and asking whether he really needed all those things are two different questions, but only because we have learned to keep the former party president and his body in two distinct conceptual compartments.[4] The deception forged by both the kleptocrats and Chiluba hinges on the merging of two otherwise incommensurable value registers.

Chiluba scaled up his needs to fit his own estimation of his status as leader of the nation on the first day of the court hearing in Lusaka, when the defence lawyer asked him for disclosures of private sponsorships. Private donors, Chiluba explained, insist on 'the golden rule of anonymity … they don't prescribe how their money will be used … for they are made aware that the party president has personal needs as distinct from general party activities' (Anon 2009: 13–14). To be sure, Chiluba's dressed body was entangled with the body politic in complicated ways. These complications involve greed, which as Robertson (2001: 31) argues, is a gut feeling that has a bodily frame of reference. The comments Chiluba made in 2005 when the contents of the trunks were first revealed to the public recognised this body reference both visually and viscerally: 'I was one of the sweetest guys in the street, an entertainer, a politician, a unionist, a man of God. Amen' (*The Post* 2005b: 4).

Laughing all the way to court and throughout the hearings, Chiluba put on a good show. The former president definitely knew how to wear clothes. Perhaps his best creation was himself. Still, it takes a good deal of courage to go to the extent that Chiluba did. Looking like a clothes horse, he was in fact a consummate politician. He had both enough money and wit to outsmart the system to ensure that he was not implicated directly in any wrongdoing, despite compelling evidence to the contrary. I therefore disagree with Kees van Donge who analysed Chiluba's politics toward the end of his rule as a display of vanity rather than as a means of building support.

What Chiluba had achieved was to surround himself with people he knew would be amenable, because of their other involvements, and who would not go after him. The acronym of the ruling party from which he and the country's next two presidents were drawn – MMD – was by then popularly known in Zambia as meaning 'Make Money Disappear'. This widespread understanding of politics signals an entangled system of corruption involving Chiluba and numerous others – politicians, civil servants and business people, both in the past and at the present. When Chiluba complained that he felt disgraced by the public display of his underwear, he in fact invoked a widely shared sentiment in Zambia that no one should hang out their dirty laundry to dry in public. Troublesome matters must be resolved privately (Hansen 1996). Yet he showed no shame, no contrition. Instead, he laughed. In the Lusaka court case, the former president continuously argued that he had not used government money, that the Zamtrop account held private money, that it was his money, money that had been given to him by friends and supporters (Anon 2009: 40). This widely shared understanding of how politics works – as private, interpersonal negotiations and exchanges of resources – helps to explain some of the passive response, the lack of public demonstration, with which former president Chiluba's acquittal was met. The case had dragged on for too long. And what was new about corruption anyway?

The closest we come in this case to Veblen's notion of conspicuous consumption in a society characterised by enormously unequal distribution of income and wealth is in the news commentaries in response to the disclosure of the contents of Chiluba's trunks. One of these, for example, queried how the former president could boast hundreds of pairs of shoes when millions of Zambians could not even afford *pata-patas* (plastic flip-flops) (*Pan African News Agency Daily News Wire* 2005). But conspicuous consumption is a drab characterisation of Chiluba's huge warehoused wardrobe. With the focus on his hoarding of clothing, popular reactions had shifted from Chiluba's acquisitive individualism to his failure to distribute and circulate the wealth of the nation to the citizenry.

Some of Chiluba's abundant wardrobe was placed in storage when he left State House in 2002. Perhaps the trunks were meant to be moved into his new home in a high-income residential area in Lusaka at a later stage but they somehow remained at the AFS warehouse. The surprising revelation of the contents of the trunks in 2005 might never have been anticipated and the sensationalism the revelation provoked might never have been foreseen. Still, the revelations proved to be a turning point on which Chiluba's fondness for spectacular dress morphed into his stored wardrobe and in turn became emblematic of corruption.

In 2011, former second republican president Dr Frederick Chiluba died. He was given a state funeral in Lusaka and laid to rest at Embassy Park, a newly designated presidential burial site, featuring monstrously large houses for the dead: Mwanawasa's, Chiluba's, and the dead body of president Michael Sata, who passed away while in office in October 2014. For a long time, the whereabouts of Chiluba's trunks and their contents were uncertain. They were rumored to be with the special task force on corruption while the cases against him were being heard in court. When the task force was disbanded, it was said that they might have been placed with the anti-corruption commission. After more than a decade in court, the Supreme Court revealed that the Bank of Zambia held some of the seized property, including the trunks, due to various oversights and weak controls (*Zambia Weekly* 2015; 2016). Chiluba's family was offered the property, but declined, demanding an explanation of how the Bank came into possession of the property and why it was not returned to the former president after his acquittal in 2009 (*Daily Nation* 2015). To give Chiluba his due, some of the contents of the trunks would undoubtedly enliven an exhibit about a consummate politician and sharp dresser in the political section of the national museum for future generations to watch the material conflation of distinction and corruption.

In July 2016, a memorial service was held to observe the fifth anniversary of Chiluba's passing during which the former president was praised for bringing democracy to Zambia and introducing a free-market economy. As he was never convicted, his deeds and public persona are vulnerable to historical revision. In an article about the slow pace in the fight against corruption across Africa, journalist Celia W Dugger (2009: A1) used the caption 'emblem of greed' for a photo of ten pairs of former president Chiluba's handmade Italian shoes. Such media depictions are at odds with the expectations of the population at large who most certainly expected their president to dress to impress. If this is conspicuous consumption, it is so without Veblen's *animus*, the invidious element (Mills 1953: xv). While his case will remain open to contending evaluations,[5] we may continue to puzzle over the political persona of former president Chiluba of Zambia and his skill at articulating power by means of his dressed body. Indeed, clothing and accessories invite more than sensationalist attention; they demand serious work by scholars.[6]

REFERENCES

Allman, J. (ed.), 2004, *Fashioning Africa: Power and the Politics of Dress*. Indiana University Press: Bloomington.

Anon., 2009, 'Here I Stand: Verbatim Testimony of Second Republican President Dr. Frederick Chiluba', ZDS Press Service: Lusaka.

Barber, K., 2007, 'When People Cross Thresholds', *African Studies Review* 50(2): 111–124.

Bayart, J-F., 1993, *The State in Africa: The Politics of the Belly*. Longman: New York.

Daily Nation, 2015, 'FJT Family Rejects Clothing', 15 July.

Daloz, J-P., 2003, 'Ostentation in Comparative Perspective: Culture and Elite Legitimation', in F. Engelstad (ed.), *Comparative Studies in Culture and Power. Comparative Social Research* Volume 21 (Comparative Social Research): 29–62.

Dugger, C.W., 2009, 'Battle to Halt Graft in Africa Ebbs', *New York Times*, 10 June, A1.

Eicher, J. B., and Roach-Higgins, M. E., 1992. 'Definition and Classifications of Dress: Implications for Analysis of Gender Roles', in R. Barnes and J. B. Eicher (eds.), *Dress and Gender: Making and Meaning*. Berg: Oxford, 8–28.

Entwistle, J., 2000, *The Fashioned Body: Fashion, Dress, and Modern Social Theory*, Polity Press: Cambridge.

Guyer, J., 2004, *Marginal Gains: Monetary Transactions in Atlantic Africa*. University of Chicago Press: Chicago.

Hansen, K. T., 1996, 'Washing Dirty Laundry in Public: Local Court, Custom, and Gender Relations in Post-Colonial Zambia', in K. Sheldon (ed.), *Courtyards, Markets and City Streets: Urban Women in Africa*. Westview Press: Boulder, 105–127.

Hansen, K. T., 2000, *Salaula: The World of Secondhand Clothing and Zambia*. University of Chicago Press: Chicago.

Hansen, K. T., 2015, 'Urban Research in a Hostile Setting: Godfrey Wilson in Broken Hill, Northern Rhodesia, 1938–1940', *Kronos* 41: 193–214.

Kantorowicz, E. H., 1958, *The King's Two Bodies: A Study in Medieval Political Theology*. Princeton University Press: Princeton.

Mbembe, A., 2001, *On the Postcolony*. University of California Press: Berkeley.

Mills, C. W., 1953, 'Introduction', in T. Veblen, *The Theory of the Leisure Class: An Economic Study of Institutions*. A Mentor Book published by the New American Library: New York, i–xix.

News from Zambia, 2007, 'Ex-President Chiluba and Others Stole £23m', No. 802, 19 April–18 May.

Ngolet, F., 2000, 'Ideological Manipulation and Political Longevity: The Power of Omar Bongo in Gabon since 1967', *African Studies Review* 43(2): 55–71.

Olivier de Sardan, J. E., 1999, 'A Moral Economy of Corruption in Africa?' *Journal of Modern African Studies* 37(1): 25–52.

Pan African News Agency Daily News Wire, 2005, 'Chiluba Claims Investigators are Bias [sic] against Him', 15 March, Copyright 2005, Financial Times Information.

Parkins, W., 2002, 'Introduction: (Ad)dressing Citizens', in W. Parkins (ed.), *Fashioning the Body Politic*. Berg: New York, 1–7.

Posel, D., 2010, 'Races to Consume: Revisiting South Africa's History of Race, Consumption and the Struggle for Freedom', *Ethnic and Racial Studies* 33(2): 157–175.

Robertson, A. F., 2001, *Greed: Gut Feelings, Growth, and History*. Polity Press: Cambridge.

Sahlins, M. D., 1963, 'Poor Man, Rich Man, Big-Man, Chief: Political Types in Melanesia and Polynesia', *Comparative Studies in Society and History* 5(3): 285–303.

Sakala, R., 2016, *A President Betrayed: Serial Murder by Slander*, Sentor Publishers: Lusaka.

Smith, D. J., 2007, *Everyday Deception and Popular Discontent in Nigeria*. Princeton University Press: Princeton.

The New York Times, 2005, 'Zambia. Investigators Seize Ex-President's Shoes', 15 March, A8.

The Post, 2005a, Editorial. 14 March.

The Post, 2005b, 'I am not Allergic to Colours … Govt [sic] has Exposed my Pants – Chiluba', 15 March, 1 and 4.

The Post, 2006, 'Cheap Demagoguery', 22 September.

Times of Zambia, 2008, 'FTJ's Geneva-Based Tailor Ordered to Repay Govt [sic]', 25 December.

Titley, B., 2002 [1997], *Dark Age: The Political Odyssey of Emperor Bokassa*. McGill-Queen's University Press: Montreal.

Turner, T. S., 1993 [1979], 'The Social Skin', in C. Burroughs and J. E. (eds.), *Reading the Social Body*. University of Iowa Press: Iowa City, 15–39.

Van Donge, J. K., 2008, 'The Plundering of Zambian Resources by Frederick Chiluba and his Friends: A Case Study of the Interaction between National Politics and the International Drive Towards Good Governance', *African Affairs* 108(430): 69–90.

Veblen, T., 1953 [1899], *The Theory of the Leisure Class: An Economic Study of Institutions*. A Mentor Book published by the New American Library: New York.

Wilson, E., 1987, *Adorned in Dreams: Fashion and Modernity*. University of California Press: Berkeley.

Wrong, M., 2001, in *the Footsteps of Mr Kurtz: Living on the Brink of Disaster in the Congo*. Fourth Estate: London.

Zambia Weekly, 2015, 'Bank of Zambia Accused of Looting', 5 June, 235(6): 4.

Zambia Weekly, 2016, 'Lawyer Reprimanded for Misadvising the BoZ', 4 November, 296(7): 6.

NOTES

1   Accounts differ concerning Chiluba's place of birth, which sometimes is suggested to be the town of Kitwe on the Copperbelt.

2   Basile informed the London Court that Chiluba's clothes were made by Italian fashion designers. Describing the former president as a man of small stature for whom clothes had to be specially made, Basile took Chiluba's measures at the Hotel Intercontinental in Geneva and forwarded them

to Italy. Boutique Basile reports visits by travelers from Zambia who pass through Geneva, wanting to take a look at the famous/infamous store.

3   Several other persons were sentenced, among them, Regina Chiluba, Dr. Chiluba's second wife, for accepting stolen property during the years of her husband's administration. Zambia's supreme court acquitted her in 2010. For reasons of space, it is not possible to provide details on all the individuals involved in the Chiluba cases.

4   Sophie Chevalier (in a personal communication) suggested that this might resonate with Kantorovicz's observations about the king's two bodies (1958). The idea of the king's two bodies, the body natural and the body politic, was founded on the distinction between the mortal and personal body and the perpetual and corporate crown.

5   Richard Sakala, the late president's former assistant, today owner of the Daily Nation newspapers, has already published his effort to 'set the record straight': *A President Betrayed: Serial Murder by Slander* (2016).

6   An early draft of this chapter was presented as a distinguished lecture to the Africanist Association of the American Anthropological Association, Philadelphia, 4 December 2009. For fact checking and for details about personal allegations, I am grateful to Ilse and Jacob Mwanza, Paul Freund and Marja Hinfelaar. I also wish to thank Jane Guyer, who always offers constructive advice and suggestions.

7 JACOB ZUMA'S SHAMELESSNESS: CONSPICUOUS CONSUMPTION, POLITICS AND RELIGION

ILANA VAN WYK

In the media, South Africa's ex-President Jacob Zuma has long been portrayed as a man who lives beyond his means and who has difficulties reining in his excessive desires. A succession of media exposés have laid bare his massive debts, his sexual appetites, the financial burden of four (current) wives and 22 children accustomed to the high life[1] (*Sowetan Live* 2016; Madisa 2016), and the family's tastes in expensive cars (Van Onselen 2012a). The media has also been fascinated by the presidential family's 'big fat' weddings and the close ties that Zuma has with the (extravagant) Swazi and Zulu royal houses (Huigen 2017).

Apart from his private extravagances, the ex-president was also profligate with the public purse while in office. By 2012, journalist Gareth van Onselen estimated that the state allowances for Jacob Zuma and his dependents were costing the taxpayer half a billion rand a year, significantly more than the amounts spent by the Thabo Mbeki and Nelson Mandela presidencies. While much of the increase could be attributed to the size of Zuma's polygamous family, his presidency saw a significant increase in claims for VIP transport, luxury helicopter rides, large motorcades and top-line private cars.[2] Similarly, his salary rocketed, making him one of the top ten best-paid politicians in the world (Van Onselen 2012a). During his presidency, the state was pressured to acquire a R4-billion presidential jet when his security detail had recommended a R150-million Boeing. Both his official and private residences were 'upgraded' far beyond the necessary security improvements. Zuma's official residences have reportedly been adorned with new chandeliers, sprawling dressing rooms, at least one sauna and a steam room (Steenkamp 2011). His private 'compound' in Nkandla, KwaZulu-Natal, has seen the installation of a large swimming pool, a helipad, a visitors' centre, a private military hospital, a parking lot and guest houses (Madonsela 2014). As the media pointed out, these expenditures were eight times more than what was spent on Mandela's two private homes and almost 18 times more than was spent on Mbeki's home (Pillay 2013). The Public Protector described it as 'opulence on a grand scale' (Madonsela 2014).

As a number of journalists suggested, the president's official salary[3] and his allowances from the state did not allow for his or his family's lavish lifestyle – especially the extravagant weddings, parties and his adult children's luxury cars and designer clothes. Perhaps not surprisingly, Zuma has faced various fraud and corruption investigations, with a 2016 report from the Public Protector (Madonsela 2016) and a string of leaked emails in 2017 detailing the extent to which the state had been 'captured' by the superrich Gupta family to whom Zuma, and his family, had been indebted in one way or another. While he has avoided any convictions to date, open speculations about the ex-president's moral compromises abound. Beyond the usual outrages about corrupt leadership, greed and extreme personal indulgence in a country where the majority of people live in poverty, a number of commentators have been dumbfounded by Zuma's inability to be 'shamed' (Madia & Evans 2016; Malala 2016; McKaiser 2017; Mulholland 2016; Williams 2016). They have repeatedly pointed out that Zuma is unapologetic about his lavish lifestyle and the probable corrupt relationships that have enabled it.

Instead of shame, Zuma's public utterances have consistently been defiant. Boasting about God's divine support, he has on numerous occasions insisted that his treatment in the media and by criminal prosecutors was the result of a dark plot by his enemies to undermine his leadership and derail his (deserved) good fortune. Even after the African National Congress (ANC) ousted him as president in February 2018, Zuma trumpeted his revolutionary work while in office (Harper & Bendile 2018). It would be easy to dismiss Zuma's claims and their embrace by sycophantic party members and certain Christian leaders as mere political opportunism. Indeed, many of Zuma's political supporters have been implicated in the scandals that have marred his presidency while most of the churches that have celebrated Zuma's 'blessings' have seen their political stars rise under his leadership (Van Wyk 2015: 136). However, harder to explain has been the enthusiasm with which many poor South African Christians have echoed Zuma's *moral* claims and celebrated his (ill-gotten) riches.

In the literature, such grassroots acquiescence or adulation of a morally suspect political leader has been explained in terms of the 'politics of the belly' (Bayart 2009 [1989]), the zombification that attends neoliberal capitalism (Comaroff & Comaroff 2001) and, in

South Africa, as a result of the racialised politicisation of economic aspiration (Posel 2013; 2014). In this chapter, I add to that body of work by paying attention to the specifically Neo-Pentecostal public context within which African leaders (and ex-leaders), such as Jacob Zuma, not only frame but also find support for their apparently 'shameless' conspicuous consumption. In *The Theory of the Leisure Class* (2003 [1899]), Thorstein Veblen focused on the leisure class in America rather than on African leaders, but his analytical emphasis on honour and the social/moral valence of wealth take us beyond well-trodden political-economic analyses. At the same time, his deep antipathy to 'wasteful expenditure' by the leisure class and his discomfort with their 'pecuniary' rituals also lays bare a Judeo-Christian tradition that has long informed a critique of conspicuous consumption – and of Neo-Pentecostalism.

A DISHONOURABLE MAN

According to Graeber (2011), one of the moral organising principles of capitalism is the expectation that someone will be shamed by their debt – and that they will settle it themselves. This principle has some purchase in South Africa – even among politicians. Within the ANC, Zuma's extravagant lifestyle has apparently long been a source of worry and embarrassment to his comrades. According to a report by KPMG auditors, Mandela and the ANC treasurer had already in 1998 'disciplined' Zuma over his financial affairs (Smith 2012). At the time, Zuma had apparently spent far more than he earned, repeatedly exceeded his bank overdraft, bought property and cars on credit, and continuously defaulted on his debt (Bauer 2012). In 2000, Mandela apparently gave Zuma R1 million because he worried that Zuma's continuing financial troubles would open him up to graft – and dishonour for the ANC (Smith 2012). Mandela's help came a year after Patricia de Lille, a member of parliament for the Pan African Congress, alleged that Zuma had received kickbacks from a controversial multi-billion rand arms deal then in progress.[4] This help did not put Zuma beyond his creditors' demands. In 2001, the media reported that Zuma had tried to quash a criminal investigation into the actions of Pieter Rootman who had allegedly used stolen donor funds to help settle Zuma's considerable debts.[5] A string of sensational fraud and corruption cases against Zuma's allies revealed that he had been receiving regular payments from a number of benefactors for anything from 'R10 car-washes to school fees and bond payments' (Williams 2016). His financial adviser, Schabir Shaik, had given Zuma R4 million for 'his children's education and upkeep' while he channeled a further R7 million to Zuma from various benefactors and businesses hoping to benefit from his ties to the state (Evans, Shamase & Brümmer 2012). Shaik's eventual conviction on charges of corruption and fraud saw Zuma dismissed as vice president in 2005. At the time, the *Mail & Guardian* (2005) reported that Zuma's bank accounts were overdrawn by more than

R400 000 – this despite a generous state salary, state allowances for living costs and generous 'help' from his various friends. After two years in the political wilderness, Jacob Zuma was elected as the head of the ANC and, in the 2009 general election, as president of the country. He was barely in office before the media started to murmur about the opulent 'security upgrades' at his Nkandla private residence (Rossouw 2009). After a number of complaints, the public protector launched an official investigation. The resulting report, entitled 'Secure in Comfort' (Madonsela 2014), was scathing about the private benefits that accrued to Zuma from the R246 million spent on Nkandla and recommended that he pay back some of the money.[6] After much political manoeuvring and a constitutional court order, Zuma finally paid back R7.8 million to the state. The media immediately speculated that the Gupta family was the most likely source of this payment (Williams 2016).

Apart from his shameful financial affairs, Zuma's private life evinced various extra-marital affairs (Pillay 2010), illegitimate children (Chidester 2012: 150–151), inappropriate sexual relationships with his friends' daughters (Larson 2010) and disloyalty to friends who had fallen on hard times – usually because of their association with him (Govender 2016). Most disgracefully, a 31-year-old family friend called 'Kwezi'[7] accused him of rape. Zuma claimed that the sex was consensual and that a post-coital shower protected him from contracting HIV. Although he was acquitted of the charges, cartoonists continued to reference his shameful conduct.[8]

With Zuma's moral failings stacking up in public, more of his critics used the language of shame and honour to pressure the ANC to replace him with a less compromised candidate (Madia & Evans 2016). At the forefront of those clamouring for his resignation using this tactic were a group of ANC veterans (Nhlabati 2016), various civil society groups, the South African Council of Churches (SACC) and the National Religious Leaders' Council (NRLC) (Katz 2016; Stone 2017). At their various protest marches and in public pronouncements, these organisations negatively compared Zuma with honourable men such as Mandela and Ahmed Kathrada (Stone 2017). And where he was compared to other politicians who had similarly been caught out in morally compromising positions, such as Pallo Jordan,[9] critics pointed out that unlike Zuma, these men had the 'decency' to be 'ashamed of [themselves]' (McKaiser 2017).

VEBLEN ON HONOUR, SHAME AND RELIGION

Veblen (2003) would not have been surprised by the weight that Zuma's critics attached to honour in their assessment of his fitness to be president. For Veblen (2003: 25), honour and its corollary 'pecuniary emulation' were at the heart of social evolution, class differentiation and conspicuous consumption. However, unlike the mobilisation of the idea of honour by Zuma's critics, Veblen's definition of honour had little to do with moral rectitude and was much closer to Nietzsche's (2001 [1882]) will to power. Veblen postulated that the aggressive struggle for honour between men gradually evolved into a system of property ownership where conspicuously displayed wealth gained 'utility as a honorific evidence of the owner's prepotence [power]' (Veblen 2003: 18). Wealth also allowed men to avoid debasing productive work in favour of (wasteful) leisure pursuits, again adding to their status (25–77). As an organising societal principle, the 'meritoriousness of wealth' (118) saw everyone participating in the pursuit and recognition of honour through the 'pecuniary emulation' of consumption standards around them (70–77).

If we overlook the racist and social evolutionary aspects of Veblen's theory (Veblen 2003: 126–182), his thesis on the meritoriousness of wealth was also used to explain why rich men who committed fraud to maintain their quality of life were often treated sympathetically while a common thief was more likely to be accused of 'moral turpitude' (79–80). Money, and the power it implies, served as a buffer against the excesses of shame.

The other part of Veblen's thesis that bears some discussion is the assertion that even the poorest of the poor are included in a status hierarchy and compete for honour/status through conspicuous consumption. A number of authors have pointed out that, historically, the South African 'poor' have been voracious and conspicuous consumers and that local black elites have long set themselves apart through their highly fashionable and opulent garb (Gardiner 1836; Hannerz 1994; Posel 2010). While successive governments (Ross 1990; Posel 2010) and religious authorities (Comaroff 1996: 19–38) tried to rein in black conspicuous consumption, commentators have long been fascinated by its hyperbolic examples among the elite – and by the lack of outrage about it on behalf of the poor (Huigen 2017; Posel 2014: 44–48). In post-apartheid South Africa, poor black people often interpret the affluence and material sophistication of political leaders as a mark of aspiration (Posel 2013: 70–2). For their part, leaders such as Julius Malema defend their extravagances as an 'effective weapon against the tenacious economic domination of the "[w]hite minority"' (Posel 2014: 46).

Undoubtedly, the racial politics of conspicuous consumption have played a role in the support of Jacob Zuma's excesses by his poor followers. But so too has Zuma's reassertion of patriarchal Zulu 'traditionalism' (see Hunter 2011), masculinity (Suttner 2009), and authoritarianism (Hamilton 2010). Zuma's ability to resonate with many poor South Africans has also been ascribed to his ability to 'connect the personal and the political' in ways that address South Africa's gendered crisis of social reproduction (Hunter 2011) and that rebel against authoritarian management (Cuthbertson 2008), neoliberalism (Hunter 2011) and an alienating technocracy (Gunner 2009). While the gendered, ethnic, economic and political dimensions of Zuma's public support have been analysed, relatively little academic attention has been paid to its explicitly religious dimensions. In a rare focus on this neglected part of Zuma's reign, Gerald West (n.d.: 1–24; cf. West 2012) argued that Zuma's religious utterances followed a post-apartheid trajectory in which the ANC increasingly inserted 'religion in the public realm'.

Unlike many contemporary scholars, Veblen (2003: 22) included religion in his discussion of conspicuous consumption, remarking that those with strong religious convictions did not see wealth as meritorious and did not participate in the same pecuniary drive as their fellows. While the devout often showed constraint at an individual level, this was seldom the case at the institutional level, as temples and ritual paraphernalia were often marked by their conspicuous opulence (80). This conspicuous consumption, however, seldom served the comfort of worshippers or those that held religious office because its pecuniary reputability attached to the divine rather than to [his] servants (81–2).[10] And yet, because they did not spend their time doing debasing productive work, religious officeholders saw pecuniary gains from their 'ennobling' life of (often austere) leisure (27–37).

Veblen's approval of religious austerity contrasted with his antipathy to the ostentation and frivolity of the (wider) leisure class. As Fenton (2012) remarked, his critique 'hinges on [the] puritanical enshrinement of labor' as an 'expression of morality, and an equally evangelical denunciation of any activity removed from productive (read: required for subsistence) labor or its immediate reproduction' (cf. Adorno 1941: 389–413). Indeed, Puritans saw hard work and frugality as important consequences of being predestined, and rejected the worldly pursuit of wealth and possessions for their own sake (Weber 2001 [1930]).

CONSUMING FOR GOD

Veblen's Puritanism is certainly at odds with new forms of Christianity that embrace the so-called prosperity gospel. It is a theology that asserts that believers have a right to boundless material earthly 'blessings' from God but that the realisation or flow of such blessings in an individual's life is blocked by evil forces that work through other people. Churches that preach the prosperity gospel, many of them Neo-Pentecostal churches (NPCs), generally hold that the world is riven by a spiritual war between God and Satan in which the latter tries to undermine the earthly establishment of God's kingdom, a place of boundless wealth, health and happiness. All humans and spirits either choose to engage in the war or, through their ignorance of it, become unwitting instruments in it (Van Wyk 2014: 37–58).

For Christians who believe in the reality of the spiritual war, the rich and powerful have achieved their blessings through individual spiritual strength and mighty spiritual intercessions rather than through individual labour. While material possessions mark spiritual victories, they also invite jealous spiritual work from enemies that could undermine these fortunes. Being 'blessed' is thus not a once-off achievement but something that needs to be continually protected from invisible sources. In this worldview, conspicuous consumption is interpreted as a celebration of divine favour and is strongly encouraged as an act of faith (Van Wyk 2014: 37–58). In the spiritual war, old Christian concerns about sin and 'upright' living pale in comparison to the immediacy of war and the willingness of brave (men) to face it. It is a theology that makes assertiveness a prerequisite of being blessed. Indeed, many NPC members believe that God only favours those who can defend his blessings (Van Wyk 2014: 162).

While the prosperity gospel emphasises God's boundless blessings, many of its proponents also fight against those who use dark forces to gain access to power and money. In South African NPCs, these dark forces are often identified as traditional healers and witches who work with various witch familiars, such as snakes, mermaids, *tokoloshes* (short, hairy tricksters with enormous penises), cats, owls and a range of otherworldly beings (Van Wyk 2014: 37–58, 145–148, 153). Good Christians fight these forces through exorcisms, vigils, prayers, sacrifices, fasts, campaigns and spiritual 'burning'.

ZUMA AND THE NEO-PENTECOSTALS

Jacob Zuma is well versed in the prosperity gospel. Apart from his longstanding membership of various NPCs, Zuma was ordained as an honorary pastor in the Full Gospel Church in 2007 (Munusamy 2013). In the run-up to the April 2009 general elections, Zuma visited a number of NPCs and preached an NPC message in the Rhema Bible Church (*Mail & Guardian* 2009; West n.d.: 10). Taking the archetypal liberation theology text of the Israeli exodus from Egypt (West n.d.: 11), Zuma turned it into a prosperity gospel message by emphasising Moses' inspired leadership and its resultant prosperous consequences for those he led (Zuma 2009a: 1–3). He encouraged his listeners to use 'the power of prayer' (and socio-economic development ventures) to 'make South Africa a land of milk and honey' (Zuma 2009a: 3). At Easter, Zuma further raised eyebrows when he eschewed the traditional head of state's[11] visit to the country's largest church, the Zion Christian Church (ZCC), in order to attend a service at the International Pentecost Church. From its pulpit, Zuma used biblical verses to make veiled swipes at his 'plotting' enemies (Zuma 2009b).

As president, Zuma increasingly eschewed the critical religious communities of more mainline churches in favour of NPCs (Van Wyk 2015: 136–7). This became particularly pronounced after the Nkandla scandal provoked angry reactions and public protests from some ANC supporters, the SACC, the NRLC and, uncharacteristically, from the ZCC (Moloto 2014).[12] First booed at Mandela's funeral on 10 December 2013, Zuma's public appearances on the campaign trail in March 2014 were marred by crowds of heckling ANC supporters (Ngalwa 2014: 4). By December 2014, the ANC's spokesperson admitted in a National Executive Council report that there were 'distant' relationships between the party and the SACC which was 'of the view that the ANC is more comfortable with wealth religion and those who are not critical of the ANC' (Hunter & Mataboge 2014).

Zuma's experience at political rallies in 2014 stood in sharp contrast to the welcome he received at the Universal Church of the Kingdom of God (UCKG)'s Easter celebrations. In front of a packed Ellis Park Stadium, Bishop Pires blessed Zuma and his entourage and gratefully received Zuma's praise of the church (Bizcommunity 2014). As more scandals came to light, the SACC and the NRLC sharpened their critique of Zuma (Katz 2016). Seemingly unperturbed, Zuma continued to attend mass NPC meetings where he was warmly welcomed and from whence he could exhort believers to 'respect those appointed to lead you' (eNCA 2016).[13] He also called on Christians to pray for politicians, as 'Satan is always around trying to derail us' (Ngoepe 2016).

In 2016, after the Constitutional Court determined that Zuma had failed to uphold the Constitution and again in 2017 with the Gupta leaks, the NRLC and the SACC called a meeting with the ANC urging them to compel Zuma to resign (Katz 2016; Pollitt 2017). They also found various public platforms to denounce him, organised public protests and supported a vote of no confidence against Zuma in Parliament (Pollitt 2017). Piqued, Zuma reminded (these) religious leaders that their role was to 'pray for our nation so respect can come back', not to meddle in politics (*The Citizen* 2017).

In June 2018, Mazibuyele Emasisweni, a pro-Zuma lobby group made up of prominent NPC leaders and bishops, 'business bodies', traditional leaders and taxi operators, announced that it would launch a new political party to 'punish' the ANC for ousting Zuma as president (Harper & Bendile 2018). While Zuma quickly distanced himself from the breakaway party, he addressed Mazibuyele members on various occasions, trumpeting his leading role in the liberation struggle and the economic transformation his presidency had inaugurated (Harper & Bendile 2018).

PENTECOSTAL POLITICS

Apart from his attendance at NPCs and the obvious ways in which their politics dovetailed with his (both during and after his presidency), Zuma's public statements were often heavily informed by Pentecostal rhetoric and modes of spiritual warfare. His supporters recognised and responded to these performances in a similar register, leading to an increasingly Pentecostalised public culture (cf. Meyer 2004; 2015).

Often drawing parallels between him and and the persecuted Jesus, Zuma and his supporters have long interpreted his legal difficulties in terms far removed from the rational language of the courts. He and his supporters have made much of the dark forces plotting against him – and of his invincibility against this onslaught. Following the graft investigations against him in 2001, Zuma's friend and then head of South Africa's secret services, Mo Shaik, likened the National Prosecuting Authority to the biblical Pontius Pilate, who conspired to have Jesus convicted in a Jewish court (Smith 2003). Three years later, as evidence against Zuma mounted in the Schabir Shaik case, his supporters at the court joined him in singing *Awuleth' Umshini Wami* (Bring my machine [gun]) (Gunner 2009), a stridently defiant anthem befitting the spiritual warrior of NPC theology (Van Wyk 2014). When corruption charges were eventually laid against him, Zuma's supporters held a prayer vigil outside the courtroom (*Mail & Guardian* 2005). In various interviews, Zuma and his supporters complained that the charges were part of a political plot to destroy his reputation and to stop him from becoming South Africa's next president (*Mail & Guardian* 2005).

When Zuma was charged with rape, a number of his supporters again saw dark forces conspiring against him, among them, Kwezi's own mother (Sesanti 2008: 371–373; Tolsi 2006). In an interview with *The Sowetan* (2006), Zuma said that 'like Christ', the media, and by implication his political opponents, wanted to 'crucify' him. He promised to strike back by appointing two lawyers to investigate his 'crucifixion by the media' (*Mail & Guardian* 2006). Zuma's spiritual war had obviously struck a chord with his many supporters who had gathered outside the Johannesburg High Court. One held up a homemade crucifix bearing a pasted picture of Zuma with outstretched arms asking: 'Why are you crucifying Zuma?' Another poster read, 'Zuma is Jesus' (Evans 2006; *Mail & Guardian* 2006). The group of mostly women also 'fell to their knees in prayer in front of a line of riot policemen posted between them and the court entrance' (Evans 2006). Zuma's supporters were elated when he was acquitted of rape and reinstated as deputy president of the ANC (Monare 2006). For many of his NPC followers, Zuma's turn in fortunes could directly be attributed to their efficacious spiritual work at the courtroom (the 'strong' hymns and prayers) and in church.

In late 2007, Judge Herbert Msimang struck the corruption case against Zuma from the court roll. When a number of opposition parliamentarians crossed the floor to join the ANC, a jubilant Zuma remarked to the media, 'That is why we believe we will be in power forever until the son of man [Jesus] comes back' (Ngoepe 2016a; Van Onselen 2016). A year later, the NPA once again reinstated the charges and again Zuma's supporters congregated outside the Supreme Court of Appeal with banners likening him to Jesus.[14] Ace Magashule, the ANC's provincial leader in the Free State, addressed the crowds outside in a now-familiar trope, saying that Jacob Zuma was 'suffering just like Jesus did … Jesus was persecuted. He was called names and betrayed. It's the same kind of suffering Mr Zuma has had to bear recently, but he's still standing strong. He's not giving up' (Cloete 2008; *Mail & Guardian* 2008). As Zuma's fortunes plummeted in

Figure 1: Garlicks store, Cape Town. First appeared in *The Cape Register*, 26 August 1893.
Courtesy University of Cape Town Libraries.

Figure 2: A wax-cloth trader arranging her stall in the Lomé textile market.
Photograph by Nina Sylvanus.

Figure 3: Photographic collage of Sasolburg cars by Jacques Bernard.
Used with permission.

Figure 4: Etienne Rousseau with Elsie Human, wife of CJF Human, Managing Director of Federale Volksbeleggings, at the company's year-end function, 28 November 1975.
Courtesy the Archive for Contemporary Affairs, University of the Free State.

Figure 5: President Frederick Chiluba, with wife Regina Chiluba in the background.
Photo by Thomas Nsama/AFP/Getty Images. Courtesy Gallo Images.

Figure 6: Wiz kid dress.
Photograph by Adeline Masquelier.

Figure 7: Faire le show.
Photograph by Adeline Masquelier.

Figure 8: The Good Fellas' designer shoes.
Photograph by Mpho Sekatane. Courtesy The Good Fellas.

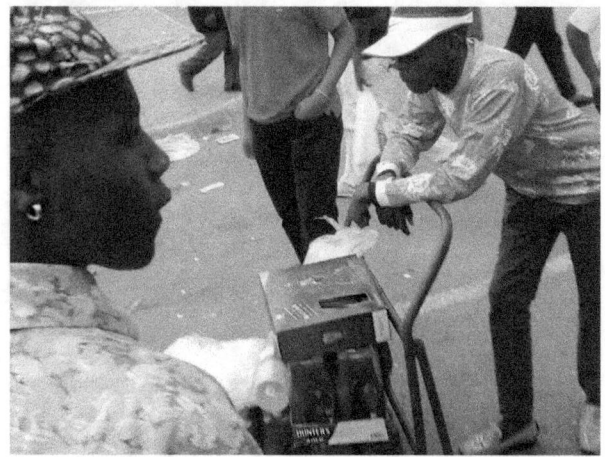

Figure 9: The Good Fellas buying expensive alcohol.
Photograph by Mpho Sekatane. Courtesy The Good Fellas.

Figure 10: The Good Fellas posing at the Civic Centre in Kempton Park.
Photograph by Siyabonga Mhlanga. Courtesy The Good Fellas.

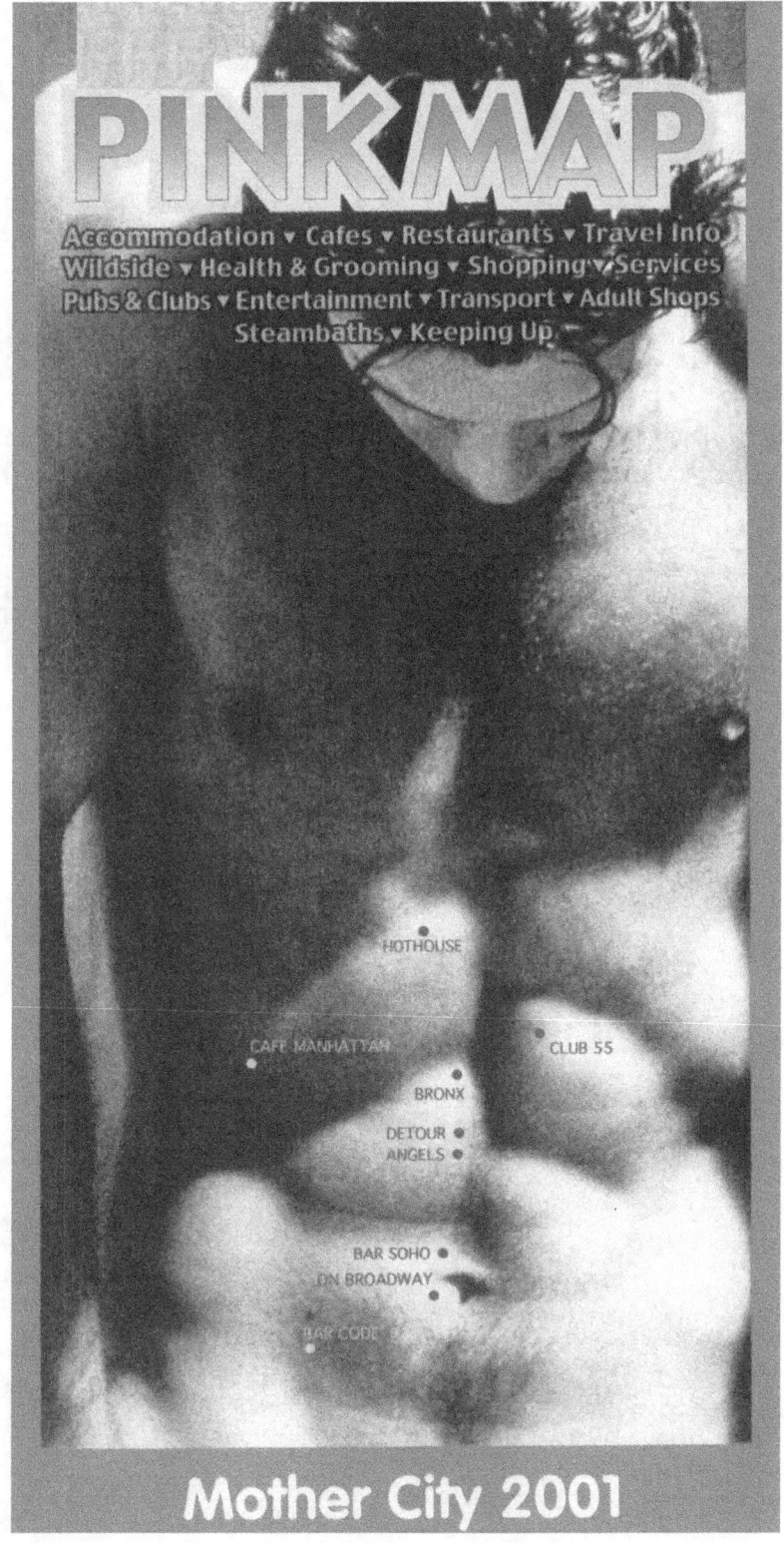

Figure 11: Cover image of 2001 edition of the *Pink Map*.
Courtesy A&C Maps. © www.mapmyway.co.za

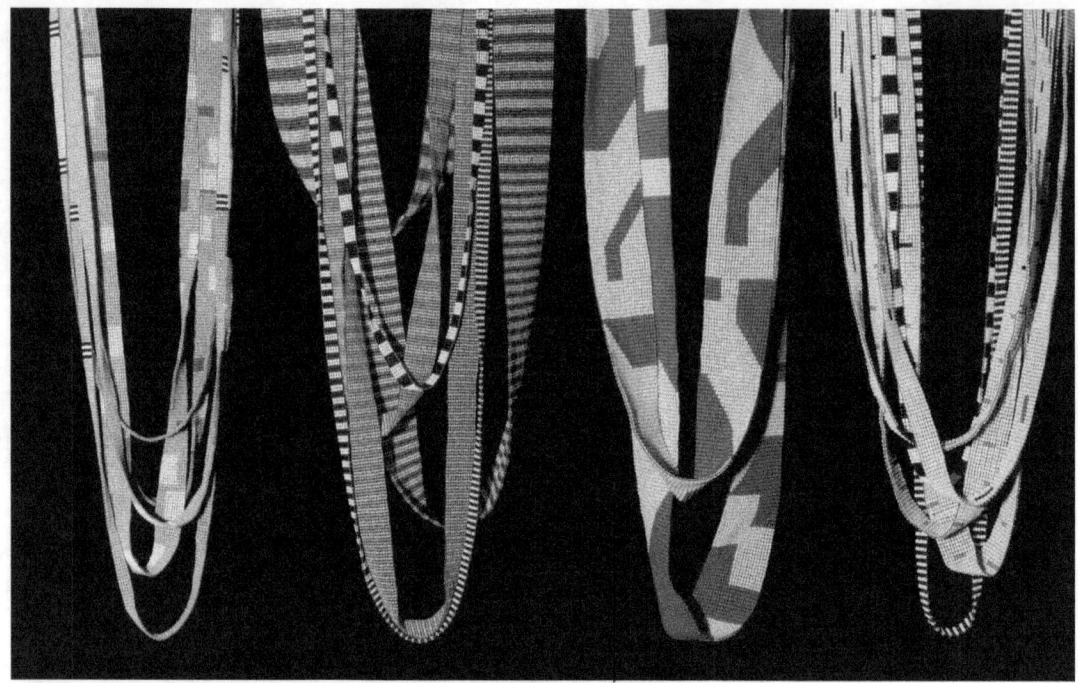

Figure 12: Strands of Marigold hand-loomed beads can be worn in endless combinations to glamorous effect.
Photograph by Liz Whitter.

Figure 13: Marigold hand-loomed beads in five variations on the pixellated 'Camouflage' design.
Photograph by Liz Whitter.

January 2009, Magashule was again at court to tell supporters, 'In church they sing that they will follow Jesus wherever he goes. That's how we should be about Jacob Zuma' (Van Onselen 2012b).

Zuma's renewed troubles coincided with the establishment of a breakaway party, the Congress of the People (Cope), and the desertion of a number of ANC members. Explicitly referring to the story of Jesus riding a donkey into Jerusalem, Zuma said of the new party, 'The people are waiting for the son of man [Jesus] who was on the donkey. The donkey did not understand it, and thought that the songs of praise were for him' (Du Plessis 2008). Magashule contributed with another biblical reference: 'Jesus had up to 70 disciples, but in the end only 12 remained' (Cloete 2008). As his Christian listeners knew, after Jesus's resurrection, the Holy Spirit rewarded the 12 disciples' loyalty with spiritual gifts.

In 2017, Zuma hit back at 'church leaders who throw stones' from his NPC platforms saying, '[e]ven our saviour was facing many challenges. He was the one who felt pain for us sinners. They called him names. They spit on him' (SABC News 2017). A few months later, as the motion of no confidence against him was defeated in Parliament, Zuma crowed to his comrades, 'You came in your numbers to demonstrate that the ANC is there, is powerful, is big. It is difficult to defeat the ANC, but you can try'. He then launched into his signature song, *Yinde le ndlela* (It's a long road ahead) (Allison 2017). In the NPCs that Zuma visited, both *Yinde le ndlela* and his infamous *Umshini wami* were repeatedly sung; both appropriate accompaniments to the spiritual war (e.g. *City Press* 2014).

Since his first appointment to Parliament, Zuma had repeatedly referred to himself as 'blessed' in public and intimated that he would be able to bless others. In a particularly NPC mode, he recalled his visit to the 'River Jordan where Jesus was baptised ... Jericho and Jerusalem were just across the Dead Sea. So, if I look at anyone, he or she will be blessed' (McKinley 2013).[15] In NPCs, believers often make pilgrimages to places with connections to the Old Testament in order to quicken the Holy Spirit and ensure a flow of blessings into their lives – and into the lives of those they bless (Van Wyk 2014: 157–163; 171–181).

Zuma's confident Neo-Pentecostal message soon emboldened other ANC members who held similar beliefs. When the ANC tried to dismiss as mere figurative speech Zuma's 2004 claim that the 'ANC will rule South Africa until Jesus comes back' (Ngoepe 2016a), Bushbuckridge mayor Milton Morema expanded:

> The ANC follows the teachings of Jesus Christ. When Jesus walked the streets of Jerusalem he identified with the poor. That is what the ANC does. Jesus Christ suffered because he wanted to see people sheltered. The ANC provides Bushbuckridge with houses. Jesus

Christ would have loved to see people living in healthy situations. The ANC provides clinics and food parcels. Jesus fought poverty and suffering in his preaching. The ANC provides grants to stop people from suffering. Like the Pharaohs, God did not support the apartheid government. That is why they did not last. But God supports this government. It does what Jesus does. It will rule till Jesus comes back. (Van Onselen 2016)

In the next few years, Zuma and his cronies repeatedly asserted that God endorsed the ANC as the party that would rule 'until Jesus comes back' – and that the party's enemies would face divine retribution (ANC 2009; Mkhwanazi 2008; Van Onselen 2012b; cf. West n.d.: 13–14). Zuma articulated this most clearly on 5 February 2011 when he told supporters in the Eastern Cape that opposition to the ANC was inherently evil and had damnable consequences:

When you vote for the ANC, you are also choosing to go to heaven. When you don't vote for the ANC you should know that you are choosing that man who carries a fork [Satan] ... who cooks people ... When you are carrying an ANC membership card, you are blessed. When you get up there, there are different cards used but when you have an ANC card, you will be let through to go to heaven when [Jesus] fetches us we will find [those in the beyond] wearing black, green and gold. The holy ones belong to the ANC. (Van Onselen 2012b)

As the ANC's relationship with old mainline churches soured, more of Zuma's allies publicly embraced the spiritual war against his enemies. In March 2014, Hlaudi Motsoeneng made headlines when he roped in a few NPC pastors to cast 'demons' out of the public protector's office (Pillay 2014). Known as Zuma's enforcer at the public broadcaster, Motsoeneng also featured in a public protector's report for awarding irregular salary hikes for himself and a few favoured underlings, making fraudulent claims that he possessed a matric certificate, and his disastrous firing of critical staff members that cost the broadcaster millions in court settlements. The Pastors of Indigenous Christian Churches, allied to Motsoeneng, responded to Madonsela's report by saying that they were 'noticing a trend in [Mandonsela's] reporting that seems to cast aspersions on critical persons in the country and thereby poisons the atmosphere'. In order to 'clear the atmosphere', they proceeded to perform a ritual exorcism aimed at the public protector's office. Another group, the Friends of Hlaudi Formation, also planned a night vigil and protest march in Bloemfontein (Pillay 2014).

In 2017, as increasing numbers of Zuma's comrades criticised him from within the ANC, Zuma stressed that only the 'enemy' [in NPC circles referring to Satan] benefitted and grew strong from the ANC's infighting. He also appealed to ANC supporters to appreciate the party's history in the same way that they appreciated the Bible (Whittles & Sigauqwe 2017).

In this increasingly Pentecostalised public space where spiritual warfare complemented politics, Desmond Tutu warned the Zuma-led government that he would pray for their demise: 'Like I warned the Nationalists … One day, we will start praying for the defeat of the ANC Government … You are disgraceful … You are behaving in a way that is totally at variance with the things for which we stood' (Pollitt 2017).

The Pentecostalisation of politics also infected the ANC's political opponents. In the second week of August 2014, news broke online that two mermaids had been killed in Zuma's controversial 'fire pool'[16] at Nkandla and that their bodies had been taken to a research facility in Durban (Anim van Wyk 2014). Originating from Nigeria, the story found enormous traction on the Economic Freedom Front (EFF)'s supporter website where many thousands of people viewed the pictures of two female figures with snake-like tails lying on a dissecting table. YouTube videos quickly sprang up with live 'proof' of the mermaids' existence.[17] The EFF site immediately accused Zuma of witchcraft, with Julius Malema quoted as saying that Zuma was 'using the mermaids to prevent him from losing his place in leadership' (Van Wyk, A 2014). Commentators asked why Malema was 'so against President Jacob Zuma … He is jealous or what?' and also: 'It might b tru wat malema s sayin abwt zuma, phela he ddnt go 2 skl he might hv gotten dis leadership thru doz mermaids' [It might be true what Malema is saying about Zuma because he didn't go to school so he might have gotten his leadership through those mermaids, i.e. through dark forces].[18]

Even in the mainstream print media, journalists started to publish sensational stories that hinted at Zuma's extraordinary spiritual powers. On 4–5 September 2015, Zuma attended the annual reed dance ceremony at the behest of the Zulu King Goodwill Zwelithini. According to front-page newspaper reports, among them *The Star* newspaper, the attending maidens started to hallucinate, cry and roll on the floor on the Friday night, but despite the work of religious leaders, 'evil spirits' possessed a large group of the girls. Apparently hearing 'strange voices', the girls rushed towards the VIP enclosure where Zuma was sitting. His bodyguards immediately whisked him away but once order was restored, the king scolded the maidens saying, 'There are some of you who came here with evil spirits to spoil this event' (Hans & Ntsele 2015: 1). In Pentecostal circles, the event could have signified Zuma's access to the Holy Spirit (in whose presence evil spirits often manifest) or shown his kinship to the spirits that tormented the young women. The journalists left that judgement to their readers.

Jacob Zuma's detractors have long been outraged at the 'shameless' ways in which he has greedily flaunted wealth for which he did not work and showed defiance in the face of various criminal charges. Zuma's shamelessness has presented a conundrum for many scholars who have tried to explain his continued support among poor South Africans. By rights, they have implied, these citizens should have been outraged by his private extravagance, profligacy with the public purse and with his various brushes with the law. While academics have looked at the gendered, ethnic, economic and political dimensions of Zuma's public support, few have taken the religious dimensions of it seriously. A number of critics dismissed his assertions of divine favour when matters went his way and dark plots when they did not as mere political populism – another shameless tactic to avoid taking responsibility for his supposed moral decrepitude. The dismissal of the religious dimensions of Zuma's public support has been especially notable given that '[q]uite where ANC politics begins and private religious convictions end has always been a difficult line to draw when it comes to the ANC President', as one commentator noted (Van Onselen 2012b).

A closer look at Neo-Pentecostal theology, and especially its prosperity gospel and spiritual warfare tenets, offers deeper insight into Zuma's continued support and his refusal to be 'shamed'. While I make no judgements about Zuma's personal commitment to Neo-Pentecostal values, I show that NPC members recognise in Zuma's reckless spending behaviour, his uncompromising fight against dark 'enemies' and his invincibility, the marks of a 'blessed' man. A very specific NPC religious ethic can be recognised in Zuma's unapologetic conspicuous consumption and the ways in which he and his supporters have reacted to his travails. Unlike the Puritan productionist ethic that informed Veblen's critique of conspicuous consumption, the NPC ethic is consumerist in its focus. It is an ethic that demands of its subscribers that they consume conspicuously and without 'shame' as part of their spiritual warfare. In contrast to his predecessors, Zuma has consistently exceeded his generous state allowances for travel, accommodation and security in favour of more luxurious and conspicuous options, while his private extravagances – the 'big fat weddings', parties and designer clothes for family members not covered by state allowances – are well known (Huigen 2017). When his frequent debts and murky debtors were exposed, Zuma was not shamed. Instead, he and his supporters attacked the dark enemies that were conspiring to undermine his deserved good fortune.

As Zuma increasingly fudged the lines between his political and spiritual struggles, and publicly allied with NPCs rather than mainline churches, his supporters and fellow politicians responded in increasingly Pentecostal ways. They sympathised with his 'persecution' and recognised in it the dark work of invisible forces and evil conspirators. Zuma's detractors were increasingly also pulled into this Pentecostalising public space.

Zuma's public life has much in common with other flamboyant political leaders and former leaders on the continent who have publicly declared their membership, leadership or support of Pentecostal churches, including Teodoro Obiang Nguema Mbasogo of Equatorial Guinea, Yoweri Museveni of Uganda, Jerry Rawlings in Ghana (Gifford 1998: 57–180), José Eduardo dos Santos of Angola, Armando Emilio Guebuza of Mozambique, Ernest Bai Koroma of Sierra Leone and Daniel Arap Moi and his successors Mwai Kibaki and Raila Odinga in Kenya (Gifford 2009). Noting the close alliance between some African leaders and NPCs, Gifford (215) has stated that this 'domesticated Christianity' is not 'concerned with a renewed order or any "new Jerusalem"' (339). Instead, Neo-Pentecostalism has emboldened 'shameless' men vying for power to celebrate their conspicuous consumption and political invincibility as scores of followers aspire to similar feats of spiritual accomplishment.

REFERENCES

Adorno, T. W., 1941, 'Veblen's Attack on Culture. Remarks occasioned by The Theory of the Leisure Class', *Zeitschrift für Sozialforschung*, 9(3): 389–413.

Allison, S., 2017, 'Jacob Zuma Narrowly Survives No-Confidence Vote in South African Parliament', in *The Guardian*, viewed 18 August 2017, available from: https://www.theguardian.com/world/2017/aug/08/jacob-zuma-survives-no-confidence-vote-south-african-president.

ANC, 2009, 'ANC President Meets with Religious and Traditional Leaders in North West', viewed 19 August 2017, available from: http://www.anc.org.za/show.php?doc=ancdocs/pr/2009/pr0318.html.

Bauer, N., 2012, 'Spend It Like Zuma: Life and Debt in South Africa', in *Mail & Guardian*, viewed 25 February 2017, available from: https://mg.co.za/article/2012-12-11-spend-it-like-zuma-a-south-african-story.

Bayart, J., 2009 [1989], *The State in Africa: The Politics of the Belly* (2nd edn.), Wiley: New Jersey.

Bizcommunity, 2014, 'President Zuma and 165 000 Church Members Attend UCKG's Good Friday Service', viewed 15 December 2014, available from: http://www.bizcommunity.com/Article/196/422/112529.html.

Chidester, D., 2012, *Wild Religion: Tracking the Sacred in South Africa*. University of California Press: Berkeley.

Cilliers, C., 2018, 'Jacob Zuma Plans to Take a New Wife', in *The Citizen*, viewed 21 June 2018, available from: https://citizen.co.za/news/south-africa/1901028/jacob-zuma-plans-to-take-a-new-wife/.

City Press, 2014, 'Politicians Get Spiritual', viewed 12 January 2017, available from: http://www.news24.com/Archives/City-Press/Politicians-get-spiritual-20150430.

Cloete, H., 2008, 'Zuma "Persecuted like Christ"', in News24, viewed 19 August 2017, available from: http://www.news24.com/SouthAfrica/Politics/Zuma-persecuted-like-Christ-20081130?cpid=3.

Comaroff, J., 1996, 'The Empire's Old Clothes: Fashioning the Colonial Subject', in D. Howes (ed.), *Cross-Cultural Consumption: Global Markets, Local Realities*, 19–38, Routledge: London and New York.

Comaroff, J. & Comaroff, J. L. (eds.), 2001, *Millennial Capitalism and the Culture of Neoliberalism*, Duke University Press: Durham and London.

Cuthbertson, G., 2008, 'South Africa's Democracy: From Celebration to Crisis', *African Identities* 6(3): 293–304.

Du Plessis, C., 2008, 'Cope Like Jesus's Donkey – Zuma', in News24, viewed 19 August 2017, available from: http://www.news24.com/SouthAfrica/Politics/Cope-like-Jesuss-donkey-Zuma-20081119?cpid=3.

eNCA, 2016, 'Watch: "Respect Those Appointed to Lead You", Zuma Tells Congregation', viewed 19 August 2017, available from: www.enca.com/south-africa/live-video-president-zuma-joins-universal-church-easter-service.

Evans, J., 2006, 'Banners Liken Zuma to Christ', in IOL, viewed 17 August 2017, available from: http://www.iol.co.za/news/south-africa/banners-liken-zuma-to-christ-270873.

Evans, S., Shamase, N. & Brümmer, S., 2012, 'Shaik Millions "for Zuma's Children"', in *Mail & Guardian*, viewed 19 August 2017, available from: http://mg.co.za/article/2012-12-14-00-shaik-millions-for-zumas-children.

Fenton, R., 2012, 'Conspicuous Consumption of the Leisure Class: Veblen's Critique and Adorno's Rejoinder in the Twenty-First Century', *Politics and Culture* 1, available from: https://politicsandculture.org/2012/05/02/conspicuous-consumption-of-the-leisure-class-veblens-critique-and-adornos-rejoinder-in-the-twenty-first-century/.

Gardiner, A., 1836, *Narrative of a Journey to the Zoolu Country in South Africa: Undertaken in 1835*, William Crofts: London.

Gifford, P., 1998, *African Christianity: Its Public Role*, C. Hurst & Co. Publishers: London.

Gifford, P., 2009, *Christianity, Politics and Public Life in Kenya*, Columbia University Press: New York.

Govender, S., 2016, 'Shaik Unfriends Zuma: "You Threw Me to the Wolves"', in *Sunday Times*, viewed 15 January 2017, available from: http://www.timeslive.co.za/sundaytimes/stnews/2016/02/21/Shaik-unfriends-Zuma-You-threw-me-to-the-wolves1.

Graeber, D., 2011, *Debt: The First 5000 Years*, Melville House Publishing: London.

Gunner, L., 2009, 'Jacob Zuma, the Social Body and the Unruly Power of Song', *African Affairs* 108(430): 27–48.

Hamilton, C., 2010, 'Framing Essay: In the Shadows of the Convened Public Sphere: Public Silences and Disavowed Debate', *Social Dynamics* 36(1): 3–10.

Hannerz, U., 1994, 'Sophiatown: The View from Afar', *Journal of Southern African Studies* 20(2): 181–193.

Hans, B. & Ntsele, P., 2015, 'Maidens Swarm Zuma: President Forced to Leave After "Demonic" Attack', in *The Star*, 7 September, 1.

Harper, P. & Bendile, D., 2018, 'JZ's Apostles to Launch New Party', in *Mail & Guardian,* viewed 21 June 2018, available from: https://mg.co.za/article/2018-06-01-00-jzs-apostles-to-launch-new-party.

Huigen, B., 2017, 'Cadres and Compatriots: An Analysis of Their Good Lives as Presented by Top Billing', *Anthropology Southern Africa* 40(3&4): 172–184.

Hunter, M., 2011, 'Beneath the "Zunami": Jacob Zuma and the Gendered Politics of Social Reproduction in South Africa', *Antipode* 43(4): 1102–1126.

Hunter, Q. & Mataboge, M., 2014, 'Why Churches Dumped the ANC', in *Mail & Guardian*, viewed 15 January 2017, available from: http://mg.co.za/article/2014-12-22-why-churches-dumped-the-anc.

Katz, A., 2016, 'Religious Leaders: Zuma Must Go "for Sake of SA"', in *South African Jewish Report*, viewed 19 August 2017, available from: http://www.sajr.co.za/opinion/surveys-most-commented-stories/2016/04/12/religious-leaders-zuma-must-go-for-sake-of-sa.

Larson, K., 2010, 'Zuma Apologises for Fathering Illegitimate Child', in *The Independent*, viewed 19 August 2017, available from: http://www.independent.co.uk/news/world/africa/zuma-apologises-for-fathering-illegitimate-child-1891515.html.

Madia, M. & Evans, J., 2016, 'Zuma Brings Shame to SA – ANC Veterans', in News24, viewed 19 August 2017, available from: http://www.news24.com/SouthAfrica/News/zuma-brings-shame-to-sa-anc-veterans-20161103.

Madisa, K., 2016, 'Keeping up with the Zumas – Get to Know the Children', in *Sowetan Live*, viewed 19 August 2017, available from: http://www.sowetanlive.co.za/news/2016/05/25/keeping-up-with-the-zumas---get-to-know-the-children.

Madonsela, T., 2014, S*ecure in Comfort: A Report by the Public Protector*, viewed 27 November 2018, available from: http://cdn.24.co.za/files/Cms/General/d/2718/00b91b2841d64510b9c99ef9b9faa597.pdf.

Madonsela, T., 2016, *State of Capture: A Report of the Public Protector*, viewed 27 November 2018, available from: https://www.scribd.com/document/329757088/State-of-Capture-Public-Protector-Report#from_embed.

Mail & Guardian, 2005, 'Zuma: Speedy Trial for Me, Please', viewed 19 August 2017, available from: http://mg.co.za/article/2005-06-29-zuma-speedy-trial-for-me-please.

Mail & Guardian, 2006, 'Zuma to Fight "Crucifixion by Media"', viewed 19 August 2017, available from: http://mg.co.za/article/2006-03-27-zuma-to-fight-crucifixion-by-media.

Mail & Guardian, 2008, 'ANC Leader Says Zuma is Suffering like Jesus', viewed 19 August 2017, available from: http://mg.co.za/article/2008-12-01-anc-leader-says-zuma-is-suffering-like-jesus.

Mail & Guardian, 2009, 'Zuma Visits Rhema, Prays for Peaceful Election', viewed 19 August 2017, available from: http://mg.co.za/article/2009-03-15-zuma-visits-rhema-prays-for-peaceful-election.

Malala, J., 2016, 'Zuma and the End of Shame', in *Rand Daily Mail*, viewed 19 August 2017, available from: http://www.rdm.co.za/politics/2016/05/09/zuma-and-the-end-of-shame.

McKaiser, E., 2017, 'Zuma, Trump and the Absence of Shame', in *Mail & Guardian*, viewed 2 October 2017, available from: http://mg.co.za/article/2017-02-10-00-zuma-trump-and-the-absence-of-shame.

McKinley, D. T., 2013, 'Zuma and the ANC's God Complex', in The South African Civil Society Information Service, viewed 2 October 2017, available from: http://sacsis.org.za/site/article/1634.

Meyer, B., 2004, '"Praise the Lord": Popular Cinema and Pentecostalite Style in Ghana's New Public Sphere', *American Ethnologist* 31(1): 92–110.

Meyer, B., 2015, *Sensational Movies: Video, Vision and Christianity in Ghana*, University of California Press: Berkeley.

Mkhwanazi, S., 2008, 'ANC to Rule Until Jesus Comes Back', in *Cape Times*, viewed 2 February 2017, available from: http://www.iol.co.za/news/politics/anc-to-rule-until-jesus-comes-back-398843.

Moloto, M., 2014, 'Don't Vote for Embezzlers: ZCC Head', in IOL, viewed 12 November 2016, available from: http://www.iol.co.za/news/politics/don't-vote-for-embezzlers-zcc-head-1679050.

Monare, M., 2006, 'Zuma Reinstated as ANC Deputy President', in IOL, viewed 12 November 2016, available from: http://www.iol.co.za/news/politics/zuma-reinstated-as-anc-deputy-president-277688.

Mulholland, S., 2016, 'The Shameless Mr Zuma', in Politicsweb, viewed 22 May 2017, available from: http://www.politicsweb.co.za/opinion/the-shameless-mr-zuma.

Munusamy, R., 2013, 'In the Name of the Father: Jacob's Law on Politics and Religion', in *Daily Maverick*, viewed 22 May 2017, available from: http://www.dailymaverick.co.za/article/2013-10-08-in-the-name-of-the-father-jacobs-law-on-politics-and-religion/#.WCRhQBS_KIA.

Ngalwa, S., 2014, 'Zuma Booed by Own Party in Limpopo', in *Sunday Times*, viewed 22 May 2017, available from: https://www.pressreader.com/south-africa/sundaytimes/20140420/281638188196972.

Ngoepe, K., 2016a, 'ANC Will Rule Until Jesus Comes, Zuma Says Again', in News24, viewed 22 May 2017, available from: http://www.news24.com/elections/news/anc-will-rule-until-jesus-comes-zuma-says-again-20160705.

Ngoepe, K., 2016b, 'Help Us Fight Satan, Zuma Asks Christians', in *Sowetan Live*, viewed 19 August 2017, available from: http://www.sowetanlive.co.za/news/2016/03/25/help-us-fight-satan-zuma-asks-christians.

Nhlabati, H., 2016, 'Shameful, Disgraceful – Elders Lay into Zuma, ANC Leadership', in *City Press*, viewed 19 August 2017, available from: http://city-press.news24.com/News/shameful-disgraceful-elders-lay-into-zuma-anc-leadership-20161103.

Nietzsche, F., 2001 [1882], *The Gay Science*, Cambridge University Press: Cambridge.

Pillay, V., 2010, 'All the President's Women', in *Mail & Guardian*, viewed 19 August 2017, available from: https://mg.co.za/article/2010-01-04-all-the-presidents-women.

Pillay, V., 2013, 'ANC: Don't Compare Zuma's Nkandla Upgrades to Mandela, Mbeki', in *Mail & Guardian*, viewed 19 August 2017, available from: https://mg.co.za/article/2013-12-19-anc-dont-compare-zumas-nkandla-upgrades-to-mandela-mbeki.

Pillay, V., 2014, 'Demons "Cast Out" of Protector's Office by Pro-SABC Church Leaders', in *Mail & Guardian*, viewed 19 November 2016, available from: http://mg.co.za/article/2014-03-14-demons-cast-out-of-protectors-office-by-pro-sabc-church-leaders.

Pollitt, R., 2017, 'Op-Ed: Keeping Faith, Speaking Truth to Power', in *Daily Maverick*, viewed 19 August 2017, available from: https://www.dailymaverick.co.za/article/2017-08-16-op-ed-keeping-faith-speaking-truth-to-power/#.WZmxnhSsOKw.

Posel, D., 2010, 'Races to Consume: Revisiting South Africa's History of Race, Consumption and the Struggle for Freedom', *Ethnic and Racial Studies* 33(2): 157–75.

Posel, D., 2013, 'The ANC Youth League and the Politicization of Race', *Thesis XI* 115: 58–76.

Posel, D., 2014, 'Julius Malema and the Post-Apartheid Public Sphere', *Acta Academica* 46(1): 32–54.

Ross, R. J., 1990, 'The Top Hat in South African History: The Changing Significance of an Article of Material Culture', *Social Dynamics* 16(2): 90–100.

Rossouw, M., 2009, 'Zuma's R65m Nkandla Splurge', in *Mail & Guardian*, viewed 19 August 2017, available from: https://mg.co.za/article/2009-12-04-zumas-r65m-nkandla-splurge.

SABC News, 2017, 'Zuma Appeals for Prayers on Good Friday', 14 April, viewed 19 August 2017, available from: http://www.sabc.co.za/news/a/b28e2a8040c6babdb5daf5d9ce9b621f/Zuma-appeals-for-prayers-on-Good-Friday-%C2%A0-20171404.

Sesanti, S., 2008, 'The Media and the Zuma/Zulu Culture. An Afrocentric Perspective', in A. Hadland, E. Louw, S. Sesanti & H. Wassermann (eds.), *Power, Politics and Identity in South African media*, 364-377, HSRC Press: Cape Town.

Smith, D., 2012, 'Nelson Mandela Bailed Out Debt-Mired Jacob Zuma, Audit Reveals', in *The Guardian*, viewed 19 August 2016, available from: https://www.theguardian.com/world/2012/dec/07/mandela-bailed-out-zuma-audit.

Smith, M., 2003, 'Mo Throws the Book(s) at Ngcuka', in IOL, viewed 17 August 2017, available from: http://www.iol.co.za/news/politics/mo-throws-the-books-at-ngcuka-117493.

Sowetan Live, 2016, 'The First Ladies of South Africa – What You Need to Know', 24 May, viewed 19 August 2017, available from: http://www.sowetanlive.co.za/news/2016/05/24/the-first-ladies-of-south-africa---what-you-need-to-know.

Steenkamp, L., 2011, 'R400m to Upgrade Official Residences', in *Die Burger*, viewed 18 August 2017, available from: http://www.news24.com/SouthAfrica/Politics/R400m-to-Upgrade-official-residences-20111020.

Stone, S., 2017, 'SA Council of Churches Release Scathing Report on State Capture', in *City Press*, viewed 18 May 2017, available from: http://city-press.news24.com/News/sas-council-of-churches-releases-scathing-report.

Suttner, R., 2009, 'The Jacob Zuma Rape Trial: Power and African National Congress (ANC) Masculinities', *Nora – Nordic Journal of Feminist and Gender Research* 17(3): 222–236.

The Citizen, 2017, 'Zuma Draws Comparison with Christ, Tells Religious Leaders How to Treat Him', viewed 19 August 2017, available from: https://citizen.co.za/news/south-africa/1489004/zuma-criticised-flip-flopping-whether-churches-political/.

The Presidency, 2017, 'President Zuma to Address TACC Easter Service', viewed 19 August 2017, available from: http://www.thepresidency.gov.za/press-statements/president-zuma-address-tacc-easter-service.

The Sowetan, 2006, 'I'm like Christ – Zuma', 24 March 2006.

Tolsi, N., 2006, 'Nkandla: Our Fortunes Are Tied to Msholozi', in *Mail & Guardian*, viewed 19 August 2017, available from: http://mg.co.za/article/2006-04-06-nkandla-our-fortunes-are-tied-to-msholozi.

Van Onselen, G., 2012a, 'The Billion Rand President: How Much Jacob Zuma Costs the Taxpayer', in Inside Politics, viewed 19 August 2017, available from: https://inside-politics.org/2012/08/20/the-billion-rand-president-how-much-jacob-zuma-costs-the-taxpayer/.

Van Onselen, G., 2012b, 'The Ten Commandments According to Jacob Zuma', in *Inside Politics*, viewed 19 August 2017, available from: https://inside-politics.org/2012/09/17/the-ten-commandments-according-to-jacob-zuma/.

Van Onselen, G., 2016, 'Jacob Zuma Actually Believes God Wants Him to Rule', in *Rand Daily Mail*, viewed 19 August 2017, available from: http://www.rdm.co.za/politics/2016/07/25/jacob-zuma-actually-believes-god-wants-him-to-rule.

Van Wyk, A., 2014, 'Nope, Nkandla's "Mermaids" Are Actually from Hollywood', in *Africa Check*, viewed 19 August 2017, available from: https://africacheck.org/reports/nope-nkandlas-mermaids-are-actually-from-hollywood/.

Van Wyk, I., 2014, *The Universal Church of the Kingdom of God (UCKG) in South Africa: A Church of Strangers*, Cambridge University Press: Cambridge.

Van Wyk, I., 2015, '"Their Message Is Not New, They Are Just Stronger": On the Phenomenal Success of a Brazilian Pentecostal Charismatic Church in South Africa', in M. Lindhardt (ed.), *Pentecostalism in Africa: Presence and Impact of Pneumatic Christianity in Postcolonial Societies*, 136–162, Brill: London.

Veblen, T., 2003 [1899], *The Theory of the Leisure Class*, Edwin Mellen Press: Lewiston.

Weber, M., 2001 [1930], *The Protestant Ethic and the Spirit of Capitalism*, Routledge: New York.

West, G., n.d., 'Forging an Ethics of Interpretation for the Re-emergence of the Bible in the South African Public Realm', in *Ujamaa*, available from: http://ujamaa.ukzn.ac.za/Libraries/Resources_for_consultation/The_ANC_the_Bible_and_economics_Gerald_West.sflb.ashx.

West, G., 2012, 'The ANC's Deployment of Religion in Nation-Building. From Thabo Mbeki, to "The RDP of the Soul", to Jacob Zuma', in M. R. Gunda & J. Kügler (eds.), *The Bible and Politics in Africa*, 115–144, University of Bamberg Press: Bamberg.

Whittles, G. & Sigauqwe, G., 2017, 'Zuma Takes Soweto to Church as he Compares the ANC to Jesus Christ', in *Mail & Guardian*, viewed 19 August 2017, available from: https://mg.co.za/article/2017-01-06-zuma-takes-soweto-to-church-as-he-compares-the-anc-to-jesus-christ.

Williams, M., 2016, 'Shameless Zuma Dumps Friends', in *The Citizen*, viewed 22 May 2017, available from: http://citizen.co.za/opinion/opnion-columns/1109885/shameless-zuma-dumps-friends/.

Zuma, J., 2009a, 'Address by ANC President Jacob Zuma at the Rhema Church Prayer Service', in ANC, viewed 19 August 2017, available from: http://www.anc.org.za/ancdocs/history/zuma/2009/jz0315.html.

Zuma, J., 2009b, 'Address by ANC President Jacob Zuma to the Easter Service of the International Pentecost Church', in ANC, viewed 19 August 2017, available from: http://www.anc.org.za/ancdocs/history/zuma/2009/jz0412.html.

NOTES

1. In 2018, the Zuma family announced the birth of his 23rd child and his engagement to a fifth wife (Cilliers 2018).
2. Whereas the state reimbursed 50 per cent of the cost of private cars under Mbeki and Mandela, it upped this to 70 per cent for Zuma (Van Onselen 2012a).

3. In March 2016, President Zuma's official salary increased to R2.7 million per year (https://africacheck.org/spot_check/spot-check-no-president-jacob-zuma-doesnt-earn-r3-2-million-per-month/)
4. See http://www.armsdeal-vpo.co.za/articles00/drowning.html, accessed 1 November 2016.
5. See http://www.iol.co.za/news/politics/presidency-remains-mum-on-claims-against-zuma-62206, accessed 1 November 2016.
6. The final report, 'Secure in comfort', was published on 19 March 2014, barely two months before the general elections.
7. The media gave Zuma's victim a pseudonym to protect her identity after his supporters publically attacked her in front of the courtroom and threatened her life.
8. After the rape trail, South Africa's most famous cartoonist, Zapiro, drew a shower on Zuma's head, attaching and detaching it as a comment on his behaviour at various stages in his political career.
9. Pallo Jordan, an ANC stalwart and liberation hero, went into self-imposed exile when he was caught out for pretending to have a PhD when he had no formal tertiary qualifications (McKaiser 2017).
10. In cases where religious officeholders served the divinity as a 'consort', however, they vicariously consumed such worldly goods on [his] behalf (Veblen 2003 [1889]: 81–82).
11. Although Zuma had not been elected as President yet, he was the ANC's only candidate and no observers expected the party to lose the election.
12. In an extremely rare public address about politics, Bishop Lekganyane asked members of the ZCC at the church's annual Easter celebrations to pray for 'the wisdom to elect leaders … who do not confuse public funds with theirs' (Moloto 2014).
13. He attended the UCKG's 2015, 2016 and 2017 Easter Friday celebrations (SABC News 2017) and spent his Easter Sundays at churches like the Twelve Apostles' Church in Christ (TACC) (The Presidency 2017).
14. See http://mybroadband.co.za/vb/showthread.php/163641-quot-zuma-being-black-jesus-quote, 23-03-2009 07:16 PM comment. Accessed 16 November 2016.
15. NPC pastors often speak in a joking manner, not to belie the truth of their sermons but as a feature of a specific Christian 'style'.
16. The Public Protector described Zuma's swimming pool as a 'questionable security renovation' after his allies insisted that it was a fire pool.
17. https://www.youtube.com/watch?v=HrCE5w6-65c. Accessed 16 November 2016.
18. See http://www.economicfreedomfighters.org/president-jacob-zuma-accused-of-witchcraft-mermaids-found-in-nkandlas-fire-pool/. Accessed 16 November 2016.

8 PRECARIOUS 'BIGNESS': A 'BIG MAN', HIS WOMEN AND HIS FUNERAL IN CAMEROON

ROGERS OROCK

On Christmas Day 2010, I phoned one of my uncles in the town of Limbe to wish him and his family a Merry Christmas. He lamented, 'We have a Black Christmas here in Limbe. Our Christmas has been spoilt this afternoon. We have a really "big die" to worry over since about an hour ago.'

'Who has died this time?' I asked in mocking exasperation, recalling our multiple conversations over the great amount of time, energy and financial commitments that Cameroonians devote to funerals.

Ignoring my invitation to banter, my uncle replied, 'Patrick Ebot,[1] a prominent son of our village, died this afternoon in Yaoundé. I'm not sure you had met him, but we're like family.'

Born in 1945, Patrick was a relatively successful mid-level elite from the Manyu Division of South-West Cameroon. Typical of many successful people in Cameroon, he was an active member of various ethnic or hometown associations that made him a notable man both in the city and among local communities back home. By the time of his demise, he was vice-president of the Manyu Elite Development Organisation, a hometown association of elites whose specific mission was to raise funds and undertake small-scale development schemes to improve the lives of kinsmen in Manyu. This role gave him significant name-recognition and visibility among many people of Manyu origin in Yaoundé and other parts of the country who held significant positions of political power in government, including ministers and members of parliament.

For much of his professional life, Patrick lived in an increasingly affluent middle-class neighbourhood of the city. His house was made up of two separate adjoining housing units in an estate purchased, refurbished and redesigned to his taste. Patrick held a PhD in Education and a host of other diplomas obtained from Nigeria and the United Kingdom. These, and his professional work experience in Nigeria, helped him to obtain employment fairly easily as a programme manager at the embassy of a major Western country's development assistance and volunteering programme. After 19 years of service, he retired in 2007 as deputy director. His comfortable financial position and security of employment allowed Patrick to try his hand at different businesses over the years, especially after his retirement. The last of his major business ventures involved the import, sale and promotion of Chinese medicine at a time when alternative lifestyles and health-seeking practices were fast becoming fashionable among the new urban elite in Cameroon's major cities. When he died, one of his most valuable assets – in addition to his houses in Yaoundé and in his native village – was a large plot of land somewhere in Yaoundé that his brothers estimated to be worth about 20 million CFA (approximately U$40 000 at that time).

Patrick's materially stable and comfortable life stood in stark contrast to his domestic or matrimonial life. He married his first wife, Jacky, the accomplished daughter of a former government minister, in the late-1980s and had two daughters. But by the late-1990s, Patrick was having a longstanding affair with a young woman in Yaoundé which resulted in the birth of a third daughter. Hearing of this, Jacky divorced him and relocated to the United States (US) with their two children. Shortly afterwards, Patrick's lover and his third daughter also moved to the United States. Following the 'flight' of these two women abroad, Patrick started another longstanding relationship with Mercy, a woman in her early forties. Although she lived and worked in Yaoundé, she was from Ebonji, a small village close to the city of Kumba. Patrick's brother, Simon, said that the family 'liked her very well' and thought of her as a 'respectable woman'. Mercy soon moved in with Patrick and convinced him to undertake various investments in her native village. Although the true extent of Patrick's investments in Mercy's village remained unclear, his family knew that she had asked her village chief to facilitate Patrick's purchase of a vast cocoa farm in Ebonji. It turned out to be a worthy investment as cocoa prices rose steadily in the 2010s. Apart from investments, Mercy also brought a young woman, Pauline, from Ebonji to live with and work for them as a maid. Shortly after her arrival and much to Mercy's chagrin, Patrick began an affair with Pauline. Understandably angry, Mercy caused a lot of trouble over the matter but eventually forgave both Patrick and Pauline over this betrayal. All three continued living together for some time, but after almost four years of domestic life with Patrick, Mercy convinced him to help her visit relatives and friends in the US. From there, she informed Patrick that she would not be returning to Cameroon.

Devastated by Mercy's betrayal, Patrick went 'public' with Pauline. To family and friends, she became his 'mistress', but upon his death, she claimed that they had contracted a marriage shortly before he died. A distant relative angrily remarked that she 'stupidly produced a piece of paper claiming it was their marriage certificate'. Embittered by these claims, Patrick's brother told me, 'Those are all fabricated stories and forged documents. The family will not be entertaining any of that. If her stories were not fabricated, why did she say all these things only now that my brother is no longer alive to support or deny any of her claims?' Thus, very soon after Patrick's demise, the complex trajectory of his domestic relationships spelled significant complications for the young Pauline.

CONSPICUOUS REGISTERS OF 'BIGNESS': WOMEN AND FUNERALS

In contemporary Cameroon, the social construction of elite status is marked by a significant degree of anxiety, especially in the case of male elites as individuals and their families seek to position themselves within the social register of 'bigness', as either 'big men' or 'big families'. Geschiere (2013: xii-xiii) has remarked that Cameroonians 'struggle to get access to new forms of consumption and enrichment' in a context where the boundaries between those who might be construed as materially really well-off and those who are not are fuzzy. As a result, '[c]onsuming is a deeply serious business in Africa' precisely because '[i]t expresses a constant struggle for affirming one's status', especially for those who are seen as 'big men' – or those who desire to project themselves as such. For such men, 'it seems all the more important to underline success with ostentatious consumption' (94).

When Thorstein Veblen first employed the concept of conspicuous consumption in the late 1800s, it was in relation to social inequalities and the demarcations between social classes in an industrial society. For him, this concept was crucial in understanding how the upper classes marked their social superiority and 'distinction' (Veblen 2007 [1899]: 12) through a combination of structural, material and ideational means. According to Veblen, the upper classes 'exploited' the lower classes' labour, and by so doing, could withdraw themselves from the drudgery of 'productive work' so as to enjoy 'conspicuous leisure' (28–29). This lifestyle was, in turn, mediated by the conspicuous consumption (and routine waste) of associated goods in the 'way of dwellings, furniture, bric-a-brac, wardrobe and meals, etc.' (47).

While the elite exploitation of the working classes remains central to contemporary capitalism, the pathways of elite accumulation are now not only more diverse but also tend to transcend territorially-bound local settings more easily and more often. While this means that we cannot apply many of Veblen's insights about elite modalities of exploitation, his most original contributions on the conspicuousness of wealth continue to be useful in reminding us that social inequality and the social meanings of wealth (recognised in cultural objects and social forms) are always contextual:

> In order to gain and to hold the esteem of men it is not sufficient merely to possess wealth or power. The wealth or power must be put in evidence, for esteem is awarded only on evidence. And not only does the evidence of wealth serve to impress one's importance on others and to keep their sense of his importance alive and alert, but it is of scarcely less use in building up and preserving one's self-complacency. (Veblen 2007: 29)

In relation to contemporary Africa, Jean-François Bayart (1993: 60–85) remarked that although thinking about social inequalities in terms of elite domination is 'singularly volatile', the case remains that the postcolonial state in Africa is highly unequal and characterised by a dichotomy between a small group of 'big men' and the majority of 'little men' (cf. Nugent 1996). Despite a communitarian emphasis on redistribution, social inequality remains largely mediated by the extent to which elites – either as individuals or families/groups – can 'impress' upon the materially deprived the signs of their personal wealth and material success. And as Geschiere (2013) has indicated, beyond such social impressions, their ostentatious forms of consumption also serve to dispel possible doubts about their status and or power.

In Cameroon, as in many West African settings, to be a 'big man' is first and foremost to display a great capacity to assemble value in disparate materials, objects, ideas and people, including women, young men, and children whose labour time can be 'exploited' without immediate compensation. 'Big men' are often 'big' in both the literal and figurative senses. If the human body has always been a metaphor of the social order within which it exists, a sign inscribed with significations of class and power, physical size matters greatly in Cameroon (see BBC Africa 2006). While a younger generation of elites increasingly sees 'slim' and 'six packs' as new standards of beauty and health, many older men and women of wealth and power still associate signs of protrusion, including curves and huge buttocks for women and a 'pot-belly' for men, with notions of value. Still within this register of the literal, the 'appetite' of big men is not limited to food. Women and sex are also important repertoires of conspicuous consumption, especially in big cities. Here, women are said to 'smell sweet' and 'ripen quickly' (Ekwensi 1963 [1954]: 23). Indeed, in these West African worlds, a woman's body is largely socially constructed as an object of male pleasure (and especially so for powerful men) and as the material sign that is itself a 'generator' of other signs that underscore the reproductive vitality of those men (cf. Levi-Strauss 1969: 496). Women are also socialised to experience 'feelings of dejection if they do not give birth to sons and [yield] to the necessity of accepting a husband's other wives and concubines' (Umeh 1981: 6).

The objectification of women as 'consumables' is not lost on Cameroonian women themselves. Longue Longue's (2011) song about the tribulations of a young woman in Douala who desires to be a wife instead of a pleasurable pastime to men was extremely popular in 2011. Bayart (1993) has shown that 'eating', as one among several metaphors of consumption, defines both the sociality and 'politics of the belly' in all its facets. And 'big men' here strive to 'eat' the best of everything that life has to offer, particularly material possessions such as cars and houses. Here, for any item worth pursuing, size and number matter greatly to enhance their distinction among their peers but also among their followers. For example, for 'big men' and their followers, having more than one woman as a sexual or domestic partner indicates wealth and power, a testament to his capacity to 'satisfy' these women emotionally and materially. 'Bigness', then, is as embodied as it is performative for those whose achievements in the areas of politics, economics or culture have elevated them to 'elites' in Cameroon.

Crucially, however, being a 'big man' and performing 'bigness' has its flipside; it comes with significant social costs (cf. Mbembe 2001). The vicissitudes associated with living 'big' are often dramatised at the death of the 'big man/woman'. There are consequences to 'big men's' 'inflated' appetites – moments when such efforts to perform social 'bigness' may fail. Funerals provide important moments of social drama associated with the burden of living and dying like a 'big man' in Cameroon, as elites pursue social distinction through various registers of conspicuous consumption, including the consumption of women.

While elite funerals are 'arena[s] for performing and validating elite status', they also 'revitalize home ties and ethnic belonging' (Lentz 2008: 7). For many Cameroonian families, funerals are opportunities for the social production of spectacles of harmony and family unity. At the death of a 'big man' (less so for 'big women') considerable energies are devoted to stage the deceased's huge, successfully 'harmonious' family 'legacy'. Funerals might thus be approached as orchestrated social dramas that work to make public shows of lives of accomplishment (for example, educational and administrative titles and other honorifics), material privilege or comfort (houses, cars, relatives arriving from distant shores, especially from Western and Asian cities), and political connections and influence (which fellow 'big men and women' are in attendance). Central to such staging is the role of a widow (possibly several) in sitting by the coffin or participating in the funeral proceedings, and that of the deceased's many (preferably adult and professionally secure) children and property. All are part of the materiality and symbolic universe that seek to mark the closing of a 'big man's' life in contemporary Cameroon. But very often these efforts to mobilise funerals as a stage for showcasing family unity and 'successful' lives of the deceased 'big man' fail. Instead, funerals are often characterised by strife and often expose the hollow claims and vulnerabilities of the deceased elites. Patrick's funeral is one such example of a failure in the staging of 'bigness'.

In themselves, funerals in Cameroon are typically and conspicuously 'wasteful' *á la* Veblen in their spending on food, drinks and other related items in an 'orgiastic' manner that Celestin Monga (1995) described as *'une mauvaise gestion de la mort'*, or the bad management of death (cf. Jindra 2011; Geschiere 2005a). But here I am not only interested in the funeral event *per se*. Rather, I also take Patrick's funeral as a starting point towards an exploration of the intimate and domestic lives of 'big men' as another, less discussed, register of conspicuous consumption. Certainly, there has been a welcome return of scholarly interest in African elites since the 1990s (see, among several others, Lentz 1994; Adebanwi 2014; Nyamnjoh & Rowlands 1998). But within this scholarship, there is hardly any discussion of their domestic and sexual lives (see Jua 2005 for a rare exception). This potentially obscures old and new figurations of domesticity in Africa given the suggestion that, contrary to the past, 'Today in Africa domesticity has less to do with the technology of household production than with ideologies of gender' (Hansen 1992: 7). Even more, such inattention to the sexual and domestic lives of elites in contemporary Africa is particularly striking considering Achille Mbembe's (2001: 110) remark that, among other things, 'the postcolony is a world of anxious virility'. Women play a particular role in the social construction of the 'bigness' of many African 'big men', and particularly, in the complex domesticities that may arise therefrom. My observations of Patrick's funeral, drawn from fieldwork among Anglophone elites in Cameroon between 2010 and 2012, emphasise this domestic and sexual register. I begin by presenting the staging of Patrick's funeral and the dramatisation of suspicions and animosities related to Patrick's complex domesticity.

PREPARING TO BURY A 'BIG MAN'

Before his death, I had seen Patrick only once, in 2007. A rather short and slightly overweight man in his sixties, he had come to Limbe to visit his older brother, Richard Ebot. Richard, a professor of biological sciences, was my uncle's boss in a medical research facility in Limbe. But his relationship with my uncle went beyond this professional context: he was my uncle's mentor and landlord.

Between Christmas and New Year's Eve 2010, Richard busied himself with plans for his brother's burial. He gave instructions and checked in with family members and friends in Yaoundé via his mobile phone. He even travelled there to assign several tasks necessary to the burial arrangements to relatives and friends. Richard also coordinated the pooling of family resources for the funeral, including huge sums of money of which he was the largest contributor. As part of these preparations, Richard had requisitioned a Toyota Hilux 4x4 Double Cab V6 truck as well as Pa Theo, one of the best drivers from their biomedical research centre. The truck would ferry the corpse and some close family members from Yaoundé to our village some ten kilometres from Mamfe, the main town in Manyu Division. This is a journey of a little over 500 kilometres that, at the time, could only be done by truck due to the bad roads. In the wet seasons, torrential rains often compelled many to bury their relatives on the way home rather than *at* home in the Manyu area (see Geschiere 2005b: 14–15). In a country where people typically insist on burying their relatives in their 'home' villages and hometowns (cf. Geschiere 2005b; Jindra 2011), such circumstances were viewed as disastrous. In addition to the truck, Richard leased a 19-seat Toyota HiAce van to ferry other members of the family and friends from Limbe to the village and back. He also had several dozen T-shirts emblazoned with Patrick's picture made in Limbe and ordered an expensive coffin from an undertaking outfit in Yaoundé.

Richard took the lead in making these arrangements because, in addition to being the eldest of their late father's children, he was also the most accomplished – if less prominent than Patrick. The two brothers had been born of different mothers: their late father married Patrick's mother after Richard's mother passed away. Patrick had two other siblings from the same mother: an older brother called Simon and a younger sister called Anne. With his five children, Simon occupied some apartments in Richard's vast compound (the same one in which my uncle was a tenant) – much to the annoyance of Richard's spouse with whom they often quarrelled. Ordinarily, in Cameroon, such families of half-siblings tend to be characterised by acrimonious relations resulting from petty jealousies and competition. It seemed that apart from the small quarrels with Richard's wife, the Ebots were markedly different in that respect.

Patrick's burial activities were scheduled to begin on 4 January 2011. Richard and his family and friends planned to leave for Yaoundé on 3 January. I arrived in Limbe on 30 December to spend New Year's Day with my uncle and his family. I hoped that this would allow me easy access to a funeral where I knew many potential key individuals such as ministers and other important political operators from the South-West Region might be in attendance. My uncle and I set off in his car early on 3 January. Richard and Simon, as well as two other young men who lived with Richard, drove in Richard's car. We arrived in Yaoundé in the evening and checked into a hotel because too many of Patrick's family members and friends, including Pauline and her relatives, were already staying in his house. At 8 the next morning, we began preparations for the removal of Patrick's mortal remains, scheduled for that afternoon. We first went to the deceased's residence to help make the final arrangements. There we found that much of the work had already been done, mainly by women. The living rooms had been draped in funeral colours, a familiar mixture of purple and white. At the centre of the larger living room, a stand covered in matching funeral drapes had been mounted, upon which the coffin would be placed for viewing by mourners and sympathisers. Many flowers and photos of the deceased had been placed around the stand. Conspicuously absent, however, was the widow or widows (in the case of polygamous marriages) who would normally be sitting on the floor next to the deceased husband's coffin. No woman was playing this role for Patrick. Although hardly anyone made direct mention of this, it was obvious that visitors and sympathisers were not sitting in the living room because there was/were no widow/s needing comfort.

As part of the preparations, many women were busy cooking different varieties of food that would be served as lunch and dinner for the multitude of mourners, friends, neighbours and dignitaries (ministers and chiefs from Manyu and other parts of Cameroon) who were expected from late morning until late at night. Mostly dressed in either black or white T-shirts adorned with Patrick's photograph, several young men were also busy setting up canopies alongside the vast esplanade shared by many houses in the estate. Richard flitted between different groups of people as he kept an eye on the preparations. His wife, I was told, stayed in Limbe to make logistical arrangements for funeral decorations, food and other catering items that would be taken with us on our next day's journey from Limbe to the village in Mamfe for the final burial.

Throughout the three or four hours we spent at the Mendong residence, I observed Pauline sitting quietly in the backyard with a little girl of three or four years old in her arms. They were, in turn, surrounded by a group of five or so older women, all sobbing intermittently, particularly any time the young Pauline began crying in gentle sobs. Seeing my interest in the sobbing women, one of the young men who helped carry plastic chairs from the backyard to the canopies out front gently said, 'That's Uncle Paddy's wife'. I also observed that while Richard came to the backyard several times and often spoke to us and the other women working there, he did not go to Pauline, his younger brother's 'widow', once, to offer any consolatory words.

A DRAMATIC 'WAKE-KEEP'

While the family had arranged to have Patrick's corpse removed from the mortuary at 3 pm, we arrived at the National Social Insurance Hospital at 1 pm to 'nudge' mortuary attendants to prepare the corpse for removal. As many other families were there for the same reason, it seemed quite chaotic, with mourners wailing, hawkers shouting, the uncontrolled movements of people back and forth into the mortuary and the incessant blaring of hearse sirens. Groups of mourners were distinguishable by their *ashuabi* (mourning uniforms).[2] I bought one of the T-shirts with Patrick's photo on it for 1 000 FCFA, although I did not wear it to the mortuary. Pauline and her family did not wear the family *ashuabi* nor did they sport the T-shirt with Patrick's photo on it. Instead, they wore plain, black, round-neck T-shirts, black long-sleeve shirts or black blouses. For most of the time at that mortuary, Pauline leaned on a wall, crying quietly and intermittently. None of Patrick's family members went to comfort her. Only a few of her own relatives, including her older brother and two women I recognised from the Mendong residence, stood by her side.

We waited for almost two and half hours before Patrick's corpse was ready to leave the hospital premises. As soon as the casket was loaded into the hearse, our group of almost 100 people headed straight for the funeral mass, scheduled to begin at 4 pm at the Catholic Church's Simbog Parish. The mass was attended by some of the most prominent political elites from the Manyu Division in particular and the South-West Region more generally. Among these were former and serving ministers, directors of different public and private corporate entities, representatives from the embassies of some Western countries and representatives from different cultural and development associations for many villages in the Manyu Division.

In Cameroon, eulogies are one of the main features of funeral masses and often continue for hours when they are about prominent people. At Patrick's mass, however, his eulogies were relatively short, lasting a little over one hour. This was largely because, embarrassingly for a presumed 'big man', none of his three grown children or 'wives' were at the funeral to deliver important testimonies about his role as a 'great' father or husband. Nonetheless, and in keeping with his status as a 'big man', a number of eulogists mentioned his largess and willingness to help those seeking assistance from him. For instance, Patrick was described by a local community chief outside Manyu Division as a 'distinguished benefactor whom we honoured with a traditional title for services rendered to our people'. A young girl, who said she was not biologically related to the Ebots, told the audience that 'God gave me a saviour to help me out and that saviour was you, Dr Patrick. You took care of me like one of your own and with this great love I was able to conquer everything.'

After the mass, we returned to the deceased's residence where the corpse was laid out for 'viewing'. The eight canopies we had set up that morning – with some 50 to 75 seats in each – were almost completely filled. Each canopy was labelled for the specific group of people occupying it. One canopy read 'dignitaries', another was reserved for 'Manyu chiefs', even the 'Simbog parishioners' had a canopy of their own. The Manyu Elements and Cultural Association (MECA) – the largest cultural organisation for people of Manyu origins – was also given a prominent place at the funeral because Patrick had been one of its most well-known intellectual leaders. MECA members sang songs and performed 'traditional' dances while great quantities and varieties of food and drink were served to the mourners.

Many of the major political figures from Manyu Division living in Yaoundé began arriving at around 9 pm. Among these were Ogork Ntui, a former minister, and Prof Peter Agbor Tabi, a serving minister working as deputy secretary-general at the presidency of the Republic at the time. Later, the family informed me that these 'big men', who were Patrick's friends, contributed towards the cost of the funeral.[3] Other prominent figures from Manyu and the South-West who could not come to the wake-keep sent cash donations. Among these was Chief Tabetando George, another major political figure who was making rival claims to political leadership of the Manyu. Tabetando, a powerful local chief of Bachuo Ntai village in Manyu Division, was also a wealthy lawyer who became a major shareholder in and then chief executive of EuroOil, an important oil exploration company in Douala. Although he did not come to the funeral in Yaoundé, he asked Richard to stop by his offices in Douala the next day on our way from Yaoundé to Limbe. Chief Tabetando gave him 150 000 CFA towards the funeral costs. Patrick's former father-in-law, a former government minister, had also donated 500 000 CFA.

Such contributions are a common feature of funerals in Cameroon and especially so for funerals of notable elite figures like Patrick. Although such donations are not typically announced, the contributors become known through rumours and gossip that pitch these elites as competitors. Undoubtedly, such donations mutualise funerary costs and are part of a broader social process within which one's 'real' wealth is measured not only in terms of the number of people who show up for the wake but also in terms of 'what kinds of people' show up. This gives concrete expression to some common aphorisms about the human condition that echo Jane Guyer's (1995) idea of 'wealth in people' and its relationship to 'wealth in things'. Cameroonians often say '*Quelqu'un est quelqu'un derriere son quelqu'un,*' which roughly translates as 'A person is a person on the back of *their* person'. This aphorism lends itself to at least a double interpretation. Firstly, it is a strong expression of the idea that personhood is the result of both the important work of human relationship-making that individuals must constantly undertake and the investment in the symbolic and material assets, titles and status distinctions that a human may have acquired or attained through their lifetime. But in another, more visceral sense, this aphorism also makes reference to the widely shared cultural assumption that relationships with people are important for their extractive value.

With particular reference to 'big men' (or women), another popular saying often used is that '*un grand n'est pas un pétit*' (a big man is incomparable to a small one). Again, this can be interpreted in at least two ways. Cameroonian elites have access to various '*réseaux*' (networks) of power and influence that allow them to resolve any social, economic or administrative obstacle that smaller men find difficult to overcome. They are expected to live large and their funerals are expected to conform to this expectation of grandeur. But '*un grand n'est pas un pétit*' is also used to mean 'big man, big trouble'. Poor and ordinary Cameroonians mobilise this saying to mock elites at times of social embarrassment.

At Patrick's wake-keep, people gossiped about the family and their reaction to his marriage to Pauline. Patrick had apparently mentioned to his family and friends that he wanted to marry Pauline in August 2010, but they strongly opposed this on the grounds that it would be highly embarrassing and unbefitting of their status as a respectable and prominent family for a highly educated and respected 'big man' to marry someone who had barely completed high school. Furthermore, Patrick's family and friends saw Pauline as 'just another gold digger'. After Patrick's announcement, Richard invited him to Limbe and presented him with a woman in her forties who was supposedly wealthy, learned, polished, and single, for Patrick to consider marrying. Patrick balked at the offer. His family maintained that Pauline's claims of marriage to their brother were bogus, or if true, that he had been tricked into a marriage barely two months before his demise so as to gain access to his property and wealth. It must be remembered that, if true, this was a marriage which Patrick contracted alone, without the support or presence of anyone from his own family.

For her part, Pauline – who looked quite intimidated by the deceased's family – and her brothers suspected their 'in-laws' of wanting to deprive them of their rightful inheritance. And so it was that throughout the wake-keep, Pauline and her family entertained their own small group of guests or mourners separately from the rest of large crowd under the designated canopies. Throughout the funeral activities, she remained largely invisible (or was deliberately made to be so), to avoid drawing attention to this rather embarrassing aspect of Patrick's domestic life. At the church service, she did not offer any testimony; neither did her tribute or one she could have written on behalf of her daughter feature in the little funeral programme booklet produced for the event. In contrast, the tributes from Patrick's two 'legitimate' daughters as well as some of their dated pictures were featured prominently in this same booklet.

At 11 pm, we began preparations for our departure to Limbe. MECA's Yaoundé branch arranged for an additional Toyota HiAce bus to ferry a delegation of 15 members to accompany Patrick's remains to his final resting place in his native village. We planned to make a stop at Richard's house in Limbe, where we would meet a second group of family and friends, including Richard's wife. The stopover was also intended to offer respite and an opportunity for a quick shower and breakfast for those exhausted by the seven- or eight-hour journey from Yaoundé to Limbe. Most people looked apprehensive at the prospect of the tedious journey ahead. But by 11.30 pm, most of the 50 or so people had taken their assigned seats and the coffin had been loaded onto the Toyota Hilux truck. The leaders of the MECA group completed some traditional rituals around the coffin to pacify the deceased and wished him 'a safe journey home'.

The main task left was to lock up every part of the house in Mendong before we left. Patrick's sister, Anne, and her brothers set about this task but noticed that the bunch of keys for the main entrance and the gate were missing. They immediately accused Pauline and her brothers of hiding the keys so that they could hand these to their 'agents to come back later and steal everything while we are in the village'. Pauline's brothers accused the Ebots of hiding the keys to make their accusations seem plausible. During this verbal exchange between the two families, many people disembarked from their cars to follow the unfolding spectacle. Visibly angry, Richard shouted, 'People are coming to fight over property when my brother is still lying there in the car, not buried. They have no knowledge how this property was acquired.'

In response, one of Pauline's brothers threatened, 'You are the rich family from Manyu with connections and the big lawyers, but we shall see.' We all stood there in the cold, unsure what would happen. Many returned to their vehicles to sleep. Meanwhile, the search for the missing keys continued.

At around 1 am, one of Pauline's younger sisters came with the keys, saying that she had found them in the backyard, in a dark corner beside the trash can. This only reinforced the Ebots' suspicion and they immediately requested that the lock be replaced before we could leave. Fortunately, two young men found a replacement lock at an all-night fuel station not too far away. A locksmith in our party quickly made the replacement. We set off from Yaoundé at 2 am under a heavy cloud of suspicion. Thankfully, the two families kept their distance during the rest of the funeral and no further incidents of the sort were reported. When we arrived at Richard's home in Limbe, I did not notice Pauline and her family there but they rejoined us when we were ready to leave for the village. We arrived in the village late on 5 January and found that a similar set of preparations had been made for a wake-keep. The grave was dug and ready for burial the next day. After a night of singing, dancing and secret rituals performed by a lodge of the *Ekpe* secret society, another short funeral service conducted by the local Catholic priest in the village was held the next morning. By 11 am on 6 January, we had buried Patrick. My uncle and I returned to the city later that evening, anxiously wondering how Patrick's complex domestic life would determine what happened next.

SEXUAL 'CONSUMPTION', MATERIAL STRUGGLES

Contrary to expectations that most educated elites in Africa secure their estates by recourse to the law, many tend to die without doing so. Patrick died without leaving a will, creating uncertainty regarding the disbursement of his estate. A few months after Patrick's funeral, I began to enquire as to the fate of both his estate and Pauline and her child. Apparently, despite claiming to be legally married to Patrick and despite her older brother's dramatic threats, no real change had occurred in terms of the control that the Ebots had begun exercising over Patrick's property from the moment he died. Pauline was either overly intimidated by the power and influence of the Ebot family or her claims to and documentation of a marriage to Patrick were indeed 'forged' and she preferred to avoid a court spectacle where she may have been found out. Either way, it seems that her fate was decided on the grounds that the child she had with Patrick at least needed to be looked after.

Following family consultations, the Ebots decided that the primary beneficiaries of their late brother's estate should be the first and 'legitimate' children he had with his estranged wife in the US, Jacky. After all, they argued, 'Most of these properties were acquired while he was married and suffering with Jacky.' Along this line of reasoning, Patrick's family allowed Pauline 'to stay in the small boys' quarters' in the big residence in Mendong but gave her no ownership rights to it nor to the main house itself. The family consented that Richard give her a 'reasonable' amount to start a small business from which she could look after herself and her little daughter while they were living in Yaoundé. As I subsequently learnt, Richard sent her additional monetary support from time to time 'for the sake of the young child'. As for Mercy – the woman who absconded to the US on the pretext of going for a holiday after she had exposed Patrick's relationship to Pauline – she returned to Cameroon a few months after Patrick's demise. Initially, Patrick's family told me that she had sought to claim the entirety of the cocoa farm that Patrick had acquired in Ebonji. After much resistance from the family and despite her attempt once again to enlist the village chief's help, she asked for at least half of the cocoa plantation. Steadfast in their resistance, Patrick's family refused. 'If at least she also had a child for our brother, that would have been a different case,' Simon told me sometime in 2012. Precisely because of this consideration, it seems, Pauline was offered full ownership rights for life of some part of this cocoa plantation. Because of the uncertainty about the extent of Patrick's property in Mercy's village, it has remained unclear to date whether she 'carved out' anything for herself from Patrick's estate by withholding this from his family.

The second woman with whom Patrick had had an affair in the late 1990s, resulting in the destruction of his marriage to Jacky, apparently made no claim to any part of Patrick's estate for her child or for herself. Neither did Jacky, the only 'real wife' that Patrick's family had known and who could 'actually claim anything because when she left she did not ask nor took anything with her despite contributing to build that estate', as Richard put it not long after the funeral. Indeed, given the potential for future conflict since Patrick's children were all young and in the US, Richard had argued during that dramatic week of the funeral that care had to be taken not to 'share his property anyhow'. This was precisely the reason why the family 'must maintain custody' of their brother's valuable assets such as the land and the houses until such a time that the children can 'sort this out for themselves in the future'.

All of the above suggests a messy funeral and post-funeral situation that the deceased's family had to manage. Geschiere (2005a: 48) observed that funerals among the Maka in the 1970s were defined by staged struggles or 'mocked fights' between *affines* (relatives by marriage). Patrick's funeral (and many like his in contemporary urban Cameroon) saw a situation in which the animosities and struggles were quite real and centered mainly around questions of access to and control over the deceased's estate. Of course, in Patrick's case, this messy situation with regard to the beneficiaries of his estate was also the direct result of his rather 'embarassing' domestic and sexual life. This was especially apparent during his funeral. But as I have also suggested, Patrick's case may be extreme and different in the important respect that he kept 'losing' his women to the appeal of that foreign country, the US.

But his case of complex domestic arrangements is hardly unrecognisable in Cameroon and in other similar West African contexts. Here, some elite men establish multiple long-standing relations with concubines that sometimes result in outright marriages even as they remain married to their first wives (going from monogamous to polygynous matrimonial domestic regimes), or they divorce the first wife to marry the well-established and 'known' concubines (serial monogamous arrangements), often producing a new set of progeny in these new relationships. As another Cameroonian scholar, Nantang Jua (2005) has shown, at their death this situation can assume a dramatic character of national proportions, depending on the stature of the 'big man' involved and the political climate of the country at the time the spectacle unfolds. In a most dramatic example, Jua recounts the tense political atmosphere in the circles of power in Yaoundé following the demise of Emah Ottou, a notable and wealthy Cameroonian political figure. Ottou had married a French wife with whom he sired three children and who came to Cameroon bearing a marriage certificate attesting to a monogamous union between her and her late husband. But Ottou had also contracted other marriages with a second as well a third and fourth wife (whose name is given as Cresence). As in the case of Patrick, whose 'fourth woman', Pauline, was his maid-turned-mistress, Ottou's fourth wife, Cresence, had also been the maid to his second wife. Importantly, Jua underlines, Ottou's 'libertinage' and the jostling for access to his significant estate of material property and financial holdings following his demise not only created a 'dispute over the ownership of his corpse' but also struggles over the large sum of money that the president of Cameroon, Paul Biya, had earmarked and made available to whatever party in the family dispute was finally victorious or adjudicated to organise the funerals for the deceased (Jua 2005: 333).

Geschiere (2013) is not particularly focused on addressing consumption as an object of anthropological concern. Rather, his remarks are situated within an anthropological discussion about the sources of the jealousies, suspicions and distrust that animate witchcraft accusations within narrow circles of domestic intimacy such as the family. Nonetheless, Geschiere's observations remind us of the contested character of desire and material property in shaping relations of kinship and friendship. In relation to this, Patrick and Ottou's cases are particularly instructive.

Cameroonian elites invest great effort in social validation through conspicuous consumption. Mbembe (2001) has argued that, amidst Cameroon's glaring inequalities, the economy of signs and symbols – ranging from money to almost anything with attribution of great value, including the textures, colouration and sizes of the bodies of men and women – are suffused with a logic of inflation. Meaning is therefore sought in the multiple processes by which people manage to attain such inflation, including the different registers and practices of conspicuous consumption. This makes sense in light of Baudrillard's (1970: 66) argument that to the extent that inequalities matter in our time, they matter not in the sense of income disparities *per se*, but in the sense of how existing social and political structures may enable or hinder access to consumption for some and not others. Geschiere's (2013) remarks on the 'seriousness' of ostentatious consumption in Cameroon and similar contexts in Africa, evoked at the beginning of this chapter, are inscribed in this line of thinking and argumentation. Particularly for elites whose currency of purchase is social distinction, great inequalities incite status insecurities and fear that others may doubt their ability to afford lavish lifestyles of consumption and therefore cease regarding them as 'big people' or '*des grands types*'. An important point to be added to Geschiere's observations above, then, is that for this ostentatious consumption to have any sociopolitical value it must be lavishly displayed *á la* Veblen. Otherwise both their less-privileged and admiring followership as well as their equally privileged competitors cannot undertake the cultural work of debating, attributing and discrediting their social value and importance through gossip, praise-singing and other similar registers.

REFERENCES

Adebanwi, W., 2014, *Yoruba Elite and Ethnic Politics in Nigeria: Obafemi Awolowo and Corporate Agency*, Cambridge University Press: Cambridge and New York.

Baudrillard, J., 1970, *La Société de Consommation*, Gallimard: Paris.

Bayart, J., 1993, *The State in Africa: The Politics of the Belly*, James Currey: London.

BBC Africa., 2006, 'Does Size Matter?', viewed 20 August 2017, available from: http://news.bbc.co.uk/2/hi/africa/4566870.stm.

Ekwensi, C., 1963 [1954], *People of the City*, Heinemann: London, Ibadan and Nairobi.

Fokwang, J., 2015, 'Fabrics of Identity: Uniforms, Gender and Associations in the Cameroon Grassfields', *Africa* 85(4): 677–96.

Geschiere, P., 2005a, 'Funerals and Belonging: Different Patterns in South Cameroon', *African Studies Review* 48(2): 45–64.

Geschiere, P., 2005b, 'Autochthony and Citizenship: New Modes in the Struggle over Belonging and Exclusion in Africa', *Quest: An African Journal of Philosophy / Revue Africaine de Philosophie* XVIII: 9–24.

Geschiere, P., 2013, *Witchcraft, Trust and Intimacy: Africa in Comparison*, University of Chicago Press: Chicago.

Guyer, J. I., 1995, 'Wealth in People, Wealth in Things: Introduction' *Journal of African History* 36: 83–90.

Hansen, K. T., 1992, 'Introduction: Domesticity in Africa', in K. T. Hansen (ed.), *African Encounters with Domesticity*, Rutgers University Press: New Brunswick.

Jindra, M., 2011, 'The Rise of "Death Celebrations" in the Cameroon Grassfields', in M. Jindra & J. Noret (eds.), *Funerals in Africa: Explorations of a Social Phenomenon*, Berghan: New York and Oxford.

Jua, N. B., 2005, 'The Mortuary Sphere, Privilege and the Politics of Belonging in Contemporary Cameroon', *Africa* 75(3): 325-355.

Lentz, C., 1994, 'Home, Death and Leadership: Discourses of an Educated Elite from Northwestern Ghana', *Social Anthropology* 2: 149–69.

Lentz, C., 2008, 'National Aspirations, Local Commitments: Elite Funerals in Northern Ghana', Paper Presented at the 10th Biannual Conference of the European Association of Social Anthropologists (EASA), Panel on 'Elite Strategies of Distinction and Mutuality', University of (Slovenia): Ljubljana, 26–29 August.

Levi-Strauss, C., 1969, *Elementary Structures of Kinship*, Beacon Press: Boston.

Longue Longue, 2011, 'Elle Cherche Un Homme,' *À bas Judas*, NBK Productions.

Mbembe, A., 2001, *On the Postcolony*, University of California Press: Berkeley.

Monga, C., 1995, 'Cercueils, Orgies et Sublimation: Le Coût d'une Mauvaise Gestion de la Mort', *Afrique 2000* 21: 63–72.

Nugent, P., 1996, *Big Men, Small Boys and Politics in Ghana: Power, Ideology and the Burden of History, 1982–1994*, Frances Pinter: London and New York.

Nyamnjoh, F. & Rowlands, M., 1998, 'Elite Associations and the Politics of Belonging in Cameroon', *Africa* 68(3): 320–337.

Umeh, M., 1981, *Women and Social Realism in Buchi Emecheta*, Unpublished PhD dissertation, University of Wisconsin–Madison.

Veblen, T., 2007 [1899], *The Theory of the Leisure Class*, Oxford University Press: Oxford and New York.

NOTES

1. All personal names used in relation to this ethnographic case are pseudonyms. Some place names have also been changed, except Yaoundé and Mamfe.
2. *Ashuabi* may consist of at least two varieties: close family members of the deceased may wear differently styled clothing sewn from a common material – usually Dutch 'wax' cloth or cheaper imitations. The word *'ashuabi'* is a deformed reference to the Yoruba description *'aso e bi'* for the same practice of uniform-making at happy celebrations such as marriages or 'born houses' as well as for sad or similarly commemorative events such as funerals or 'death celebrations' (cf. Fokwang 2015). In addition to this, more distant family members may wear simple, round-neck T-shirts emblazoned with photos of the deceased. Such T-shirts are often given or sold to friends and sympathisers at moderate prices to help support the costs for the burial.
3. For example, Prof. Peter Agbor Tabi, a major political leader of the Manyu people under the banner of the ruling Cameroon People's Democratic Movement (CPDM) party led by President Paul Biya donated 100 000 CFA in support to the bereaved family.

9 YOUNG MEN OF LEISURE? YOUTH, CONSPICUOUS CONSUMPTION AND THE PERFORMATIVITY OF DRESS IN NIGER

ADELINE MASQUELIER

'When we were young, we would spend a lot of money', Moustapha, a 20-something-year-old nursing student,[1] said to me as he watched his adversary roll the dice and move one of his chequers across the backgammon board. We were sitting at the entrance of Moustapha's family home in Lamordé, a former village on the edge of the Niger River that has since been absorbed into Niamey, Niger's capital city. The sun was slowly setting into the hazy horizon. It was time for the *mangariba* prayer (Hausa equivalent of the Arabic *maghrib*; one of the five prayers Muslims perform daily). Two young men sitting next to the players were making their ablutions, pouring water from a plastic kettle, in preparation for worship. The air around us was thick with the smoke of women's cooking fires and the dust raised by young boys running after a deflated soccer ball just up the street. Absorbed in their game, neither player gave any sign that they had heard the muezzin's call to prayer. Moustapha rolled the dice and moved his pawn swiftly across the board. Then he turned to me:

> We'd have dance parties. We'd go to nightclubs, we'd go to *la pilule*.[2] *On gaspillait beaucoup d'argent* [we wasted a lot of money]. Now we're more mature, we don't want to waste money that way. We're thinking about marriage, we want to get married, have a family, buy a house and have a nice life. We must leave behind this life of waste we used to lead.

Moustapha was alluding to his younger days, when he and his friends, all members of the Titanic *fada* (conversation group or 'tea circle'), met every evening to listen to popular music, drink tea and plan their next evening of wild fun. *Fadas*[3] unite *samari* (young men) who have grown up in the same neighborhood or attended the same school. They constitute a refuge from formal social constraints and function with their own moral codes, ethics of accumulation and expenditure, and their own pathways to self-fashioning.

At the *fada* un(der)employed young urbanites, whose daily lives are overshadowed by uncertainty, can unburden themselves away from parental pressures and, as one of them once put it, 'enjoy [their] youth while [they] can'. Aside from partaking in the daily pleasures the *fada* affords (playing cards, sharing jokes and so on), *fadantchés* (*fada* members) also pursue a quest for visibility and recognition through more costly forms of entertainment that invite controversy in this overwhelmingly Muslim country – because they often entail drinking alcohol and mingling with young women. At infamous beach picnics, neighbourhood dance parties and local bars, young men engage in social battles for prestige through which they redraw social trajectories and redefine the meaning of masculinity.

Muslim religious leaders condemn these gender-mixed gatherings as sites of decadent consumption that contravene the moral discipline, self-restraint and frugality pious Nigerien men (and women) should ideally embody. Reformist Muslim preachers – who, since the Islamic revival of the 1990s, have frowned on the pursuit of pleasure, the Westernisation of local values and ostentatious displays of wealth – are particularly critical (Masquelier 2009).[4] In their sermons, they excoriate the 'worthless' *samari* who 'sit idly' while their fathers toil, implying that idleness is a form of self-indulgence that leads to dissolution and delinquency. Parents themselves at times bemoan young men's unbridled consumerism and question how they obtain resources.

At first blush, these critiques of youthful hedonism seem to echo Thorstein Veblen's indictment of materialism among wealthy and aspirantly wealthy classes in nineteenth-century American society. In his study of American consumerism, Veblen (1994 [1899]) demonstrated that ownership was critical to developing social recognition or 'honour'. Honour here was not derived from a person's 'moral' value or productivity but was predicated on the display of accumulated wealth – what Veblen called 'conspicuous consumption'. Conspicuous consumption, that is, the public display of expensive goods (and services) not deemed essential to survival, Veblen argued, was one way through which people could demonstrate pecuniary standing. The other way was by engaging in leisurely activities that suggested exemption from work. While, for Veblen (28), conspicuous consumption was 'a waste of goods', conspicuous leisure was 'a waste of time and effort'. Together, they constituted the 'canon of conspicuous waste' (30) that guided the pursuit of honour and status among members of the so-called leisure class: 'The basis on which good repute in any highly organized industrial community ultimately rests is pecuniary strength; and the means of showing pecuniary strength, and so of gaining or retaining a good name are leisure and a conspicuous consumption of goods' (28).

Although consumption and leisure initially enabled members of the leisure class to differentiate themselves from the working class, the 'standards of worth' (72) they created through their lifestyle became a model of reputability and success for all other members of society. Thus everyone, no matter what their station, 'accept[ed] as their ideal of decency the scheme of life in vogue in the next higher stratum, and ben[t] their energies to live up to that ideal' (28). No one, 'not even the most abjectly poor' (28), escaped the temptation to consume, for all wished to emulate those above them and earn social recognition, no matter the cost. 'Pecuniary emulation', as Veblen called the tendency to imitate the spending habits of wealthier classes, created an appearance of prosperity among the middle and lower classes that was deceptive. The domestic life of most classes, Veblen noted (37), 'is relatively shabby, as compared with the *éclat* of that overt portion of their life which is carried on before the eyes of observers'.

The cost endured by individuals who feel pressured to engage in lavish displays of wealth they can ill afford is one reason Islamic reformism quickly gained a foothold in Nigerien society when it first appeared in the 1990s. For those Nigeriens who promote frugality as a sign of renewed commitment to Islam, conspicuous consumption is a form of waste because, rather than fulfilling a fundamental human need, it is motivated by 'the struggle for pecuniary reputability' (16), that is, the impulse to position oneself advantageously in the eyes of one's peers. In short, it is a way of indexing status as well as class. Further scrutiny of the wider context in which critiques of young Nigerien men's practices unfold nevertheless reveals that, if Veblen's model of class and consumption points us in the right direction, it cannot fully account for the *fada*'s significance as a site of cultural production and a vector of self-realisation. Nor does it help us understand how, as Moustapha suggests, conspicuous consumption as a 'wasteful' practice in some contexts is specifically associated with youth.

Veblen's concept of conspicuous consumption also opens the door to a critical exploration of what 'straining to excel others in pecuniary achievement' (17) might mean for those who, far from enjoying the wealth of the so-called leisure class that he studied, struggle in conditions of severe material scarcity. Young men in Niger spend money they often do not have in order to create the 'respectable appearance' (77) that signifies access to some form of capital. As a place of competitive sociality, the *fada* provides a Veblenian platform for consumerism in some of its most vivid, performative manifestations. Yet it is also a haven from the harshness of a neoliberal present where prospects for the young, no matter how educated, are grim.

As much as they want to grow up and take hold of their future, young men also paradoxically cling to their youth as a place of fun and experimentation that offers respite from the world of responsibilities. In the face of precarity, negotiating between lighthearted hedonism and weighty activities is a tactical move designed to escape the brutal vagaries of the labour market. Conspicuous consumption is a useful lens through which to explore the workings of age and intergenerational relations – issues which do not feature in Veblen's strictly class- and status-based analysis. Certain accounts of gender, and specifically masculinity, go beyond the strictures of Veblen's narrow preoccupation with female ostentation as a tool of male 'honour'.[5]

The settings for this ethnographic study are Dogondoutchi, a provincial town of some 40 000 heterogeneous Hausa speakers, and Niamey, a multi-ethnic and multilingual metropolis.

'SITTING AT THE FADA': IDLENESS, SOCIALITY AND THE LIFE COURSE

In Hausa, Niger's lingua franca, the term '*fada*' conventionally designates the *sarki*'s (chief or emir) court, a masculine place of public audience and deliberation. In the early 1990s, the concept of the *fada* as a customary form of community assembly was recuperated by young male urbanites to designate their own social gatherings.

According to some, young men's *fadas* first appeared in Niamey in 1990 when students went on strike to pressure the government to institute a multiparty democracy. Against the backdrop of growing popular discontent, they provided a forum where striking students could pass time and debate the future of the country. Like the Yemeni *qāt* chews described by Wedeen (2008), they became privileged sites for the performance of citizenship. Over time, the *fadas* spread to other urban areas where male youths struggled with unemployment, boredom and social exclusion. A competing narrative locates the birth of *fadas* in Zinder, the country's second largest city, where in recent years, many of these youth groups, locally known as *palais* (French for 'palace'), have become synonymous with gangs. In some instances, when *palais* were mobilised by local politicians seeking to consolidate their power, civic marches turned into violent protests, further contributing to *palais*' reputation as dens of thuggery (Schritt 2015).

Although some *fadantchés* have a history of vigilantism, the equation of *fadas* with gangs is misleading because it glosses over the diversity of projects young men initiate. *Fadas* often bring together young men with shared interests; yet not all *fadas* are united by the same vision of sociality and citizenship. Some are but informal conversation spots – tea circles. Most are far more structured organisations, supervised by an executive team and animated by a spirit of civic-mindedness. The names they often bear – such as Black Warriors, Money Kash, Las Vegas, Jamming Rasta, or Boss

Karate – reveal their cosmopolitan aspirations and their fondness for the gritty images of heroic masculinity produced by global popular culture. A few of them are *de facto* non-governmental organisations aiming to improve neighbourhood residents' quality of life. Others function as rotating credit associations, helping members earn a living through the purchase of a sewing machine, a motorbike, or a plane ticket to a distant city. Yet others provide informal training for developing certain professional skills. Not all *fadas* have a civic mission: some serve as nodes in drug distribution networks or meeting grounds for petty thieves. During elections, a number of *fadas* become campaign headquarters for political parties. Others are more interested in generating social capital through artistic or musical channels. In recent years, many *fadas* have become part of the security infrastructure: since young men sit in the street until late, they can be on the watch for possible criminal activity at night. As a space of sociality, the *fada* thus encompasses a diverse range of projects and pursuits. Their diversity notwithstanding, the significance of these projects and pursuits cannot be fully grasped outside the context of austerity and anomie within which the *fada*, as a crucible of introspection and a space of experimentation, emerged.

After independence in 1960, Nigeriens who sought upward mobility through education were assured of being admitted to the civil service. In the past three decades or so, however, the state was forced to adopt neoliberal policies that constrained its recruitment of educated youths. While educational credentials have not translated into stable employment, they have created aspirations that prevent youth, especially young men, from accepting jobs they view as degrading. *Fadas* are filled with idle *samari* waiting for the 'right' job – or a job *tout court* [period].[6] *Sai da dogon hannu,* unless someone with a 'long arm' intervenes on their behalf, young men say, they will not find formal employment. They are unable to transition into the world of adult responsibilities because they lack the resources to marry and provide for dependents. Those who navigate the informal economy or end up trapped in low-level white-collar jobs are not much better off; what they earn cannot adequately sustain a household. Honwana (2012) described this condition as 'waithood'. Going beyond the linear life-course model to which Honwana's waithood is indebted, I consider how waiting emerges as both an experiential condition and a tactical posture for imagining viable futures.

The *fada* is a place where idleness is transformed into 'leisure' thanks in part to the way that teatime – during which tea is prepared and consumed – punctuates the boredom of idleness and gives waiting a purposeful dimension (Masquelier 2013a). For *samari* who, in the absence of stable income, must postpone their plans of marrying and achieving the social respectability that comes with becoming a household head, the enforced immobility that accompanies joblessness is experienced as a burden and weighs heavily on them. In a neoliberal world boasting of forward momentum and global potentialities, it is, in fact, the ultimate form of displacement. Young Hausa speakers have an expression to capture the misery of an existence that has them burdened by immediate needs yet unable to plot a way out: *zaman kashin wando,* which translates literally as 'the sitting that kills the pants'. Figuratively speaking, to 'kill one's pants' is to wear them out. In the past, manual labour frayed or stained garments but in the absence of jobs, it is immobility that wears out a person's trousers.[7]

The image of idle young men who fray their pants by 'just sitting' captures the vulnerability of large segments of the younger generation whose precarious livelihoods become naturalised into a permanent disposition.[8] Unlike Veblen's (1994: 56) leisure classes who display their prosperity by wearing 'neat and spotless garments' that signal their exemption from 'productive labour', the *samari*'s 'leisure' directly contributes to their worn garments. Granted, the deterioration *samari* invoke by deprecatingly labelling themselves as *masu kashin wando* ('those who wear out their pants') is metaphorical. But their frustrated fantasies of middle class consumerism – and their anguished wait for jobs that do not materialise – are real.

DRESS, CONSUMPTION AND 'PECUNIARY STANDING'

Samari are sharply aware of the centrality of dress in social life. In urban Niger, every social event is an occasion to dress up. New outfits are must-haves for wedding and naming ceremonies, even if it means buying cloth on credit or borrowing money from money lenders. During religious and national celebrations cash-strapped men may be seen wearing crisp, new *manyan riguna,* the costly robes traditionally worn by political elites to assert their *girma,* bigness. Up to 2.5 m wide, the flowing, richly embroidered gown endows its wearer with regal bearing. Through its association with *alhazai* (pilgrims from Mecca), it connotes piety, wealth, and respectability, making it the *de rigueur* dress on Islamic holidays. Some women are known to go heavily into debt – or pressure husbands (or suitors) for cash – for the sole purpose of engaging in public displays of sartorial elegance and outshining potential rivals at social functions. Young men too borrow money from kin to purchase costly attire. They share an intense preoccupation with clothes and invest much of their resources in the acquisition of stylish outfits (see Figure 6). They take photos of themselves dressed in fancy outfits and post them on social media. The clothes, the dress performances they enable, and the photographs that are produced can be said to constitute a 'prestige economy' (Fuh 2012: 501) that is as vibrant as it is competitive.

Urban *samari* have access to a wide selection of dress styles, whether they commission outfits from local tailors, buy cast-off imports from secondhand merchants, or acquire more expensive knockoffs at fancier *boutiques* (shops). For the great majority of them, keeping up with fashion means buying clothes of foreign provenance. Foreign styles strategically bridge the gap between the world of poverty in which they live – Niger is one of the poorest countries on Earth, routinely being placed last on the United Nation scale of human development – and the world 'out there' filled with exciting, yet remote, potentialities. With the emergence of hip-hop in the mid 1990s many *samari* adopted the baggy pants, oversized T-shirts, neck chains and baseball caps of their favorite rap artists. The ghetto life peddled by African American rappers in their music videos loomed large in the imagination of *samari* who saw themselves as a disenfranchised population fighting for visibility. The black American rapper symbolised the contradictory legacy of the African diaspora as a space of both victimisation and empowerment. As such, he suited *samari*'s aspirational sensibilities. To this day, he remains a critical icon of masculine agency.

A decade or so later, *coupé décalé*, a musical culture of Ivorian provenance with proponents who favoured skin-tight pants and T-shirts, rapidly conquered the local fashion market. After watching *coupé décalé* performers on television incite their audiences to enjoy life, *samari* wanted to look like them. 'We dress like Ivorians,' a young man told me. 'It's what's cool now.' If figure-hugging clothes are all the rage among the younger generation, rap shorts (that fall below the knee) nevertheless remain a staple, together with the ubiquitous sunglasses and baseball caps associated with black American culture. Meanwhile the Rasta look (dreadlocks, Rasta caps and T-shirts bearing the colours of the Ethiopian flag) associated with reggae music and Jamaican cool remains popular among young men who identify with the message of Bob Marley and Rastafarians disseminated by radios and glossy magazines. Popular as well is the classic look favoured by urban dandies: dark pleated trousers, white dress shirt, and dress shoes (see Figure 7).

Veblen (1994:103) recognised that 'admitted expenditure for display is more obviously present, and is, perhaps, more universally practi[s]ed in the matter of dress than in any other line of consumption'. According to the logic of conspicuous waste, the wealthy purchase expensive apparel that they can display on their own personas as proof of their ability to acquire these goods in the first place. While people are naturally inclined to avoid futile expenditures, Veblen noted that fashion motivated them to set aside barely worn garments and purchase new apparel. Aside from creating desire for novelty, fashion shifted the 'canons of reputability' (Veblen 1994: 49), justifying the frequent acquisition of garments of which consumers had no need.

Samari would undoubtedly agree with Veblen that dress can be used to communicate information about social identity, ultimately helping position people hierarchically on the basis of sartorial expenditure. Dress, *samari* will tell you, can be read in the sense that it displays legible signs attesting to a person's social position. A garment's style, the choice of fabric, its design and quality, the possible presence of iconic brand logos, all participate in the evaluative process through which a person's financial resources (and sartorial competency) are measured. The deciphering may also yield facts about one's educational background, age, adherence to religious values and so on. A young man's clothes may thus signal that he is an *intellectuel* (school educated), a hip-hop artist, or a pious Muslim. They may suggest he is an urbanite, or conversely, a villager, a chief or a *talaka* (commoner). Youths are proficient in the language of fashion: they scrutinise a friend's outfit to evaluate how much money was spent and draw conclusions about his social circumstances.[9] In this respect, fresh-looking clothes, suggesting a recent purchase, may well be indicative of 'pecuniary standing' (Veblen 1994: 16).

One cannot always draw such conclusions, however: for one thing, many *samari* tend not to wear their best clothes daily so as to preserve them for as long as possible, although they will wear them to drop in on a girlfriend, attend a concert, or visit a high-ranking official. Moreover, what they wear may have been borrowed. As Veblen noted, if dress can enact social classification through the deployment of various aesthetic registers, it also has the potential to deceive, enabling people to create an illusion of wealth that conceals their less than prosperous circumstances.

CONSPICUOUS CONSUMPTION IN THE PAST AND PRESENT TENSES

Far from being a new phenomenon, conspicuous consumption, that is the public display of wealth for the purpose of earning social recognition, has a long history in the region. In precolonial times, Hausa ruling elites[10] wore voluminous robes made of imported cloth to demarcate themselves from commoners who could not afford such fineries (Nicolas 1986). Imported textiles – acquired from long-distance traders in exchange for slaves, leather, or ivory – were a luxury. By 'creating isolating, protective spatial envelopes for leaders' (Worden 2010: 219), codes of dress and regalia conceptually separated them from the world, thereby reinforcing social hierarchies. Paradoxically, they also enhanced rulers' visibility. By conspicuously parading in their finery, religious and political elites asserted their superior status.

Today, ordinary Nigeriens find much to criticise in local elites' lavish display of wealth. As they struggle amidst soaring food and fuel prices, the extravagant (and much publicised) lifestyle of the rich is a bitter reminder that the gap between the haves and the have nots is widening. However, it is not the display of wealth per se that is considered problematic. Ostentation is already inscribed in material culture as a critical mode of singularisation: in the past, some individuals engaged in extravagant displays during which vast amounts of wealth (grain, objects and so on) were given away in competitive rivalry for prestige (Nicolas 1986). Far from being considered wasteful, the potlatch-like performances these individuals staged were seen as creating value through the social recognition or 'fame' (Munn 1986) they received.

As is the case elsewhere in West Africa, cloth remains one of the main 'bodily signifiers of wealth' (Barber 1995: 214). As soon as imported textiles became more affordable, commoners sought to emulate rulers by adopting their dress. The spread of Islam, which associated Muslim identity with expansive robes, facilitated the process. In Islam, wealth is a sign of God's blessing. By accomplishing the pilgrimage to Mecca, wealthy Muslim Nigeriens demonstrate not only their piety but also their good fortune. As such, they are models to be emulated. In the way they embody simultaneously religious commitment and material success, they signal the extent to which wealth and virtue are intertwined. Granted, prosperous individuals are occasionally accused of witchcraft (on the basis that their riches were acquired through nefarious means). Nevertheless it is widely accepted that, as a friend put it, 'you owe your success to God'.

Lest conspicuous expenditure be seen as a male prerogative, I should note that women too engage in extravagant displays of wealth. Nowhere is this more vividly demonstrated than in the *kan kaya* ('carrying the things'), during which wedding gifts are ceremoniously brought to the Hausa bride's marital home. Mothers invest considerable time, labour and resources to acquire the household goods that will fill their married daughters' rooms. The joyful procession of ululating women bearing cloth, furniture and cooking implements conveys an image of 'head-borne wealth' that is critical to the social recognition women earn as brides (Cooper 1997:94; Masquelier 2009). Though they are regularly targeted by moral campaigns aimed at ridding Nigerien society of 'gluttonous' traditions, most women ignore these calls for frugality and restraint. For the conspicuous parade of *kayan daki* ('things of the room') is what establishes a mother's worth and, with it, her capacity to produce wealth for her daughter. The *kan kaya* must therefore dazzle onlookers with the sheer quantity of stuff exhibited. If competitive displays of wealth have long participated in local processes of self-realisation, many Nigeriens nevertheless agree that today this has reached new heights, forcing many to spend resources they do not possess.

As it should be clear by now, conspicuous consumption is not restricted to youth. Given how they disproportionately spend their money on flashy items and entertainment, the young urbanites whose lives revolve around the *fada* could, in fact, be called typical conspicuous consumers. To be sure, they spend excessively compared to their rural counterparts and other urban *samari* who must contribute to the parental household. Yet, they do not see these expenditures as being merely indulgent: their ultimate aim is often to impress young women and secure their affection. Growing up means marrying. It also means becoming thrifty. 'I have stopped buying nice clothes. I no longer buy jeans, just regular pants,' a recently married man told me. 'Who am I going to impress?'

GENERATION, 'FUN,' AND THE FASHIONING OF YOUTH

Household heads are – in theory at least – responsible for providing clothing for their dependents. Typically, male youths receive money from their parents – or an older sibling – to update their wardrobe, especially if they attend school and do not draw a regular income. During adolescence, young men are nevertheless expected to demonstrate increasing self-reliance by finding ways to pay for their own clothes, especially if they come from a large family. Many of them take odd jobs, earning the cash required to buy items – expensive shoes, a fancy sports jacket – their parents are unable or unwilling to pay for. It is not unheard of for a young man to spend weeks hauling goods for a merchant so he can buy the Adidas high tops or the Sebago dress shoes he covets. In fact, this is a typical way of claiming youthfulness. 'I buy lots of clothes for myself. That's what youth do,' is how a young man put it, implying that once he married, his purchasing pattern would likely shift.

For *samari* who cannot rely on the support of kin, keeping up with fashion is costly. Among other things, not being able to dress fashionably may diminish their romantic prospects. A young man confided to me the torments he endured when the girl he loved rejected his overtures because he could not compete sartorially with his peers. Though many parents sympathise with their sons' struggles and approve of their *fada*-centered initiatives, others suspect that *samari* engage in illicit activities to win the affection of young women.[11] A Qur'anic teacher told me the pressure to appear fashionable may lead young men 'to do improper things'. From his perspective, the *fadas* amounted to the 'devil's workshop' where temptations abounded: rather than enabling young men to follow the straight path, they were hotbeds of crime and corruption.[12]

Fadas are occasionally vilified for supposedly promoting a culture of idleness and self-indulgence that stands in contradiction with conventional ideals of masculinity based on work, financial autonomy, and self-determination (Masquelier 2013a). Young men, critics argue, spend their waking hours engaging in unproductive forms of gratification while others labour. Just as worrisome, they are fixated on fashion. For *fada* critics, these forms of sociality also impose burdensome social and sartorial requirements on participants. In a society where social recognition is contingent on conspicuous expenditure and dress practice is a 'potent form of wealth' (Bastian 2013:15), such criticism seems out of place. It nevertheless signals how some elders perceive young men's sartorial practices as self-indulgent, wasteful.

Given the country's unemployment rate among the young, *samari* resent the social control elders exert over them through their tight grip on leadership positions. Such intergenerational tensions are a typical manifestation of how processes of social reproduction establish structural opposition between young people and an older generation.

Within the tangle of power relations in which they are embedded, youths enjoy certain rights, such as the right to be provided for by elders. In return they are expected to demonstrate deference and obedience to the older generation. Given how youth defines itself in opposition to elders, it is no wonder young people feel prompted to assert their superiority over 'deadwood', challenge established hierarchies and spend their money as they see fit.

Young men often invoke their junior status to offer justification for their pastimes and pursuits. '*Nous sommes des petits* [we are juniors],' they counter in the face of insinuations that they are squandering resources on flashy consumer goods or getting so absorbed in card games that they do not hear the call to prayer. *Samaris*' actions, these claims imply, are removed from consequentiality and fatefulness. If mistakes are made, there will be time in the future to repair them. Young men's lack of piety, for instance, is not as consequential as that of grown men. Once they marry, they will make up for lost time by praying five times a day. Since a married man's prayer is worth more than a bachelor's, they will earn numerous blessings – enough to gain entry into paradise. By deferring to their youth, *samari* also suggest they are not ready to make the commitment that social adulthood requires. Such commitment hinges on both a steady income and the moral agency required to serve as a role model for the next generation.

Whether they play soccer, attend a hip-hop concert, or simply enjoy a round of fragrant water pipe with friends, young men bracket their activities from the world of adults. They also remind us that, however restrictive juniority may be, it is also a means of asserting certain privileges. *Samari* claim youth for the freedom it provides to experiment with a range of identities before settling into mature social roles. Tied as it is to both processes of self-fashioning and the aspirational logic of global consumer culture, dress provides an especially vivid illustration of this process of experimentation. A number of *fadas* commission special uniforms (the styles vary from mass-produced basketball jerseys with the number of their favorite player to locally tailored, multicolored outfits) through which to demarcate membership and accumulate prestige. They hold dance competitions during which members perform as a unit against other rival *fadas*. While mastering a set of choreographed moves is critical to the performance, so is the 'look' of the dancers.

Using dress to assert one's youth often means transgressing imposed regimes of bodily discipline (Masquelier 2013b). In Niger, young men's fashions often mix playfulness with provocation. Rather than wear the locally tailored, long-sleeved tunic and drawstring pants worn by a number of adult men, many *samari* opt for the controversial dress style known as *checkdown*; a pair of very low-riding pants that require its wearers to move cautiously and deliberately so as to prevent the garment from slipping further down their hips while they sit, walk, or stand. Far from projecting the aura of respectability associated with the voluminous, embroidered gowns of Muslim men, *checkdown* unsettles the normative codes of dress and demeanour.

OBAMA'S SANDALS

By suggesting that their pastimes are not part of *la vie sérieuse*, young men highlight the (im)provisational nature of their endeavours while carving spaces of enjoyment beyond the control of their parents and Muslim religious authorities. Consider the case of Sani,[13] who once bought a pair of sandals simply because the name Obama was written on them. Lacking stable employment, the young man occasionally worked odd jobs, such as hauling fruit, for one of his uncles. That day, he had gone to market with some recently earned cash, planning to buy a goat for his mother. He had returned home with the 'Obama' sandals instead.

In the wake of Obama's accession to the White House there was much hope in Africa that a black American president would alter the fate of poor countries like Niger. Many youths and children sported Obama T-shirts that spoke of their aspirations to inhabit the same hopeful world as Obama. Similar motivations no doubt drove Sani to buy the Obama sandals. What interests me is the spontaneous, affective dimension of Sani's purchase. 'When I listen to Obama, I shake. It's the emotion. I'm happy. His voice does something to me,' Sani told me when I asked him about the sandals. He had been overwhelmed, he implied, and unable to resist the temptation of owning something with Obama's name on it, despite the fact that he had limited cash to spare. 'It was silly, I know. But every time I look at them, I'm happy,' he concluded.

Sani's gesture exemplifies the joyful, occasionally extravagant, spending associated with *samari* who signify their immaturity – that is, their avoidance of responsibility – through loud sartorial statements. The sandals were overpriced, but Sani did not think twice before handing his money to the merchant. He lived under his parents' roof and had no dependents; he could therefore afford to indulge. In the way it casts aside planning and parsimony, Sani's stance is emblematic of the way that youths 'claim youthfulness' (Bayat 2010: 30) through their exuberant participation in consumer culture. It differs radically from the kind of wastefulness Veblen had in mind when he criticised the practices of fashion-minded elites. Note that young men's appropriation of Western consumer goods remains ambivalent, mediated as it is by their sense of exclusion from the world of opportunities. *Samari* often speak of the shoddy quality of the goods they purchase, implying that they see 'the dynamism and force of the global world … lie elsewhere' (Weiss 2009: 127). As much as they were a positive reminder's of Sani's connection to the United States president, the Obama sandals also confirmed his marginalisation from the global order of values he fantasised about.

WASTE AS WORK

In Niger, young men who, through consumption, distance themselves from what they define disparagingly as 'tradition' are referred to admiringly as *branchés* (plugged in). They are attuned to emerging fads and display this awareness through the way they dress, speak and carry themselves. The *fadas* they belong to often become a primary forum for the cultivation of their *branchés* reputation. Some *fadas* are known for their excessive 'style' through their membership's entanglement with particular aesthetic subcultures (hip-hop, rasta and so on), their blind embrace of cosmopolitanism, their sense of entitlement and arrogance. Most *fadas*, however, have a disparate membership that cuts across social and educational divides. How their members experiment with new subjectivities through dress, language and so on varies significantly. Being *branché*, in such settings, is more often than not an act of stylish individuation.

Like the *bluffeurs* of Abidjan (see Newell 2012), who spend without restraint on costly foreign brand-name clothes, cell phones and nightlife entertainment to impress their peers (and girlfriends), *samari's* reputation as *branchés* hinges not on financial stability so much as on the 'display of potential' (Newell 2012: 1). As Sasha Newell argued, in the world of *bluffeurs*, looking fashionable is not a sign of success. It is success itself, produced through 'the magical efficacy of clothing' (Newell 2012: 165), a power that Ivorians associate with foreign things, including brand-name clothing. In the face of a chronically depressed labour market, the *branché*'s strategy is to spend all his money on a few expensive consumer items, such as new Adidas sneakers or a fancy watch, to suggest that he has resources when he is penniless.

Faroteur (show off) is another word for those who spend extravagantly to impress others. It is a derogatory term, associated with the excesses of *coupé décalé* (scam and scram), the Ivorian musical culture that has brought conspicuous consumption to a heightened level (Kohlhagen 2006; Masquelier n.d.). In the nightclubs of Abidjan *coupeurs décaleurs* (performers of *coupé décalé*) forged short-lived networks of patronage by showering DJs with cash and buying champagne for everyone. They drew attention to themselves by spreading cash around and bringing joy to their audiences. In this context, to waste (*gaspiller*) was to work (*travailler*). Decked out in the latest fashion, some young men in Niamey show up at bars and perform *farotage*. Drawing on the performative power of clothing, they engage in silent 'dress duels' with similarly elegantly attired rivals in the hope of gaining 'fame' (Munn 1986), however short-lived. In these competitions for prestige, those present witness the spectacular use to which dress is put. While *farotage* usually denotes (resented) excessive indulgence because it is simply 'too much', the *faroteur* is also an object of admiration. To win hearts, a young man may buy drinks for everyone even if that means spending his last franc. By conjuring, if only momentarily, the grand lifestyle he would enjoy if he had a steady source of income, he turns an illusionary performance of wealth into tangible evidence of success.

Like the Ivorian *bluffeur* who confounds the distinction between illusion and authenticity through his masterful display of brand-name products, the Nigerien *faroteur* is an expert at managing impressions. The clothes he wears are calculated to create an appearance of wealth and success regardless of whether he has actually achieved prosperity. He is a master of *la dépense* (spending) in the sense that the consumption in which he engages is characterised by passion and excess.[14] Yet, far from having no end beyond itself – as Bataille (2011 [1933]) would have it – the ostentatious consumption in which the *faroteur* engages generates rewards.

THE LIMITATIONS OF VEBLEN'S MODEL

Focusing on what is produced rather than what is 'wasted', in this chapter I have traced some of the ways in which young men in Niger respond to disaffection and *désoeuvrement* (idleness) through the idiom of consumption. In contexts of chronic un(der)employment and increasingly volatile economic circumstances, the quest for recognition has generated an obsession with fashion; it has given rise to – formal and informal – competitions for prestige during which material wealth (or its appearance) is converted into forms of social capital.

Initially, Veblen's notion of conspicuous consumption appears to resonate with the practices that contribute to the prestige economy centered around young men's *fadas*. After all, these practices are motivated by a quest for visibility and recognition that is itself rooted in longstanding traditions of competitive display of wealth. Similar to the process of pecuniary emulation described by Veblen, they often speak of *samari*'s aspirant rather than actual prosperity. Nevertheless, the Veblenian model is so focused on class distinction and emulation that it ignores the dynamics of generation. As such, it fails to elucidate why, in replacing predictable forms of social mobility, some new self-directed means of achieving adulthood are measured in terms of access to commodities rather than productive labour. Focusing on conspicuous consumption should not imply ignoring the powerful economic constraints that shape youthful practice. By giving pride of place to emulation, Veblen's model ignores the role of resistance. According to Veblen, it was because the lower classes appropriated their style that elites in turn abandoned it and adopted a new trend. Youth fashions, the practice of *checkdown* suggests, do not follow this logic. The trickle-down model renders invisible the intergenerational modes of resistance that often shape young men's practices of self-fashioning. As such it cannot account for the way that style is used by *samari* to differentiate themselves from – rather than imitate – elders at the same time that elders urge youngsters to imitate them. In sum, it cannot encompass generational tensions and the process of social reproduction.

Hampered by a Protestant outlook that equates excess with dissipation, Veblen's model of consumption does not easily accommodate *samari*'s self-indulgent consumerism. Nor can it make room for the role of affect in these practices. A more encompassing perspective, attuned to the role of pleasure in consumption, would help us understand how, for instance, Sani's emotional state – that can perhaps be described as a mixture of optimism, excitement and adventurousness – resulted in the impulse purchase of a pair of sandals with Obama's name on it. It would also clarify how the delight Sani experienced as the proud owner of a pair of Obama sandals differs from the 'honour' (that is, the sense of one's distinctiveness) whose pursuit, Veblen argues, constituted one of the primary motivations for conspicuous consumption in nineteenth-century American society.

It is tempting to assume that young men who splurge on clothes are mistaken about their priorities or to reduce the hedonistic pursuits of *faroteurs* to a form of escapism, a mere distraction from real-life struggles.[15] I want to suggest instead that *samari*'s relentless focus on presentist pleasures must be understood as a part of the 'tactical' apparatus young men deploy in the face of an ever more receding horizon. So tenuous is their grasp on processes of temporal unfolding that some young men postpone the transition to adulthood to capitalise instead on the potentialities of youth. As they see it, making long-term plans is simply not feasible in the face of such a precarious outlook. Given how readiness to assume the disciplined constraints of adult life is measured in economic terms, claiming to be a youth and cultivating dependency upon elders is, for some young men, a more viable option than asserting social maturity. Out of the *branché* tactics youth thus emerges as a product of marginalisation as much as a mode of participation – a way of navigating the structures of possibility and impossibility that have arisen in contexts of economic restructuring.

REFERENCES

Barber, K., 1995, 'Money, Self-Realization, and the Person in Yorùbá Texts', in J. I. Guyer (ed.), *Money Matters: Instability, Values and Social Payments in the Modern History of West African Communities*, 205-224. Heinemann: Portsmouth.

Bastian, M. L., 2013, 'Dressing for Success: The Politically Performative Quality of an Igbo Woman's Attire', in K. T. Hansen & D. S. Madison (eds.), *African Dress: Fashion, Agency, Performance*, 15-29. Bloomsbury: New York.

Bataille, G., 2011 [1933], *La notion de dépense*. Éditions Lignes: Le Kremlin Bicêtre, France.

Bayat, A., 2010, 'Muslim Youth and the Claim of Youthfulness', in L. Herrera & A. Bayat (eds.), *Being Young and Muslim: New Cultural Politics in the Global South and North*, 27-47. Oxford University Press: New York.

Cole, J. & Durham, D., 2007, 'Introduction: Age, Regeneration, and the Intimate Politics of Globalization', in J. Cole & D. Durham (eds.), *Generations and Globalization: Youth, Age and Family in the New World Economy*, 1-28. Indiana University Press: Bloomington.

Cooper, B., 1997, *Marriage in Maradi: Gender and Culture in a Hausa Society in Niger, 1900-1989*. Heinemann: Portsmouth.

Fuh, D., 2012, 'The Prestige Economy: Veteran Clubs and Youngmen's Competition in Bamenda, Cameroon', *Urban Forum* 23: 501-526.

Honwana, A., 2012, *The Time of Youth: Work, Social Change and Politics in Africa*. Lynne Rienner: Boulder.

Kohlhagen, D., 2006, 'Frime, escroquerie et cosmopolitisme: Le succès du "Coupé-Décalé" en Afrique et ailleurs', *Politique Africaine* 100: 92-105.

Masquelier, A., 2009, *Women and Islamic Revival in a West African Town*. Indiana University Press: Bloomington.

Masquelier, A., 2013a, 'Teatime: Boredom and the Temporalities of Young Men in Niger', *Africa* 83(3): 470-91.

Masquelier, A., 2013b, 'Forging Connections, Performing Distinctions: Youth, Dress and Consumption in Niger', in K. T. Hansen & D. S. Madison (eds.), *African Dress: Fashion, Agency, Performance*, 138-152. Bloomsbury: New York.

Masquelier, A., 2019, *Fada: Boredom and Belonging in Niger*. University of Chicago Press: Chicago.

Munn, N. D., 1986, *The Fame of Gawa*. Cambridge University Press: Cambridge.

Newell, S., 2012, *The Modernity Bluff: Crime, Consumption and Citizenship*. University of Chicago Press: Chicago.

Nicolas, G., 1986, *Don rituel et échange marchand dans une société sahélienne*. Institut d'Ethnologie: Paris.

Schritt, J., 2015, 'The "Protests Against Charlie Hebdo" in Niger: A Background Analysis', *Africa Spectrum* 1: 49-64.

Smith, A., 1759, *The Theory of Moral Sentiments*. London: Andrew Millar and Edinburgh: Alexander Kincaid and J. Bell.

Sommers, M., 2010, Urban youth in Africa, *Environment & Urbanization* 22(2): 317-332.

Veblen, T., 1994 [1899], *The Theory of the Leisure Class*. Dover Thrift Editions: Mineola.

Wedeen, L., 2008, *Peripheral Visions: Publics, Power and Performance in Yemen*. University of Chicago Press: Chicago.

Weiss, B., 2009, *Street Dreams and Hip Hop Barbershops: Global Fantasy in Urban Tanzania*. Indiana University Press: Bloomington.

Worden, S., 2010, 'Clothing and Identity: How Can Museum Collections of Hausa Textiles Contribute to Understanding the Notion of Hausa Identity?', in A. Haour & B. Rossi (eds.), *Being and Becoming Hausa: Interdisciplinary Perspectives*, 213-234. Brill: Leiden.

NOTES

1. Moustapha is not the young man's real name. I have adopted pseudonyms throughout to protect the anonymity of my interlocutors.
2. *La pilule* (birth control pill) is a sheltered beach on the Niger River favoured by youths. The name is a veiled reference to the sexual activity that supposedly takes place there.
3. The plural of the Hausa term *fada* is *fadodi* but it is often frenchified in the media as *fadas*. To highlight the cosmopolitanism of these forms of sociality, I use the French plural form.
4. The emergence of the Jama'at Izalat al-Bid'a wa Iqamat ai-Sunna (the Society for the Removal of Innovation and Reinstatement of the Sunna) in Niger translated into widespread efforts to tackle the perceived corruption of Sufi orders and purify society from a host of 'sinful' practices, including excessive public consumption. Originating from Nigeria, the reformist movement was embraced by large numbers of Nigeriens, among them young men, wary of the costs of getting married.
5. For Veblen, it is by consuming conspicuously that the wives of rich men provide tangible proof of their husbands' wealth in a social hierarchy of invidious distinctions.
6. Not all *fadantchés* are underemployed or jobless. Some attend school. Others work full time.
7. *Masu kashin wando* (those who wear out their pants) are male. *Wando* (pants) are traditionally marked as male garments. Moreover, young women do not loiter on the street. Their mobility is constrained by social norms and they have burdensome domestic responsibilities and, therefore, less leisure time.
8. The distinction conventionally made between employment and unemployment does not capture the range of income earning activities *samari* perform. Some of these activities take place in improvised spaces, such as the street, and are difficult to measure (Sommers 2010).
9. Many youths can estimate at a glance the price of the garments another youth is wearing.
10. The Hausa are the largest ethno-linguistic group of Niger.

11 In Niger, affect is intertwined with materiality in complicated ways in romance and marriage. A young man hoping to cultivate a young woman's affection must shower her with gifts, thereby demonstrating that he has the ability to provide for her once they wed.
12 In the eyes of some parents, young men's lack of occupation leads to violence, alcoholism and drug addiction.
13 Not his real name. I have adopted pseudonyms throughout to protect the anonymity of my interlocutors.
14 In the conventional model of utilitarian ethics adopted since Adam Smith's publication of *The Theory of Moral Sentiments* (1759), the concept of economy is ruled by the conservative principles of production and acquisition, thrift and accumulation. Turning this restrictive model of economy on its head, Georges Bataille (2011 [1933]) defined the need for waste or *la dépense* (expenditure) as an end in itself, of which utility was a secondary derivation. Rather than obeying rules of economic constancy, this form of expenditure privileges immoderation and extravagance.
15 I have heard young men who spent much of what they earned on clothing being accused by elders of delaying maturation so they can continue to 'play'.

10 BOOTY ON FIRE: LOOKING AT *IZIKHOTHANE* WITH THORSTEIN VEBLEN

JABULANI G MNISI

Thorstein Veblen's (2003 [1899]) critique of the nineteenth-century American leisure class makes it apparent that their costly, wasteful and showy expenditure was, while somewhat distasteful, in keeping with class expectations of normal behaviour. While he did not focus on the so-called lower classes, he asserted that they did not stand outside the matrix of 'honour' mediated by conspicuous consumption. Although their consumption was constrained by more meagre incomes, they emulated the higher classes as they too vied for status (Veblen 2003: 58). The poor were marginal to Veblen's original thesis, as was a form of consumption that was virtually unknown in Veblen's time, namely the spectacular total destruction of expensive commodities by poor people in front of an assembled audience. The South African township youth subculture of *ukukhothana* (literally, 'to lick', figuratively in this context, 'to boast') involves groups of youths from disadvantaged socio-economic backgrounds theatrically destroying expensive consumer items in competitive dance-offs. The destructive conspicuous consumption of *izikhothane* (participants in *ukukhothana*) represents a fascinating case study of people who consume well beyond what they can comfortably afford, a possibility that Veblen did not explore.

BACKGROUND TO THE SUBCULTURE OF *UKUKHOTHANA*

Elements of *ukukhothana* have historical precedents in Europe and South Africa. During the Industrial Revolution, working class men who mimicked the dress of aristocrats were called dandies, a disparaging term for 'pseudo-aristocrats' (Botz-Bornstein 1995). As Corrigall (2015) argued, dandyism went beyond transgressing class boundaries: it was a political act that questioned the conventions that governed society. South Africa met its dandy in the mid-1880s in Kimberly with the rise of the so-called 'diamond field dandies' (Magubane 2004). Like their counterparts in Europe, the diamond field dandies sought to challenge social conventions, and especially the racially inscribed identities and stereotypes that were central to South African society at the time (Corrigall 2015). Mine work allowed black men 'to buy certain markers of distinction' (Magubane 2004) that until then were reserved for whites.

Seventy years later, a different kind of dandy emerged in Johannesburg. First visible in Jeppestown during the 1950s, *oswenka* (from the word 'swank'[1]) were predominantly Zulu-speaking, working-class South African men who migrated to Johannesburg from the rural areas of KwaZulu-Natal. Living in harsh hostel conditions, these men would dress up in expensive tailored suits and colourful, European-made two-toned brogues to compete in bi-monthly amateur fashion shows. At these shows, *oswenka* competed to be crowned the finest dresser and put a lot of stock in the outcome of competitions (Fleminger 2007).

Fifty years later, *izikhothane* first appeared in townships on the East Rand of Gauteng and gained popularity in Katlehong. The trend quickly spread to other South African townships but it was only in 2011 and 2012 that *ukukhothana* gained widespread media attention.[2] In Johannesburg's townships, *izikhothane* are generally referred to as 'those boys who destroy what they cannot afford to destroy'. *Izikhothane* are mainly black adolescent youths from working-class township backgrounds who engage in competitive, destructive conspicuous consumption 'battles' (Nkosi 2011; Mkhwanazi 2011; Jones 2013; Howell and Vincent 2014). At planned, and sometimes spontaneous, *izikhothane* gatherings, loud house music is played from minibus taxis and many spectators are drawn to the performance. The male *s'khothanes* dance flamboyantly while showing off expensive designer clothing brands (some of which still have their price tags attached), such as Nike, as well as Italian brands such as DMD, Carvela, Casa di Arbiter (also known as Arbita) and Rossimoda. DMD is known for its brightly coloured floral T-shirts and tight-fitting trousers that cost in the region of R600[3] and R700 respectively. To contextualise this: T-shirts and 'skinny' trousers at cheaper chain stores in South Africa cost between R80 and R150. The *s'khothanes'* Rossimoda shoes cost upwards of R2 600 while Arbita shoes could set someone back R2 800 a pair (see Figure 8). A *s'khothane*'s complete outfit averages about R4 500, often much more. While styles could differ quite considerably between *s'kothanes*, the one constant is that their clothes are usually brightly coloured. As one young *s'khothane* called Max[4] explained, 'you see, *boi*,[5] our clothes must be bright in colour and grab people's attention and show that they are expensive. Without even asking, a person should be able to see money.' Occasionally, *izikhothane* combine expensive attire with cheaper, unbranded clothes, especially on days when they do not perform.

Izikhothane normally organise themselves into crews that vary in number, but usually have a maximum of about 20 members. Group members get together to discuss the look that they want to go for, often honing in on a particular fashion trend. This requires quite a bit of research on the part of *izikhothane* who take photos of people on the streets of Johannesburg whose dress sense they admire and who do a lot of window-shopping in order to see what is trending and to get an idea of prices. It is important that the whole group has the same look, a fact that requires quite a lot of coordination. This group identity is then further developed in their dance routines and choice of music.

At *ukukhothana* performances, participants occasionally tear or burn bank notes as well as their own and their rivals' clothes. They also wash their hands with luxury alcohol and douse expensive food with it after throwing the food on the ground. Common types and brands of alcohol included in these performances include whiskeys, like Jameson, and cognacs, like Bisquit and Hennessy, as well as imported beers and ciders (see Figure 9). As these young men often like to say, 'We drink beer that's only in green bottles not the brown bottles', an oblique reference to the fact that most beers in brown bottles are produced locally and retail for less than the imported green-bottle beers. Unlike most working-class township people who drink Castle Lager, Hansa Pilsner and Carling Black label, *izikhothane* buy Heineken, Amstel Lager and Windhoek. They also buy popular fast foods normally associated with affluent people in the township, such as Kentucky Fried Chicken (KFC), Debonairs pizza and Panarottis pizza – franchises that in recent years have infiltrated the township market.

It is important for these young men to attract a female audience base, and rival groups compete to impress the most attractive spectators. Emboldened *s'khothanes* often try to court those women who catch their eye during the performance. The women on the sidelines of the performance are often seen as coveted ornaments that add to the performer's credibility as a man worthy of the 'salute'. As the young men often remark of their comrades, '*lo mjita ublind and unstwembu*' (literally: this is a blind man and a fool), which is Zulu slang to indicate that a person is worthy of respect, the same kind of respect they crave from the audience.

Izikhothane performances happen against a backdrop of poverty. Their expensive outfits often cost more than some of their working-class parents' monthly incomes. Most *izikhothane* come from homes that have single parents working as domestic cleaners, factory workers, retail assistants and the like.[6] They often live in shacks, Reconstruction and Development Programme (RDP) houses, or rented backyard rooms. While some *izikhothane* live with both parents, others are from child-headed families or have precarious living arrangements with relatives. Against this backdrop, people commonly ask how *izikhothane* fund their lifestyle. In some instances, they receive money from their parents, uncles, and other relatives who may or may not know about their engagement in this subculture. In other instances, they earn money through small informal businesses, such as car washing and selling snacks and drinks. While there are rumours that *izikhothane* rob people and businesses, I am not aware of a case where the *izikhothane* I studied engaged in criminal activities to fund their participation in *ukukhothana*. Instead, they often insisted, '*Itariyane liyaspina ngedlela e grand*' (literally: 'an Italian man must hustle to be grand' – that is, you must be willing to work hard to become reputable). Their money-making and saving was, however, not 'victimless'. A number of *izikhothane* reported that they concealed money at home and did not contribute as much as they should have to the common purse in order to take part in the performances.

Given their low socio-economic status, it is important to consider *izikhothanes*' saving and sacrificing activities. Individuals that make up a crew tended to save money over a long period of time before a performance. Interestingly, very few of them had bank accounts and most saved at home, stashing their cash in secret places where others could not get at it. Normally hidden in saving jars, this proximity to their savings, as many of them assured me, offered many temptations and required a lot of discipline to persist. Some young men also saved by buying their clothes on lay-by, a practice whereby local businesses allow customers to pay off an item over a set period and only 'release' the item once it has been fully paid off. The risk with lay-bys though was that one needed to pay them off within three months or lose both the money and the coveted item of clothing.

It is also important to note that not all *izikhothane* events were accompanied by destruction. The crews were very strategic about the timing of 'burn events' as it took time to accumulate sufficiently large amounts of valuables to make for a spectacle. Burning a few items too soon or items with relatively low value could diminish the success of an event and the reputation of the crews involved. Once they accumulated the right outfits and created a sufficient amount of anticipation from their followers, they organised big events in public spaces that were widely marketed. For the most part, *izikhothane* crews preferred to hold their big events at places like Witbank Dam (for those who live near the East Rand), Dries Niemandt Park near Tembisa, Fountains Valley in Pretoria and other public parks. Recently, they also started having events at local community halls. Increasingly, these events are incorporated into the entertainment section of other community or public events. For instance, in 2016, The Good Fellas participated in the Miss Masakhane beauty pageant, and in October 2107, they performed at the Miss Tembisa beauty pageant. Apart from these local events, *izikhothane* have featured in commercials and as part of large music festivals. *Izikhothane* choose dates that allow their fellow schoolmates and peers to attend in large numbers. While some crew members might be older, this is largely a subculture for people of school-going age.

More mundanely, *izikhothane* have spontaneous gatherings on Friday afternoons just after school. They form big circles on popular road intersections and start dancing and insulting other crew members (so-called 'trash talking'). Occasionally, a T-shirt might be torn, but the main activity is the competitive dancing and insults. When a rival runs out of words to 'trash' his opponent, when his clothes are deemed inferior, when he no longer has alcohol to spill, when he refuses to burn or tear his clothes, and when women audiences 'go crazy' for the other participant, he knows he has lost. The prize for a victory is the short-lived honour of having outdone an opponent, at least until the next meeting. As these gatherings attract more and more people, taxis with loud sound systems stop to play music for the dancers. The crowds soon disrupt the flow of traffic, with many impatient and annoyed motorists trying to inch through the crowds, which part reluctantly.

CONSPICUOUS CONSUMPTION

Veblen wrote *The Theory of the Leisure Class* (1899) at a time of mass industrialisation and social inequality in America. Focusing largely on the leisure class, he asserted that their consumption of goods was seldom, if ever, motivated by utilitarian concerns. Rather, in the competition for honour and social distinction, men consumed expensive goods (and participated in visible leisure habits) to signal their wealth. In this system, the possession of property functioned as a basis of popular esteem, which then became a requisite of self-respect or honour (Veblen 2003: 31). But '[i]n order to gain and to hold the esteem of men,' Veblen asserted, 'it is not sufficient merely to possess wealth or power. The wealth or power must be put in evidence, for esteem is awarded only on evidence' (131). He found much of this evidence in the lavish parties of the leisure class, which allowed friends and competitors to witness the host's wealth, underscoring his pecuniary strength. Veblen (75) likened these costly entertainments to potlatches. A potlatch was an economic system of competitive hosting and gift giving among the indigenous people of the Pacific Northwest Coast of Canada and the United States, as famously described by Franz Boas (1888; cf. Benedict 1934; Harris 1974). During a potlatch, the hosting chief and his people demonstrated his wealth (and honour) by showering guests with gifts, lavish entertainment and by burning expensive consumer items. Anthropologists have also recorded cases where hosting chiefs burnt their own homes during the potlatch (Benedict 1934; Harris 1974). Guests at these potlatches had to reciprocate in a similar manner at a future date lest they lose honour (Benedict 1934; Harris 1974).

Such 'waste', according to Veblen, was central to the ways in which the leisure class demonstrated its wealth. Their choice of food, costly clothes, property, banquets, alcohol and cigars went far beyond utility – the 'waste' was primarily honorific (Veblen 2003: 108). Like the potlatch and the lavish entertainments of the nineteenth-century American leisure class, *ukukhothana* is a spectacle of wasteful consumption geared to impress audiences. However, unlike those spectacles of yore, it is funded by young men who are relatively marginal in terms of social status and wealth.

Veblen's model did not address the possibility of poor people destroying or 'wasting' luxury goods to gain honour. However, he did state that while the competition for distinction through conspicuous consumption was particularly acute among the leisure class, it permeated all levels of society. Men from all walks of life commonly emulated consumption styles and patterns that would distinguish them from people of the same social class. In looking at the 'lower classes', Veblen (2003: 78) pointed out that ambitious men would emulate those of a higher social class by wearing cheaper versions of elegant clothes. While these copies did not evince the workmanship of the originals, they were distinctly unsuitable for manual labour, an important requirement to gain pecuniary honour. In discussing the consumption patterns of ambitious 'lower class' men, Veblen allowed for emulation but not for the possibility that these men would consume the same expensive items as the leisure class – or that these expenses would exhaust all their wealth. Indeed, he makes the point that for those poor people in nineteenth-century America 'for whom acquisition and emulation is possible' it was only so 'within the field of productive efficiency and thrift' and that 'the struggle for pecuniary reputability will in some measure work out in an increase of diligence and parsimony' (18). However, he later suggests that conspicuous consumption claimed a significant portion of urban dwellers' income because the desire to impress transient observers in these areas was much stronger than it was in rural areas (87).

Despite these qualifications, Veblen's model of emulation has been criticised for its reductionism and for overlooking the complex ways in which people imitate and adapt various consumer goods within different cultural contexts (Sassatelli 2007). Critics have also pointed out that his model of emulation does not allow for the poor to invent their own fashions (Sassatelli 2007: 68). Contemporary understandings of consumption hold that identification and imitation take place alongside more creative and selective procedures of reproduction (Sassatelli 2007: 69; see also Bourdieu 1984).

THE CRITICS

In *The Theory of the Leisure Class,* Veblen (2003: 18) was scathing about the frivolous and wasteful expenditure of the rich but praised the parsimony of the lower classes. Similarly, most people in Johannesburg's townships do not participate in *ukukhothana* and are, like Veblen, disdainful of this 'wasteful' and 'unnecessary' practice. The difference between Veblen's disdain and that expressed in the townships is that the disapproval of *ukukhothana* centres on their being 'matter out of place' (Stanhope cited in Douglas & Isherwood 1979); as poor young men, they behave unlike others of a similar class who carefully husband their money – or if indebted, do not flaunt their consumption. Indeed, *izikhothane's* consumption has tended to demonstrate identities removed from their 'real' economic circumstances. As children of working-class parents, the general expectation was that they behave as their parents did by buying modest clothes and constraining their expenditures to fit their meagre means (Burger, Louw, De Oliveira-Pegado and Van der Berg 2015; Melber 2017). Participants also tended to expect that their parents would always disapprove of the 'waste' involved in their performances. In fact though, a number of parents financially assisted their sons in this lifestyle as an expression of love, although they were not supportive of the destructive aspect of the subculture (Hamilton & Catterall 2006).

Such expressions of filial affection are not explored in the media's treatment of *ukukhothana*. Often the subject of investigative journalism programmes, *izikhothane* have frequently been depicted as irrational, selfish and driven by the obsession to have their proverbial 15 minutes of fame – at whatever cost. In a section of the hard-hitting *3rd Degree* television programme, Debora Patta focused on *ukukhothana* and commented that it was 'bling gone obscenely mad' (Mnisi 2015). Her comments on the subculture were in keeping with a wider trend in the media to focus only on the negative aspects of *ukukhothana*. In general, the most common media narrative is that this is a superficial youth culture in which naïve young men destroy expensive consumer items to attract fleeting attention (TVSA 2012; BBC 2016). Many of these narratives are manufactured to create outrage at the supposed moral corruption that sees impressionable young men destroy what their needy audiences could productively have consumed. Not surprisingly, media footage of *izikhothane* is always sensationally filmed against footage of the grinding poverty of the people and settings in which they perform. Apart from investigative programming, *izikhotane* have also featured as uncouth braggarts in television advertisements[7] and local soap operas.

THE GOOD FELLAS

The Good Fellas[8] is an all-male *izikhothane* crew from Phumulong in Tembisa, Johannesburg. Initially named Thembisa, Tembisa is the second largest township in Gauteng after Soweto. It was founded in 1957 when the National Party government started to implement its separate development or apartheid policy in the suburbs of Edenvale and Kempton Park. Black people forcefully relocated from these suburbs were resettled on a piece of land on the northern outskirts of the city. In an act of apparent hopefulness, the newly homeless called the place Thembisa, which means 'promise' (South African Historical Archives 2016). Like other South African townships, Tembisa was marked by black suffering under apartheid, a legacy that is still visible in the high unemployment, poverty and modest and informal housing that characterise much of Tembisa today.

Phumulong is a recently developed section of the township with newly constructed RDP-type houses. There are 18 members in the Good Fellas crew ranging from 18 to 21 years old (see Figure 10). All of them are still in high school but enjoy quite a bit of fame because of their successful performances at various events and beauty pageants. The Good Fellas are known for their brightly coloured outfits and their penchant for Italian fashion. They often show off their Rossimoda shoes and are known for the liveliness of their events (see Figure 8).

Lury (1996) suggests that consumption patterns should be read as communication messages with consequence and social meaning (cf. Douglas & Isherwood 1979: 11; McCracken 1990). So how do did the Good Fellas view *ukukhothana* and what is it that they were communicating?

The Good Fellas referred to their expensive purchases in the same way as warriors or plunderers would refer to booty: these items were symbolic of their 'victory' and bestowed honour and respect because they evidenced successful contestation through aggression. Their 'white man's liquor' (Edwards 1988; Blignaut & Sithole 2014), expensive clothes, girls and choice food all represented booty. In an interview with a member of the Good Fellas, he noted:

> Being a *s'khothane* is a competition – you see we have to let our clothes do the talking. They must tell people that we have money so they can respect us. We know that in reality we don't have money, boss, we are just guys who hustle in order to be respected as real men ... but during our performance we are wealthy full stop!

In this 'competition', the achievement of having clothes that 'spoke' for their owner was hard won. Indeed, for many *izikhothane,* their clothes represented an achievement, particularly when one considers the sacrifice that went into acquiring them. According to Veli, an outspoken member of the Good Fellas, 'we know what is trending and then *itariyane kwamele lispine* [an Italian man must hustle to be grand] in order to have enough money for the clothes'. Hard work and an ability to hustle, however, was often not enough. Many *izikhothane* had to make persistent sacrifices in daily life and forego basics that their peers took for granted. Mpho[9], for instance, explained that his sacrifice involved not eating during break time at school so that he could save his lunch money for clothes. 'And on top of that, I also sell the Strikers biscuits in order to supplement my saved lunch money', he said.

Merely having expensive clothes was not enough. As the Good Fellas stated, anyone could acquire expensive clothes through sacrifice. It took courage to publicly burn those same clothes. As Men-E noted, 'we try not to burn or tear clothes, man, because they are very expensive but when it gets really tough you would strategically destroy something because that would be the final step in getting people to notice you and see that you are *there*'. This is why it was so important for crews to impress with their dance routines and to hone their skills at trashing – the better these skills were, and the more they impressed with their presence, with being *there*, the less the chances were that they would have to burn their expensive clothes. But this was a careful balancing act; if the boasts were too fulsome, they invited 'testing'. In public contests, the only real way to test their rivals' boasts was to tear or burn their clothes. Indeed, this often happened when a rival competitor carried his extra clothes in a backpack; a powerful symbolic signal of excess. In these cases, the backpack was often seized and burnt. To win esteem, the 'victim' had to keep calm when this happened because if he quarrelled about his possessions, he would immediately lose the contest – and face – in front of his peers. Vegga, a proud Good Fella, expanded on this when he said:

> During the mock battle, man, you must be ready for anything. For example, a guy can just be dancing then come to you and tear your T-shirt from the neck down and you can't fight him because doing that means you can't really afford to be a *s'khothane* – you are simply claiming *nje* (just) you are not a real man.

The same manly wastefulness marked The Good Fellas' consumption of alcohol. They did not just drink expensive spirits but incorporated this liquor into their performances, spraying it on their clothes and washing their hands with it. According to one crew member, they did this to say, 'I have more and can afford to waste'.

But beyond its honorific utility, alcohol played an important social role in *ukukhothana*. The Good Fellas enjoyed alcohol as something that 'men do'. Interestingly, when it came to consuming expensive spirits, Maxwell stated that these 'are the bottles, the real alcohol that real men who are wealthy and worthy of respect drink'. Extending the prestige of expensive whiskeys, Snamzo mentioned that you could not expect people to respect you if you, like other commoners, drank alcohol like *Is'kali*[10] or *intankunyisa;* home brewed alcohol normally sold to old people in *shebeens*. Essentially, the Good Fellas' consumption of expensive alcohol was economically aspirational; a stylised act that involved the impersonation of an ideal masculinity associated with wealth and success.

On another level, alcohol also played an important role in creating bonds between friends in the group (cf. Friedman 1994; Dittmar 2008; Harnett, Thom, Herring

& Kelly 2000; De Visser, Wheeler, Abraham & Smith 2013). The Good Fellas associated drinking with being happy, with coming together and 'being free to do as you please without fearing anything'. Members of the Good Fellas frequently stated that alcohol allowed them to socialise freely and to prove their loyalty and friendship by taking care of friends who were drunk. Their shared intoxication also allowed for the sharing of stories about the previous night when everyone was hungover. Apart from large quantities of alcohol, the Good Fellas also liked smoking a hookah pipe. They insisted that it made them 'cool'. Ever aware of trends in the city's swanky nightclubs, they pointed out that all the fancy lounge bars had hookah pipes. The hookah gave them a 'head rush' at a much cheaper price than alcohol and, in lean times, hid their lack of cash. Women thought them sophisticated and worldly for smoking the hookah rather than cheap roll-ups (hand rolled cigarettes) or *los draws* (single cigarettes bought at local *spaza* shops).

HONORIFIC FAILURE?

While the Good Fellas insisted that *ukukhothana* performances, and especially the spectacular burning events, gained them 'respect' as rich men or men of a higher status, they were aware that many outsiders saw them as 'wasteful boys who buy things that they cannot afford'. In this respect, their performances, unlike those of the leisure class, could be said to fail in conveying the intended message. Mthingo complained about this:

> Yoh! The problem is that people have an uninformed perception about *izikhothane*, especially when they see us do what we do. They say we are claiming and [that we are] fake people and *siya fosta* [literally, we are forcing a version of ourselves that we are not], [they] even suggest that we should rather do useful things with the money we waste. But there is more to us, man – we are not bad guys! I mean, as the name of our group implies, we are the Good Fellas!

Mpho added: 'Among *izikhothane* you will surely be saluted but people who are not *izikhothane* will only comment that these kids are burning clothes and this and that. If you really want to be famous among *izikhothane,* you must burn clothes and then you will be a legend.'

The Good Fellas did not seem to be deterred by negative perceptions of their behaviour. As Maxwell said, 'I don't care about people who criticises [sic] me because I know what I'm doing and where I'm going'. Like his fellow Good Fellas, he saw being a *s'khothane* as a fleeting phase of his youth, a period of enjoyment before he went on to fulfil his life goals. These goals were very similar to those of his peers at school: to get a well-paying job, to buy a house in a more upmarket area, to marry, have kids and to have a good quality of life. As Snamzo summed up these aspirations:

> I'm currently in Grade 11. Next year I'll be finishing school and after that university follows immediately. I want to go to UJ [University of Johannesburg]. I'm not sure about what I want to study but one thing for sure I want to get a good office job and a wear a tie to work.

But these were goals for a distant future and being *izikhothane* was imagined as a care-free hiatus between childhood and responsible adulthood.

Of particular importance to the Good Fellas was that their competitions put them in a position where their impoverished backgrounds were concealed. As many a young man in the group remarked, it was the visibility of poverty laid bare that was painful. Again, the ability to hide their real circumstances was tied to ideas of a masculinity untouched by poverty. As Veli remarked, 'Your challenges as a man should not be laid bare for all to see. You need to push your stuff.' But this was not always possible because most *izikhothane* did not have enough expensive clothes to 'push' and had to resort to wearing less expensive items on non-performance days. On an ordinary day, the Good Fellas would hang out at the local taxi rank, chatting to one another wearing old clothes, patched T-shirts and caps. In this guise, it was evident that they came from underprivileged backgrounds – but for the lone branded items that punctuated their outfits. It was in these ordinary contexts, when *izikhothane's* brash assertions were threadbare, that older people felt empathy for them.

Veblen (2003) thought the 'leisure class' particularly guilty of wasteful conspicuous consumption because, in their pursuit of honour, they put their 'wealth in evidence' through spectacular parties and expensive clothes. While showing off to their peers, the leisure class' excessive consumption also served to underline clear class differences, distancing them from the lower classes' productive labour and parsimony. People lower down the socio-economic scale emulated leisure-class styles, but Veblen (2003) noted that their consumption was largely derivative and constrained by their limited means.

Neither Veblen nor social commentators in South Africa could have foreseen the rise of *ukukhothana*. Although the diamond field dandies and *oswenka* offer historical examples of poor black men who spent inordinate amounts of money on clothes (and in the latter case, competed for sartorial honours), commentators have been puzzled by *ukukhothana's* destructive wastefulness – for seemingly dysfunctional and vain ends. Read from a Veblenian perspective, one could also see their performances as failed attempts to gain honour, especially since the young men fooled no one into thinking that they were, contrary to general knowledge, rich or an aspirant leisure class. In this chapter, I have tried to dispel some of the perceptions that frame *ukukhothana* in solely negative light by looking at the ways in which *izikhothane* viewed their competitions and gave meaning to their conspicuous consumption. I argued that while *izikhothane* wanted to escape their poverty, they did not see the *ukukhothana* lifestyle as a (deluded) way out of poverty. Instead, while wildly aspirant, most *izikhothane* saw their participation in this youth culture as a fun part of their youth and as a way to generate social status among their peers. Behind the scenes, crews such as the Good Fellas worked hard to buy their expensive clothes and made a lot of sacrifices to allow them to participate in this lifestyle. The rewards included popularity and respect (honour) for being stylish 'hustlers', especially when their hard-earned booty caught fire. Unlike Veblen's lower class imitators, these young men were deeply creative in the ways that they assembled outfits and mixed branded clothes with cheaper ones. Their consumption also pointed, unlike Veblen's individualists, to groups of young men who used their conspicuous consumption to create a group identity and cohesion. There is thus much more to the *izikhothane's* performances than simply a misplaced hankering after 'honour' or fame.

REFERENCES

BBC, 2016, 'The Female Wrestlers of Bolivia', in BBC, viewed 11 September 2017, available from: http://www.bbc.com/culture/story/20160321-the-female-wrestlers-of-bolivia.

Benedict, R., 1934, *Patterns of Culture*, The Riverside Press: Boston and New York.

Blignaut, C. & Sithole, S., 2014, '*The Twisted Tale of Alcohol and Apartheid*', in News24, viewed 22 April 2016, available from: http://www.news24.com/Archives/City-Press/Twisted-tale-of-alcohol-and-apartheid-20150429.

Boas, F., 1888, 'The Indians of British Columbia', *Popular Science Monthly* 32: 631.

Botz-Bornstein, T., 1995, 'Rule-Following in Dandyism: "Style" as an Overcoming of "Rule" and "Structure"', *Modern Humanities Research Association* 90(2): 285–295.

Bourdieu, P., 1984, *Homo Academicus*, Minuit: Paris.

Burger, R., Louw, M., De Oliveira-Pegado, B. B. & Van der Berg, S., 2015, 'Understanding Consumption Patterns of the Established and Emerging South African Black Middle Class', *Development Southern Africa* 32(1): 41–56.

Corrigall, M., 2015, 'Sartorial Excess in Mary Sibande's "Sophie"', *Critical Arts* 29(2): 146–164.

De Wisser, R. O. & Smith, J. A., 2006, 'Alcohol Consumption and Masculine Identity Among Young Men', *Psychology and Health* 22(4): 595–614.

De Visser, R. O., Wheeler, Z., Abraham, C. & Smith, J. A., 2013, '"Drinking Is Our Modern Way of Bonding": Young People's Beliefs About Interventions to Encourage Moderate Drinking', *Psychology and Health* 28(12): 1460–1480.

Dittmar, H., 2008, *Consumer Culture, Identity and Well-Being: The Search for the 'Good Life' and the 'Body Perfect'*, Psychology Press: Hove.

Douglas, M. & Isherwood, B., 1979, *The World of Goods*, Allen Lane: London.

Edwards, I., 1988, 'Shebeen Queens: Illicit Liquor and the Social Structure of Drinking Dens in Cato Manor', *Agenda* 3: 75-97.

Fleminger, D., 2007, 'Swanky Swenkas: Dressing Sharp Regardless of Cost', viewed 23 March 2012, available from: http://www.vice.com/read/swank-b14n5.

Friedman, J., 1994, *Consumption and Identity*, Harwood Academic Publishers: Chur.

Hamilton, K. & Catteral, M., 2006, 'Consuming Love in Poor Families: Children's Influence on Consumption Decisions', *Journal of Marketing Management* 22(9-10): 1031–1052.

Harnett, R., Thom, B., Herring, R. & Kelly, M., 2000, 'Alcohol in Transition: Towards a Model of Young Men's Drinking Styles', *Journal of Youth Studies* 3: 61–77.

Harris, M., 1974, *Cows, Pigs, Wars and Witches: The Riddles of Culture*, Random House: New York.

Hebdige, D., 1979, *Subculture: The Meaning of Style*, Routledge: London.

Howell, S. & Vincent, L., 2014, '"Licking the snake": The i'khothane and contemporary township youth identities in South Africa', *South African Review of Sociology* 45(2): 60–77.

Jones, M., 2013, 'Conspicuous Destruction, Aspiration and Motion in the South African Township', *Safundi* 14(2): 209–224.

Kimmel, M. S., (ed.), 1987, *Changing Men: New Directions in Research on Men and Masculinity*, Sage: London.

Kimmel, A. J. & Issier-Desborde, E., 2000, 'Masculinity and Consumption: A Qualitative Investigation of French and American Men', in C. Otnes (ed.), *GCB – Gender and Consumer Behavior 5*, 1–18, Association for Consumer Research: Urbana.

Lury, C., 1996, *Consumer Culture*, Rutgers University Press: New Jersey.

Magubane, Z., 2004, *Bringing the Empire Home: Race, Class and Gender in Britain and Colonial South Africa*, University of Chicago Press: Chicago.

McCracken, G., 1990, *Culture and Consumption*, Indiana University Press: Bloomington.

Melber, H., 2017, *The Rise of Africa's Middle Class: Myths, Realities and Critical Engagements*, Wits University Press: Johannesburg.

Mkhwanazi, P., 2011, *Conspicuous Consumption and Black Youth in Emerging Markets*, Master's degree dissertation, University of Pretoria: Pretoria.

Mnisi, J., 2015, 'Burning to Consume? *Izikhothane* in Daveyton as Aspirational Consumers', *Communication* 42(3): 340–353.

Nkosi, L., 2011, '*Izikhothane* Burn Swag Burn Mahala', in *Mahala*, viewed 3 March 2012, available from: http://www.mahala.co.za.

South African History Archive, 2016, *Tembisa Community Oral History and Photographic Project (2010–2011)*, viewed 19 January 2019, available from: http://www.saha.org.za/projects/tembisa_oral_history_photography_project.htm.

Sassatelli, R., 2007, *Consumer Culture: History, Theory and Politics*, Sage Publications: London.

South African Reserve Bank., n.d., 'Reserve Bank Act', viewed 13 September 2017, available from: https://www.resbank.co.za/BanknotesandCoin/Upgrade1Banknotes/Documents/SA%20Reserve%20Bank%20Act%2090%20of%201989.pdf.

TVSA., 2012, 'Jaw Dropped by Izikhothane – Reloaded', in TVSA, viewed 11 September 2017, available from: https://www.tvsa.co.za/user/blogs/viewblogpost.aspx?blogpostid=29743.

Veblen, T., 2003 [1899], *The Theory of the Leisure Class*, Edwin Mellen Press: Lewiston.

Wehmeier, S., McIntosh, C., Turnbull, J. & Ashby, M. (eds.), 2007, *Oxford Advanced Learner's Dictionary: International Student's Edition*, Oxford University Press: New York.

NOTES

1   See Wehmeier, McIntosh, Turnbull & Ashby (2007: 1492).
2   https://en.wikipedia.org/wiki/Izikhothane
3   At the time of writing this article.
4   Not his real name. I have adopted pseudonyms throughout to protect the anonymity of my interlocutors.
5   While this term is used in the LGBT community, township youth use it to refer to someone who has asked a stupid question, probably borrowed from American popular culture. See https://www.urbandictionary.com/define.php?term=boi

6   There are some *izikhothane* that come from families that are relatively well off, but these are very few.
7   The most famous of these advertisements was a 2012 Nandos advert, part of its '25 reasons we love South Africa' campaign that featured two rival crews whose competition eventually sees one crew burning a taxi seat before the other drives a whole taxi towards the flames, when the tagline comes on: 'Reason #15: We still tell stories around the fire' (See https://www.youtube.com/watch?v=KVIiVrhf_Jg).
8   I chose to interview this crew and attend their performances over eight months because they appeared to be one of the largest and most famous groups in Tembisa. They were also easily accessible and were happy to talk about their lifestyles.
9   Mpho is not his real name. I have adopted pseudonyms throughout to protect the anonymity of my interlocutors.
10 *Is'kali* is home brewed beer. The name is derived from the word 'scale', which refers to how the beer is measured when poured into tumblers or jugs. In some areas it is called *intakunyisa* [literally, 'make them shit'], as it is known that those who drink it are likely to do so until they are so drunk that they soil themselves.

11 CONSPICUOUS QUEER CONSUMPTION: EMULATION AND HONOUR IN THE PINK MAP

BRADLEY RINK

The cover of the inaugural 1999 edition of the *Pink Map: The Gay Guide to Cape Town* featured an image of a colourful peacock – a flamboyant creature itself – made more extraordinary by the addition of a dazzling pink triangle crest on top of its head. The *Map*, as well as the ostentatious image itself, was not the start of queer leisure consumption in Cape Town, but certainly served as a sign of the emergence of a more tangible queer[1] pleasure periphery in the city as South Africa transitioned from decades of apartheid rule. While queer individuals and communities in Cape Town began to emerge slowly into mainstream society, they also became more conspicuous consumers and as tourists, the definitive leisure class (Veblen 2008 [1899]), emulated a global standard of queer identity and consumption amongst the numerous others exercising their freedom to consume (Posel 2010). As the city of Cape Town began to realise the potential impacts of the lesbian, gay, bisexual and transgender (LGBT) oriented tourist industry on the local economy, the city's tourism authority began to market Cape Town actively as a gay-friendly destination. This active and identity-based place promotion materialised in the form of the *Pink Map*, an annual publication that, since 1999, has attempted to map the city's queer leisure spaces for LGBT visitors, while also serving as material evidence of the shaping of queer destination space (Rink 2013).

My analysis of 14 editions (from 1999 to 2012) of the *Pink Map*, using Thorstein Veblen's (2008) theory of conspicuous consumption as a lens marks the emergence of the queer consumer at the dawn of queer liberation in South Africa through the emulation of an idealised subjectivity based on standard tropes within a global LGBT identity. More than simply mapping the 'pink' tourist experience, the *Pink Map* also serves as an archive of changes in consumption amongst those that Oswin (2006), following Altman (1997), terms the 'global gay'. In Oswin's analysis, this diffusion of a globalised (and male-centric) queer identity from the West to the non-West is problematic for a number of reasons – not least for its failure to recognise the diversity and lack of buying power across a range of queer individuals. Patterns of conspicuous consumption are linked to changes in the politics of queer identity – in particular a shift in consumption at a time when same-sex rights were legally recognised, gaining broader social acceptance. At that critical juncture of citizenship and consumption, the queer consumer gained honour and acceptance within what Murray (1995) calls the 'ambient heterosexual'. The movement from sexual citizenship to consumer citizenship is evidenced through modes of consumption and the resulting emulation and pursuit of honour. The archive provided by the *Map* thus demonstrates how consumption starts with desiring and loving the bodies of fellow sexual dissidents and then charts new pathways to freedom in the form of purchasing, displaying and performing objects of desire.

QUEER CONSUMPTION: OUT OF THE CLOSET THROUGH THE PINK MAP

The *Pink Map* was first produced in 1999 as an outgrowth of publisher Philip Todres' special-interest maps including the *Arts & Crafts Map*, the *Antique Map*, the *Food Map*, *Victoria Falls Map*, *B&B Map*, *Rainy Day Map*, *Sports & Leisure Map*, and the *Museum Map* for Johannesburg. The time had come, said Todres, for the *Pink Map* to emerge from 'under the counter' in the form of a design-oriented, respectable and queer-oriented publication (Todres 2008, personal comments). The growth of a visible and vibrant queer leisure scene in Cape Town had coincided with popular annual events such as the Mother City Queer Project's (MCQP) costume party, as well as the development and concentration of gay-owned and focused businesses in Cape Town's De Waterkant enclave (Rink 2016). The combination of such high-profile events with growing social acceptance of queer individuals (Tucker 2009), and the city's desire to be seen as a gay-friendly tourist destination (Visser 2003b), meant that it was time for the *Pink Map* to 'come out of the closet' in a similar metaphorical journey of self-discovery experienced by many queer individuals. While the *Pink Map* may not be solely responsible for metaphorically bringing queer Cape Town out of the closet, it at least offered broader visibility to the existence of queer spaces within the city. It promised to open the borderlands of queer Cape Town to a willing audience, while differentiating homosexual space which excluded heterosexual space, presumably in order to ensure a pleasant stay by filtering out the queer landscape from the rest (Elder 2004).

The map implicitly assumes for its reader that all space is heterosexualised space unless otherwise indicated.

Published every year since 1999, the *Pink Map* has remained a free publication that relies on revenue from advertisers and service providers listed within the map. The prominence of advertising, and the use of the map as a tool for the tourism industry and tourists alike, means that the *Pink Map* implicitly posits consumption as its central purpose. It is distributed through Cape Town Tourism information kiosks, hotels, guesthouses, clubs and other venues that are listed within its covers. More than simply a commercial venture, however, the *Map* also provides relevant information to queer communities that it is intended to serve. This includes information such as the gay, lesbian and bisexual helplines, HIV and AIDS support groups, and gay-friendly places of worship. While it maps queerness in Cape Town, Todres does not see it as an exclusively gay or lesbian publication. In fact, as the arbiter of content, he bristles at the discourse of exclusivity. As he says:

> One of the things that we had concerns about were establishments that claimed to be 'exclusively gay' and I thought that was a very derogatory thing to have on our maps. I still insist that 'exclusively gay' is something that we would not like to have … it's as bad as saying 'exclusively white' or 'exclusively whatever'. Constitutionally it just doesn't sit well with me. (Todres 2008, personal comments)

Todres and his *Pink Map* have sought, however, to make queer Cape Town visible and mainstream for a broader audience while framing queer spaces as welcoming to outsiders. The tension of normalising queerness whilst also setting it apart – by mapping it differentially as 'pink' – is something that will change over time and that will itself be evidenced by changing modes of consumption. The utility of the *Pink Map* is informed by questions of mobility, consumption and the notion of the global gay.

MOBILITY, CONSUMPTION AND CITIZENSHIP: A FRAMEWORK FOR ANALYSIS

The *Pink Map* has become a document of queer mobility: in respect of consumer-based status, as well as more broadly. Mobility, according to Cresswell (2006), includes freedom, progress, the physical movement of bodies as they experience displacement over space and time. As a central defining feature of social life, mobility also serves as a lens through which we may understand the movement of humans, non-human animals, objects, capital and information (Hannam, Sheller & Urry 2006). Thus mobility includes the upward social mobility brought on by the de jure status of queer members of society, as well as the corporeal mobility of tourists more generally and a global queer elite specifically that can be traced in the contours of the *Map* over time.

The social and physical mobility evidenced through the *Map* is partly a product of the struggle South African other LGBT individuals endured to seek legal equity and social acceptance. Historically, laws that governed South African cities had a history of enacting spatial barriers to performing sexuality in the city. Apartheid laws brought with them not only forced removals, pass laws and segregation, but also a strict disciplining of same-sex desire in both public and private space (Elder 1995). However, as Elder (1995) notes, the inconsistent response from the State to issues of homosexuality along lines of race was an example of how apartheid-era political leaders struggled to conceptualise more fluid and flexible expressions of sexuality in the multi-racial South African context. Thus South Africans have long defied the dictates of the State to express their sexual identity and same-sex desire (Gevisser 1994). In a similar vein, Leap (2002) demonstrates how South African men of all races were able to subvert state control and enact their same-sex desire in public spaces which were intended as heterosexual, as well as racially segregated, space. By doing so, Leap argues that gay men in South Africa were forerunners in the struggle against apartheid and champions of sexual citizenship. Such notions of citizenship are central to being part of the city. The search for citizenship is, however, complicated by issues of identity, mobility, politics and consumption. These issues situate citizenship, like place, in a state of constant change.

The same phenomenon can be observed in Cape Town. While Cape Town has a reputation as the preeminent tourist city on the African continent, it has also gained the reputation as Africa's 'gay capital' (Visser 2003b). Within the city of Cape Town itself an urban enclave called De Waterkant gained an international reputation as the heart of the gay capital (Rink 2016) due to its dense assemblage of clubs, bars, and restaurants that catered to queer leisure consumers – locals and tourists alike. Cape Town's reputation as the premier gay destination in Africa grew in tandem with De Waterkant's development as the locus of those queer quests. In the process De Waterkant became discursively 'quartered' (Bell & Jayne 2004), in the sense that it was shaped as the locus for its symbolic framing as a gay village (Rink 2016). Once sites primarily for performance of sexual identity, gay villages around the world have become important loci of consumption implicated in the economic development of cities through their focus on the leisure class. As Gorman-Murray and Nash (2016) argue:

> Conscripting gay villages as commodified quarters of the neoliberal city is consequential for their function and inclusivity. No longer just LGBT territories, gay villages are part of the leisure and tourist market … (Gorman-Murray & Nash 2016: 4)

The *Pink Map* shapes and archives these parallel modalities. It is an unapologetically commercial, free publication that generates income through advertisers who offer details of their bar, restaurant, guesthouse or service in exchange for being plotted on the map. Through their visibility on the queer pleasure periphery of the *Pink Map*, businesses expect to attract clients and to solidify the territory of 'pink' Cape Town. While the tourist-to-consumer trajectory may be an unsurprising outcome of most tourist maps, the result becomes more complicated when applied to a map intended primarily – although not exclusively – for sexual minority groups. The complication arises through the commodification of gay spaces that 'can be read as an instance of "the new homonormativity", producing a global repertoire of themed gay villages, as cities throughout the world weave commodified gay space into their promotional campaigns' (Bell & Binnie 2004: 1808). Those using the *Pink Map* are thus simultaneously positioned as tourists *and* as sexual citizens (Evans 1993), the latter being rooted in the development of sexual politics and utilising 'the idea of citizenship as a space for thinking about sexual identities, desires and practices' (Bell & Binnie 2006: 869). Sexual citizenship is thus inherently geographical, but is nonetheless characterised by conflicts and a struggle for representation when played out in the real world. Tourist nodes depicted in the *Pink Map* are therefore central to sexual citizenship, particularly as they are also sites of consumption: an idea that is both central to how citizenship is defined, and implicit in the management and disciplining of the self that occurs through the choices that consumers make (Binnie 2004: 167). Modern urban citizenship is incumbent upon how and where citizen-consumers position their consumptive practices (Binnie 2004). Citizens thus seek and find new conceptions of self and assertions of power (Binnie 1995) through consumption, and in doing so, merge destination space into consumption space.

As a destination for tourists and locals alike, De Waterkant serves as a locus of citizenship and consumption in post-1994 South Africa. Scholarship in gay-related tourism in South Africa (Elder 2004; Visser 2002; 2003a; 2003b) sheds light on the consumptive practices in De Waterkant, while recognising the impact of gay-oriented tourism that the *Pink Map* intends to promote. In this instance the term 'gay' is more appropriate than 'queer' in that much of the 'pink' tourist infrastructure is focused upon and limited to an elite group of mostly white, mostly gay, male clientele (Rink 2008; 2016). The growth of such globalised gay spaces, as Elder (2004) notes, can create a 'myth of community' while also masking the lives of gay and lesbian people and the material inequalities of globalization' (Elder 2004: 580). Those material inequalities include what Binnie (2004: 167) calls 'the limits and myths of the pink economy discourse'. As such, queer consumerism must be taken in context of the greater heterosexed world – that which is situated in the many silences of the *Map*. Those silences include the lack of visibility across the diversity of South Africa's racial demographics, limited inclusion of lesbian and transgender identities, an absence of mundane consumption (grocery stores, chemists, non-tourist related services), and the omission of large swathes of

Cape Town's urban landscape that queer individuals call home. Examining the range of queer consumption in the *Pink Map* demonstrates how emulation and honour-seeking through queer consumption have shifted over time.

CONSPICUOUS QUEER CONSUMPTION: EMERGENCE AND EMULATION

If conspicuous consumption evidences wealth and power, as per Veblen (2008), then it was the emergence of the queer consumer at the dawn of LGBT liberation in post-1994 South Africa that signalled queer Cape Town's arrival on the world stage. Emulating an idealised LGBT subjectivity based on globalised tropes of LGBT identity, evidence from the *Pink Map* exemplifies consumption *of* the body whereby individuals desire and seek sexual encounters to underpin their own identities; consumption *for* the body whereby a global gay ideal encourages corporeal self-discipline in bodily regimes; and finally shopping that is elevated to retail therapy, evidenced by a decline in sexual transgression and a focus on fashion, jewellery, furniture and décor for the home. It is in this final mode of consumption for domestic space and mimicry of heterosexual marriage and domesticity whereby LGBT individuals seek honour through consumption in the context of gaining equal status both legally and through broader social acceptance.

Early editions of the *Pink Map* highlight the opportunities for encountering one's sexuality whilst also signaling the emergence of Cape Town on the global gay circuit. Two examples from the *Map* illustrate this: firstly, in the representation of sexual citizenship as 'lifestyle' through bathhouse culture in Cape Town; and secondly, in the embodied representation of the *Map* itself. The Hot House, a gay male bathhouse, quite literally made its first splash in the first edition of the *Pink Map* in 1999. Under the listing for the Hothouse Steam & Leisure is a photograph of three men in a spa bath. Two white men are sitting facing the camera, submerged to their shoulders, while a naked black man sits perched in an elevated position on the edge of the bath, holding a cocktail in a tall glass garnished with a large slice of lemon. His feet are in the water and his back is turned to the camera, while he faces the two other men in the spa. The two white men look at each other while the black man's gaze is clearly focused on the other two. The caption notes: 'A new club & definitely a new lifestyle at Hot House' (*Pink Map* 1999), and heralds the possibility of same-sex desire across racial lines.

In his historical look at the bathhouse, Tattelman (1997) focuses on some of the key elements that constitute the unique, sexualised spaces of the bathhouse. The perception of the baths, he notes, is about a lack of limits or of prohibition, while the strategy of these spaces was 'to prioritize sex over all else' (Tattelman 1997: 394). Such limitlessness opened new relations between men and erased the boundaries between people from different socio-economic and racial backgrounds, and perhaps, in some hopeful way, characterised the intended freedoms of a democratic South Africa. Bathhouses are therefore sites of boundary-crossing and social equalisation, as Tattelman (1997: 394) suggests:

> The principle of the bathhouse was that you brought nothing inside with you. Ideally the bathhouse tried to erase the boundaries that divide people; clothing was removed, and issues of class were left at the lockers. By stripping bare, new experiences became possible.

By stripping bare, consumption was also limited to the body itself – in this case the idealised, muscular gay male body. These elements are evident on the *Pink Map*. Reflecting on the first images of gay bathhouses in 1999, the power of the bathhouse to potentially overcome boundaries is clear. The image of the men in the spa bath – the naked black man fixing his gaze on the two white men submerged in the water – stands out from the many other images in the *Pink Map*. Even though the gazes of the men in the image do not seem to meet, this is one of only two images within 12 years of the *Pink Map* in which men of different races are portrayed in a sexually charged position. In later images of the Hot House, from 2000–2002, we see a similar trio of two white men and one black man, who appear stripped bare except for the same white towels. The interior spaces of the Hot House may then function as the intended 'playground'; a playground that, according to Tattelman (1997) allows greater latitude of fulfilled desire than the streets outside.[2] However, later editions of the *Map* depict the Hot House in a narrower light, showing images of young, well-toned white men only, limiting expectations of participation in such potentially liberating spaces. This example, in conjunction with a broad examination of gay leisure spaces within the *Pink Map*, would corroborate Visser's (2003a) contention that, in the history of gay Cape Town, there has been little public interaction between gay communities across racial lines.

The second example relating to consumption of the idealised body in the *Pink Map* can be seen in the 2001 edition where a portion of De Waterkant is mapped on the body of the cover model (see Figure 11). The image features a white male, seemingly naked, with dark hair, hairy chest and a 'six pack' of abdominal muscles. The hirsute cover model is looking 'south' – both in relation to the plane of the map and toward the nether regions of his own corporeal geography. Most of the model's face is obscured, lending an air of anonymity, while focusing the objectifying gaze on the contours of the embodied map. In the midst of his navel-gazing, De Waterkant venues emulating place names from the capital of gay liberation, New York, are superimposed over the model's upper body – from the top of his abdominal muscles to the area above his pubis. The venues are superimposed as if on a map, with the model's body being the landscape of De Waterkant. The venues are located in relation to each other as they are situated in De Waterkant, with the midline connective tissue of the *rectus abdominus* muscle serving as the cartographic depiction of Somerset Road, the busiest thoroughfare of the area. The eye of the viewer is drawn down the bodily landscape from thorax to pubis across map references to the Hot House; Bronx (a gay 'action bar' that features dancing); On Broadway (a cabaret venue); Café Manhattan (a gay-owned restaurant and bar); and a variety of bars/dance clubs including Club 55, Detour, Angels, Bar Soho and Bar Code, a gay bar that caters to leather and fetish aficionados that is, perhaps owing to its geographic location or symbolically due to its transgressive sexuality, situated at the lowest point on the verge of the pubis.

The corporeal cartography that is depicted on the cover of the 2001 edition sexualises the landscape of De Waterkant while it emulates a cosmopolitan city with legendary centrality to the queer liberation struggle. The contours of the body become the contours of De Waterkant's landscape, and the journey through both is positioned as one and the same.

While embodiment is central to early versions of the *Map,* emulation of the idealised queer body through grooming has been a concern of the *Pink Map* since its inception. The number of 'health & grooming' listings has fluctuated over the years, and the changes are telling. In the 1999 edition, the listings under 'health & grooming' included two general practitioners, a hair stylist, a pharmacy and a non-surgical facelift consultant. With the exception of facelifts, these services can be characterised as utilitarian bodily regimes. By contrast, in the 2008 edition, the 'health & grooming' listings were augmented by the inclusion of a 'good selection of sex aids and poppers' and a 'large range of designer men's underwear'; a wellness centre that offers 'a wide range of treatments including shiatsu, reiki, reflexology, manicures and more'; a 'grooming station' with treatments from an 'international skincare guru'; and a laser eye centre (*Pink Map* 2008). Like shopping that has become 'therapeutic', health and grooming have also become complicated by sexual function, style and the assistance of laser technology.

These practices of health and grooming fall within the realm of corporeal self-discipline, in keeping with Foucault's (1977) assertion that citizens invigilate themselves, their bodies and their movements through space. The bodily practices range from laser hair removal that tames the wildness from the beast (*Pink Map* 1999) to non-surgical face lift consultants that promise to 'reverse the ravages of time' (*Pink Map* 2001), and a dentist who uses the latest technology to enable your smile 'to create the perfect first impression' (*Pink Map* 2012). Changes in the *Pink Map* suggest that health and grooming practices become more than utilitarian regimes. Caring for one's body later becomes an issue of 'wellness' that involves crystals, pendulums and elaborate settings that feel 'like entering a submarine from the newest James Bond movie' (*Pink Map* 2008) – all the while overseen not by a mere medical practitioner but by an internationally renowned 'guru' of skincare (*Pink Map* 2008). The consumption of grooming and healthcare services as seen in the *Pink Map* evidences both emulation of the idealised body and honour-seeking when 'perfection' is achieved. While the general sense of corporeality is central to the *Map,* the visibility of queer individuals is limited to those who are white, young and male, ascribing a sense of belonging to those who align to a global gay identity.

While the consumption *of* the body may be waning in terms of its presence on the *Map,* sex is still alive and well in the form of food *for* the body. In 2005, Col'Cacchio, a local chain of pizzerias, is described in a small listing as 'a funky vibey restaurant' that makes 'the best pizza, pasta and salads in the world' (*Pink Map* 2005). In the 2008 edition, however, the line between restaurants and the wild side becomes blurred:

> It's not only *size*, but the combination of taste and flavour sensations that makes Col'Cacchio Pizzeria stand out in the crowd. *Hunky* pizzas, *satisfying* pastas and *sexy* salads plus great locations and friendly service add up to a fun and relaxed good food experience. (*Pink Map* 2008 – emphasis added)

The sexual innuendos indicate a clear change in how the *Map* situates desire. *Hot, friendly, diverse, pleasure* and 'licensed for wine and malt' describe Knights M2M (male-to-male) massage in the 1999 edition; while *hunky, size, satisfying* and *sexy* describe Col'Cacchio Pizzeria in the 2008 edition. One might be forgiven for mistaking the words that describe culinary pleasure for corporeal desire. The overall effect however is to sexualise the entire landscape into a corporeal geography of consumption (Valentine 1999) through the use deliberate double-entendres.

CONSPICUOUS QUEER CONSUMPTION: SEEKING HONOUR THROUGH RETAIL THERAPY

Along with the growth of consumption as well-being comes a relative decline in what might be considered sexual transgressiveness. The sexualised imagery of the 2001 edition lent an air of seduction and transgression to the cityscape. Looking at the *Maps* over time, however, one can see a gradual neutering of this sexual discourse. The *Pink Map* category known as the 'wild side' serves as one example of these changes. By 2006, this category has dwindled to two entries relegated to a sidebar without map references; it is no longer a prominent aspect of the pink cityscape. In 2007 and 2008, the wildness is almost absent from the *Map,* the one remaining listing and its accompanying map reference stand alone in their transgression, located on the periphery of the pink landscape furthest from the notion of the 'good gay' (Richardson 2004), evidencing a self-policing notion of heteronormativity that limits expression within the boundaries of queerness. After 2008, the 'wild side' category disappears from the *Map* to be replaced a new category called 'get connected', relocating transgression from the map to cyberspace.

The images and iconography used both on the cover and within the maps indicate further changes. After the drag queen on the cover of 2000 edition and the corporeal cartography of the 2001 edition, the maps that followed feature increasingly less provocative, non-corporeal imagery and artwork. Imagery and artwork refer less to sexual identity and more to sexually neutral leisure consumption. In 2007, for example, the icons that point to the map reference numbers change from the iconic pink triangles (a recognisable symbol for many gays and lesbians around the world, but perhaps not as universally understood or identifiable), to simple squares, appealing to a broader audience. The unambiguously queer iconography that helped to frame sexual citizenship and signal an emergence makes way in later editions for graphics that appeal to a broader audience of both heterosexual and homosexual readers. The cover of the 2008 edition signals a further mainstreaming of the *Map*'s imagery. The cover features an image of a woman submerged in a cocktail glass adorned with a pink lily on the rim. The woman is holding her breath, a birdcage containing a pink 'goldfish' in her right hand. Although she appears to be wearing very little, if no clothing, the woman's body is obscured, covered by a wispy underwater sea of white feathers. The glass is set on a pink surface with the image of a sunset (over the exclusive seaside suburb of Camps Bay, not far from De Waterkant – perhaps owing to the Camps Bay location of sponsoring restaurant Paranga) in the background. There is a lack of overtly gay or lesbian iconography or symbolism in the 2008 edition. The image is one that conveys a sense of luxury and exclusivity without directing suggesting that a gay or lesbian identity is connected to those notions or spaces.

The 2008 version stands in stark contrast to the sexually embodied cartographic image of the 2001 version. These changes point as much to changes in the way the publisher saw his role as to transitions taking place in Cape Town and in South African society. These transitions include a broader acceptance of gays and lesbians in society as a whole and an increasingly mixed (gay and straight) following in the city's clubs, bars and restaurants. Previous covers of the *Pink Map* brought both criticism and praise for its publisher. As sentiments changed and the pink market expanded, however, the publisher looked for something different. So, when a high-profile Cape Town restaurant with an upmarket clientele wanted to sponsor the cover, the *Pink Map* opened itself up to new possibilities. For Todres, it was a signal of the recognition of the value of the pink constituency and a sign that Cape Town had become more liberated. It could also be understood as a symbol of the *Map*'s reframing of its constituents: a shift from sexual to consumer citizenship.

After 2008, successive editions of the *Map* begin to eschew transgressive or overly sexualised imagery in favour of content that evidences Richardson's (2004) 'good gay'. The 'good gay' materialises:

> ... primarily through an adherence to dominant intimate norms. That is, by lesbians and gay men demonstrating at both individual and collective levels a desire for, and commitment to, loving, stable, marital-style couple relationships. (Richardson 2004: 397)

It is at this time that the *Map* exhibits shopping that is elevated to 'retail therapy', evidenced by a focus on fashion, jewellery, furniture and décor for the home. In later editions of the *Map*, listings by jewellers showing pairs of wedding rings and diamonds by 'Prins and Prins' (*Pink Map* 2012), amongst others, suggest the growing trend in same-sex marriages, made legal in South Africa in 2006, and a closer alignment with heteronormative values. As LGBT individuals gain the right to legal marriage, the *Pink Map* signals this achievement through the display of wedding rings amongst the items on offer in Cape Town's retail therapy marketplace.

INTO THE MAINSTREAM: THE SPECTACLE OF CONSUMPTION

Shifts in consumption patterns and in the nature of the citizen-consumer can be seen through the ever-changing listings in the *Map*. In a Veblenian analysis, honour is achieved by means of conspicuous consumption and the display of goods. If seen in this light, LGBT individuals could be seen to have gained social acceptance and standing through the display of goods that are the hallmark of mainstream heterosexual consumers. *The Pink Map* lends itself to this kind of account. What was once a map that appealed to readers through shared notions of sexual citizenship has become one for which the common pursuit of consumption is the overarching focus, as a feature of a presumed consumer elite. In that regard, the *Map's* readership appears to be eating more and transgressing less. Among the trends is a growth in restaurant listings – from nine listings in 1999 to a high of 27 listings in 2008 – and a decline in venues that are exclusively 'queer'. Consumerism itself has changed its name and perhaps its role in society: from the utilitarian yet descriptive 'shopping' from 1999 through 2005, it was elevated to 'retail therapy' from 2006 onward. This gives the sense that being a consumer-citizen is more than just buying your daily bread or your Diesel footwear 'for successful living' (*Pink Map* 2000); it is a mode of active healing and self-preservation. The act of shopping gains a level of respect and importance in one's daily life that is implicitly necessary for well-being and identity formation.

At the same time, the 'gay village' has been replaced by the consumer 'lifestyle village', a shopping mall that has been elevated to a community of shoppers pursuing consumption as a lifestyle experience. The Cape Quarter Lifestyle Village brings shopping, transforming the mundane experience of being in De Waterkant to the extraordinary. It makes the search for a new pair of shoes an adventurous pursuit in 'historic' surroundings that evoke Cape Town's early history. It is more than just shopping; it is a lifestyle experience that goes beyond the ordinary. Yet, as Miles (2010: 98) notes, '[t]he shopping mall is indeed living testament to the physical domination of consumption upon the urban fabric'. Such is the case with De Waterkant, an enclave presented prominently as the heart of the 'gay Capital of Africa' in early editions of the *Pink Map*. By 2011, it is home to only a handful of queercentric venues which have been replaced by the Cape Quarter Lifestyle Village.

The commercial development of the Cape Quarter Lifestyle Village, comprised by Cape Quarter 'the Square' and Cape Quarter 'the piazza', exemplifies Pinder's (2000) notion of spectacle in that it is a form of capitalist urban development that re-imagines place in commodifiable ways. For Pinder, the spectacle is critical in understanding the commodification of everyday life, where 'electronic media, advertising, television and other cultural industries are said to be increasingly shaping everyday life' (Pinder 2000: 357). The sexual freedoms that were emancipatory in the late 1990s have been replaced by the 'power of capital to emancipate desire in the contemporary' at a level that is merely 'skin deep' (Miles 2010: 52), leaving the consumer wanting more.

The consumer landscape depicted by more recent editions of the *Pink Map* is one that may feel more familiar and comfortable for the 'good gay' and the broader queer and straight publics he/she would emulate. The *Pink Tongue*, a monthly newspaper geared toward Cape Town's queer market segment, has itself heralded changes in the definition of the 'pink' community in Cape Town. As a report from Independent Newspapers noted, the advertising and marketing director who initiated the idea for the speciality newspaper 'said it would not be about "steam rooms, gay dating and HIV-positive people". Rather it would fill a gap for a more *stylish* platform' (IOL 2007, emphasis added). Such repositioning of the queer community aligns it with the characteristics of Richardson's 'good gay' (2004) while masking some of the characteristics that define the leisure activities, social needs and health concerns of queer individuals in Cape Town. This framing of the *Pink Tongue* also signals a shift in the gay community – from overcoming stereotypes to emulating the 'stylish' life of an 'ordinary' consumer. These shifts are evident in the *Pink Map* and in the consumer landscape of De Waterkant depicted within it. De Waterkant has undergone notable changes since the days when the only opportunities for consumption were at corner shops, panel beaters, massage parlours and gay clubs. Formerly industrial buildings, such as the warehouses on the corner of Jarvis and Dixon Streets, were converted for retail and entertainment use in the late 1990s. Similarly, in the early 2000s, cottages along Dixon and Jarvis Streets [in De Waterkant] turned their use toward retailers and estate agents as light industry was forced out of the area due to large-scale property development and the emergence of multi-use commercial hubs known as 'lifestyle centres'[3] (such as the Cape Quarter Lifestyle Village).

The gay bars and dance clubs that once lined Somerset Road (in the area) were the symbols of a sexual citizenship formed around emulation of the idealised body and the expression of desire. Now that most of those clubs have either moved out the De Waterkant or completely off the *Pink Map*, they have been replaced by temples of consumerism: shopping arcades, restaurants and upmarket spas. A consumer ideology and the attraction of the property boom of the early 2000s coupled with the lack of available land in the CBD led to large-scale development in the area. 'Lifestyle' was once a word that connoted sexual identity; now it refers to shopping, eating, drinking and socialising within a certain socio-economic context. In the increasingly dense and competitive consumer landscape, the trope of consumption is more and more important and thus more likely to be strategically deployed. As business interests compete for their share of the consumer's discretionary spending, segments of the fractured city begin to do battle with each other. Thus, there are discourses that paint De Waterkant not simply as a unique destination in the world or in Africa, but, according to the promise of the consumer spectacle – the promise that the Cape Quarter Lifestyle Village will be 'the place to be … shopping … relaxing … working … eating … meeting … playing … in Cape Town'.

Neither the *Pink Map* nor the enclave of De Waterkant are immune to the shifting modes of consumption that have become prevalent in recent years – from commercial spaces in the public sphere to the private space of the home via the Internet. Such changes eliminate the need to seek same-sex desire in homo-normalised spaces in the public sphere while allowing social connections to be made in cyberspace. Similarly, the nature of desires may also be changing: from food and entertainment to a focus on hearth and home. This takes Kraftl's (2007) 'utopia of the homely' literally – where the pursuit of the perfect place has its locus in domestic spaces rather than in the public spaces of bars and clubs.

Recent discourses of consumption in De Waterkant through the *Pink Map* have played on the notions of 'upmarket' and 'lifestyle' (Rink 2016). Both are mentioned frequently in discourses that seek to elevate place-making to a utopian ideal, where everyday and commonplace market choices and consumerism are replaced with a form of consumption that is step beyond the present, to the point of being a way of life. The ideal of upmarket consumerism is utopian in that it creates a separation from the mundane and the promise of a shopping experience that is beyond the ordinary. The upmarket notion is also a buffer from the inequities that characterise the city beyond the centre. De Waterkant's upmarket image acts to separate itself from the rest of the city in which it stands. At the same time, it allows wealthy (and mostly white) South Africans to manage the contradiction between the identity to which they aspire and the city in which they live (Ballard 2005) through the exclusionary comfort of a secure shopping destination that acts as an 'identity-affirming space' (Ballard 2005: 5) for those who can afford to feel 'at home'.

The emergence of the queer consumer concurrent with queer liberation in post-1994 South Africa highlighted a subjectivity that was hewn from a global LGBT identity. The 'global gay' as evidenced in the *Pink Map* was a gay male New Yorker – the idealised liberated queer subject. As LGBT individuals have merged more and more into the mainstream of society through a combination of legislation and changing social values, the *Pink Map* traces the shifting politics of sexuality through changing modes of consumption and the branding of homosexuality as style and a marked mimicry of heterosexual relationships and domestic life. Indeed, as Gorman-Murray and Nash (2016) argue, LGBT neighbourhoods have become progressively more integrated into urban cultures and economies. That integration is expressed as a change from the consumption of same-sex desire to the consumption of goods and services that transcend sexual citizenship in favour of consumer citizenship. These shifts echo Franklin (2007: 136), who argues that satisfaction begins with consumption that is 'orientated to physical, embodied forms of satisfaction such as with use or satiating hunger'. However, as he concludes, desire replaces satisfaction as a primary motivation:

> With desire, it was the anticipation of consumption and the associated intense pleasures of thinking, imagining and dreaming about acquisition and ownership that became paramount. This of course detaches the consumer from the object in a purely physical sense releasing them for the intense pleasures of reverie. (Franklin 2007: 136–137)

As Veblen (2008) reminds us, such reverie is an esteem-building exercise. The arc from satisfaction to desire might be explained as a generational one, driven by changing tastes and needs, or it might be an editorial one driven by the inclusion or exclusion of advertisers due to limits imposed by advertisers who might not want to be associated with alternative sexualities. Likely a combination of all of the above, the changes demonstrate a variety of shifts taking place in society that have bearing on both sexual and consumer citizenship which ultimately conspire to shape the leisure-seeker's consumer experience and the queer pleasure periphery within which it takes place.[4]

REFERENCES

Altman, D., 1997, 'Global gaze/Global gays', *GLQ* 3: 417-436.

Ballard, R., 2005, 'Bunkers for the Psyche: How Gated Communities Have Allowed the Privatisation of Apartheid in Democratic South Africa', *Dark Roast Occasional Papers Series*, 24. Isandla Institute.

Bell, D. & Jayne, M., (eds.), 2004. *City of Quarters: Urban Villages in the Contemporary City*, Ashgate: Aldershot.

Bell, D. & Binnie, J., 2004, 'Authenticating Queer Space: Citizenship, Urbanism and Governance', *Urban Studies* 41(9): 1807-1820.

Bell, D. & Binnie, J., 2006, 'Geographies of Sexual Citizenship', *Political Geography* 25(8): 869-873.

Binnie, J., 1995, 'Trading Places: Consumption, Sexuality and the Production of Queer Space', in D. Bell & G. Valentine (eds.), *Mapping Desire: Geographies of Sexualities*, 182-199, Routledge: London.

Binnie, J., 2004, 'Quartering Sexualities: Gay Villages and Sexual Citizenship', in D. Bell & M. Jayne (eds.), *City of Quarters: Urban Villages in the Contemporary City*, 163-172, Ashgate: Aldershot.

Cresswell, T., 2006, *On the Move*, Routledge: London.

Elder, G., 1995, 'Of Moffies, Kaffirs and Perverts: Male Homosexuality and the Moral Order in the Apartheid State', in D. Bell & G. Valentine (eds.), *Mapping Desire: Geographies of Sexualities*, 56-65, Routledge: London.

Elder, G., 2004, 'Love for Sale: Marketing Gay Male P/leisure Space in Contemporary Cape Town, South Africa', in L. Nelson & J. Seager (eds.), *A Companion to Feminist Geography*, 578-589, Blackwell: London.

Evans, D., 1993, *Sexual Citizenship: The Material Construction of Sexualities*, Routledge: London.

Foucault, M., 1977, *Discipline and Punish: The Birth of Prisons*, Penguin: Harmondsworth.

Franklin, A., 2007, 'The Problem with Tourism Theory', in I. Ateljevic, A. Pritchard & N. Morgan (eds.), *Advances in Tourism Research*, 131-148, Elsevier: Oxford.

Gevisser, M., 1994, 'A Different Fight for Freedom: A History of South African Lesbian and Gay Organisations – the 1950s to the 1990s', in M. Gevisser & E. Cameron (eds.), *Defiant Desire: Gay and Lesbian Lives in South Africa*, 14-86, Ravan Press: Johannesburg.

Gorman-Murray, A. & Nash, C., 2016, 'Transformations in LGBT Consumer Landscapes and Leisure Spaces in the Neoliberal City', *Urban Studies* 54(3): 786-805.

IOL, 2007, 'Get ready for the Pink Tongue', 31 August, viewed 25 March 2008, available from http://www.iol.co.za/index.php?set_id=1&click_id=3045&art_id=nw20070831145601280C305506.

Hannam, K., Sheller, M., & Urry, J., 2004, Editorial: Mobilities, Immobilities and Moorings, *Mobilities* 1(1): 1-22.

Kraftl, P., 2007, 'Utopia, performativity, and the unhomely', *Environment and Planning D: Society and Space* 25(1): 120-143.

Leap, W., 2002, 'Strangers on a Train: Sexual Citizenship and the Politics of Public Transportation in Apartheid Cape Town', in A. Cruz-Malave & M. Mannalansan (eds.), *Queer Globalizations: Citizenship and the Afterlife of Colonialism*, 219-235, New York University Press: New York.

Miles, S., 2010, *Spaces for Consumption*, Sage: London.

Murray, A., 1995, 'Femme on the Streets, Butch in the Sheets (A Play on Whores)', in D. Bell & G. Valentine G (eds.), *Mapping Desire: Geographies of Sexualities*, 66–74, Routledge: London.

Oswin, N., 2006, 'Decentering Queer Globalization: Diffusion and the "Global Gay"', *Environment and Planning D: Society and Space* 24(5): 777–790.

Pinder, D., 2000, 'Old Paris is no more: Geographies of spectacle and anti-spectacle', *Antipode* 32(4): 357–386.

Pink Map: Gay Guide to Cape Town, 1999, Published by A&C Maps: Kalk Bay.

Pink Map: Gay Guide to Cape Town, 2000, Published by A&C Maps: Newlands.

Pink Map: Gay Guide to Cape Town & Surrounds, 2001, Published by A&C Maps: Newlands.

Pink Map: Gay Guide to Cape Town & Surrounds, 2002, Published by A&C Maps: Newlands.

Pink Map: Gay Guide to Cape Town & Surrounds, 2003, Published by A&C Maps: Newlands.

Pink Map: Gay Guide to Cape Town & Surrounds, 2004, Published by A&C Maps: Newlands.

Pink Map: Gay Guide to Cape Town & Surrounds, 2005, Published by A&C Maps: Newlands.

Pink Map: Gay Guide to Cape Town, 2006, Published by A&C Maps: Newlands.

Pink Map: Gay Guide to Cape Town, 2007, Published by A&C Maps: Newlands.

Pink Map: Gay Guide, Cape Town & Surrounds, 2008, Published by A&C Maps: Newlands.

Pink Map: Gay Guide, Cape Town & Surrounds, 2009, Published by A&C Maps: Newlands.

Pink Map: Gay Guide, Cape Town & Surrounds, 2010, Published by A&C Maps: Newlands.

Pink Map: Gay Guide, Cape Town & Surrounds, 2011, Published by A&C Maps: Newlands.

Pink Map: Gay Guide, Cape Town & Surrounds, 2012, Published by A&C Maps: Newlands.

Pink Map: Gay Guide, Cape Town & Surrounds, 2013, Published by A&C Maps: Newlands.

Pink Map: Gay Guide, Cape Town & Surrounds, 2014, Published by A&C Maps: Newlands.

Pink South Africa Guide, 2007, Second Edition, Cape Info Africa: Cape Town.

Pink South Africa Guide, 2008, Third Edition, Cape Info Africa: Cape Town.

Posel, D., 2010, 'Races to Consume: Revisiting South Africa's History of Race, Consumption and the Struggle for Freedom', *Ethnic and Racial Studies* 33(2): 157–175.

Richardson, D., 2004, 'Locating Sexualities: From Here to Normality', *Sexualities* 7(4): 391–411.

Rink, B., 2008, 'Community as Utopia: Reflections on De Waterkant', *Urban Forum* 19(2): 205–220.

Rink, B., 2013, 'Que(e)rying Cape Town: Touring Africa's Gay Capital with the Pink Map', in J. Sarmento & E. Brito-Henriques (eds.), *Tourism in the Global South: Heritages, Identities and Development*, 65-90, Centre for Geographical Studies: Lisbon.

Rink, B., 2016, 'Quartering the City in Discourse and Bricks: Articulating Urban Change in a South African Enclave', *Urban Forum* 27(1), 19–34.

Tattelman, I., 1997, 'The Meaning of the Wall', in G.B. Ingram, A. Bouthillette & Y. Retter (eds.), *Queers in Space*, 391–406, Bay Press: Seattle.

Todres, P., 2008, *Interview*, 12 February 2008, Cape Town.

Tucker, A. 2009, *Queer Visibilities: Space, Identity and Interaction in Cape Town*. Blackwell: London.

Valentine, G., 1999, 'A Corporeal Geography of Consumption', *Environment and Planning D: Society and Space* 17(3): 329–351.

Veblen, T., 2008 [1899], *The Theory of the Leisure Class*, at Project Gutenberg, viewed 19 January 2019, available from http://www.gutenberg.org/ebooks/833.

Visser, G., 2002, 'Gay Tourism in South Africa: Issues from the Cape Town Experience', *Urban Forum* 13(1): 85–94.

Visser, G., 2003a, 'Gay Men, Leisure Space and South African Cities: The Case of Cape Town', *Geoforum* 34(1): 123–137.

Visser, G., 2003b, 'Gay Men, Tourism and Urban space: Reflections on Africa's 'Gay Capital', *Tourism Geographies* 5(2): 168–189.

NOTES

1. Here, I invoke the term 'queer' to be inclusive of multiple sexual identities including lesbian, gay, bisexual, transgender, and intersex. My use of the term 'queer' follows Tucker's (2009) recognition that same-sex-attracted communities and individuals in Cape Town know/practise their own type of subversion. In this chapter, I employ the term 'queer' beyond a shorthand for sexual dissidents with reference to the ephemeral and fluid nature of space and place, leading to an understanding of tourism destination spaces that lack fixity in the sense that they are highly mobile.
2. Elder's (2004) analysis concludes that the experience of the gay bathhouse as depicted in the *Pink Map* runs counter to the unprescribed, liberating experience that Tattelman (1997) attributes to such spaces. Elder's reading concludes that the *Pink Map* provides limited possibilities for participation in the bathhouse experience unless you are white, twenty-something and physically well defined.
3. The 'lifestyle centre' concept is attributed to Memphis, Tennessee (USA) property developers Poag & McEwen. According to company sources (www.pm-lifestyle.com), their centres are designed to '[serve] a growing and affluent community as the primary center for quality shopping and dining'. They are places where, 'life meets style' and where 'the customer is never overwhelmed but is, instead, able to escape the pressures of the day to relax, dine and shop in style'.
4. I owe a debt of gratitude to Philip Todres of A&C Maps, the publisher of the *Pink Map,* for providing access to and permission for using the *Pink Map* in this research.

12 THE POLITICS AND MORAL ECONOMY OF MIDDLE-CLASS CONSUMPTION IN SOUTH AFRICA

SOPHIE CHEVALIER

When I began studying South Africans, I was struck by the political force of debates about consumption. The emancipation of black people in post-apartheid South Africa was closely linked to and reflected in the emergence of an African middle class, which, given recent history, inevitably had racial connotations (Chevalier 2010b). The black majority have hitherto lacked substantial property, inheritance and savings; and fuelling their desire to consume commodities through moneylending has led to widespread indebtedness (James 2014). Public debate concerning this development has usually hinged on two criteria: black people's access to consumption patterns previously reserved for whites; and residential mobility, especially those households that have left the townships and segregated areas to live in the formerly white suburbs. The growth of a new middle class of consumers has been, and still is, taken as a measure of success in transforming the country's society and politics. If consumption has not exactly made this group (Herpin 1986), it has certainly been used to define it, more than other criteria.

For nine years now, I have carried out intermittent ethnographic research[1] in eThekwini/Durban on the lower middle class. Since 2008, I have maintained a second home in a multi-racial apartment building in the city, visiting for periods ranging from one to six months. I have interviewed members of some 50 households, some more than once. Most interviewees had children; and one in three households included extended family members. The adults were all between 30 and 50 years old. For the last three years, a major focus has been on consumption, especially on food provisioning, preparation and consumption.[2] My informants were from all racial categories (now usually referred to as 'communities'); and the blacks, Indians and coloureds in the study had moved out of the townships where they were once compelled to live in favour of formerly white areas. In this social class, food was the main budgetary item[3] and its provisioning and consumption were divided between home and visits to malls, supermarkets and restaurants – and sometimes to shops in their old township (Chevalier 2012; 2017).

My recent focus on the moral economy of food among lower-middle-class consumers in Durban has led me back to my original interest in media discourse about South Africa's middle classes. Public discussion about the new African middle class at first crystallised around the type known as the 'black diamonds', likewise emphasising consumption. I became interested in how this stereotype was reproduced in the South African press, especially in terms of the image it promotes of a certain kind of consumer (Chevalier 2010b; Krige 2011).[4] The black diamonds' presumed lifestyle apparently left little to be desired when compared with the 'conspicuous consumption' of Veblen's (1992 [1899]) American leisure class; for each group prestige was the only consideration.

Walter Benjamin (2006), when writing about the construction of urban social types in nineteenth-century Europe, likened the moral portraits typically produced by a 'panoramic literature' to 'phantasmagoria'. He extended this metaphor, taken from a kind of magic lantern show, to Paris's shopping arcades, built at the birth of modern capitalism in the 1840s, which he saw as spectacular theatres of the new commodity culture. In contemporary South Africa, there is no shortage of shopping malls or of moral portraits describing their denizens. Following Benjamin (2006), I regard these images as being projected through a magic lantern fuelled by white fear and suspicion. The black diamonds' supposed profligacy and lack of knowledge underpins much talk about their alleged conspicuous consumption.

Empirical evidence for this caricature is non-existent; yet it is often reported as an objective fact. Given my wish to explore personal variations in consumer behaviour, the fact that so much public discussion in South Africa assumes that consumption is socially programmed and has no scope for individual subjectivity or agency is particularly irritating. Breaking up the idea of the 'middle class' as a unitary category is long overdue in South Africa and this is a prime focus of my wider ethnographic study. No distinction is usually made between the black upper middle class, which is often close to political power, and a black lower middle class whose roots long precede the end of apartheid. The latter constitutes the bulk of the middle class, yet the media prefer to focus on the former, often drawing on imagination rather than empirical analysis, while eliding the difference between upper and lower divisions of the class and ignoring the time gap between their emergence in history (Chevalier 2010b). We should always keep in mind that, while there has been striking growth of a black elite and middle class more generally since the early 1990s (Seekings and Nattrass 2006: 308), the African majority sustained a lower middle class of professionals and shopkeepers before then; and this grew significantly from the 1960s, above all from the mid-1970s when a shortage of qualified white workers opened up access to a number of professions that had hitherto been reserved for whites (Crankshaw 1997).[5]

The people I interviewed in Durban belonged to another world to that of the new elite. Their consumer behaviour took its meaning from the life they shared with their family and intimate social circle and was embodied in the objects they consumed. For this class, food provisioning and consumption were shaped by a 'moral economy' (Thompson 1966; Scott 1976) which they experienced as being culturally differentiated.[6] Having considered the relevance of Veblen (1992) on 'conspicuous consumption' to my study of lower-middle-class food habits, I find that his emphasis on waste and excess played little part in their 'moral economy'. Like people everywhere, they had their moments of ostentation. But the main point of this chapter is a plea for a more plural approach to who the South African middle classes are and what motivates them.

In addition to my Durban informants, I have consulted numerous media sources that offer advice to middle-class consumers, such as television programmes, cookery books and women's magazines – mostly *Bona* and *Your Family* (Iquani 2015 approaches consumption through the media and secondary sources). The public advice they dispense on how to manage a budget or to cook healthy and economical meals reinforces the 'moral economy' of typical readers. I also introduce comparative reflections on analogous social processes drawn from my ethnographic research on several European societies before I came to South Africa.[7]

THE MORAL ECONOMY OF LOWER-MIDDLE-CLASS ACTOR-CONSUMERS

Even though most of my informants were lower middle class, the ubiquity of the term 'black diamonds' and the descriptions this elite class attracted in the media affected them too, since the distinction between lower and upper middle classes was rarely observed.[8] Partly for this reason, they often rejected being called 'middle class', preferring to be known as the 'professional' class – it is important to use categories that reflect the lived experiences of those whom we classify. Focusing on Soweto, some authors (Phadi & Ceruti, 2011; Phadi & Manda 2010) have approached class through the language used to denote the social class positioning of individuals there; and Khunou (2015) emphasises the dynamic and contingent construction of class (cf. Krige 2012). My informants were teachers, nurses, technicians, librarians, secretaries, police officers, independent consultants, and so forth. They came from all 'communities';

I started out by focusing exclusively on black people and later decided to include all races. This was because I wanted to understand the emergence of a multi-racial petite bourgeoisie[9] through an analysis of consumer behaviour that did not entail a focus on race.

What features defined this professional class? Some of my black and Indian informants said that they were glad to have the chance of a house and a job, not to have to worry about food, and to have something left over for discretionary purchases that they could share with their family. To be able to afford a little more than the basics made a difference for them; having some purchasing power gave them a sense of agency. Their upward social mobility lay in the contrast between their present circumstances and their more constrained origins.

But this sense was often linked to the fear of losing what they had gained, and the absence of a secure platform (in the form of savings, for example) distinguished this social class from the upper middle class. The people I interviewed still clung more to their community of origin than to a common middle-class identity, which was in any case fragile. They knew that their purchasing power was quite limited, even if it made them a little superior to the poor masses. My focus on food consumption in Durban was in turn an extension of my long-term European research.[10] Here I examined urban food-supply chains – markets, supermarkets, shopping malls and so on – as well as individual shopping and cooking preferences. Looking at food allowed me to bring together a wide range of issues since, although we need to eat to live, eating is also a basic way of participating in social life and it gives expression to a wide variety of lifestyles. More than most things, food is a deep symbol of inherited identities. Nothing illustrates the precarity of lower-middle-class lives more vividly than fluctuations in their food consumption habits.

Discussing consumer behaviour with my informants and watching it in practice, I became aware that their routines were shaped by certain values, by a sense of justice to which they were emotionally attached that might be called a 'moral economy'. James Scott (1976) adapted Thompson's (1966) use of the term to show how Southeast Asian villagers were motivated by safety-first principles and a subsistence ethic, rather than profit. This claim is somewhat idealistic; we could say rather that both self-interested calculation and moral norms may be found in all economies and at all economic levels, so that what matters is their variable interplay (Hann & Hart 2011: 83ff). This was certainly the case with my Durban informants. Scott locates the roots of a moral economy in unequal power relations and resistance by the dominated to their oppressors; but, as Fassin (2009: 1257) points out, it would be wrong to suppose that the only group with a concern for moral economy are the poorest members of society.[11] Every social class has its moral economy, including the elites. Nor does a moral economy necessarily involve resistance to capitalism. Certainly, my informants were not opposed to the mass consumption that surrounded them, but rather adapted it to their own values and strategies of self-improvement.

Even if moral economies may be found in all corners of the world, it would be mistaken to approach society as a set of conflict relations between opposed moral universes (Abélès 2014). Focusing on the cultural and moral dimensions of economic behaviour would lead us to lose sight of classes and of society. If a moral-economy approach puts the spotlight on meaning and subjectivity, these elements should still be combined with an approach from history and political economy. Finally, it is vital to understand economic relations in their global context.

Keeping in mind the 'power of everyday actions' (De Certeau 1984), I identify three ways in which my informants' lives were shaped by their moral economy as a guide to good consumer behaviour: budgeting, sharing and attachment to their community of origin.

BUDGETING: MONEY IS NOT AN ABSTRACTION

Coloured, Indian, white and black consumers took great care when budgeting for food and other regular items, often observing strict limits to their expenditure. People were anxious to maintain a budget for food, their single largest outlay. Regardless of its share of their budget, most of them were keenly aware of food prices and could calculate their family's food costs, if asked to do so. These South African households took advantage of cost reductions made possible by large-scale marketing, relying on end-of-month 'specials', bulk purchases, comparing prices and buying some food for the whole month – often the weekend after they received their salary. 'I check out all the promotional literature by the supermarkets to identify specials; I plan my purchases accordingly and then I stock up on them!' said Bronwyn[12] (coloured, married, early 30s, one child, clerk in a police station). Gladys (black, 43 years old, divorced, three children, a captain of police) went to Makro, a large hypermarket, where she stocked up on a month's supplies, especially meat, which she froze. Mpumi (black, widow, single, 42 years old, trader and dental nurse) went shopping with her sister Jabu (37 years old) and her daughter. They bought the same things every month at Makro, and the rest at a Pick n Pay supermarket (for example, 10 kg of onions and potatoes). They went there by minibus and took a taxi home.

Some women had a system of envelopes with money linked to specific goods, what Zelizer (1997) calls 'earmarking': money is not just an abstraction, but is tied to specific items of expenditure. And of course, some of the women participated in saving clubs (*stokvels*) with the specific aim of buying groceries in bulk for Christmas. As is common everywhere, routine food consumption with an eye on the budget was interspersed with more ceremonial occasions, such as feast days, anniversaries, parties and so on, which no doubt offered opportunities to show off in a limited way that I did not observe directly.

Consumption and budgetary management have generated a whole branch of education in South Africa, as elsewhere. One must be a prudent consumer and, if indebted, a responsible debtor. In order to be a fully self-controlled consumer, one must learn how to manage a budget. Self-appointed authorities, like women's magazines, took it on themselves to teach women, especially black women, how to consume. This recalls historical studies of the birth of a mass consumer society in the United States and Europe in the late nineteenth century, when both middle and working classes were put through a sort of apprenticeship in this regard (Strasser 1998; Zelizer 1997).

I have studied two women's magazines, *Bona* (successor to *Zonk* studied by Posel[13]) and *Your Family*. Although they address an historically specific 'community' readership, their columnists' advice on money and cooking recipes was remarkably similar across the board, even though, when dealing with other issues (fashion, personal advice and so on), their line was quite closely targeted at one group only. *Bona*, a very popular monthly with a readership of mainly younger black lower-middle-class women,[14] always had a section on 'finance'. Over a number of years, a double-page spread offered advice, such as '10 money-saving tips from our grandparents' or 'buy less, stay at home, do without'.

The first food item to be cut when households had to economise was meat: the women's magazines understood this well, since they provided many recipes without meat or explicitly pushed slogans like 'veggie and good' or 'veggie winners'. For some years now, *Your Family* has suggested some 'meals for the week' with a 'Monday meat-free' recipe. 'Budget family meals: feed four for under R50' was just one very successful section (*Your Family* September 2013). Often, these budget meals were linked to advertisements – Pick n Pay suggested some meals based on items available in their supermarkets that would help consumers to control their expenses (*Bona*, April 2014).

The list is long! These magazines also suggested menus and recipes for Christmas and other festivals: but there was always a careful balance between respecting the household budget and any desire for luxury and glitter. And the 'finance' section before Christmas would always be on how to save and stay within budget.

This literature emphasises the role of advertising and brands in the formation of consumer behaviour. Similarly, the people I interviewed, especially those over 40, expressed an attachment to brands that had been around for a long time: 'because we have always seen them around us'. Knowledge of these brands was a kind of shopping guide for many. Black informants in particular often described themselves as novice consumers because shopping and access to services more generally were difficult and restricted in the townships during apartheid. While sticking to the basic supermarket chains for bulk purchases, a number of my informants liked to visit upper-middle-class food chains, such as Woolworths. They did so mainly for the shopping experience there and perhaps to show off a plastic bag with their logo, rather than buying the more expensive items. They tended to go for cheap and familiar goods, such as potatoes and onions, rarely for a special treat (sweets or cakes) as a reward for doing the shopping (Miller 1998).

Magazines and television programmes gave priority to identifying the standards that made individuals 'good' consumers, always within an assumed framework of personal responsibility. But pooling resources was another central feature of my informants' moral economy.

SHARING AND ATTACHMENT TO ONE'S COMMUNITY OF ORIGIN

The tasks of food provisioning were normally shared: young couples went shopping together, women with a daughter, sister or mother. Even though it was largely a female duty, a lot of men participated in food provisioning by buying (and carrying) items like bottles or meat. The big monthly or weekly food shopping expeditions to supermarkets often ended up with lunch in one of the numerous fast-food chains or restaurants located in shopping centres or malls. The attraction of the malls was to luxuriate in a world of consumption, carrying purchases in bags that displayed brands from all over the world, each of them providing links to everywhere. This was once a country with limited access to imported goods, especially for black people; now many were cheered when a new international chain store appeared in a mall.

My informants never bought food only for their own household, mainly because in most cases its composition was fluid, consisting of more than a couple and their children. They often shopped and prepared food for other family members who did not live with them, especially parents who remained in the townships or lived elsewhere. Some had to provide for their employees or even for their religious community. In all these ways, food was shared. Cooking was also coordinated, especially during festivals: every year Priya cooked with her mother, sister and sisters-in-law for Diwali, a Hindu festival. They would consult cookbooks for new ideas about pastries. Bronwyn joined her mother-in-law in the kitchen when she got married, and since they belonged to the same religious community, she regularly cooked with her female in-laws from then on.

Cooking together involved not only handing on cooking techniques, but also learning how to incorporate new recipes. Bronwyn had to learn how to cook vegetarian food. Isobel (white, married, 57 years old, two children) was a librarian and her mother-in-law lived with them; she made some meals for her, as well as for the maid. Amanda (white, married, 38 years old, three children) bought and cooked food for her religious community who then distributed this food to needy families. Eating out in a restaurant was usually restricted to close family and friends, but rarely just to a couple or a lone individual.

Informants from all communities assiduously kept up family relations by making frequent visits. The old in particular were rarely neglected. Most people visited their parents every weekend and sometimes after work. They supported them financially, through money transfers, by doing their shopping or by inviting them for a meal on a regular basis. Muntu (black, widower, 39 years old, high school teacher) placed his 13-year-old son in Umlazi with his grandmother because she had recently lost her husband and daughter and was lonely. He brought his boy home every weekend and took food to his mother. Many black and Indian consumers were happy to return to their old neighbourhood at weekends to attend a church service and to shop for specific items, such as meat (see Chevalier 2007 for a French example) or a haircut.[15] They would sometimes cross the city to visit a particular shop, such as a seafood specialist or a halal butcher. In such cases, budgetary considerations were suspended since the point of their trip was the quality or uniqueness of the product: 'We are going to shop for meat at Star Meat, the big halal supermarket, in Overport Centre. Why is halal meat so expensive? The rocketing prices have really hit our grocery budget!' (MV, Indian, married, early 40s, three daughters). MV went to greet his parents-in-law every day after dropping off his daughters at school. Some informants retained economic interests in the townships, renting out accommodation or running commercial enterprises there.

CONVERGENCE, NOVELTY AND TRADITION IN FOOD HABITS

Attachment to one's community of origin was also supposedly revealed in a preference for cooking a community's 'soul food', even if tastes were slowly changing. But when I interviewed women about their daily cooking practices, most of them described the same range of meals as their favourites: macaroni cheese, sausages and potatoes, roast chicken, lasagne, roast lamb and cottage pie. Children's lunch boxes were filled with polony (a processed meat roll), peanut butter sandwiches and sausage rolls. Bona and Your Family also recommend everyday cooking recipes that cover very similar ground. At lunch time, queues line up in front of takeaway stands mostly selling the same dishes: chicken or mutton curry, grilled chicken, macaroni bolognaise, rice with minced meat, sausages and sometimes fish and chips. It was not easy to define this everyday food repertoire, but, apart from the recent rise of Italian food, most of these recipes shared a British colonial heritage.[16]

If daily eating habits had much in common for many, this was because, despite being open to experimentation with new foods, people often used the same manufactured options and attended the same chain restaurants and takeaways. Most households had takeaways as a family meal at least once a week: cooking styles of all kinds were diffused across restaurants, especially as takeaway dishes that most people were keen to try. The choice of takeaway restaurants was wide, with South African and international chains and local restaurants to choose from. Despite what some might consider their banality, Maureen (black, 48 years old, divorced, three kids, consultant) loved to treat herself to something from Wimpy, Steers or KFC. Some informants, however, were suspicious of what they considered to be 'European' or 'Western' food, such as pizza and sushi.

Two new foods were becoming universal. In the past, fish was consumed by only a few, while a European minority ate pasta. Despite being a port and seaside resort, Durban had hardly any fishmongers, since demand had until recently always been low. This paradox was due to the food traditions of the various local groups: whites, coloureds and Indians traditionally consumed fish, but the black majority, especially Zulus, mainly ate meat. Sipho (early 40s, married, three kids, independent consultant) confirmed this: 'Most of the black people here don't eat fish day-to-day. We are more meat eaters'. Even so, probably in a move towards healthy eating, everyone now said that they ate fish or would like to. But most of my informants, especially blacks, knew little about how to cook it and preferred to eat fish in restaurants or as a takeaway. They bought tinned fish – pilchards and tuna were very popular – or frozen fish.[17] Ocean Basket – a national chain of seafood restaurants – was a favourite of many: a family, such as Jube and her sister, would eat fish and shrimp there after shopping in a mall. My Indian informants, however, had their own shops where they bought fish and seafood, and they were quite fussy about it. Women's magazines encouraged their readers to eat fish like tuna, pilchards, hake and snoek, from tins.

Pasta was another food that had been taken up recently. It has joined the main staples, even though it was more expensive than maize, for example. Mpume (36 years old, married, two girls, clerk at the electricity utility) told with some irony of how she once served pasta to her mother-in-law for Sunday lunch instead of the traditional *pap* (maize porridge): 'She complained loudly, but she ate the pasta (for the first time ever), while my husband and daughters adore pasta and, since I am the cook, I get to choose'. Of course, pasta could be cooked in a variety of ways, sometimes in line with more traditional tastes; thus Lameez (married, 38 years old, two girls, housewife) said, 'Spices are essential to Indian cooking. I mostly cook curries; at least I use spices all the time, even if I am cooking pasta. My daughters find Italian sauces too bland, for example.' You could also use tinned sauces, like chakalaka in tomato sauce, for your pasta. How the lower middle class ate outside the home was fairly standard, but the way they prepared food at home was often distinctive of their 'community'.

The most striking feature of the lower-middle-class moral economy of everyday consumption, highlighted in their food habits, was the persistence of community norms, of an ethic of sharing and of practical and emotional attachment. Even though my informants were willing to push at the boundaries of their community culture, making it semi-fluid around a traditional core, the confidence they needed for this was always qualified by awareness of the fragility of their economic position. Any temptation to show off by buying or cooking more expensive or fashionable foodstuffs had to be squared with specific notions of solidarity within their family and inner social circle. Moral duty to less well-off members was a central feature of their economy; whether or not such transactions among kin were 'conspicuous consumption' is disputable. If representing democracy as individual consumption is a general neoliberal project, Durban's lower middle class did not readily conform to it, since their moral economy was anchored in maintaining relations with their kin group and their racial and religious communities.

ON CONSUMPTION, CONSPICUOUS OR OTHERWISE, AND NATION-BUILDING

In *The Theory of the Leisure Class*, Thorstein Veblen (1992) saw evolutionary significance in the development of leisure and excess. This was a product of two interconnected processes. Elite status was based on exploiting the labour of others, which allowed the emergent leisure class to advertise their own freedom from toil through leisure activities, including every sort of play (the more wasteful the better). Veblen's leisure class also attracted attention by spending lavishly and this was widely emulated. Taken together, these trends pushed the markers of leisure in ever more arcane and recursive directions.

I have drawn attention here to how lower-middle-class consumers in Durban calculated means-ends relations and showed restraint in their spending within the framework of a moral economy. If they ever had a chance for conspicuous consumption, this normally took place in the constraining context of an extended family and community of origin where an ethos of sharing was valued more highly than competition for status. Of course, ceremonial occasions – such as weddings, birthday parties and feast days – provided an opportunity to relax budgetary constraints somewhat, when more members of the extended family might be present and favourite luxuries were indulged, especially meat and alcohol. Some might label such occasions not as gatherings of families who share, but as performances whose purpose is winning status and attention. The lower-middle-class Durbanites of my acquaintance took pleasure in their own ingenuity, imagination and generosity when sponsoring celebrations. This is largely a matter of judgement and not of antagonistic social principles. Social reality permits a number of interpretations and this case study adds my voice, along with the voices of my informants, to the conversation about Veblen's relevance to understanding class and race in South Africa today.

REFERENCES

Abélès, M. 2014, *Penser au-delà de l'Etat*, Belin: Paris.

Benjamin, W., 1999 [1939], *The Arcades Project*. Harvard University Press: Cambridge.

Benjamin, W., 2006, *The Writer on Modern Life: Essays on Charles Baudelaire*, ed. M. W. Jennings, Belknap: Cambridge.

Bona, April 2014, Caxton Magazines: Johannesburg.

Chevalier, S, 1997, 'L'idéologie culinaire en Angleterre ou comment séparer le blanc du jaune', *Ethnologie Française* 27(1): 73–79.

Chevalier, S., 2007, 'Faire ses courses en voisin: Pratiques d'approvisionnement et sociabilité dans l'espace de trois quartiers de centre ville', Lyon et Besançon: Paris. http://metropoles.revues.org/107

Chevalier, S., 2010a, 'The Spatial Anchorage of Kinship: The Dole Case Study', with Amiotte-Suchet, L., in P. Heady and P. Schweitzer, *Kinship in the 21st Century Europe 2: Family, Kinship and Community at the Start of the 21st Century – Nineteen Localities*. Campus Verlag: Frankfurt/New York.

Chevalier, S., 2010b, 'Les "Black Diamonds" existent-ils? Médias, consommation et classe moyenne noire en Afrique du Sud', *Sociologies Pratiques* 20: 75–86.

Chevalier, S, 2012. 'Comment partager les mêmes espaces? Les classes moyennes à Durban (Afrique du Sud)', *Espaces et Sociétés* 148–9(1): 129–44.

Chevalier, S., 2014, 'Pile *et* face: consommation et endettement: L'émergence d'une nouvelle classe moyenne en Afrique du Sud (Durban)', in V. Guillard (ed.) *Boulimie d'objets: L'être et l'avoir dans nos sociétés*, De Boeck: Bruxelles, 137–151.

Chevalier, S., 2015, 'Food, Malls and the Politics of Consumption: South Africa's New Middle Class', *Development Southern Africa* 32(1): 118–129.

Chevalier, S. 2017. 'Participer à la nouvelle Afrique du Sud? La dimension politique des *shopping malls*'. In *Shoppings Malls: l'avènement de la modernité? Ateliers d'anthropologie* 4, viewed 23 November 2018, available from: http://journals.openedition.org/ateliers/10377.

Chevalier, S. & Escusa, E., 2011, *Les pratiques alimentaires des classes moyennes sud-africaines*, Rapport de recherche pour l'entreprise Bel, Septembre, Entreprise Bel: Paris.

Comaroff, J. & Comaroff, J., (eds.) 1993, *Modernity and Its Malcontents: Ritual and Power in Postcolonial Africa*, University of Chicago Press: Chicago.

Crankshaw, O., 1997, *Race, Class and the Changing Division of Labour Under Apartheid*, Routledge: London.

Darbon, D. & Toulabor C., 2014, *L'invention des classes moyennes africaines, enjeux et défis*, Karthala: Paris.

De Certeau, M., 1984 [1980], *The Practice of Everyday Life*, University of California Press: Berkeley.

Dlamini, J., 2009, *Native Nostalgia*, Jacana: Johannesburg.

Duflo, E. & Banerjee A., 2007. *What Is Middle Class About the Middle Classes Around the World?* Bureau for Research and Economic Analysis and Development (Bread) *Journal of Economics Perspectives* 22(2): 3–28.

Fassin, D., 2009, 'Les économies morales revisitées', *Annales. Histoire, Sciences Sociales* 6: 1237–1266.

Hann, C. & Hart, K., 2011, *Economic Anthropology*, Polity Press: Cambridge.

Herpin, N., 1986, 'Socio-style', *Revue Française de Sociologie* 27: 265–272.

Hyslop, J., 2000, 'Why did Apartheid's Supporters Capitulate? Whiteness, Class and Consumption in Urban South Africa, 1985–1995', *Society in Transition* 31(1): 36–44.

Hyslop, J., 2003, 'The White Poor at the End of Apartheid: The Collapse of the Myth of Afrikaner Community', *Itinerario* 27(3–4): 226–242.

Iquani, M., 2015, *Consumption, Media and the Global South*, Palgrave MacMillan: London.

James, D., 2014, *Money From Nothing: Indebtedness and Aspiration in South Africa*, Stanford University Press: Redwood City.

Johnson, R., 2009, '"The Girl About Town": Discussions of Modernity and Female Youth in *Drum* Magazine, 1951–1970', *Social Dynamics* 35(1): 36–50.

Khunou, G. 2015, 'What Middle Class? The Shifting and Dynamic Nature of Class Position', *Development Southern Africa* 32(1): 90–103.

Krige, D., 2011, *Power, Identity and Agency at Work in the Popular Economies of Soweto and Black Johannesburg*. Unpublished PhD dissertation, University of Witwatersrand: Johannesburg.

Krige, D., 2012, 'Histories and Changing Dynamics of Housing, Social Class and Social Mobility in Black Johannesburg', *Interdisciplinary Journal for the Study of the Arts and Humanities in South Africa* 19(1): 19–45.

Miller, D., 1998, *A Theory of Shopping*, Polity Press: Cambridge.

Phadi, M. and Ceruti, C., 2011, 'Multiple Meanings of the Middle Class in Soweto, South Africa', *African Sociological Review/Revue Africaine de Sociologie* 15(1): 88–108.

Phadi, M. and Manda, O., 2010, 'The Language of Class: Southern Sotho and Zulu Meanings of 'Middle Class' in Soweto', *South African Review of Sociology* 41(3): 81–98.

Posel, D., 2010, 'Races to Consume: Revisiting South Africa's History of Race, Consumption and the Struggle for Freedom', *Ethnic and Racial Studies* 33(2): 157–175.

Scott, J., 1976, *The Moral Economy of the Peasant: Rebellion and Subsistence in Southeast Asia*, Yale University Press: New Haven.

Seekings, J. & Nattrass, N., 2006, *Class, Race and Inequality in South Africa*, UKZN Press: Pietermaritzburg.

Strasser, S., McGovern, C. & Judt, M. (ed.), 1998, *Getting and Spending*, Cambridge University Press: Cambridge.

Southall, R., 2016, *The New Black Middle Class in South Africa*, Jacana: Johannesburg.

Thompson, E. P., 1966, *The Making of the English Working Class*, Vintage: London.

Veblen, T., 1992 [1899], *The Theory of the Leisure Class*, Transaction Publishers: New Brunswick.

Your Family, September 2013, Caxton Magazines: Johannesburg.

Zelizer, V., 1997, *The Social Meaning of Money*, Princeton University Press: Princeton.

NOTES

1   I contacted informants through personal networks based on neighbourhood, school and workplace. I also interviewed shopkeepers and managers of supermarkets and malls. I studied

consumption and class in the media – especially women's magazines, television programmes and cookbooks. I bring three decades of research in France, England and Bulgaria, including several projects in Paris. My South African ethnography draws on a mixture of French and Anglophone traditions of field work.

2   Duflo and Banerjee (2007) focus on consumer behaviour and, more vaguely, ways of life when trying to pin down 'the middle class'. See also Southall (2016).

3   Some of my informants claimed that they spent nearly half of their income on food, but nobody confessed to borrowing money for food.

4   An English version of this article may be found on the London School of Economics website: http://www2.lse.ac.uk/anthropology/research/popular_economies/35b_Sophie_Chevalier.doc

5   For this reason, I examined oral histories collected during 1979–1982 from members of what was then the black elite in Durban's townships in the Killie Campbell archives in Durban.

6   Although 'class' is a term widely used in post-apartheid South Africa, 'race' is more common in private than in public. When referring to the residue of the old South African racial categories, the generic term 'community' is most often used. This is understood to have a 'cultural', not biological foundation.

7   I previously undertook field work in France, England and Bulgaria for two decades and continue to carry out research in France. See my habilitation thesis: 'Towards a Political Anthropology of Everyday Economic Practices' (*Ecole des Hautes Etudes en Sciences Sociales*, Paris, October 2014).

8   The main difference conventionally lies in the amount of property owned and the related contrast in exposure to market fluctuations. The lower middle class or petite bourgeoisie are thought to swing between identifying with the upper middle class and workers. When the French (attributed to Napoleon) called the English a 'nation of shopkeepers', they were probably referring to the size and fluidity of this class.

9   French sociologists now write of a *petite prosperité* (class with a modicum of prosperity) to describe this petite bourgeoisie in West Africa (Darbon & Toulabor 2014).

10 For France and Britain, see Chevalier (1997, 2007); on South Africa, Chevalier (2015, 2017), Chevalier and Escusa (2011).

11 Some authors (for instance, Posel 2010) argue that the new dominant black class also bring their own version of moral economy to consumption conceived of as a significant marker of their emancipation and freedom struggle.

12 I have used pseudonyms throughout to protect the anonymity of my sources.

13 Posel, D., 2014, 'Seeing Apartheid as a Consumerist Project: The view from Zonk! Magazine in the 1950s and 1960s', Institute for Humanities in Africa, University of Cape Town, 27 March.

14 The other magazine that I have studied, *Your Family*, has the same publisher; its appearance is very similar, right down to many of the same section headings, but the fashion and make-up models are always white. It is read by members of all communities, especially by mothers, even if at one time it addressed only white women.

15 I do not want to explore the nostalgia issue here, as in the debate initiated by Jacob Dlamini's (2009) book. It was however a striking feature in Bulgaria during the 1990s when I did field work there.
16 Another example is the basic food basket which generally includes Ceylon black tea, tins of baked beans and a loaf of white bread.
17 The basic food basket now contains tinned fish and fresh fish.

13 MARIGOLD BEADS: WHO NEEDS DIAMONDS?!

JONI BRENNER AND PAMILA GUPTA

It is day one of the 2016 Johannesburg Art Fair and the 12 drawers, three freestanding glass display stands and ten wall-mounted units for the Marigold hand-loomed beaded necklaces have already been replenished with fresh stock after the frenzy of the opening event the night before.

Replenishment of the supply happens frequently over the coming three days of the Fair, in response to the waves of consumers. Discerning and focused, many return repeatedly over the course of the event to enjoy and inspect the changing displays. Each new purchase seems to inspire or inform the next – as if these necklaces need each other.

The booth at the Art Fair, a shocking-pink cubicle, is shared with the Friends of JAG (Johannesburg Art Gallery) and has been tightly conceptualised to draw connections between genres of art, design, craft and adornment. The Friends of JAG – at the Fair to raise awareness of their important collection and to increase membership – present a fine example of an Ndebele *nyoga* (a beaded bridal train) and a pair of *umlingakobe* ('long tears' or head hangings, worn by mothers whose sons are at initiation school). Seen in relation to these earlier Southern African examples, and echoing in some way their form, the Marigold necklaces are presented as contemporary manifestations of traditional beadwork objects possessing a shared but different use-value (in that they are both worn) and symbolic value (in that they both express particular kinds of social status). A new limited edition design, directly inspired by the work of Serge-Alain Nitegeka, a featured artist at the Fair, is also presented.

The Friends of JAG happens to be directed by iconic South African fashion designer and arts activist Marianne Fassler, and as a result, the booth exemplifies high style: distinctive pink walls, designer furniture, wall texts, long slim mirrors, a single green leaf in a mid-century, violet-coloured glass vase and a large-scale stylised moody photograph of a model draped in Marigold beads with just one necklace extended between her outstretched arms. A tightly curated space, it creates a particular kind of platform for viewing the beads.

For three days, visitors to the Art Fair stop in at the booth to make their choices. Many are familiar with the necklaces and already hold significant existing collections. These people have encountered the Marigold necklaces at private 'pop-up shops' in Johannesburg, or at Kim Sacks' African Art and Design Gallery on Jan Smuts Avenue, Johannesburg, seen them on the Leopard Frock/Marianne Fassler catwalks, or heard about them via a range of public lectures, radio interviews, university seminars and conferences.[1]

The frenzy to acquire has been marked in other settings too, including the perhaps unlikely forum of an academic conference. Johannesburg-based artist Joni Brenner, one of the authors of this chapter, has made several presentations on various aspects of the production and consumption of the beads – and invariably, many in the academic audience, while interested in the content of her talk, are intent on buying the beads. Immediately following these seminar or conference papers, the first audience question is always, 'Can I have that one?' or 'How much is it?' or 'Do you take credit cards?'. A colleague, Kopano Ratele, observes with bemusement, 'It doesn't matter what you say in your paper, people just want them!' Recognising this possibly awkward synergy between academic interest and the desire for consumption in a workshop held in the run-up to this very publication, Deborah Posel – wearing a good few strands herself – put forward the notion that as researchers, we must all 'fess up' to our own consumption impulses. In a workshop full of anthropologists, it is a given that these kinds of first-hand and personal experiences are telling. In the workshop in preparation for this book, the overwhelming impulse to examine, touch, feel, try on, select, combine and ultimately own could be justified as good practice – an academic as participant rather than detached observer is surely a good thing!

Seldom is a buyer's encounter with the beads a bland, matter-of-fact affair. The decision to acquire the beads is mostly made by people who love them and 'must' have them – with the knowledge that each additional purchase extends their options for making new visual combinations/statements.

Equally telling, however, is that this rapt fascination for these beads, and the desire to accumulate them, seems limited to a very specific stratum of buyers – a particular social type: women who style themselves as outside the fashion mainstream, as creative mavericks and/or as women dissenting from sexualised versions of jewellery. The subtitle for this chapter – 'who needs diamonds' – is also then a tossing off of the associations embedded in the 'getting rid of headaches since 1888'[2] type of advertising campaigns for diamond jewellery, which invariably/deliberately position diamonds in the realm of highly sexualised – and economic – power relations between men and women.

How do Marigold beads, which are made of (relatively) inexpensive materials – thousands of tiny glass beads that, individually, have little material or financial worth – even begin to function as a form of conspicuous consumption in Thorstein Veblen's terms? Is the buying and wearing of Marigold beads a form of Veblenian conspicuous consumption? If so, in what sense, and to what extent, is Veblen's lens on the phenomenon a useful one in this case?

Certainly at the Johannesburg Art Fair, the Marigold necklaces were among the most affordable purchases to be made, but they are not acquired because they are cheap. They are, in fact, expensive in relation to much other beaded jewellery. Though not as expensive as gold and diamonds, it is indeed easy to amass quite a few thousand ZAR around your neck.

There may be a degree of conspicuous consumption attached to the acquisition and display of these necklaces, but are they acquired for their capacity to signal wealth? Do they even remotely signal wealth in Veblen's framework? If not material wealth, then what kind of wealth might they signal? Is there some kind of stylistic kudos accrued by wearing them that attaches one to an elitist social group defined by superior, discriminating taste and knowledge (of other kinds of value), borne of education?[3]

If more obviously ostentatious forms of jewellery signal wealth and prosperity – gold and diamonds for example, or semi-precious stones and their elaborate settings – what do Marigold beads signal, and what drives this evident, focused, bead-need?

How does the exuberant and robust demand for these beads measure up against Veblen's somewhat one-dimensional notion of that which drives consumption? Who buys and wears these beads and why (and who does not), and is there a difference between the thoughtful acquisition of something that is not a passing fad and (an)other form of buying where the things are 'consumed', having relatively short term value and novelty?[4]

VEBLEN: OWNERSHIP AND DISPLAY; WEALTH, WASTE AND WOMEN

In Veblen's cynical view of the leisure class, the consumption of goods that can indicate taste, style, design, and by extension wealth, is even better when these 'wasteful' qualities can be visibly and conspicuously displayed to others. Why have a practical and ordinary spoon when you can have a hand-wrought silver one? For him, forms of adornment and embellishment are limited to their capacity to signal class, status and wealth. His disregard of sensuous tactility and aesthetic pleasures or beauty as mere evidence of material value is there in his claim that 'beauty is commonly a gratification of our sense of costliness masquerading under the name of beauty' (Veblen 1994 [1899]: 79) – or in other words, that we tend to find things beautiful because they are expensive. His is a limiting reduction of worth to fiscal value, and of the harnessing of beauty, style and aesthetic taste to display wealth – the more conspicuous, the more 'bling', the better. Aside from his flat equation of beauty with expensiveness, built into the view of the conspicuous display of goods as indicators of financial power is the gendered notion, very much of his time, that a woman's role is to 'sustain the good name of the male household to which she belongs' (83). Veblen states, 'Still in the full sense the property of the men, the performance of conspicuous … consumption … came to be part of the services required of them' and that 'not [being] their own masters, obvious expenditure and leisure on their part would redound to the credit of their master rather than to their own credit' (83).

This patriarchal view is, astonishingly, the same view that is behind the contemporary De Beers advertising campaign for diamond jewellery mentioned above, another example of which reads, 'Exactly how badly do you want to play golf this weekend?' Embedded in the campaign is the notion of such jewellery being bestowed on women for purposes of male social aggrandisement as well as an implied control over women – keeping them quiet.

The purchase of gold and diamonds by men to adorn and harness their women is likely understood in relation to the gold index and the share price of mining corporations – that is, in terms of a financial return. Arguably, many of the men who buy diamonds set in gold for women, do so as indicators of their own wealth and power. Expensive materials, generally sourced and crafted by men into delicate feminine settings where floral motifs and curlicues abound, are made into pretty necklaces that men – integral to the production and purchase – invest in and are invested in.

In the Veblenian sense, jewellery as an expression of wealth and status inhabits a realm of classist, gendered and highly sexualised power relations that are a far cry from the kind of statements made by wearers of Marigold beads. In this respect, the Veblenian lens is useful as a foil for the ways in which Marigold beads operate. Made by women, and on the whole (although not exclusively) personally selected, acquired and worn by women, these necklaces bypass sexualised power relations. They signal a different set of allegiances and values altogether.

The Marigold necklaces are the product of collaboration between a long-standing beadwork cooperative in Bulawayo, Zimbabwe, and Brenner, who was born in Bulawayo. Their collaboration, begun in 2011, has developed slowly but surely, and in response to demand. This demand has never been orchestrated by advertising, never actively marketed. It has grown through informal exposure to the beads, and by word of mouth, within very particular and select circles and circuits of information. It started small: a set of three necklaces, designed, commissioned and worn by Brenner, was widely remarked on, repeatedly enquired about. This led, eventually, to further commissions, which sold even more. In response, the project grew, the cooperative directors employed and trained more craftswomen and it is now a sustainable beadwork cooperative producing between 150 and 200 highly regarded and much-wanted necklaces every month.[5] It remains a small, focused operation that is alive to design changes and innovations, one emerging from the other, while maintaining a product that is the same but also different with each iteration, and continuing to resist overt marketing and advertising (See Figure 12).

Indeed, the necklaces, made in Bulawayo and sold in Johannesburg via the select outlets described above, have to a large degree only been accessible through the social networks that Brenner is part of. So the primary consumers have been – at least initially – fellow-artists and academics,[6] museum curators, collectors, art lovers and designers. But there is a wider network too, and exactly who responds to, wears, loves and collects these necklaces has given pause for thought. The more public showcasing at the Johannesburg Art Fair certainly expanded the clientele and the interest has stretched beyond local shores.

I NEED, I WANT: WHO DOES, WHO DOESN'T AND WHY?

There are, of course, varying reasons driving the consumption. Many overlap and intersect, while others challenge and complicate presumed readings of why people want these beads so intensely, and of what they get from wearing these simultaneously simple and complex long flat strands of hand-loomed beads, which are produced in a range of varying widths and lengths, and stitch-joined one end to the other without clasps or fasteners.

Marigold beads, by nature, are exclusive: the monthly production is small, and they are only available in three places in Johannesburg, one of which is by appointment only. One wearer noted that, for her, this element was an important factor, she likes the fact that not everyone has them, that they are not commonly available; in fact she admits to being elusive about where to find them when pressed for this information!

There is, in any event, an embedded uniqueness in each loomed strand, a function of their being handmade and by definition different every time – a feature reinforced by what artist and African art collector Karel Nel (2017) has termed the 'constant drift': the ever-shifting colour palette supplied in the form of raw beads, and the ever-evolving changes to the designs/patterns. This, along with each consumer's personal choices and combinations, ensures a high level of individuation, while also signaling allegiance to a like-minded group.

The beads are key tools in some people's constructions of their sense of self. In the very early days of the project, architect Briget Grosskopff tried on one strand of pure black beads, then added another, another and yet more until she had nine strands around her neck, finally concluding that no architect should have less than nine black strands. We recently discussed this early intuitive response of hers, and she reflected that there is something in the combined simplicity of the form with the structural three-dimensionality of a group of necklaces that becomes sculptural; it echoed an oft-made description of herself as a sculptor on a very large scale.

Grosskopff further observed that 'adornment is making yourself more', something that resonated with the selfie received from artist Clive Van den Berg sporting an outfit completed by a mass showcasing of striped and shiny Marigold strands at a conference in Venice, with the short statement, 'they caused a stir'.

The noticing can also be constituted by more private or intimate acts: several buyers have noted how daughters either long to wear, or participate in the selections of, strands to be worn by their mothers, that these exchanges are prized moments of shared creative looking and decision making.[7]

By all accounts, from patients and colleagues alike, Anne Stanwix is a deeply creative medical practitioner. Her professional mind and working life are rooted in science, yet she has often recounted that choosing the combination of Marigold beads to wear constitutes her single most creative act of each day. She is one of the earliest collectors of the beads and has followed the project with great commitment, always at the pop-up shops, and regularly bringing groups of other dedicated wearers from shores near and far to see the new collections at Brenner's apartment.[8] Stanwix is also a generous giver of the beads, and she has almost single-handedly constructed an international following for these necklaces. The necklaces connect women: makers and wearers, and wearers to one another. The reach and presence of Stanwix's generosity, and the direct association of the beads with the giver, is clearly made in George Tobias' amusing Facebook comment in response to a photograph of New York curator Beckie Warren wearing a Marigold necklace: 'She's wearing one of Anne's necklaces!' In various conversations over the years Stanwix has reflected that she likes to give these beads to people across the globe because they signal Johannesburg specifically. Although people have received them from her as a gift, she tells, they have then requested more of them. On a recent trip to Europe, three disappointed women friends exclaimed, 'What do we have to do to get these beads from you!?'

Are they desired because they are noticed and admired? Donna Bryson, journalist and author, recounted how, several times, she has struck up conversations with strangers in cafés that she has spotted wearing Marigold necklaces, saying, 'You must know Joni?' Similarly, Penny Hoets greets fellow wearers with 'friend of Joni!' In several ways, the beads forge connections. Estelle Trengove, fellow Wits academic, was followed in a supermarket and then stopped by a woman she did not know who admired her necklaces and enquired where she might acquire some for herself – and Joni's number was given. The woman was Deborah Womack, head of relationship marketing at SABMiller, who was briefly passing through Johannesburg. Following her visit to the apartment, she sent an email: 'I am wearing four of the pink/green/deep red beads today and people cannot stop looking at them. Four people so far in the office asked about them! I am so delighted. They make me so happy'. Looking and being knowingly looked at, with recognition, approval, possibly envy from fellow wearers points to the fact that even though, as Posel notes, these beads might be invisible to many jewellery consumers – and, she adds, to most men – they are immediately apparent to a kind of self-constituted sub-set or inner circle. Other wearers notice and the pleasure of this fuels the need.

Fiona Southwood, an advocate, reflected that she wears the beads to work as 'an act of creativity and of self-expression, perhaps a subtle way of being seen'. She also observed though that 'people don't often comment on them, except in an environment where it's acceptable, for example when I come to one of your open-house gatherings. My colleagues, particularly my male colleagues, are quite careful about commenting on women's appearance and what they're wearing (and I'm not sure how many notice). I think my work environment (colleagues, attorneys, clients), generally, is not conducive to eliciting a response. I have become aware that people do notice the beads when I give them as presents. The recipients are truly delighted and will then tell me how much they like the ones that I wear. I wear them because it feels like I'm wearing art works, more so than with other pieces of jewellery. Also, given that I've got quite a few, every opportunity for wearing them is an opportunity to play, putting different combinations together with different clothes.'

It is perhaps unavoidable that a small project like this, which has emerged through, and taken its shape within, what Pierre Bourdieu (1984) calls a 'circle of legitimation', looks a particular way, and resonates with or reaches a particular type of person. In Bourdieu's circuit of inter-legitimation, a complex web of experiences, each answering and reinforcing all the others, creates enchantment (Bourdieu 1984: 53). In practice then, the fact that Nel acquired the first dozen Marigold necklaces for his impressive African art collection, and has continued to acquire select pieces, is in keeping with the fact that Lily Goldblatt chose to gift three strands to the curator of photography at SFMoMA which led to their prestigious design store carrying Marigold beads. These 'experiences' are reinforced again by Fassler's inclusion of them on her catwalk, by their being featured at the Johannesburg Art Fair, and by the countless examples of artists and intellectuals who wear these beads.

As an artist who regularly makes exhibitions of her own and of others' works, including the products from the Marigold cooperative (where her role in buying beads and developing new designs is collaborative and extends to the responsibility of positioning/exhibiting the work), Brenner's 'cultural capital' – that 'accumulated stock of knowledge about the products of artistic and intellectual traditions, which is learned through educational training and, crucially for Bourdieu, also through social upbringing' (Trigg 2001: 104) – is of course deployed in shaping how the beads are seen.

Such 'circles of legitimation' may be seen negatively, divisively even, as producing an elitist closed social group/circuit, but it is possible too to see the project, and the beads, as a binding and bonding social network with possibilities and creative opportunities for makers and wearers alike, with the potential to traverse barriers rather than produce them. Even if they are not affordable to everyone, they are also not priced to be elitist, certainly not in relation to the price point of branded flashy accessories.

Whether one sees the Marigold necklaces as inclusive or exclusive, they undoubtedly have become something of a social code; one that is read differently from the way that gold and diamonds are read.

OFFERING SOLACE, PERSONAL CONNECTIONS BETWEEN WOMEN

Some of the ways in which the beads are understood rub against Veblen's reading of embellishment/adornment as mere symbol of money.

Attorney Janine Bredenkamp is among others in remarking that she would rather buy Marigold necklaces than any other gift for her women friends because knowing something of the source, of where they are made, and by whom, makes a difference to her, makes her gifts personal in a many-layered way. Indeed, her first visit was to purchase one for each of the women who cared for her while she was in recovery from a hip surgery.

Several comments in the visitors' book at Brenner's apartment reveal recognition of the presences embedded in this work: 'So many lives and loves in these beads'; 'Magnificent and such love and talent in the making, will treasure them'.

Several buyers have commented on the tactility of the necklaces, and on the way in which the beads roll between the fingers; researcher Penny Hoets and professor in political studies Shireen Hassim both speak of the necklaces as 'worry beads',[9] connecting their fluid form to a meditative practice of focus and presence, processing thoughts/worries through the repeat action of the fingers. Some buyers have gifted a necklace to friends, including those who are undergoing chemotherapy. The healing role that the

Marigolds sometimes perform surfaced in a conversation with Dr Mmatala Mabeba, who called to say that she had had an unspeakable year of loss and grief and she needed to see what was in the drawers.

On other occasions, the therapeutic impulse was more familiar – as 'entrancing retail therapy' – to which several consumers have wittily, and sometimes self-critically, owned up.

PURPOSEFUL MODES

The acquisition of the beads – whatever the underlying impulses to have them – is not merely, if at all, about being 'in vogue'. Veblen's disdain for being fashionable, for the rapidity with which fashions change and the conspicuous wastefulness embedded in the constant replacement of one trend with the next, may be a position shared with several Marigold consumers. But they would reject entirely Veblen's disavowal of the aesthetics of conspicuous consumption and all repertoires of desire. The pleasure and importance of personal expressions of style – which are central to the somewhat compulsive, but always purposeful, accrual of more and more Marigolds – is not something that Veblen considered in his line of argument.

Distinguishing the personal/individual construction of style from the externally determined dictates of fashion, actress and model Lauren Hutton famously remarked that 'fashion is what you're offered four times a year by designers. And style is what you choose' (Ramsdale 2017). The same sentiment is there in Edna Woolman Chase's observation that whereas 'fashion can be bought, style one must possess' (ibid).

Though sometimes frenzied and lustful, the selection and purchase of Marigold beads is by no means thoughtless or random. Selections are made pointedly with existing collections and wardrobes in mind (and sometimes in hand!), and in relation to mood, to what one feels comfortable wearing, or with the specific qualities of the recipient in mind. Finally making it to the Johannesburg drawers from her Cape Town base, art historian Sandra Klopper remarked, 'I realised when I had to choose for myself yesterday just how difficult it is to do so, but also how very well others have chosen for me in the past'.

The sites of viewing and purchasing are carefully selected. All of the spaces – Kim Sacks African Art and Design Gallery, Cinda Hunter's Beloved Things and Joni Brenner's apartment – are quiet, calm spaces filled with art, books, (mirrors!) and carefully displayed Marigolds, where a shopper receives personal attention, usually coffee or tea, and as much information as is required about the the cooperative in Bulawayo and about the Marigold beads and how they are made. They are constructed environments that embed an understanding that it matters what you say about things, it matters how you present and display things and it matters that these strategies encourage close looking and deep knowing. While the product may transcend such strategies – it would be hard to miss their beauty even at a jumbled flea market – buying from someone who knows about the source, where the objects are produced, and by whom, works against the anonymity or abstractions that are attached to the sale of much craftwork. In these spaces the purchasing is a slow experience, people look long, and they look hard. Only on occasion is a bead visit brief. Mostly, a visit is paced with pauses between looking and relooking. Shoppers spend time looking at the often overwhelming options, narrowing down their choices, trying them on, reconfiguring them; rescanning the full range of options to see what might have been missed or overlooked the first time. It is always a deliberate process of looking and relooking.

Not all buyers are interested in the invested processes of making, or in the story of the development of the cooperative and the circle of women who make the necklaces and are sustained by the project. But they all notice and respond to the beauty, quality, labour, time and the creative choices represented in each strand. They all recognise the refinement of the product and the perfection of the handwork, and it resonates with Fassler's assertion that 'craft is the new luxury' – something that also underpins the statement by Giovanni Corvaja, an Italian goldsmith artist:

> I like to think about my work as a mixture of various elements: time, diligence, skill, passion, ideas and gold. And of all those things, gold is probably the most easily attainable. (Banks 2015: 3)

His statement is insightful in that it makes clear what some of the embedded values are in objects of desire today. If the Marigold necklaces can be seen as a form of conspicuous consumption, then arguably what is being conspicuously displayed is the wearer's recognition of the embedded time, diligence, skill, passion and ideas – these are the qualities that form the beauty and drive the demand.

If this is so, then the Marigold necklaces sit squarely outside of Veblen's notion of conspicuous consumption as described in his *Theory of the Leisure Class*. While conspicuous consumption and its attendant Veblenian clauses of emulation and one-upmanship – as seen in many of the case studies in this volume – is alive and well in twenty-first century Africa, the need for Marigolds seems less about having more than anyone else than it is about satisfying a hunger for beauty, the aesthetic, and the scope that material and craft-based art forms have for fulfilling desire, pleasure and connections – across class barriers and outside of emulation and aspiration.

And yet, ruffling that neat distinction and distance from Veblen's notion of conspicuous consumption, there is surely some part of the drive to have these beads that affirms one's own artistic and intellectual prestige; that asserts allegiance to the exclusivity, rarity and thoughtful beauty represented by the Marigold beads. If this is so, perhaps they do not sit so absolutely squarely outside of Veblen's order. Occupying a slightly uncomfortable space, or having some degree of ambiguity, produces complexity and enquiry, demands a questioning and a reckoning about who we are and what we value. There are no neat edges.

AFRICAN COSMOPOLITAN: BEADS, PLACE AND IDENTITY

The acquisition of Marigolds grows and expands a collection rather than replacing an earlier necklace with a newer one; they have no shelf life. Similarly, the South African fashion house Leopard Frock, directed by Fassler, with whom Marigold has been associated in a number of public events, has often asserted that they do not value the concept of 'last season'; that their garments do not date because Leopard Frock is very much about revisiting and reimagining the central themes and approaches that have defined their work – a slow construction of a particular, idiosyncratic style or identity rather than a series of unrelated seasonal and disposable fashions. Over and again you will see Vlisco wax-print fabrics in mad combination with Basotho blankets, tartan and camouflage, animal print, neon, rick-rack trim and beadwork – each symbolic or reminiscent of trade, exchange, colonisation, warfare, urban and rural identities, identities and experiences in conflict, hybrid frissons and a dynamic and embracing interpretation of what it means to be South African now.

The hybridity makes a political point about what constitutes 'Africanness' and extends to a reading of beads, themselves manufactured in Europe, but traded and styled in Africa for centuries, as embodying a dynamic, antistatic understanding of African creative production.

Global materials reconstituted and repurposed locally take on an identity of the local that is always an interpretation, alive to creative change and extension. The Marigold necklaces, like Fassler's garments, have both local and global appeal, resonating with consumers in their projection of identification with things well crafted, with a complexity of form and design, and arguably with the allusion to intersecting influences that ruffle any notion of hermetically sealed static identities.

The point to be made is not that Marigold beads are associated with a fashion house in an attempt to position them in the realm of the rich leisure class; it is a specific fashion house, with an intellectual alignment to the values undergirding the Marigold project. The association strategically reinforces the shared values of change and continuity, of highly crafted well-made objects, and of intelligent sometimes-disruptive playfulness.

Glenn Adamson makes the observation that 'craft is usually seen as existing in opposition to globalization' (Adamson 2010: 272), and by implication, as something limited by its sheltered/insular practice. In Posel's view, the Marigold beads appeal exactly because the pure form, the sensual tactility of the strands of beads, could not be further from any such staid notion of craftwork. For her, they transcend any popular, closed, notion of what might be a stereotypical or ethnically rendered African aesthetic, and bear no connection to place.

Hassim's phone call differently reflects the complex hybrid nature of identity and place: 'Please put aside that long wide necklace I looked at earlier today – I am presenting an award at the end of the month and it will be nice and showy; it will make a great impact. The occasion has a dress code "formal traditional" so this seems like the right response to wear with black silk kurta!' We laughed about the complexity of identity; that if we are all mongrels, at least we are stylish ones!

Others insist on a clearer view of beads as African: Dandrige 'Pops' Mahlamvu, a fine art installer, said 'beads are indigenous … these work very well with traditional clothing'. He is among many who associate beads with Africa and who combine Marigolds with traditional clothing.

The group/type of consumer is clearly diverse, as are the reasons that Marigolds are acquired, traversing differences in age, race, gender and levels of socio-economic mobility. If there is indeed a type of wearer, the type holds only loosely, perhaps under the broad rubric of close observers, recognisers of skill, labour, and creativity, and those with a taste for this kind of aesthetic.

GREED-NEED: IS THERE MORE TO IT?

Though knowledge of the cooperative and the 16 women whose livelihoods depend on the continuing sales may justify increased expenditure for some consumers, no one buys out of a sense of charity. Arguably, some consumers may feel compelled to mask their unstoppable need – 'These are for gifts' – though, even with the best of intentions, many of these never make it to the recipient, real or imagined.

Undoubtedly, people want, and they want a lot, but is there more to the need than the sheer beauty of the necklaces and a hunger for participatory creative play?

People seem to be moved by looking at, touching and handling these tactile, mobile objects. Cari Romm asserts that 'it makes sense that the word *feeling* can refer to an emotion and a sense of touch' (Romm 2016). In retail studies, the environmental psychologist Paco Underhill, in a chapter titled 'The Sensual Shopper', suggests that touching something produces a mini-bond with the object, making you more likely to buy it (Underhill 1999: 179). As an extension of this idea, and especially with regard to deeply personal hand-wrought objects like the Marigolds, it is possible to imagine that touching and handling them produces a bond between people – between makers and wearers – where there is an instantaneous, often moving connection with the passion, skill and diligence of another person.

Research on mirror neurons, undertaken by Vittorio Gallese and others (2009: 519–536), affirms the idea that there is some kind of transmission of presence embodied in these necklaces or that they elicit an empathic response. Mirror neurons are responsible for the faculty of empathy, of being able to interpret another's feelings through their expression or demeanour and to respond by mirroring it. Nicole Shaer, medical doctor and artist, explains that:

> Gallese proposes that this same unspoken understanding/interpretation and mirrored response or feeling, happens with the unconscious perception of material marks of creation in an object. Of course, if we look closely, we can see the sort of marks a maker is using ... careful, careless, confident and fluid or tightly precious and so on. And it makes sense to me that the unconscious perception of the spirit of making – roughly translated to the degree of care – might be automatic.
>
> Of course, being slow and meticulous or whatever *may* yield a more materially valuable item by virtue of its painstaking production, but it is much more exciting to think that this value might be an indescribable quality which equates as the amount of 'love made visible' that is imbued in the not-so-inanimate-after-all object.
>
> I was thrilled to discover this because I have long mused on what makes 'useless' (art) objects feel loveable and I prefer this theory to others that necessarily emphasize greed and ego as the predominant link between me and a nice thing. (Shaer, email 2017)

In connecting Gallese's work on mirror neurons/empathy with consumption practices, Shaer points to a nuanced and more complex understanding of why we buy/want beautiful (handmade) things.

VEBLEN AND THE HAND-WROUGHT OBJECT

Certainly, responding to the mark of an individual maker is tied to the notion of the unique/exclusive object, something that is valued by most Marigold consumers. In Veblen's hard view, however, the necklaces may well constitute a fanciful and wasteful practice – the slow, hand-wrought production as something that invests an object with a conspicuous display of 'honorific waste', for him a mere indicator of wealth and status:

> The point of material difference between machine-made goods and the hand-wrought goods which serve the same purposes is, ordinarily, that the former serve their primary purpose more adequately. They are a more perfect product – show a more perfect adaptation of means to end. This does not save them from disesteem and deprecation, for they fall short under the test of honorific waste. *Hand labor is a more wasteful method of production; hence the goods turned out by this method are more serviceable for the purpose*

of pecuniary reputability; hence the marks of hand labor come to be honorific, and the goods which exhibit these marks take rank as of higher grade than the corresponding machine product [italics added].

Commonly, if not invariably, the honorific marks of hand labor are certain imperfections and irregularities in the lines of the hand-wrought article, showing where the workman has fallen short in the execution of the design. The ground of the superiority of hand-wrought goods, therefore, is a certain margin of crudeness. This margin must never be so wide as to show bungling workmanship, since that would be evidence of low cost, nor so narrow as to suggest the ideal precision attained only by the machine, for that would be evidence of low cost. (Veblen 1994: 96–7)

Though the Marigolds are handmade, they in no way 'fall short in the execution of their design'. Indeed, it is their flawless quality – no 'certain margin of crudeness' here – but handmade nature that makes them so extraordinary and desirable. Veblen's argument, though contestable in many ways, is one that values economical practical modes of production and consumption, need and function above the fanciful and wasteful. Of course, a mass-manufactured stainless-steel teapot that is poorly designed, for example, does not show 'a more perfect means to an end', and a well-designed teapot whether mass-manufactured in steel or crafted by hand may be equally perfectly adapted to the end imagined (Burroughs, email 2014). Though he values a 'bare necessities' approach, elsewhere in his text, Veblen reflects that:

consumption may of course be conceived to serve the consumer's physical wants – his physical comfort – *or his so-called higher wants – spiritual, aesthetic, intellectual, or what not;* the latter class of wants being served indirectly by an expenditure of goods, after the fashion familiar to all economic readers [italics added]. (Veblen 1994:17)

This 'concession' is not exactly an affirmation of the actual existence of such higher needs, reduced as they are, by implication, to fulfillment by commodities, but it is at least a limited recognition that consumption practices can have complex origins, driven by multiple and sometimes overlapping desires and needs.

Marigold necklaces, like much other handmade, craft-based art forms run counter to the experience of chain commodity. These are personal and personalised objects, and the detail and the complexity in each carefully constructed strand often solicits questions about who the makers are. By contrast, when one buys a diamond ring for example, the ring does not evoke the miners underground extracting the metal and the stones, or the person sitting with a grinder and a loupe spending hours faceting the stone or the one refining the metal or its being made by yet another person into a ring.

Somehow, the 'forever' diamond seems to have sprung fully and mechanically formed from somewhere and its value seems to lie almost exclusively in the amount paid for its purchase (Burroughs, email 2014). It seems that to make or buy the Marigold necklaces is to enter a slow world of craft, design and personal interaction. It is to enter a charmed circle, which allows one to step out of the abstractions of capitalism (Hofmeyr, email 2014) where one is embedded in the impersonal relations of the market, and the commodity chain of purchasing, say, diamonds instead (See Figure 13).

In *Five Poems for Grandmothers*, Margaret Atwood writes: 'Sons branch out, but / one woman leads to another. / Finally I know you / through your daughters, / my mother, her sisters, / and through myself (Atwood 1987: 14). Initially, her words may seem to jar with the Veblenian sense of consumption for self-elevation, rather than for, say, more empathic reasons. There may well be some acquisition of Marigolds that happens for reasons of emulation and aspiration, but there are also other factors involved, many of which point to complex personal and communal expressions of identity.

The subtitle of this chapter, 'Who needs diamonds', suggests identification with a different value system; one that foregrounds – or conspicuously displays – recognition of skill, craft-based art forms, time, passion, beauty, creative ingenuity and connectivity among people across time and place. Defamiliarising the notion of conspicuous consumption, we draw attention to modes of consumerist 'conspicuousness' that unsettle the Veblenian presumption through their emphatically anti-bling register.

REFERENCES

Adamson, G. (ed.), 2010. *The Craft Reader*. Berg: Oxford and New York.

Atwood, M., 1987, 'Five Poems for Grandmothers', in *Margaret Atwood Selected Poems II, 1976–1986*, 11–16, Houghton Mifflin: Boston.

Banks, L., 2015, 'Defining Luxury for a Modern Era', *The New York Times*, viewed 31 October 2016, available from: http://nyti.ms/1HKkbWG.

Bourdieu, P., 1984, *Distinction: A Social Critique of the Judgement of Taste*, Harvard University Press: Cambridge.

Bredenkamp, J., 2017, Conversation with Joni Brenner, 27 February.

Bryson, D., 2017, Conversation with Joni Brenner, 6 February.

Burroughs, E., 2014, Email correspondence. Received by Joni Brenner, 6 November.

Fassler, M., 2016, Email correspondence. Received by Joni Brenner, 12 September.

Gallese, V., 2009, 'Mirror Neurons, Embodied Simulation, and the Neural Basis of Social Identification', *Psychoanalytic Dialogues* 19: 519–536.

Grosskopff, B., 2017, Conversation with Joni Brenner, 14 March.

Hassim, S., 2017, Conversation with Joni Brenner, 19 March.

Hoets, P., 2017, Conversation with Joni Brenner, 09 March.

Hofmeyr, I., 2014, Email correspondence. Received by Joni Brenner, 23 November.

Klopper, S., 2016, Email correspondence. Received by Joni Brenner, 1 February.

Mabeba, M., 2016, Conversation with Joni Brenner, 25 October.

Mahlamvu, D., 2017, Conversation with Joni Brenner, 22 March.

Nel, K., 2017, Conversation with Joni Brenner, 12 March.

Posel, D., 2016, Writing workshop: Conspicuous Consumption in Africa, 23 November.

Posel, D., 2017, Email Correspondence. Received by Joni Brenner and Pamila Gupta, 10 March.

Posel, D., 2017, Conversation with Joni Brenner and Pamila Gupta, 20 March.

Ramsdale, S., 2017, '"I don't do fashion. I am fashion": The 50 best style quotes of all time', in *Marie Claire*, viewed 9 April 2017, available from: www.marieclaire.co.uk/fashion/the-40-best-style-quotes-of-all-time-122453#jTzkChyd2iqhso66.99.

Ratele, K., 2014, Symposium session: Conspicuous Consumption in Africa, Institute for Humanities in Africa, University of Cape Town, 4 December.

Romm, C., 2016, 'The people who store their emotions in their fingertips', in *New York Magazine*, viewed 17 January 2017, available from: https://www.thecut.com/2016/05/the-people-who-store-their-emotions-in-their-fingertips.html.

Shaer, N., 2016. *The Paradox of Uncertainty*, MFA dissertation, University of Cape Town: Cape Town.

Shaer, N., 2017, Email Correspondence. Received by Joni Brenner, 21 March.

Southwood, F., 2017, Email Correspondence. Received by Joni Brenner, 24 March.

Stanwix, A., 2017, Conversation with Joni Brenner, 5 April.

Tobias, G., 2014, Facebook feed. 27 October.

Trengove, E., 2014, Conversation with Joni Brenner, 16 March.

Trigg, A. B., 2001, 'Veblen, Bourdieu, and Conspicuous Consumption', *Journal of Economic Issues* 35(1): 99–115.

Underhill, P., 1999, *Why We Buy: The Science of Shopping*, Simon & Schuster: New York.

Van den Berg, C., 2016, Email correspondence. Received by Joni Brenner, 16 August.

Veblen, T., 1994 [1899], *The Theory of the Leisure Class: An Economic Study of Institutions*, Dover Publications: New York.

Womack, D., 2014, Email correspondence. Received by Joni Brenner, 14 March.

NOTES

1. African art collector and dealer Cinda Hunter stocks a selection of Marigold beads in her boutique store, Beloved Things, in Midrand, Johannesburg. Occasionally they have been featured in international museum and gallery stores in Europe and North America.
2. De Beers print media ad campaign, September 2002, agency: J. Walter Thompson, Madrid.
3. With thanks to Nicole Shaer for her valuable observations and insights on what she called 'necklace-related human intrigues'.
4. With thanks to Elizabeth Burroughs for her astute observations on this issue.
5. The Marigold beadwork cooperative is 16 women strong. The current members are: Nothando Bhebhe, Simangele Dube, Siphiwe Dube, Ridia John Samson, Gcunuthando Ndlovu, Dzidzai Shemaiah Hwende, Blessed Lunga, Thokozile Maseko, Sifiso Mathe, Cassandra Mkhwebu, Similo Moyo, Concilia Mukarobwa, Lethukuthula Ncube-Ndou, Sikhangele Nkomo, Teresa Nkomo and Jestinah Nyoni.
6. Anthropologist and Wits colleague Pamila Gupta was among these early admirers and acquired her first strands at a pop-up shop in 2013. Pleasure and interest in the beads prompted her involvement in the scholarly research into and analysis of their production and consumption.
7. Several young daughters have visited the drawers with their mothers, making their own selections and trying on various combinations. Over the years some mini-Marigolds have been commissioned for these very young wearers, including for Padma Orrantia, Ruth Alice McIlleron, Luciana Somma and Noa Nitegeka.
8. With thanks too for her insightful comments on various drafts of this paper and for prescribing the Atwood poem about bonds between women.
9. For Hoets (2017), the action of revolving the rows of beads reinforces her connection to the beads, to the way they have been crafted, and to their makers who are fellow Zimbabweans.

CONTRIBUTORS

Joni Brenner is a practising artist and a principal tutor in History of Art at the University of the Witwatersrand. Her practice, and much of her teaching, is centered on portraiture and its attendant issues of mortality and transience. Revisiting the same subject – whether live model or skull – over and again underpins her belief in learning through doing, looking closely, recognising shifts. These same values inform her collaboration with the Marigold beadwork cooperative in Bulawayo, Zimbabwe. She has a master's degree in Fine Arts from The University of the Witwatersrand. She has taught at Wits, in Visual Literacy and then in History of Art, since 1999.

Sophie Chevalier is a professor of Anthropology at the University of Picardie. Her main interest is in economic life, consumption and the comparative history of anthropology. Her fieldwork includes sites in Paris, London, Sofia and, since 2008, Durban. In the latter case, her focus is on the new middle classes, with reference to food, the media, shared social spaces and recently horse racing and betting. Her recent books include: (editor) *Anthropology at the Crossroads: the View from France* (2015) and, with E Lallement and S Corbillé, *Paris, résidence secondaire* (2013).

Claudia Gastrow is a lecturer in the Department of Anthropology and Development Studies at the University of Johannesburg. Her research focuses on urban politics in Angola with specific emphases on questions of governance, citizenship, housing, land, material culture, and aesthetics. More broadly, her work happens at the intersection of urban studies and political anthropology with a geographical focus on Lusophone, Central and southern Africa. She has published in *Antipode*, *Politique Africaine*, *Citizenship Studies*, and in *Africa is a Country* and *The Conversation*.

Pamila Gupta is an associate professor at WISER at the University of the Witwatersrand. She writes about Portuguese colonial and missionary history in India and Africa, decolonisation, heritage tourism, visual cultures and islands in the Indian Ocean. She has published in *Interventions*, *African Studies*, *Journal of Asian and African Studies*, *Critical Arts*, and *Public Culture*. She is the author of *The Relic State: St Francis Xavier and the Politics of Ritual in Portuguese India* (2014) and co-editor of

Eyes Across the Water: Navigating the Indian Ocean with Isabel Hofmeyr and Michael Pearson (2010).

Adeline Masquelier is a professor of Anthropology at Tulane University. She is author of *Prayer Has Spoiled Everything: Possession, Power, and Identity in an Islamic Town of Niger* (2001) and *Women and Islamic Revival in a West African Town* (2009), which received the 2010 Herskovits Award and the 2012 Aidoo-Snyder Prize. She edited *Dirt, Undress, and Difference: Critical Perspectives on the Body's Surface* (2005). She is co-editor, with Benjamin Soares, of *Muslim Youth and the 9/11 Generation* (2016) and, with Gaurav Desai, of *Critical Terms for the Study of Africa* (2018). Her recent publications have focused on Muslim identity as well as youth and popular culture. She recently completed a book entitled *Fada: Boredom and Belonging in Niger*, due for publication in May 2019.

Jabulani G Mnisi, known as Sifiso, has a master's degree in Communication Science from the University of Johannesburg, and is doing his doctorate in the same field of study with a focus on conspicuous consumption and masculinities in the activities of the subculture of *ukukhothana*. He is employed as a programme head at the Independent Institute of Education. Previously he worked as a lecturer at the University of Johannesburg and the University of South Africa respectively. He has also worked in the government sector as a media liaison officer for the Gauteng Department of Infrastructure Development.

Rogers Orock is a lecturer in Social Anthropology at the Department of Anthropology, University of the Witwatersrand. His work examines elites, political culture in relation to democratisation and development in Cameroon.

Deborah Posel is a professor of Sociology at the University of Cape Town, based in the Institute for Humanities in Africa (HUMA), of which she was the founding director. Her research and writing have focused on many facets of South Africa's past and present, with an abiding interest in the variegated regulation of race. Her publications include *The Making of Apartheid, 1948-1961* (1991), *Commissioning the Past: South Africa's Truth and Reconciliation Commission* (2002; co-edited with Graeme Simpson); *Apartheid's Genesis* (1994; co-edited with Phil Bonner and Peter Delius), *Ethical Quandaries in Social Research* (2015; co-edited with Fiona Ross).

Bradley Rink is a senior lecturer in the Department of Geography, Environmental Studies and Tourism at the University of the Western Cape (UWC). His teaching and research in the sub-discipline of human geography explores the role of mobilities in everyday life, and their contribution to shaping the city and citizenship. His recent outputs have been published in leading journals within his field, including *Mobilities, Transfers, Tourism Geographies, Urban Forum*, as well as in various edited collections. He is the recipient of the 2016 UWC Faculty of Arts Research Award, as well as the 2017 CHE-HELTASA National Excellence in Teaching and Learning Award.

Stephen Sparks is a senior lecturer in the History Department at the University of Johannesburg, having studied History at the then University of Natal and completed his DPhil in Anthropology and History at the University of Michigan, Ann Arbor. His research focuses on industrial development, science and town planning, as well as everyday life under apartheid. He is writing a book provisionally titled *Apartheid Modern: Science, Industry and Society in South Africa*, and has recently published on South Africa's oil-from-coal project, Sasol, in the *Journal of Southern African Studies* and the anti-apartheid oil boycott in the *South African Historical Journal*.

Nina Sylvanus is associate professor of Anthropology at Northeastern University. Her book, *Patterns in Circulation: Cloth, Gender and Materiality in West Africa* (2016), theorises the dense materiality of African print cloth as a national and global framework for understanding colonial/postcolonial patterns of exchange and value production. She is currently working on two new research projects: Tech Color, an anthropological study of how colour and material science influenced emerging textile markets (between Europe and Asia/Africa) in the nineteenth and twentieth centuries, and Harboring the Future, on the emergence of new technoports and logistics infrastructures in West Africa.

Karen Tranberg Hansen is an anthropologist with extensive research experience in Zambia. Her work focuses on the material, social and cultural dimensions of urban livelihoods in the context of historical, regional and global dynamics. Her books include: *Distant Companions: Servants and Employers in Zambia 1900–1985* (1989), *Keeping House in Lusaka* (1997), and *Salaula: The World of Secondhand Clothing and Zambia* (2000). She edited *African Encounters with Domesticity* (1992), co-edited, with Mariken Vaa, *Reconsidering Informality: Perspectives from Urban Africa* (2004) and is lead author of *Youth and the City in the Global South* (2008). She edited, with D Soyini Madison, *African Dress: Agency, Power, Performance* (2013), and with Walter E Little and B Lynne Milgram, *Street Economies in the Urban Global South* (2013).

Ilana van Wyk is a lecturer in Anthropology at Stellenbosch University and former editor-in-chief of *Anthropology Southern Africa*. She has researched and written on Neo-Pentecostal Christianity, gambling, and the South African Lottery. Her first book was entitled *The Universal Church of the Kingdom of God in South Africa: A Church of Strangers* (2014/2015). She is currently working on precolonial money exchange at the Cape and is co-writing a book on the academic biographies of two retiring anthropologists.

INDEX

A

acquisition and display of wealth 1, 3, 5, 8, 13–14, 16, 19, 45, 47, 50, 57
    through clothing/fashion and adornment 45, 47–51, 55, 98, 101, 156–157, 216–217, 219
    link to status 3, 14–15, 17, 20–21, 64, 68, 97, 153, 135
    through potlatch performances 17, 157, 172–173
    see also esteem/honour seeking, Veblen's concept of; Marigold beads, acquisition and display of; *ukukhothana* performance; Togolese consumerism; West African sartorial landscape
Adorno, T 11, 117
'Africa rising' narrative 1, 14, 84
    access to internet/mobile phones 1–2
    see also new middle class in Africa
African elite conspicuous consumption 14, 97
    in context of inequality 55, 80, 84–85, 89, 147
    anti-black racism defence 15, 80, 82, 88–91
    link with corruption 14–15, 81–82, 97
    as mark of aspiration 3, 13, 28, 50–52, 54, 57, 59, 114, 116
    Neo-Pentecostalist justification of 16
    relevance of Veblenesque model to 3, 12, 14, 20, 46, 59, 69, 86, 97, 108, 115–116, 124, 152–153, 163, 209, 217, 223, 226–228
    and status vulnerabilities/insecurities 16, 147
    see also acquisition and display of wealth; African leisure class; Angolan conspicuous consumption; modernity
African elites 2–3, 136
    Angolan 80–85, 88–91
    Cameroonian 133–134, 136–138, 141–142, 144, 146–147
    Nigerian 85, 95n6
    South African (black) 116, 202
    Togolese 52, 58–59, 61n6
    see also; new middle class in Africa; white South African elite
African leisure class 114
    lives of 'big men' 16, 45, 136, 138
    see also conspicuous registers of 'bigness', Cameroon

African National Congress (ANC) 113–115, 117–124
    breakaway party (Cope) 121
African tradition/traditionalism 53, 57, 116, 118, 141, 143, 155, 225
    dialectics of modernity and 48–49, 54, 61n5&7, 162, 214
Afrikaner identity
    modernisation of 63–67, 70
Afrikaner nationalism 13, 63–64, 69, 71
    cross-class alliance 65–66, 72, 74
    verkramptes 64–66, 70–72, 74
    verligtes 64–66, 70–71
Afro-pessimist tropes 89, 90, 95n13
Aguilar, R 82–83
Aku, Martin 51–52
America *see* United States of America
Angolan economy
    candonga system 83
    diamond business 82, 86–88
    impact of civil war on 82–84
    oil business 80–85
    privatisation of the state 81, 83
Angolan conspicuous consumption
    dos Santos family excesses 81, 85–87, 90–91
    link with corruption/patronage/clientelism 14–15, 81–85, 87, 90–91, 95n7
    Naulila Diogo 79–80, 90
    public criticism of 80, 85–86, 88–91
apartheid 63–65, 67, 73–74, 122, 186
    job reservation policies 65–66, 72
    separate development policy 174–175, 205
    policy on same-sex desire 183, 186
    post-Sharpeville survivalism 70–71, 74, 78n7
ashuabi 140, 149n2

B

Barber, K 105, 158
Bayart, J 3, 81, 97, 113, 136–137
Bell, D 186–187
Benjamin, Walter 27–28, 201
black elite *see* African elites
body politics 15, 45, 48–49, 53, 102
Bourdieu, Pierre 58, 173, 220–221
Britain/UK 2, 27–28, 32, 35, 99, 101
broedertwis see under Rousseau, Etienne
Burgis, T 85, 87

C

Cameroon 16, 88
    Manyu area 133, 139–142, 144
    Yaoundé 133–134, 138–139, 141–146
    see also conspicuous registers of 'bigness', Cameroon

Cape Dutch 26, 35–36

Cape Town
    Atlantic seaboard 18
    colonial identity of 41–42
    nineteenth century modernisation of 12, 25–27, 29–31
    see also De Waterkant, Cape Town; queer conspicuous consumption in Cape Town

Cape Town's department stores, 12, 27, 30, 36
    building design and technology 31–33, 36
    competition between 35–36
    motif of abundance 12, 32, 37–38, 41
    racial repertoires 39–41, 44n5
    Stuttafords 29–30, 35–36, 38, 40
    symbolic juncture of art, design and commerce 38–39
    see also Garlicks department store

capitalism 8, 18, 28, 81, 84, 114, 135, 194, 201, 203, 228
    Anglo-Afrikaner 64, 66, 70, 73–74
    consumerist 11, 89
    emancipatory value of 54
    and racial regulation of consumption 98
    see also neoliberal capitalism

Chiluba, Frederick 98–99
    corruption charges/trial of 15, 96–97, 99–100, 103–104, 106–107
    death/memorial service 107–108
    dressed body as symbol of political power 15, 96, 101–108
    first wife Vera 99, 102
    second wife Regina 100, 102, 111n3

class
    differentiation 4, 6, 12, 25, 40–42, 101, 135, 163, 189
    hierarchies in Togo 47, 50–52, 58–59
    lower 13, 17–18, 45, 163, 168, 173, 178–179
    middle 18–19, 28–30, 37, 64, 67, 34–35, 203, 206
    see also leisure class, Veblen's critique of; lower middle class, Durban; new middle class in Africa; white Afrikaner working class; working class

Cloete, H 120–121

clothing and adornment *see under* acquisition and display of wealth

colonial elite 12, 30, 34, 36–37, 40, 51, 53

colonial dandies
    diamond field 169, 178
    Togolese 13, 45, 47, 51–53

colonialism
    civilising mission of 3, 13, 30, 39–42, 51–52
    entanglement of conspicuous consumption and 13–14, 31, 39–40, 49, 51
    see also under gender politics

Comaroff, J 3, 113, 116

Congo/Congolese *see* Democratic Republic of Congo

conspicuous consumption
    definition of 4, 7–10
    in racialised societies 25, 36, 40, 42, 46, 88–89
    see also queer conspicuous consumption in Cape Town; Veblen's notions of conspicuous consumption

conspicuous consumption, colonial Cape Town
    among white elite 12, 25
    as declaration of modernity 12, 25–27
    see also Cape Town's department stores

conspicuous registers of 'bigness', Cameroon 16, 142, 147
    funerals 135, 137–146
    women 135–138, 146

Consitutional Court, South Africa 115, 119

consumerism 3, 10, 15, 47, 55, 89, 124
    American 151–152, 155
    gay 18, 187, 193, 195, 228
    superficiality of 11
    see also Togolese consumerism

D

Darwin, Charles 5, 10, 39, 41
de Morais, Marques 86–87, 91
de Sousa, Bornito 79–80
de Villiers, David 66, 69
De Waterkant, Cape Town 184
    Cape Quarter Lifestyle Village 18, 194–195
    as heart of gay capital 186–187, 189–190, 192, 195–196
debt 15, 71, 100, 112, 114, 124, 155
see also indebtedness
Democratic Republic of Congo 45, 87, 97, 99–102
department stores 27–29
Diederichs, Nico 67–68
Dokolo, Sindika 87–90
Durban 19, 123, 200–203, 208–210
    1973 strikes 74
    see also lower middle class, Durban

Index

E
Elder, G 184, 186–187, 199n2
esteem/honour seeking, Veblen's concept of 7, 14–15, 135–136, 196
    importance of ownership to 6, 8, 67, 116, 151
    through pecuniary emulation 8–11, 47, 64, 115–116, 152, 163, 172–173, 188, 223
    racialised/social evolutionary aspect of 5–6, 10, 25, 46, 39, 116, 209
    see also acquisition and display of wealth; queer conspicuous consumption in Cape Town
Evans, J 113, 115, 120

F
fadas
    being *branché* in 162
    criticisms of 151–152, 159, 167n15
    culture of idleness in 151, 153–155, 159
    as escape from uncertainties/precarity of youth 16, 151–155, 166n6
    generation of social capital and 154
    performance of citizenship and 153–154
    see also *samari*
Fanon, F 3, 81
Fassler, Marianne 215, 220, 223–224
France 27, 51, 54, 98
    Parisian fashion 27–28, 32

G
Garlick, John 30–34
Garlick's department store 29–30, 37–38, 40
    aggressive marketing of 34–36
    architecture of 31–34, 36, 39
gay conspicuous consumption *see* queer conspicuous consumption in Cape Town
gender politics
    of acquisition and display of wealth 13, 16, 53, 57, 98, 138, 151, 217
    of colonial public sphere 13, 46, 50, 52–53, 61n3
    and crisis of social reproduction 116, 124
    of urban dress and style, Togo 13, 45–52, 54–55, 58
gendered constructions of conspicuous consumption 2, 4, 16, 67
    Veblen and 8, 13–14, 18, 47, 51, 153, 217
generation 2, 4, 20, 66
    intergenerational dynamics 17, 58, 136, 153, 155–156, 159–160, 163–164
Geschiere, P 135–136, 138–139, 145–147
Ghana 2, 45, 53–55, 58, 125
global gay identity *see under* politics of identity
Gorman-Murray, A 186, 196

Grundlingh, Albert 65, 71
Guyer, Jane 105, 142

H
Hodges, T 83–84
homosexuality, commercialisation of *see* queer conspicuous consumption in Cape Town: commodification of gay space; *Pink Map*
human evolution 5–6, 10, 25

I
indebtedness 84, 100, 113, 174, 200, 205
inequalities 1, 16, 21
    deepening/rampant 2, 4, 46–47, 55, 80
    nineteenth century exacerbated 5, 9, 28
    see also under African elite conspicuous consumption
Institute for Humanities in Africa (HUMA) 3
International Monetary Fund 1, 24n1, 99
Iscor 68–69, 77n5
izikhothane
    money-making/hustling activities 171, 175, 179
    poverty/low socio-economic status of 17, 168, 170–171, 174, 178–179, 182n6
izikhothane, conspicuous consumption of 17, 168–169, 173, 177–179
    alcohol 170, 176–177
    designer clothing 169–170, 175, 178–179
    women 17, 170, 176
    see also ukukhothana destructive performances/burn events

J
Johannesburg, South Africa 17, 63, 120
    Art Fair 19, 214–216, 218, 221
    oswenka 169, 178
    Soweto township 174, 202
    Tembisa township 171, 174–175

K
Kabwe, Faustin 100–101, 103
Kaunda, Kenneth 98–100, 102
Kimberley 40
    diamond fields 26, 31, 41
KwaZulu-Natal, South Africa 113, 169
see also Durban; lower middle class, Durban

L
labour aristocracy 72, 74
leisure class, Veblen's critique of 5, 8–13, 15, 18, 45, 51, 59, 117, 168, 201
    wastefulness, notion of 6, 9, 16, 31, 63, 71, 97, 114, 116, 135, 151–152, 156, 161, 173, 178

Lomé, Togo 48–50, 58, 61n2
    baptisms 55–57
    lower class dandies in 13, 45, 51–52
Lourenço, João 87, 90, 95n12
lower middle class, Durban 200, 203, 205, 208–209
    'black diamonds' 19, 201–202
    precarity of 19, 203
    see also moral economy of food consumption

M

Madia, M 113, 115
Madonsela, T 113, 115, 122
Magashule, Ace 120–121
Magubane, Z 41, 169
Malema, Julius 45, 116, 123
Mandela, Nelson 112–115, 118
Marigold beads, acquisition and display of 19, 214–215, 217–218, 224–225
    circles of legitimation 20, 220–221
    exclusivity 20, 216, 218–219, 221, 223–224, 226
    as expressions of identity 224, 228
    as personal/individual construction of style 217, 219, 222–225, 227–228
    symbolic value 19, 214, 216–217, 219, 221–222, 224
Marx, Karl 5–6, 8, 47
    concept of false consciousness 8–9
    Marxism-Leninism 82–83
masculinity 116, 151, 153, 178
    heroic/ideal 17, 154, 159, 176
Mbembe, Achille 2, 81, 95, 97, 137–138, 147
missionaries 3, 53, 231
modernity
    colonial 31, 46–47, 49, 51–52
    conspicuous consumption and 4, 12–13, 21, 25–26, 28, 42, 46, 53–54, 73
    Togolese 53–54
moral economy of food consumption 19, 201–203, 208, 209
    budgeting 19, 204–206, 209
    persistence of community norms and ethic of sharing 19, 204, 206–209
MPLA (Popular Movement for the Liberation of Angola) 82–85, 90
Munn, N 157, 162
Mwanawasa, Levy 99–101, 107

N

Nash, C 186, 196
National Party, South Africa 65, 70–71, 174
National Religious Leaders' Council (NRLC), South Africa 115, 118–119
Nel, Karel 218, 220

neoliberal capitalism 17–18, 113, 116, 152, 154, 186, 209
    structural adjustment programmes 55, 99
Neo-Pentecostal Churches (NPC) *see* Zuma, Jacob: Neo-Pentecostalist ethic of
new middle class in Africa 1–2, 12, 81, 134, 152, 155
    distinctions within 201–203
    see also lower middle class, Durban
New York 33, 79, 189, 196, 219
    Conference Board 72
Niger 151–152, 154, 156–157, 160–163
    conspicuous consumption of youth in 16–17, 150–151, 153
    Hausa 150, 153, 155, 157–158
    Islamic revival in 151–152, 155, 158
    joblessness/youth unemployment in 154–155, 159
    Niamey 16, 150, 153, 162–163
    search for upward mobility in 154
    Zinder 153
    see also generation: intergenerational dynamics
Niger, conspicuous consumption in 152
    centrality of dress to 17, 155–158, 160–162
    in precolonial times 157
    pursuit of social recognition/status and 157–159
    women's displays of wealth 158
    see also fadas
Nigeria 45, 47, 98, 123, 134, 166n4
see also African elites: Nigerian
Ngoepe, K 119–121

O

Olympio, Dinah Grunitsky 54–55, 62n9
O'Meara, D 64, 66, 69–70
ownership
    of property 6, 8, 116, 145
    of women 8

P

Paradise Papers exposé 2, 24n2
Parkins, W 101–102
patriarchy 8, 18, 217
    traditional Zulu 116
Pink Map 18, 184–199
    and emulation of idealised body 188–192
    differentiation of homosexual space through 184–185
    LGBT tourist promotion through 183–186
    silences/limitations of 187–188, 199n2
    'wild side' category 191–192
    upmarket lifestyle focus of 192, 194–196

politics of identity 18
    intersection with conspicuous consumption 14, 20–21, 179
    notion of global gay/queer/LGBT identity 18, 183–186, 187–188, 192, 196
    notion of personhood 54, 142
    racial 169
    see also sexual citizenship
Portugal 84–85, 89
privatisation 81, 83, 99, 103
    power relations 160, 203–204
    sexualised 216–217

Q

queer conspicuous consumption in Cape Town
    emulation and honour-seeking through 183–184, 188, 190–191
    commodification of gay space 18, 186–187, 194–195
    see also Pink Map; sexual citizenship
queer/LGBT liberation, post-1994 188–190, 196

R

race 40
    colonial hierarchies 12–14, 39, 50–52
    and dynamics of conspicuous consumption 4, 19–20, 36, 80, 82, 88–91, 98, 114, 116, 200, 203, 225
    and same-sex desire 186–187, 189
    see also Veblen's notions of conspicuous consumption: and race; whiteness
racial inequality/segregation 27, 39–41, 64
    in South Africa 64, 71, 114, 200–201
    see also apartheid
racial stereotyping 88–91, 169, 201, 225
see also Afro-pessimist tropes
racism 14–15, 82, 88–91
Reconstruction and Development Programme (RDP) South Africa 170, 175
Robertson, AF 105–106
Rosenthal, E 31–36, 38, 40
Rousseau, Etienne 13–14, 63–64, 67–69, 72–74
    and *broedertwis* contestations 64–66, 70–71

S

samari 157, 160–161
    self-indulgent consumerism of 16–17, 150–151, 155–156, 158, 160–164, 167n15
    status/social recognition-seeking among 17, 151–152, 156, 158–159, 162–163
    see also *fadas*
Sasol 13, 63, 65–69, 73–74
    managerial revolution at 70

Sasolburg
    Calvinist sensibilities of 14
    consumerist trajectory of 13–14, 63–64, 66–68, 71, 73–74
    elite 64
    emerging Anglo-Afrikaner identity in 70
Schubert, B 83–84
Scott, James 202–203
Sese Seko, Mabuto 3, 87, 97
sexual citizenship 186, 188, 190
    shift to consumer citizenship 184, 187, 192–196
Simmel, G 50, 61n5
Smith, D 3, 97, 114
Smith, Will 85–86
Smuts, Jan 66, 70, 78n6
Soares de Oliveira, R 81, 84–85
South African Council of Churches (SACC) 115, 118–119
Spindler, M 5, 9–10
Stellenbosch University, South Africa 65–66, 68–69

T

Tattelman, I 188–189, 199n2
Thompson, E 202–203
Tilman, R 9–11
Todres, Philip 184–185, 192
Togolese consumerism
    link with identity formation 47, 50, 54, 58–59
    and new social hierarchies 50–51, 58, 61n1
    pagne aesthetic 13, 46–50, 52–58
    politics of reputation and recognition 58–59
    urban context 46, 48–50, 54, 61n4
    see also gender politics: of urban dress and style, Togo
Tornai, Pnina 79–80
Trentmann, Frank 27–29, 64

U

ukukhothana destructive performances/burn events 17, 45, 169–172
    Good Fellas crew 17, 171, 174–179, 182n8
    negative perceptions of 174, 176, 178–179
    respect/honour-seeking aspect of 170, 175–179
    see also *izikhothane*
Union for the Total Liberation of Angola (Unita) 83–84, 95n5
United States of America (USA) 19th century 1, 4, 10, 27, 66, 69, 85, 114, 168, 172
    mass industrialisation in 5, 97, 172
    poverty/economic depression in 5
    upward mobility in 1, 14
Uys, Jamie 63–64

V

van Donge, Jan Kees 99–100, 103–104, 106
van Onselen, Gareth 112, 120–122, 124
Venice Biennale 87–88
Veblen, Thorstein
    biography 4–5
    influence of Darwin on 5–6, 10
    interdisciplinary scholarship of 9–10
Veblen's notions of conspicuous consumption 1, 3–4, 42, 45, 151
    different readings of 10–12
    link with patriarchy 8, 18, 217
    marginality of poor to 168, 173–174
    pecuniary reputability through 6, 18, 80, 117, 152, 156, 173, 226–227
    and race 12, 20, 25, 42, 116
    puritan productionist ethic of 15, 117, 124
    symbolic drivers of 10, 20, 25, 41, 216
    and transition to 'barbarian society' 6, 9–10
    see also esteem/honour seeking, Veblen's concept of; queer conspicuous consumption in Cape Town; leisure class, Veblen's critique of

W

Weber, M 47, 117
West African sartorial landscape 2, 16, 158
    boubou 47
    female aesthetic of excess in 45–46, 50–51, 55, 59, 155
    wax-print/Dutch wax cloth aesthetic 46–49, 55, 149n2, 224
    see also conspicuous consumption in Niger: centrality of dress to; Togolese consumerism: *pagne* aesthetic
white Afrikaner working class 64, 66
    car culture of 13, 65, 67–68
    impact of upward mobility on 65, 71–72, 74
white South African elite 12, 30
    business 64, 66, 68–69, 71–73
whiteness 12, 41–42, 64, 89
Williams, M 113–115
working class 8, 46, 135, 152, 168, 205
    black/Zulu 169–170, 174
    elite exploitation of 135, 209
    see also white Afrikaner working class

Y

youth culture, South African township 17, 168–169, 174–175, 179
see also *ukukhothana*

Z

Zaire see Democratic Republic of Congo
Zambia 15, 96
    Access Financial Services (AFS) 100–104, 107
    colonial 51, 96
    copper-based economy of 97
    New Culture in 15, 98, 102–103, 105
    Movement for Multiparty Democracy (MMD) 98, 106
    task force on corruption 101
    Zamtrop account 100, 106
    see also Chiluba, Frederick
Zelizer, V 204–205
Zimbabwe 19, 230n9
    Bulawayo beadwork cooperative 217–218, 222–225, 230n5
    former president Mugabe 2
Zuma, Jacob 15
    civil society/public criticism of 115, 118–120
    indebtedness of 112–115
    Nkandla upgrade 113, 115, 118, 123, 132n16
    Neo-Pentecostalist ethic of 16, 113, 117–125, 132n15
    popular support for 115–117, 119–120, 124
    reassertion of patriarchal Zulu traditionalism 116
    salary and state allowances 112, 115, 131n2, 132n3
    shameless conspicuous consumption of 16, 113–114, 123–125
Zuma, Jacob, criminal and corruption charges against 113–114, 120
    arms deal 114
    'capture' by Guptas 113, 115, 119
    rape charge 115, 120, 132n7&8
    Schabir Shaik case 114, 120

www.ingramcontent.com/pod-product-compliance
Lightning Source LLC
Chambersburg PA
CBHW081506080526
44589CB00017B/2663